The Genesis of Arabic Narrative Discourse

The Genesis of Arabic Narrative Discourse

A Study in the Sociology of Modern Arabic Literature

Sabry Hafez

Saqi Books

British Library Cataloguing-in-Publication Data
A Catalogue record for this book is available from the British Library

ISBN 0 86356 149 7

First published 1993 by
Saqi Books
26 Westbourne Grove
London W2 5RH

Typeset by Kalimatexts, London

For My Parents

Contents

Preliminary Note 9
Foreword 10
Introduction: The Sociology of Narrative Discourse 17

1. The Infrastructure of Cultural Transition *37*
Early Signs of Cultural Revival 38
Confrontation with the French Expedition 42
The Pioneers of Cultural Transition 45
Accelerating the Process of Modernization 48
Changes in the Levant and Iraq 52
Printing and the Change in Patronage 54
Urbanization and New Social Norms 58
Transformation of the Sociocultural Atmosphere 60
2. The Reading Public and the Change in Artistic Sensibility *63*
Educating the New Reading Public 65
Education and Women's Emancipation 68
The Awakening of National Consciousness 71
Cultural Societies: A Vision in Search of a Role 79
Journalism and Cultural Change 82
Translation and the Contact with the West 85
The Impact of Russian Literature 91
The Composition of a New World-View 97
The New Reading Public and Its Sensibility 102
3. A Modern Narrative Discourse in Embryo *105*
Oral, Traditional and Translated Narrative 106
The Revitalization of the *Maqāmah* 108
The Emergence of Indigenous Narrative 111
Nadîm: The Qualification of the New Writer 113
Language and the New Sensibility 117
The Early Narrative Sketches 120
Exploration of Further Grounds 123
Elements of the New Narrative Discourse 125
The Rejuvenation of the *Maqāmah* 129
The Romantic Break with the Past 136
The Dream as a Narrative Discourse 140
The Sentimental Slant of the Romantic 142
Muṣṭafā 'Abd al-Rāziq: A Neglected Pioneer 149
The Herald of Realistic Narrative 152

4. The Quest for National Identity and the Birth of Narrative Genres *157*
Nationalism and New Artistic Endeavour 158
The Emergence of the Short Story 159
Muḥammad Taymūr's Pioneering Work 162
The Gap Between Theory and Practice 164
Thematic and Artistic Contribution 167
Nu'aymah and the *Mahjar* Experience 170
Ḥaddād and the Stories of Expatriation 175
The Brothers 'Īsā and Shiḥātah 'Ubaid 178
Real People in Plausible Situations 182
Literary Symbols and a Sense of Structure 185
Al-Sayyid: The Return to Russian Literary Influence 189
5. Narrative Genres in Search of an Identity: Maḥmūd Taymūr *199*
Introducing a New Narrative Discourse 200
Revisiting Old Themes 201
Experimenting with New Themes 204
The Culmination of his Early Career 207
Artistic and Conceptual Qualities 210
The Problematic Language of Narrative 212
6. The Maturation of the New Narrative Discourse:
Maḥmūd Ṭāhir Lāshîn *215*
Jamā'at al-Madrasah al-Ḥadîthah 216
Narrative Survey of the Society 219
Characterization, Themes and Settings 222
A Critical Vision of People and Society 225
Lāshîn's Lasting Significance 227
Narrative Discourse and the Reader's Consciousness 229
7. The Culmination of a Sophisticated Discourse: Ḥadîth al-Qaryah *233*
Naming as a Prefatory Narrative Device 235
The Beginning and Its Assumptions 236
Dialectics of *Fabula* and *Sjuzhet* 238
Skaz and Characterization 242
Molestation, Duplicity and Authority 247
The Polyphony of Discourses and Intertextuality 249
Thematic Interpretation and the Use of Description 252
The Open Ending and Its Significance 255

Appendix: *Village Small Talk*: an English translation of
Ḥadîth al-Qaryah 262

Notes 269
Bibliography 307
Index 317

Preliminary Note

1. The standard system of transliteration has been adopted throughout, albeit with minor modifications. The aim is to produce simple, recognizable and easily pronounced forms of Arabic names and words that can be traced to the original form. Therefore the initial *hamza* is not marked, nor are final vowels except long vowels and when the word may be misread without the marking, or when it could be easily confused with another word. Because of the occurrence of some colloquial words, both *i* and *y* are used interchangeably for the Arabic letter *yā, i* being generally used in connection with colloquial words or when the sound of the word is of some significance. The final *tā' marbūṭah* is marked as *h* except in an *iḍāfah* construction where it naturally appears as *t*. The final *alif maqṣūrah* is also marked and fully transliterated as *ā*. For ease of reading and rendering any Arabic word or name back to its original form, however, the diacritical marks are fully used in every occurrence. Full references with diacritical marks are also given in the notes and in the bibliography. When Arabic words, whether special terms or titles of works, appear in the text, they are fully transliterated and translated in the first instance, but are subsequently used only in their transliterated form.
2. The Egyptian pound £E which is called in Arabic *junayh* has a slightly higher exchange value than sterling. Its name was originally derived from the English guinea and was thus equivalent to 21 shillings. This continued to be its approximate value throughout the period of this study.
3. The translation of all quotations from Arabic stories and essays are the author's own. But the translation of Lāshīn's short story, "Village Small Talk", in the appendix is by Catherine Cobham.

Foreword

For many years, the question of the concurrent rise of the various genres of narrative in modern Arabic culture has engaged the minds of scholars. However, it has always been treated either in the context of a specific genre in a single Arab country, or from a purely ideological viewpoint. Those who wanted to emphasize the impact of the West attributed to it significant influence, while those who wanted to deny the West's influence looked for older Arabic narrative forms. This study endeavours to break with the established tradition in this field by investigating the genesis of narrative discourse across the Arab world, and particularly in the countries that formed the centre of its cultural activities in the last century and the early decades of this century. The main emphasis is therefore on Egypt, for it played the major role in this respect, and also on the countries of the Levant (Lebanon, Palestine and Syria) and Iraq. The role of other Arab countries at the time was negligible and can easily be overlooked. In its investigation of the formation of the new narrative discourse, this study will use a different critical approach from that used either in Arabic scholarship, or in the various studies of the subject in English and other European languages. The tenets of this approach are elaborated in the introduction in a manner that indicates their sources in Western scholarship.

This study breaks with the common propositions of either relating the genealogy of modern Arabic narrative to the classical genre of the *maqāmah* or perceiving it as an import from the West. It establishes the study of this topic in the domain of the sociology of literature and post-structuralist theory and posits the concept of genesis with its sociocultural dimensions versus the old concepts of origin, genealogy or mimesis. The dialectic interaction between the transformation of a world-view, the change in artistic sensibility, the emergence of a new reading public and the formation of a new discourse is seen in this study as a complex process that motivates and structures the production of the new discourse. The term narrative discourse is therefore used here to describe any referential text in which temporality is represented, and to widen the implication of the theoretical assumptions of the study to encompass all narrative genres: the novel, the novella, the short story and drama; and suggests a different approach in dealing with the early works of these genres in modern Arabic literature. The term "narrative discourse" is preferred to others not merely because of its association with modern critical theory, but mainly because the term "discourse" better indicates the specific social and ideological contexts and relationships involved in historically produced uses of language. In its construct form "narrative discourse" it denotes the coherent body of statements that constitute its own field, produce a self confirming account of reality and generate textual strategies with which to analyse it.

The aim of this study is to apply modern critical theory to answer the crucial question: how new literary genres emerge in a particular culture at a specific time, and why. It attempts to answer this question not merely on the theoretical plane, though some abstract postulations are inevitable, but mainly through the specific case of the genesis of modern Arabic narrative discourse, particularly the short story, a narrative genre which played a major role in changing the canons of taste and shaping the new literary sensibility in modern Arabic culture.

The period of time covered by this study starts with the early signs of cultural transition in the eighteenth century and extends up to 1930. It challenges the widely held assumption of the stagnation of Arabic culture before its contact with the West in the beginning of the nineteenth century, then traces the revival to the mid-eighteenth century and follows its development throughout the Arab world showing how the emergence of a new reading public with its distinct world-view induced the process of the transformation and genesis of a new literary discourse. The book then engages in a detailed study of the dynamics of this process and outlines the various stages of the formation and transformation of the new narrative discourse which started to emerge in the second half of the nineteenth century until it culminates in the production of a highly sophisticated and mature narrative in the 1920s.

The short story has been selected as the main field of enquiry for several reasons. First, it offers an answer to the central question of how and why a new literary genre emerges which can be easily applicable to other literary genres, since "the materials and their organization in a short story differ from those in a novel in degree and not in kind",[1] and also since "literary genres are to be understood not as *genera* (classes) in the logical sense, but rather as groups of historical families".[2] Second, it has been the testing ground for many of the novelists, novella writers and dramatists in the Arab world, whose early works owe a great deal to the technical and stylistic solutions developed and skills mastered during their experimentation with the genre. Third, among all narrative forms in Arabic, and with the exception of some attempt at drama, it was the first to appear and, more importantly, the first to reach maturity, for by 1929 there were excellent examples of mature work in the genre, while in other literary genres works of such maturity did not appear before this date. Fourth, the short story is, in a sense, the genre of those on the fringe of society, and this as we shall see is the condition of the newly educated middle class which occupied a rather large and overcrowded margin, but, in terms of power, recognition, or status, remained a fringe. It was this group that created narrative discourse and consumed it in Arab society. Fifth, because of its size the short story was easier to publish than other genres, one of which, drama, required elaborate preparation to see the light of day. In addition, the short story has the shortest dissemination period (the period between writing the text and communicating it to the reader) of all narrative texts, or, indeed, of any literary text, bar the poem, and this enhanced its instantaneous interaction with both the reading public and society.

The short story is a popular and respectable genre in Arabic literature. Many outstanding writers attained fame and eminence by dedicating most of their literary careers to the short story.[3] It was the only modern narrative medium with some roots in the Arabic tradition and could avail itself of the vast opportunities opened up by the advent of the press and the rapid growth of a new reading public. Although short narrative forms — fabliaux, sketches, yarns, tales, anecdotes, *exempla,* parables, fables, etc. — had been prominent oral or written genres for centuries,[4] around the turn of the century an expanding reading public gave their written replacement — the short story — a real impetus. This reading public which emerged as a result of radical changes in the educational system, expanding journalism, growing urbanization, and rising national awareness made increasing demands on the literary establishment, yet it had not developed regular reading habits and hence preferred the short story to the novel. Some critics even argue that "short stories can help create an audience, or a larger audience, for novels".[5]

The Arab reading public favoured the short story, perhaps, because of the singularity of its effect, or its unity of impression, and because it was well suited to the conditions and needs of such newly developed readers emerging from the canons of oral reception. Its brevity demands little time, but its coherence is sufficient to hold the readers' unflagging attention from beginning to end. The short story therefore appealed to a restless audience, brought up on the theatricality and collectivity of the oral tradition, which needed a medium capable of holding readers by the hand, enmeshing them in its structure, and training them, in small doses, to get used to the lonely art of reading. The short story suited the Arab readers, whose crowded social life allowed only for short periods of solitude, and whose strict and socially controlled life enabled them to appreciate its biting criticism. The short story's critical power, especially in its satirical form, was particularly popular with readers who demanded from literature a change, an insight, an articulation of their feelings, and a contribution to their own knowledge.

As a literary genre, the short story is closely related to the two major art forms on which the Arab reader was nourished before its birth: poetry and folk narrative, both of which have a strong oral element. The short story shares this oral tradition, for "the limits and distinguishing characteristics of the short story as we know it today are the limits and distinguishing characteristics of the spoken story as it has existed from the beginning of time".[6] This facilitated the new reading public's acclimatization to its conventions and habituated readers to its world, a world that offered them not merely a haven from their own crowded life, but a role when a role had been denied them elsewhere. Because of its dependence on suggestive devices and its revelatory nature, the short story demands the most active participation by its reader. This was essential for an audience brought up on a diet of oral literature and used to playing an active role in its reception. The short story alerts its readers' imagination so that they are able to perceive, in its shadowy outlines, the complete pattern.

Indeed, "short stories require great concentration from the reader, for every word, if the job is being done properly, must carry weight and help to intensify the impact of other words".[7] The careful selection of vocabulary and the emphasis on the poetic function of language are major components of the textual strategies of the short story with its marked inclination to discard photographic presentation for elliptical and symbolic representation which brings it closer to poetry. Even in its earlier forms, it manifested a tendency to be more metamorphic and to avoid emulating reportage. In its mature forms, its suggestive and revelatory powers push it further into the realm of poetry, and this brought it more into harmony with the dispositions of readers who had a long tradition of poetry, but were newly introduced to journalism. Both poetry and journalism are major factors in developing the new narrative discourse.

Another significant consideration is the status of this literary genre in modern Arabic culture, and its versatility, vitality and relevance to the major social and literary issues of the day. Unlike its Western counterpart, the short story is both a serious and popular genre in Arabic literature, with a sustained vitality and vigour. This is hardly surprising, since the evidence provided by *The Kenyon Review*'s publication of the proceedings of the "International Symposium on the Short Story",[8] the most impressive and comprehensive survey of the genre, demonstrates that while the genre is suffering from marginalization in advanced Western societies, with the exception of Germany,[9] it enjoys popularity and health in developing cultures.

In Arabic, as indeed in many other literatures, the short story, and indeed narrative discourse in general, has still a flavour of newness and vigour. One can trace its descent from other traditional forms of narrative going back to *Alf Laylah wa-Laylah (The Arabian Nights)*, which is full of examples that can rival any modern narrative text in dexterity and coherence, yet when one speaks of narrative discourse in the modern sense of the term one is talking about a new literary genre whose early examples were conceived in the last few decades of the nineteenth century and reached maturity in the early decades of this century. Like its Western counterpart, the Arabic narrative tradition is centuries old. Modern Arabic narrative is closely connected with its European counterpart, by which it has been influenced. Thus it is appropriate to start by investigating the various channels through which this influence filtered through to the Arab world. This study also investigates the sociocultural scene at the time and the lengthy process of cultural transition in order to isolate the elements that gave rise to the new genres of narrative.

My selection of the short story for the illustration of the genesis of narrative discourse emerged from a long fascination with it as an art form endowed with supreme simplicity, charged with poetic power, and capable of portraying the innermost depths of the human soul in the most compact manner. I became interested in the short story at the outset of my literary career, and my interest in the genre has continued ever since. The vast developments in the field of literary theory in general and the theory of narrative discourse in particular have been applied, on the whole, to the novel, and the short story was left out. This study endeavours to redress this balance by applying the new critical approaches to the study of this genre.

The introduction of this study therefore investigates the principles of the sociology of narrative discourse, outlining the basic theoretical assumptions which inform the study and justify its structure. It offers a critical account of the prevalent approaches in both Arabic and Western scholarship to the question of the genealogy of modern Arabic narrative genres, and then defines the major concepts of the study including those of the "world-view" and "discourse and discursive field" which played a vital role in the genesis of new narrative genres in Arabic literature. The order of the basic theoretical concepts treated in the introduction corresponds to the structure of the whole study. The role of the change of world-view in the modification of literary discourse and the various elements of Goldmann's and Bakhtin's sociology of narrative offer the theoretical foundation behind the first two chapters, while those of intertextuality, discursive field and Jauss' concepts of genre, the horizon of understanding and the deciphering of codes are relevant to Chapters 3—6, in which the elaborate process of the formation of a new discursive field is studied, and the rubrics of drawing its conventions and preparing the reader for its reception are probed.

Chapters 1 and 2 investigate the developments underpinning the cultural transition which led to a radical change in world-view and called subsequently for a new discourse capable of articulating its tenets. They investigate the interaction between the awakening of national consciousness, the composition of the reading public, its role in the creation of new sensibility and the rise of narrative genres. This survey of the sociocultural preparation for the genesis of narrative discourse starts in the eighteenth century. The book's concern with the cultural transition spans a long period from the revival of the eighteenth century through the nineteenth and up to the end of the third decade of the twentieth century. It identifies the routes through which the two major cultural influences (French and Russian literatures) travelled and changed the horizons of literary expectations.

The third chapter sifts through various early attempts to express the new sensibility. Nadīm's early narrative sketches were the first significant venture in this field, for they set the tone and prepared the ground for the following endeavours. The chapter follows the trail from Nadīm's work through various other attempts to create an indigenous narrative discourse in the Arab world in an attempt to demonstrate the dynamic and complementary nature of the discursive field and the vital interaction between the narrative endeavours in various Arab countries. This chapter sheds light on the role of the rejuvenation of the *maqāmah* and the romantic break with the past and culminates in the discovery of two neglected pioneers of the genesis of narrative genres: 'Abd al-Rāziq and Baydas.

Chapter 4 demonstrates the vital relationship between the emerging new discourse and the quest for national identity and follows the development of the new discourse through the work of six writers. Chapter 5 is devoted to the work of Taymūr and 6 to that of *Jamā'at al-Madrasah al-Ḥadīthah*, and its most talented member Maḥmūd Ṭāhir Lāshīn, whose work provides the best examples of the mature phase of the narrative discourse.

It was Lāshīn who wrote the first mature and artistically coherent short stories and brought the genesis of the new genre to its close. This is the reason for selecting his short story *"Ḥadīth al-Qaryah"* for the detailed textual analysis in the concluding chapter of this book in order to demonstrate how the various factors which participated in the process of the genesis of narrative discourse come together on both the structural and thematic planes. The other reason for concluding the study with a close reading of one of Lāshīn's texts is that the proof of literary history is best demonstrated through practical criticism. The critical approach adopted by this study implies that the conclusion of any "literary history" can no longer confine itself to making the implicit aims of the historical study explicit in a final note which is often redundant and states the obvious. It has to demonstrate the validity of its various assumptions through a detailed critical analysis of a representative text. The concluding chapter demonstrates through its close reading of the story how the various elements of the literary historical process, including the new reading public and the conflict of the new discourse with the old, filtered through the text and participated in the shaping of its complex structure and fine literary composition. It also shows how intertextual elements are fused into the fabric of the story in a manner that enhances its ability to absorb and articulate the diverse sociocultural processes which gave rise to the new narrative discourse. Lāshīn was strongly influenced by Russian literature and my critical analysis of his text benefits from the contribution made by Russian critics around the time in which he wrote his major work. In order to enable the reader to follow this critical reading, a full English translation of Lāshīn's story is included in the appendix.

My grateful acknowledgements are due to the School of Oriental and African Studies of the University of London, and to Dr R.C. Ostle and the late Professor T.M. Johnstone, the two scholars who meticulously read certain portions of an earlier version of this study. I am very grateful for the help, support and encouragement of Dr B.M. Conway, Dr M.M. Badawi, Dr O. Wright, Mrs C. Cobham, Mr Yaḥya Ḥaqqi and Dr Laṭīfah al-Zayyāt. They have given invaluable advice, which I must confess, in fairness to them, I have not always followed. I am particularly grateful to Mrs Cobham for translating Lāshīn's story in the Appendix. I should like to express a word of thanks to those who have encouraged me and helped me throughout my stay in Britain: Professor J. Wansbrough, Professor A.K.S. Lambton, Professor P.J. Vatikiotis, Dr D. Hopwood, Dr R. Owen, Dr S. Radwan and Mr and Mrs al-'Abbās. I would like also to express my thanks to my two friends, the short story writer Mr A. Abu-l-Najā and the poet Mr M.I. Abū-Sinnah, for obtaining for me valuable information on the life of a number of the writers discussed. Finally, my debt to my family, especially my immediate family who bore with me the burden of this work, is beyond expression. While I express my deepest thanks and gratitude to these institutions and persons, I naturally absolve them from any responsibility for my opinions and errors.

London, February 1991

Introduction
The Sociology of Narrative Discourse

The question of the genealogy of the various genres of Arabic narrative discourse has attracted the attention of many scholars. The simultaneous rise of new literary genres (the novel, the novella, the short story, and drama) previously unknown in Arabic literature has engaged many minds. The Western ancestry for the new narrative discourse has been resolved on the sociological plane by Watt and Leavis,[1] on the socio-philosophical plane by Lukács and Bakhtin[2] and on the socio-psychological plane by Girard.[3] Yet scholars of modern Arabic literature are still searching for a convincing explanation of the unprecedented rise of new narrative discourse in Arabic culture around the turn of the century. Some endeavour to establish a long linear connection between modern Arabic narrative discourse and its medieval narrative antecedents. Although classical and medieval Arabic is relatively rich in archetypal prose fiction, the *maqāmah* (session), a special form of traditional narrative, has been chosen by most scholars as the ancestor of virtually all genres of narrative: the novel, the novella, the short story and even drama.[4] Others object to stretching the blood line of modern narrative discourse so far and reject, on the basis of structural as well as functional differences, any connection with the past. They assert simply that it was "borrowed from the West",[5] or at least conceived under its weighty influence in a manner that makes it a direct descendant of Western narrative forms.[6]

The two arguments represent different facets of a critical dilemma resulting from close adherence to diachronic methods of study, complete denial of the usefulness of synchronic approaches and the imposition of extrinsic explanations on the complex phenomenon of the genesis of modern narrative discourse in Arabic literature. Both arguments not only raise issues of literary history and its interaction with literary theory, but also invoke problems of ideology in connection with their perception of the question of national identity. The former argument has its roots in the desire of many scholars to deny or at least minimize the impact of the West on the cultural life of the Arabs and to strengthen its bonds with classical and medieval Arabic tradition. The latter stems from a conviction that the classical and medieval legacy is onerous and can only impede the process of progress and modernization. For reasons of brevity and convenience I shall call the first argument traditional and the second modernist in the following discussion.

Behind the traditional argument one detects some characteristics of what Goldmann calls the "tragedy of refusal";[7] that is, a state of mind which is a symptomatic expression of a group of people facing increasing social powerlessness and condemned by the vigorous process of change to ineffectiveness. They recognize the drastic developments, and yet are incapable of taking any action to prevent or curtail them. Instead, their only attempt is to confer on them the blessings of the old, in order to think of them not as radical departures from the past, but as new manifestations of its perpetual essence. In this manner they can comprehend the new by integrating it into the old. We shall see later how the process of modernization which swept through every facet of Arab society displaced a whole class of traditional intellectuals whose intellectual heirs figure prominently among formulators of this argument. The exponents of this argument recognize the change yet are unwilling to embrace it, and so dictate their terms for accepting its cultural product: by declaring them to be a continuation of their own tradition.

The modernist argument is the complete opposite of the former, yet it suffers from the same shortcomings though in a reverse order. The exponents of this view recognize and are often part of the mechanisms of change, yet their very involvement in the process, and in its triumphant ascent, obscures their understanding of the complex dialectical relationship between the "emergent" and "residual" cultures. Such dialectics permeate the whole cultural scene, particularly at times of social and cultural transition. As the argument of the traditionalists is intermingled with a certain denial of the present, this argument uncannily denies the power of the past and its impact on the present. Both arguments, though diametrically opposed, stem from a similar reductive methodology that attempts to explain a complex and intricate phenomenon, that of the genesis of a new literary discourse in Arabic culture, by resorting to simplifications and extrinsic reasoning.

Neither argument explains the emergence of Arabic fiction at the time when it appeared. If its roots stretch back to the medieval *maqāmah,* why did we have to wait for nine centuries for the form to reappear, though with major modifications? What were the reasons for such modifications? What do they signify, and what function do they perform? Why were the early examples of modern narrative discourse different in interest and outlook from the new *maqāmāt* of the same period? How can we explain the structural and philosophical differences between the *maqāmah* and the new narrative forms? Was it purely coincidental that the *maqāmah* was chosen as the legitimate ancestor of the new narrative and not, say, the *nādirah* (anecdote), *usṭūrah* (legend), *khurāfah* (myth), *sīrah* (biography), *risālah* (narration), *khabar* (sketch), *wāqi'ah* (yarn), *qiṣṣah* (story), *ḥādithah* (happening), *ḥikāyah* (tale) or *ḥikāyāt al-amthāl* (exemplum)? More importantly, why choose the *maqāmah* and not *The Arabian Nights,* which is not only richer and far more sophisticated in terms of structure and narrative strategies, but also contains both long and short narrative pieces that arguably could have given rise to both major forms of narrative discourse, the novel and the short story? Is the designation of ancestry purely random, or does it signify a thought process inherent in, and affecting the formulation of, both the argument and the perception of the new genre?

Similarly, had the modern Arabic narrative been a direct product of Western influences, why did it need almost a century after the confrontation with Europe to emerge; and, more importantly, how does one account for its originality and difference from its European counterpart? Is the importation of literary genres possible and, if so, what is actually imported and what is left out in the process? What is the role of the various factors which create a milieu conducive to borrowing or importation and, more precisely, what is usually imported? Is it a form devoid of content, a set of narrative strategies, or a total vision and a way of thinking? Each answer to the last question would invoke a new set of problems, for if it was a form, is the form independent of its content? Semiotic studies have proved that forms and codes are laden with meaning and play a vital role in shaping views and understanding. And if it was a vision, is it possible to separate a vision, and specifically a cultural one, from its formal embodiment? Furthermore, the whole question of importation cannot simply be resolved in connection with cultural products, without discussing the possibility of divorcing such products from their milieu, and, more importantly, from what Edward Said calls "beginning conditions".[8]

Western narrative forms are both time-and culture-bound and stem as a result from a specific view of the world. In *The Theory of the Novel,* one of the most insightful and seminal works on narrative discourse, Georg Lukács suggested that "the novel is the epic of a world that has been abandoned by God", and that "the mental attitude of the novel is virile maturity, and the characteristic structure of its matter is discreteness, the separation between interiority and adventure".[9] This means that the writer's resort to narrative suggests the "virile maturity" that believes in, or at least posits, man's ability to alter events, if not to control them completely. It means in addition that the narrative form itself is part and parcel of the social process of transformation that led to the emergence of "a world that has been abandoned by God" or at least the writer's perception of the world as such, a perception that implies a certain process of questioning, and thus is inseparable form the world-view which is implied in its conception. The novel's virile maturity "is maintained by an author whose maturity depends on distinctions, inherited from the novel's history, between pure subjective fantasy and pure factual chronicle, between directionless brooding and an unlimited episodic repetition".[10]

The term "world-view", which has been widely used by Dilthey and his school, but which later acquired a certain association with Goldmann's notion of "homologous structures" that are generally manifested in the "form of the content", with his sociology of literature in general, "is not an immediate, empirical fact, but a conceptual working hypothesis indispensable to an understanding of the way in which individuals actually express their ideas".[11] Goldmann's concept of world-view stems from both Marx and Mannheim's belief that ideas are formulated and conditioned socially and they are thus collective rather than individual. It is a trans-individual concept that aspires to elaborate the working of the collective subject behind the individual one, for it means "a *coherent* and *unitary* perspective concerning man's relationship with his fellow men and with the universe. Since the thought of individuals is rarely coherent and unitary, a world-view rarely corresponds to the actual thought of a particular individual".[12] Such a view can neither be transported nor divorced from the milieu in which it originated, it is also inseparable, as Goldmann demonstrates from the form of its content. Goldmann's demonstration of the "interrelationship of structure and function" is of vital importance to this study, since its elaboration of the changeability and continual formation and deformation of structures explains the inner mechanism of the process of genetic materialization of structures operative in the genesis of narrative discourse. The deformation of the *maqāmah* form in the work of many nineteenth-century Arab writers showed clearly the rupture between the function and structure of the old mode of discourse, and expedited the emergence of a new narrative discourse.

The argument that a literary form can be transplanted from one culture to another overlooks the coherent and unitary nature of the world-view, and turns a blind eye to the fact that the host culture has a different set of beliefs, which in this case spring from the tenets of Islam and have been subjected to the vast historical developments of Arabic culture, and consequently a dissimilar, if not antagonistic, world-view. In a passing remark that completely overlooks his own notion of "beginning conditions", Said acknowledges the difficulties pertaining to this position. Ironically, he starts by stating that "modern Arabic literature includes novels, but they are almost entirely of this century. There is no tradition out of which these modern works developed; basically at some point writers in Arabic became aware of European novels, and began to write works like them".[13] Although Said is unusually reticent when it comes to the interesting, and in some respect crucial, process of moving from the state of awareness of the existence of a certain foreign cultural product to that of producing "works like them", he is too sophisticated to fall into the trap of the concept of "imitation" let alone the more naïve one of "borrowing" or "importation", for he recognizes, in a later work, that "the closeness of the world's body to the text's body forces readers to take both into consideration".[14]

Indeed, he hastens to say, "obviously it is not that simple; nevertheless, it is significant that the desire to create an alternative world, to modify or augment the real world through the act of writing (which is one motive underlying the novelistic tradition in the West) is inimical to the Islamic world-view. The Prophet is he who has completed a world-view; thus the word *heresy* in Arabic is synonymous with the verb 'to innovate' or 'to begin'. Islam views the world as a plenum, capable of neither diminishment nor amplification".[15] Although his remarks on the Islamic world-view confirm the static features of the doctrine, they tend to overlook the contributions of Islamic philosophy with its sophisticated undermining of this static vision. His evaluation of the stories of *The Arabian Nights* as "ornamental variation on the world, and not completion of it; neither are they lessons, structures, extensions, or totalities designed to illustrate the author's prowess in representation, the education of a character, or ways in which the world can be viewed and changed",[16] is more relevant. Although it slights and even neglects some of the major textual strategies of this great work of narrative, it shows, even if indirectly, a different and more subtle way of interaction between narrative and the real world. Yet Said is neither concerned with the mode of this specific form of interaction, nor interested in explaining how, in the face of such an inimical world-view, Arab writers produced not only mature novels, but also fine short stories and drama. Nor does he explain how it is that the views inherent in many of these works are not completely discordant with those innate in an Islamic world-view.

Nevertheless, his main proposition, which poses "authority" and "molestation" as the root of the fictional process and the operative principle maintaining the autonomy of the novel as an institution, may offer a solution to the problem. In fact the very process of modifying, complementing or augmenting the real world through the act of writing is prevalent not only in *The Arabian Nights* but also in the interpretive act of understanding Islam, adopting its teachings, and producing its secondary discourses, with the inevitable consequence of creating numerous versions of Islam. In this interpretive process, the secondary discourse, which often plays a vital and more active role than that of the primary and holy text, is motivated by complex social and textual considerations that bring plurality into the monolithic world-view of Islam. These in turn create conditions conducive to the accommodation of different world-views within a flexible Islamic framework.

The elaboration of pluralistic discourse is even more intricate in the secular practice of narrative writing. Said acknowledged that Arabs who wrote narrative and secular discourse in general "undertook a fundamentally heroic enterprise, a project of self definition and autodidactic struggle".[17] They "struggle against political chaos and foreign domination, a struggle in which national identity was at its most precarious initial stage — with religion, demography, modernity, language enmeshed confusingly with each other".[18] But they also struggled against a literary tradition whose inherent world-view and stylistic canon required radical transformation to become conducive to the development of narrative discourse. The "heroic" nature of their enterprise is nowhere as evident as in the understanding that narrative discourse is a purposive action and cognitive process of rationalization in which the most extreme flights into fantasy have their in-built reason. "Philosophers of history have shown that narration is not just an impressionistic substitute for reliable statistics but a method of understanding the past that has its own rationale".[19] Any particular aspect of reality can only be understood in connection with the particular means of representing it. The genesis of narrative discourse in Arabic culture is therefore synonymous with the genesis of a new way of rationalization and perception of both the self and the other. As a process, it is inseparable from the emergence of the new social and cultural experiences which gave rise to a new perception of national identity.

However, the question of the genesis of narrative discourse in Arabic literature requires a more comprehensive approach that takes into account a host of factors. Such a question did not, and indeed cannot, find a satisfactory answer in any of the simplistic genealogical arguments of either camp. Even if one was to retain the genealogical terminology, it is important not to take it literally, to emphasize the polygenetic rather than the monogenetic nature of this genealogy, and to couple it with Jacques Berque's affirmation that "the genealogies of creativity do not, and need not, follow a straight line. The history and variations of artistic genius presuppose discontinuity, interaction, an unexpected intersection of lineages rather than a simple linear succession. Why look among the *ta'ziyas,* popular skits, or magic lantern shows for the ancestors of the contemporary theatre if the latter does no more than provide a modern language to life's theatricality that formerly assumed quite different forms?"[20] There are two important arguments in Berque's statement: one is the discontinuous and interactive nature of the genealogy of creativity, and the other is a complete denial of the textual for the sake of the social.

Berque's emphasis on the discontinuous and interactive nature of the genealogy of creativity is of vital importance, for close study of the genesis of narrative discourse suggests the key role of discontinuity and the constant break with established tradition in order to elaborate the basis for an emerging one. Yet his second argument undermines the importance of genealogy and moves the emphasis from the textual plane to the sociological one. While the shift is welcome, the problem with this permutation is that it tends completely to obscure the significance of textual or rather intertextual aspects of the complex polyphyletic process of the origination of modern narrative discourse in Arabic literature. Indeed, the question of linear genealogy in the realm of literary genres is simply reductive, for it tends to resort to easy and mechanical explanations for a complex and polymorphous phenomenon. Yet it is also simplistic to wash one's hands completely of the textual elements. Without undermining the importance of the sociological approach, one can still benefit from the work advanced by genealogical arguments that takes into account the discontinuous and interactive nature of the genealogy of creativity.

Understanding the genealogy of creativity in this manner enhances the sociological treatment of the subject and the awareness of the various rubrics of the context in which the process takes place. Inherent in the concept of discontinuity there is an acknowledgement of a cultural rupture which involves a break with certain traditions and the development of others. Such a rupture can indirectly shed some light on the intertextual process whose dynamics offer, when conducted in a changing socio-historical context, a more coherent explanation of the genesis of new narrative discourse. This is so because intertextuality brings a vital dimension to the process, for it designates the various relationships that a given text may have with other texts and its transformation of distinct textual elements within its discourse. The very term *rupture* implies an established mode of understanding and at the same time a break with its basic conventions. The break cannot be comprehended without prior knowledge of the system that it aspires to subvert, for the established system acts as a vital part of the meaning-generating process, a part that is vital for the understanding of what is new in the new mode. Bakhtin suggests therefore that "poetics should really begin with genre, not end with it. For genre is the typical form of the whole work, the whole utterance. A work is only real in the form of a definite genre. Each element's constructive meaning can only be understood in connection with genre".[21] In the absence of an established genre and a recognized frame of reference, as is the case with the genesis of narrative discourse, appropriation of other genres and their approximation to the needs of the new discourse in order to create a horizon of understanding is necessary. This was achieved in the context of the genesis of modern narrative discourse in Arabic literature through the elaboration of the genealogical argument.

The sociological approach to the analysis of narrative discourse has long been elaborated by both Bakhtin and Goldmann in a manner that has purged it of the simplistic notions of Marxist theory, which saw literature as a mere reflection of social reality. They established a homological relationship between narrative and social structures that recognizes the specific nature of the literary text and the uniqueness of its poetic composition, and, at the same time, investigates and elaborates its ability to mediate social reality. Their major contribution was achieved by associating the study of literature with that of semiotics, structures and ideology. Bakhtin's attempt to synthesize the semiotic contribution of the Russian formalists with that of sociological thinking resulted in the fusion of the study of semiotics into that of ideology. He states that ideological structures coexist with the semiotic field, for

> everything ideological possesses meaning: it represents, depicts, or stands for something lying outside itself. In other words it is a sign. Without signs there is no ideology ... A sign does not exist as part of a reality — it reflects and refracts another reality. Therefore, it may distort that reality or be true to it, or may perceive it from a special point of view ... The domain of ideology coincides with the domain of signs. They equate with one another. Wherever a sign is present, ideology is present too. Everything ideological possesses semiotic value.[22]

When he applied this equation to his study of narrative, he demonstrated that narrative discourse in any literary work is never self-contained or self-generating, but refracts through its content or material a unified ideological environment. "For Bakhtin, the specific nature of literature, its internal organization, was closely connected with, and penetrated by socio-historical forces not identical in their specificity with their transposition into the imminently literary ... Bakhtin advanced a concept of the social nature of literature which unified the internal and external without collapsing one into the other".[23] This is radically different from previous sociological theories of reflection, for it suggests that the validity of the sociological analysis of literary discourse is conditioned by its ability to reveal the social nature of literature from within the whole poetic construction. Like the sign, a literary work is simultaneously internal and external, its content and devices social and literary. As the sign depends on its context for meaning, it follows that the constitutive nature of the sign itself embodies a multiplicity of meaning which is realized only in the process of active, responsive understanding. Understanding is thus dialogic in nature, and Bakhtin's theory of communication emphasizes the central role played by this dialogic process of understanding and generating meaning as the active medium of social values.

For Bakhtin, narrative discourse is dialogic by nature; thus, a crucial precondition for its development is the internal stratification of national language into distinct linguistic levels, a stratification which in turn is associated with a certain degree of social development that allows for the polarization of such linguistic strata. Narrative discourse "can be defined as a diversity of social languages and a diversity of individual voices, artistically organized. The internal stratification of any single national language into social dialectics, characteristic group behaviour, professional jargons, generic languages, languages of generations and age groups, tendentious languages, languages of the authorities, of various circles and passing fashions, languages that serve the specific socio-political purposes of the day ... this internal stratification present in every language at any historic moment of its existence is the indispensable prerequisite for the novel as a genre",[24] or, indeed, for any genre of narrative discourse. The internal stratification of the national language corresponds to similar stratifications of literary styles in the composition of narrative. Narrative discourse "as a whole is a phenomenon multiform in style and variform in speech and voice. In it the investigator is confronted with several heterogeneous stylistic unities often located on different linguistic levels and subject to different stylistic controls".[25]

Bakhtin lists several types of compositional stylistic unities prevalent in narrative discourse, such as direct authorial literary artistic narration, stylization of the various forms of everyday narration, stylization of the various forms of semi-literary (written) everyday narration (the letter, the diary, etc.), various forms of literary but extra-artistic authorial speech (moral, philosophical, or scientific statements, oratory, ethnographic descriptions, memoranda and so forth), and the stylistically individualized speech of characters. The language of narrative discourse incorporates a multitude of different languages, and, by implication, of the genres associated with these languages. The study of these compositional stylistic unities demonstrates that they come to narrative discourse from a multiplicity of sources, and in the process they bring with them various literary and textual strategies. The heterogeneity of these elements enforces the polygenetic rather than the monogenetic nature of the genesis of narrative discourse. Narrative discourse aspires to "represent all the social and ideological voices of its era, that is, all the era's languages that have any claim to being significant; it must be a microcosm of heteroglossia".[26]

Goldmann's sociology of narrative is based on four main maxims. Firstly, "the literary work is not the mere reflection of a real, given collective consciousness, but the culmination at a very advanced level of coherence of tendencies peculiar to the consciousness of a particular group, a consciousness that must be conceived as a dynamic reality, orientated towards a certain state of equilibrium".[27] The main difference between this assumption and that of the theory of reflection is that it transforms the very concept of consciousness into an evolving process, and sees the key concept not in the *real* collective consciousness existing separately and outside the work, but in the constructed concept (*zugerechnet)* of *possible consciousness* which alone makes an understanding of the first possible. Secondly, "the relation between collective ideology and great individual literary ... creations resides not in an identity of content, but in a more advanced coherence and in a homology of structures, which can be expressed in imaginary contents very different from the real content of the collective consciousness".[28] The complexity of this relationship is such that it allows a multiplicity of its manifestations, yet beneath this multiplicity it is possible to detect a pattern. An understanding of the composition of such a "collective ideology", or "world-view", is necessary for the deciphering of the process of the genesis of narrative discourse. The emergence of a different world-view is homologous to that of its new forms of expression which draw many aspects of their composition from such a view.

This is enhanced by Goldmann's third precept that the narrative work which "corresponds to the mental structure of the particular social group may be elaborated in certain exceptional cases by an individual with very few relations with this group. The social character of the work resides above all in the fact that an individual can never establish by himself a coherent mental structure corresponding to what is called a world-view. Such a structure can be elaborated only by a group, the individual being capable only of carrying it to a very high degree of coherence and transposing it on the level of imaginary creation."[29] Apart from offering a sociological interpretation of the concept of the gifted individual without denying the significance of individual talent, this assumption posits the interaction between the literary work, its author and the society on a more sophisticated and dialectical plane where all mechanical and static concepts are invalidated. The sophisticated nature of this interaction suggests the fourth maxim that "the collective consciousness is neither a primary reality, nor an autonomous reality; it is elaborated implicitly in the overall behaviour of individuals participating in the economic, social and political life".[30] Although these four maxims of the sociology of literature remained at the centre of Goldmann's sociology of narrative, their modification by his concept of the *category of mediation* in which the thinking of certain *problematic* individuals (artists, writers, philosophers, etc.) remains free from the predominant characteristics of the collective consciousness and dominated by qualitative values (even though such problematic individuals are unable to extract themselves entirely from the degraded mediation whose action permeates the whole of the reified society) freed Goldmann's approach from the pitfalls of traditional sociology of literature and enabled it to illuminate various forms of cultural creation. For him, "there is valid literary and artistic creation only when there is an aspiration to transcendence on the part of the individual and a search for qualitative trans-individual values".[31]

The relation of modern Arabic narrative to either Western narrative discourse or classical Arabic archetypal fiction is, therefore, not one of genealogy but of dynamic intertextuality. Indeed, "intertextuality comes into play when those approaches which insist on the text as a self-regulating unity and emphasize its functional independence are felt, for one reason or another, to be inadequate or untenable. Thus, in many instances it has gained currency as an umbrella term, covering all and any *external* relationships a text may have and embracing most conceivable ways of contextualizing it within a broader frame of reference".[32] Yet its main concern is the investigation of the way in which texts, in the widest sense of the term, interact with and shape each other; for in the intertextual plane the literary work is taken to be in constant dialogue with other texts, particularly those of similar literary traits. It posits the dialogical principle with its dynamic and dialectic nature in place of the genealogical argument, which is linear and static. Thus, one does not need, as the genealogical argument dictates, to choose only one literary ancestor, or even to consider the question of ancestry as a valid proposition. This is so because the dialogical process is pluralistic rather than singular, and presupposes that it takes place in a certain context, for dialogues do not take place in a void. Kristeva suggests that within the literary text several other discourses are legible which create round the text a multiple intertextual space whose elements can be applied in the text, and through which the text becomes a subordinated system of a larger whole which is the space of the texts applied in this whole.[33]

"André Malraux's affirmation that the work of art is not created on the basis of the artist's vision but on the basis of other works opens up the possibility for better understanding of the phenomenon of intertextuality. This phenomenon implies the existence of autonomous semiotic systems — or discourses — within which more or less explicit processes of construction, reproduction, or transformation of models take place".[34] All such processes, and they are evidently marked by plurality, are governed by, and take place within, the autonomous, hierarchical network of internal relations of dependence and interdependence operating in narrative discourse. Hence, intertextuality does not consider prior texts as direct sources of a given text nor does it concern itself with the study of influences in its traditional sense, for this is yet again the domain of genealogy, but it investigates the texts' contribution to a code which makes possible the various effects of signification on the one hand, and the emergence of new forms of discourse with their varying codes on the other. "Intertextuality thus becomes less a name for a work's relation to a particular prior text than a designation of its participation in the discursive space of a culture: the relationship between a text and the various languages or signifying practices of a culture and its relation to those texts which articulate for it the possibility of that culture".[35]

However, intertextuality should be taken, here, in its Bakhtinian sense of a complex and rich dialogical process which operates within a changing social horizon. This is particularly so because claiming, "as some do, that intertextuality exists between different text-occurrences, when it is only a matter of semantic and/or syntactic structures common to one type or genre of discourse, is tantamount to denying the existence of social discourse and semiotic systems transcending interpersonal communication".[36] It is therefore important to emphasize that intertextuality takes place dialogically and within the social world, or, more precisely, within a changing social horizon. The dialogical aspect accentuates the vital role of the individual writer and enables one to avoid displacing authors or allocating to them merely the role of midwife assisting in the birth of literary work whose real parents are society, social class, or collective conscience.[37] It also enhances the role of the text as an agent of a continual process of change that affects both its codes and the horizons of it reception, for

> the relationship between the individual text and the series of texts formative of a genre presents itself as a process of the continual founding and altering of horizons. The new text evokes for the reader the horizon of expectations and 'rules of the game' familiar to him from earlier texts, which as such can then be varied, extended, corrected, but also transformed, crossed out, or simply reproduced. Variation, extension, and correction determine the latitude of a generic structure; a break with the convention on the one hand and mere reproduction on the other determine its boundaries.[38]

The fact that this process takes place within the social world points to the social nature of literary production and eliminates all the romantic or mystical notions about the writer as a genius mysteriously inspired by unknown and illusory muses, whose work, therefore, is an independent product transcending society and time and completely metaphysical and beyond analysis. Any theory of the social nature of art and literature depends on two assumptions: "(1) that the fundamental impulses to these activities are themselves social, and (2) that those aspects of human responsibility significant to them are the creation of society. The first idea is often expressed in the form that art is essentially communication and thus a response to other people, if not to social facts or cultural patterns".[39] This is one of the basic propositions that led to the investigation of the role of the reading public and the nature of cultural transition that paved the way for the rise of modern narrative discourse around the turn of the century. The second idea stems from the fact that the basic impulse for the creation of art is a response to other people and artistic works produced by them. Even the question of subjectivity is itself open to a social interpretation, for "the assumption that subjectivity is constructed implies that it is not innate, not genetically determined, but socially produced in a whole range of discursive practices",[40] and literature is one of them. The social nature of art is enhanced further by the role of the social and cultural forces in directing, controlling, modifying and limiting the creative tendencies of individuals. This does not deny the importance of individual differences which distinguish writers and artists not only from each other but also from the rest of their fellow citizens, but the social and cultural forces which keep the divergence within limits give these individual differences a social significance.

"This suggests that the process through which a literary form emerges is the work of innumerable individuals rather than of immense anonymous force, that it resembles a coral rather than a volcanic island".[41] Some of those innumerable individuals, such as writers, critics, publishers and readers, are involved directly in the process, while others who constitute the rest of the society in which the process takes place and for which it is generally directed are vicariously involved. Yet this vicarious involvement is more significant than it appears to be, for it participates in the elaboration of values, social systems and tastes upon which the first group draw for the organization of the process of creativity and its marketing and reception. Like that of any social action, the degree of involvement of the several categories of the first group varies considerably, and so does their interaction with the second. Anthony Giddens posits the concept of "the duality of structure" as an explanation for the interaction of these varied degrees of involvement. It recognizes that men produce society, but they do so as historically and socially located individuals within a context that is not entirely of their own choosing, and of which they can never be completely independent. Yet, "structures must not be conceptualised as simply placing constraints upon human agency, but as enabling, and this is what I call the duality of structure".[42] This is clearly evident in the process of literary and artistic production in which the constraints of the social context are balanced by its enabling power. Yet creativity uses this enabling power to subvert control and change the very structure from which it has emerged. In addition, the duality of structure in this process is both operative within the social context and in its complex interaction with the literary work. The homology between the structures of both is further enhanced by the concept of duality of structures.

This requires the investigation of other factors participating in the shaping of the sociology of literary genre, prominent among which is language. The use of language for the creation of literary texts reinforces the social nature of literature, for "what is represented in the play of language is objects, conditions, and relations which are immanent in particular structures of discourse and particular conditions of enunciation carrying the complex play of social power".[43] As Bakhtin suggests, "every concrete utterance is a social act. At the same time that it is an individual material complex, a phonetic, articulatory, visual complex, the utterance is also a part of social reality. It organizes communication oriented towards reciprocal action, and itself reacts; it is also inseparably enmeshed in the communication event. Its individual reality is already not that of a physical body, but the reality of a historical phenomenon".[44] The social and the autonomous qualities are inseparable aspects of language; in this respect, language, like art, is one of the means for mediating reality, that maintains a constant dialectics between its autonomous aspects and its referential dimensions.

It is also through the pervasive power of language that individuals acquire the traditions and outlook of their cultures. Since the work of Ferdinand de Saussure demonstrated that meaning is produced within language rather than having a separate existence reflected by it, the work of post-structuralists paid attention to the elaborate interaction between language and textuality. "Language, far from reflecting an already given social reality, constitutes social reality for us. Neither social reality nor the natural world has fixed intrinsic meaning which language reflects or expresses. Different languages and different discourses within the same language divide up the world and give it meaning in different ways which cannot be reduced to one another through translation or by appeal to universally shared concepts reflecting a fixed reality".[45] But since language is not a semiotic system that exists in a vacuum or without history, objects, situations and categories of knowledge and values which we encounter or experience are always to some extent preinterpreted and preclassified for us by our particular culture and language in a manner bearing the marks and signs of their prior evaluation by our fellow men, and coded into the language they use.

Yet the role of the individual in changing and modifying language in order to manipulate meaning is recognized, but in order that this modification becomes effective it has to be seen as part of what Michel Foucault calls discursive fields,[46] whose realization relies on an intricate process of interplay between language, social institutions, subjectivity and power. In any discursive field, the range of modes of subjectivity, though great, is controlled by the dynamics of the field and its interaction with the society. But in order for any of these modes to attain power, they have to be articulated into a discourse that proves to be persuasive in the heterogeneous mass of discourses within its discursive field. As a result, not all discourses will carry equal weight or power; thus, the construction of a certain discourse into a discursive field is controlled by an elaborate process of selection, foregrounding and backgrounding. The rubrics of this construction are governed by four principles: *reversal, discontinuity, specificity* and *exteriority*. The principle of *reversal* leads to the investigation of the source of discourse. "Where, according to tradition, we think we recognize the source of discourse, the principles behind its flourishing and continuity, in these factors which seem to play a positive role, such as the author discipline, will to truth, we must rather recognize the negative activity of the cutting out and rarefaction of discourse".[47]

Both processes of flourishing and rarefaction have within them and in their interplay in the construction of discursive field the principle of *discontinuity*. Thus,

> discourse must be treated as a discontinuous activity, its different manifestations sometime coming together, but just as easily unaware of, or excluding each other. The principle of *specificity* declares that a particular discourse cannot be resolved by a prior system of significations; that we should not imagine that the world presents us with a legible face, leaving us merely to decipher it; it does not work hand in glove with what we already know; there is no prediscursive fate disposing the word in our favour. We must conceive discourse as a violence we do to things, or, at all events, as a practice we impose upon them; it is in this practice that the events of discourse find the principle of their regularity.[48]

The fourth principle, *exteriority,* gives the appearance of discourse and its regulating aspects a prominent place in its investigation. It spares us the arduous task of burrowing into the hidden core of discourse or delving into the heart of the thought, meaning and intention manifested in it. Instead, "we should look for its external conditions of existence, for that which gives rise to the chance series of these events and fixes its limits".[49]

Foucault's principle of *exteriority* brings back into the modern study of discourse the rubrics of its social context. In a literary discourse the context is not purely textual; it is linked with the social conditions as much as with the language, for it is impossible to use language as a creative medium without bringing to the final literary product both its social connotations and its aesthetic legacy. The sociology of literature has established that "prose is a more socially conditioned form of writing than verse".[50] As a result, it is perhaps easier to determine the period in which any piece of prose was written. Yet the individual differences in style, though they may vary enormously, must remain comprehensible to at least a few others in the society. If such individual styles aspire to be appreciated, let alone to be influential, then this brings into consideration the social process by which various forms and styles come to have value ascribed to them by certain groups in particular contexts, and this is what is meant by the canon. Janet Wolff argues convincingly that "assumptions and judgements which operate in traditional aesthetics are socially located and, in an important sense, ideological. The very products which aesthetics and art history posit as 'works of art' cannot be uncritically taken as somehow distinguished by certain intrinsic features, but must be seen as produced in that history by specific practice in given conditions".[51]

In the course of this study we shall see how the change in language, aesthetics and literary canon plays a significant role in the elaborate process of the genesis of narrative discourse. Although aesthetic values have their own autonomy and play a significant role in the process of the genesis of a new narrative discourse, they are shaped, modified and enhanced by their constant interaction with the various social and cultural aspects of this process. By viewing this process dialectically, this study comes closer to Jauss' concept of the *horizon of expectations* which determines both the nature of the changing aesthetic value and the reader's reception of the literary work. The horizon of expectation is seen as the accumulation of heterogeneous values (generic conventions, experiential norms, language types, and modes of representation) which are socially mediated in the process of the formation of discursive fields. The relationship between this "objectifiable system of expectations that arises from each work in the historical moment of its appearance, from a preunderstanding of the genre, from the form and themes of already familiar works, and from the opposition between poetic and practical language",[52] and the literary text is not static but dialectical and dynamic, for as the horizon of expectations shapes literary works, it is also formed and changed by them. Literary discourse does not simply exist but is generated in relation to other discourses, and its structure is also generated in the same manner, and this makes the literary text an intersection of textual surfaces, a dialogue among several writings rather than a point or a fixed meaning.

On the literary plane the linguistic code becomes an element in a more elaborate system of codes that draws upon a multiplicity of semiotic structures in its attempt to forge them into a new system. "In disrupting and transforming the semiotic system governing social exchange, and displacing social instances into discursive instances, the text produces a *referential* function as a particular effect of language: social reference occurs on the level of contradictory relationship between different structures of discourse".[53] The textual coding functions as a transformational process which changes previous semiotic structures and assimilates them into its own system. Thus, it defies any attempt to reduce it to one particular code or source. Many of these codes are themselves complex, constituting whole genres of discourse in their own right. The formation of a new discourse can therefore draw upon several codes and even varied genres of discourse at the same time.

The investigation of the genesis of narrative discourse through the specific case of the modern Arabic short story, a narrative genre which played a major role in changing the canons of taste and shaping the new literary sensibility of modern Arabic culture, requires a discussion of the concept of genre and its development within a specific context. Genre is generally defined as a set of rules and restrictions operating in the process of codification and production of literary texts. The problematic questions regarding the emergence of a new literary genre, a new set of literary rules and their familiarization to both readers and writers in a certain culture necessitates some prefatory notes regarding the use of the concept of genre in this study. This is inevitable in the face of the mounting attack on the very usefulness of the term and its validity in modern criticism.

Most anti-genre criticism concentrates on the fact that it has outlived its usefulness as a concept of classification, and that creative practices tend always to break with any set of preimposed rules, a criticism that is not void of positive insight. Yet such criticism is unable convincingly to reject the useful function of the concept of genre as a bridge capable of uniting, according to Hirsch, "the particularity of meaning with the sociality of interpretation .... Using this term, the paradox regarding the individuality of meaning and the variability of interpretation can be solved by saying that a speaker and an interpreter must master not only the variable and unstable norms of language but also the particular norms of a particular genre".[54] Here Hirsch approaches the question of communication which constitutes a vital part of the function of genres as an integral part of the semiotic system. The genre as a particular system of internal relations serves to structure expectation and interpret variables by reference to a set of invariables.

In his study, the *Theory of Genres and Medieval Literatur,*[55] Hans Robert Jauss argues for the importance of the concept of genre for the understanding of literary texts and their aesthetic reception.

> Just as there is no act of verbal communication that is not related to a general, socially or situationally conditioned norm or convention, it is also unimaginable that a literary work set itself into an informational vacuum, without indicating a specific situation of understanding. To this extent every work belongs to a genre — whereby I mean neither more nor less than that for each work a preconstituted horizon of expectations must be ready at hand (this can also be understood as a relationship of "rules of the game" [*Zusammenhang von Spielregeln*]) to orient the reader's (public's) understanding and to enable a qualifying reception.[56]

Genres are still, then, important even after a long history of the attempt to undermine their usefulness. Bakhtin forcefully stated that "poetics should really begin with genre, not end with it".[57] With the advent of semiotics and the interest in structures and forms the theory of genres has benefited greatly from its association with these new studies, for it has become part of a wider investigation of the semiotics and the communicative nature of the literary text.

Croce's old critique of the universal validity of the canon of genres, and his assertion that "every true work of art has violated an established genre, and in this way confounded the ideas of critics who thus found themselves compelled to broaden the genre",[58] do not suffice to do away with either the nominalist or typological functions of genres. In the depth of his attack there is a clear understanding of the concept of genre in its classical form of an essence, *Wesensbegriff,* assuming a timeless validity. In this respect this study shares Croce's criticism of this version of the concept, for it understands it not as a static essence or even as *genera* (classes), but as an open, self-regulating and dynamic system of associations. The concept of genre whose recognition depends on associating a complex of elements is a transtextual one that is retrospectively constructed, for genres are enmeshed in the historical context — it is a historically bound concept. There is a large number of variables in a set of invariables operative in any concept. These variables are also operative in the domain of the relationship between any single manifestation of the concept and the body of rules which makes its complex features; in other words between actuality and possibility, or to use Saussure's epoch-making distinction between *parole* and *langue.* As autonomous entity, it maintains relations of dependence and interdependence, and is equipped with an internal organization of its own typology of relations.

As Jauss points out

> the relationship between the individual text and the series of texts formative of a genre presents itself as a process of the continual founding and altering of horizon. The new text evokes for the reader the horizon of expectations and "rules of the game" familiar to him from earlier texts, which as such can be varied, extended, corrected, but also transformed, crossed out, or simply reproduced. Variation, extension, correction determine the latitude of a generic structure; a break with the convention on the one hand and mere reproduction on the other determines its boundaries.[59]

This explains both the dialectics of establishing genres, and breaking with them at the same time. Indeed, the genre as a horizon of communicative expectations is as necessary for understanding a work that is a mere reproduction of the common features of the genre as for comprehending the works that attempt to achieve a complete rupture with its canon. In order for the rupture to be completely understood as a rupture and a radical departure from the norm, the norm needs to be firmly established. Furthermore, the establishment of genre rules is *a priori* to the tightening of these rules, for it is not possible to finalize a set of coherent rules culminating in the formation of the genre without the gradual elaboration of its elements in their development and transitionary phases.

The study of the genesis of narrative discourse is in one sense the elucidation of the rise of these elements in response to various cultural needs, and the explanation of the process of its crystallization through a continuous process of change and transformation in which elements from diverse literary sources come together in a certain moment of time to establish the limitations of the genre. We shall see that the lack of established conventions of the different genres of narrative discourse was responsible for the proliferation of unnecessary preambles in both long and short narrative genres operating as a bridge between the yet to be completed set of rules and the rudimentary and transitory set of rules which act as a prefatory sketch for the genre. This is what Jauss calls the "continual founding and altering of horizon",[60] a process in which new genres emerge, not only sub-categories of the old ones, but also completely new ones. It is an *a posteriori* classification whose recognition and the familiarity of its conventions are essential to the process of communication and the generation of meaning, for the genre involves a formal structure whose traits, patterns and internal relations are not necessarily found in one text but can be easily drawn from a body of texts. The term genre is different from those of form or mode though they are not mutually exclusive, but genre has both a wider and more comprehensive scope. It designates a category of classification which is less explicitly dependent on stance, motif, or occasional touches of rhetorical texturing. But, more importantly, "it is independently able to constitute texts, whereby this constitution must be synchronically comprehensible in a structure of nonsubstitutable elements, as well as diachronically in a potential for forming a continuity".[61]

I am aware that some literary theorists regard the concept of genre as obsolete, but this is a post-Romantic idea, and this study is dealing with a phase synonymous with that of the Renaissance. Furthermore, "Genre ideas have a necessary heuristic function in interpretation ... a generic conception is not simply a tool that can be discarded once understanding is attained because understanding is itself genre-bound. The generic conception serves both a heuristic and constitutive function. It is because of this that the genre concept is not hopelessly unstable".[62] This study demonstrates that, at the early phase of the genesis of a literary genre, the writers who participate more effectively in the formulation of its embryonic phase are not necessarily those who make it their business intentionally to develop a new genre, but rather those who were more aware of the needs of the emergent reading public and sensitively receptive to its vision. This is so because literary genres emerge as an answer to a literary need more than as a result of a deliberate attempt to innovate or introduce new cultural products. Such innovations may widen the scope of an existing genre or at best realize some of its unrealized potential, but they rarely give rise to genres. Since genres, according to Jauss, are necessary for the process of understanding, their rise is thus linked to the schism in artistic sensibility which generates in turn a new world-view and a fresh way of expressing and consequently understanding it. The relationship between variable and constant structural elements that come to light in the radical historical change which has swept Arabic culture since the turn of the last century can be established only from a diachronic perspective, and this is the reason for linear and consecutive ordering of materials in this study.

1
The Infrastructure of Cultural Transition

Arabic narrative discourse has been the creation of both a particular historical process and the rise of a new reading public. Without any denial of the importance of the writer's individual imagination, Arab writers were, like their British counterparts, "profoundly conditioned by the new climate of social and moral experience which they and their readers shared".[1] In an attempt to break with the one-sided view of work and audience prevalent in certain practices of the sociology of literature, it is important to emphasize the dialectical nature of this relationship between writer and audience. Literature is written to meet the demands of a particular public, but also the converse: "there are works that at the moment of their appearance are not yet directed at any specific audience, but that break through the familiar horizon of literary expectations so completely that an audience can only gradually develop for them. When, then, the new horizon of expectations has achieved more general currency, the power of the altered aesthetic norm can be demonstrated in that the audience experiences formerly successful works as outmoded, and withdraws its appreciation".[2] The consequent development of a discursive field with its generic rules and horizons of expectation is the focus for the rest of the study.

Change in perception is one of the major catalysts for literary innovation which often leads to radical change in the nature of literary discourse. The vigorous and sweeping process of change which altered the social and moral experience of both writers and readers in the Arab world over the last century and writers' perception of themselves and of their nations' place in the world are the subject of the first two chapters of this book.

During times of social and cultural transition of such magnitude, "the production of what purports to be an authentic account of the actual experiences of individuals ... involved many departures from the tradition of fiction".[3] The pre-eminence of the social, cultural and moral process, which is operative on both writers and their readers, does not undermine the importance of the role of the reading public. The "interplay between reader and writer has been unique in prose fiction: it has its origin perhaps in Part Two of Cervantes' *Don Quixote,* where the errant protagonist encounters men and women who have read Part One and expect-indeed, dictate-certain actions from him. In some sense readers of fiction through the years of its maturity have played almost as great a role in the form's flourishing as have the writers".[4] This type of interplay can also be found in the very structure of the classical Arabic *maqāmah.*

Early Signs of Cultural Revival

Arabic narrative discourse draws simultaneously upon various narrative codes inherent in Arabic literary tradition and upon new modes of experience, developed through the process of modernization and the interaction with Europe, which led to substantial changes in literary sensibility. It emerged as a result of a long and painful interaction between two cultures with two contradictory world-views and has retained the tension of these contradictions. The beginning of the dramatic encounter of the Arab mind with Western civilization at the time of the French expedition to Egypt in 1798 is widely accepted as a convenient point of departure for the study of the interaction between the two cultures. But long before that date, European travellers had come to the Arab world, rubbing shoulders with its notables and exchanging ideas with its intellectuals. In 1734 a Lebanese priest, a graduate of the Maronite College in Rome, founded the 'Ayn Ṭūrah Academy, the first European-style school in the Arab world.[5] The influence of Europe slowly infiltrated every aspect of social and cultural life in Egypt and the Levant, and later, to a lesser extent, in Iraq.

The impact of Europe on this particular part of the Arab world was a result of several historical and cultural factors. Since the time of the crusades Egypt and the Levant have borne the brunt of the interaction with the West, which was often bloody and rarely without tension. They played a major pioneering role in synthesizing its results and harmonizing its various elements with those of the indigenous culture. In this respect Egypt and the Levant, though politically distinct, constituted a harmonious cultural entity. Intellectuals and cultural ideas flowed freely from one part to the other in an active movement that reached its peak in the nineteenth century. The leading intellectuals of the Levant in the late eighteenth cencury and throughout the nineteenth century not only travelled to Egypt as a centre of culture and intellectual life; but many of them settled and worked there for shorter or longer periods of their lives and some adopted it as their second home. Egypt's position as the leading centre of Arab intellectual activity continued well into the twentieth century. "The country reared not only patriotic and political leaders but intellectual ones whose influence was felt beyond its narrow confines".[6]

The dialogue with Western culture entered a new phase during the nineteenth century because it took place as a result of a genuine desire to revive Arabic culture. Long before the the arrival of the French expedition, Egypt, the eminent scholar Maḥmūd Shākir argues,[7] was witnessing a grand cultural revival whose outstanding intellectuals were 'Abd al-Qādir ibn 'Umar al-Baghdādi (1620—83), the author of *Khizānat al-Adab* (Treasury of Literature); Ḥasan ibn Ibrāhīm al-Jabarti al-'Aqīli (1698—1774);[8] and Muḥammad ibn 'Abd al-Razzāq al-Ḥusayni, known as al-Murtaḍā al-Zubaydi (1732—90), the author of the famous encyclopaedic dictionary, *Tāj al-'Arūs*. As his name indicates, al-Baghdādi was originally from Iraq and played a reviving cultural role there before moving to Egypt. His work was developed in Iraq by 'Abdullah al-Suwaydi (1701—74), who was a gifted scholar and discerning writer; 'Abdullah al-Bītūshi (1748—98), and Abū-l-Fawz al-Suwaydi (d. 1830).

The nature of this revival has been elaborated in Peter Gran's admirable study of the period,[9] which outlines the socio-political background of this revival as well as its religious and cultural manifestations. His study establishes the socio-economic base of cultural production in eighteenth-century Egypt, and elucidates the inner workings of the patronage system at the time and how the merchants and upper class were involved in the cultural movement and providing for its prosperity. He demonstrates how in the eighteenth century the gradual breakdown of the Ottoman system, the internationalization of the commercial sector, and the rising importance of agricultural exports changed the composition of the ruling class and led to the crumbling of old solidarities based on corporate structures and their replacement by new ones more characteristic of an urban class structure.

This was also confirmed through the various studies of Aḥmad Ṣādiq Sa'd,[10] which attempt to outline the lengthy process of Egypt's transition from the Asiatic mode of production to a capitalist economy and its social and cultural ramifications. Applying a mixture of Marx's concept of the Asiatic mode of production and Wittfogel's theories of the hydraulic society and oriental despotism to the study of Ottoman Egypt, Sa'd elaborates the "tributary" social formations of Egyptian society and the nature of the specific social, economic and cultural transformations in the relationship between the land owners' cabal, merchant capital, the Ottoman bureaucracy and the intellectual institution of al-Azhar (the oldest and major Islamic university) in a manner that led him to identify two distinct phases in Ottoman Egypt. The first extends from the Ottoman conquest of Egypt in 1517 to the end of the seventeenth century, and the second spans the rest of the period until the ascension of Muḥammad 'Ali in 1805. The former is characterized by its plunder of Egypt's human and economic wealth and the ruin of its cultural heritage. It produced a new bureaucratic class which gradually integrated itself in the Mamelukes and started, together with them, to demand a larger share of the cake.[11]

By the late seventeenth century a number of political revolts within the ruling cliques took place, and by the beginning of the eighteenth this had become the norm for the transition of power. Popular uprisings followed in succession, and the gradual growth of urban population made the city their natural arena.[12] The intellectual establishment of al-Azhar, which acted as an arbiter between the people and the ruler, was tempted by the promise of wealth, which became apparent during the period of social transformation, and started to lean more towards the ruling establishment.[13] This led to the emergence of new cultural forums to articulate the views and the needs of the oppressed masses, and gradually to the polarization of conflicting world-views or assessments of reality. "The emergence of urban class structure, which gave wealth or the promise of wealth to some while withholding it from others on a new basis, needed legitimisation. This fact played a large role in the revival of *ṭarīqah Ṣūfism*. The new economic differentiation expressed itself during this period for the first time in the creation of suburbs where wealth, not occupation or origin, was the sole criterion for admission".[14]

The process of legitimizing the new socio-economic changes ushered in the ensuing cultural revival and structured its various institutions as expression of the different social forces of the period. The *Ṣūfi* orders were the organized institution of this revival, and their proliferation to more than eighty *ṭarīqah*[15] led to the frequent conflict between them and al-Azhar.[16] By the beginning of the eighteenth century, *Ṣūfism* had become an institution leading the tendency for spiritual independence and revolt in the face of officials, *'ulamā'* and corrupt administrators.[17] It established a new institution for the poor in Egypt in juxtaposition to, and often in conflict with, the Ottoman institutions. Indeed, this *Ṣūfi* institution with its fine network in every village was more powerful and influential than the Ottoman one.[18] The *Ṣūfis* started with the extensive study of *Ḥadīth* (the traditions of the Prophet) in order, on the one hand, to ascertain the acceptability of the new socio-political reality and to motivate the various interpretations of reality, on the other. But "*Ḥadīth* studies depend on a range of ancillary disciplines, including literature, language, sciences and history. As a consequence of the need for more specialized knowledge in these fields, religious scholars organized a new cultural institution within the *ṭarīqah*, the *majlis*. The function of the *majlis* was to serve as a meeting place f-r scholars and littérateurs."[19]

A study of the composition and cultural production of the *Ṣūfi* orders in the eighteenth century demonstrates the vital link between their work and the social context in which it was produced.[20] Their activities "turned their *majlis* into a religio-cultural institution, a literary salon. These *majālis* permitted the coming together of Azhar sheikhs, literary figures from outside al-Azhar, and traveling scholars for frank interchanges free from the artificialities of formal institutions."[21] The first literary salon, the *majlis* of Riḍwan, was started in 1738 by al-Amīr Riḍwan al-Jalfi and lasted for fifteen years until his death in 1753. "The formation of the *Wafā'iyyah*[22] salon, the first modern cultural institution in Egypt, occurred very soon thereafter ... and was characterized by two emphases, its interest in later Andalusian culture and its interest in mystical poetry, especially that of Fāṭimid Egypt."[23] The number of these salons increased and their activities continued well into the nineteenth century until the changes of Muḥammad 'Ali's reign led to their demise.

These salons reflected the ideological views of the various forces in society and participated actively in the cultural debates of the period. Some, such as the *ṭuruq* of *Bakriyyah* and *Wafā'iyyah,* justified the new urban class structure. The former was a movement led directly by the merchants; the latter was based on upper-class merchant patronage. The *ṭarīqah Bayyūmiyyah* was a prototype of the "popular" order, and its cultural production continued to earn the admonishment of the establishment up to the time of 'Abd al-Raḥman al-Jabarti (1754—1822), who was a student of Muḥammad al-Ṣabbān, a leading member of the Wafā'iyyah, and was himself a member of the *ṭarīqah Shadhiliyyah.* His harsh and repeated criticisms of them as the representatives of the rabble and as the masters of the vulgar crafts (*arbāb al-mardhūlah*) provide a glimpse into the conflicting ideologies at the time. But the most important accomplishment of these orders and their literary salons was "the rebirth of a critical consciousness among writers of the middle classes",[24] for without this sharp critical consciousness and the ensuing polarization of views and articulation of arguments, the intellectual movement would not have responded in such a mature and discriminating manner to European culture when first encountered at the end of the century.

Though it was mainly a traditional revival concerned with classical literature, theology and language, some of its members, like al-Jabarti, the father, had interactions with Europeans that gave it a modern slant. He had been visited throughout his active life by a steady stream of European travellers and orientalists, and his house, as his son tells us, was like one of those literary salons constantly in session. The strength of this revival was soon to demonstrate itself in the staunch resistance to the French on the one hand, and in the direction the cultural movement took after their departure on the other. Had the French come into a cultural vacuum, as many have suggested,[25] their impact would not have produced the same results either in form or in direction.

In the Levant the revival had begun even earlier and was of a different character, for since the time of Fakhr al-Dīn II (1572—1635), the great Druse emir of Lebanon, a clear awareness of the importance of the achievements of the European Renaissance had prompted extensive interaction with the West. This led to the establishment of several schools and produced a number of enlightened intellectuals who played a significant role in paving the way for a cultural revival such as Jirmānūs Faraḥāt (1670—1732), the author of more than one hundred books on language and literature; Buṭrus Mubārak (1660—1747); Yūsuf Sam'ān al-Sam'āni (1687—1768), the acclaimed scholar and philosopher who became the librarian of the Vatican;[26] Yuḥannā al-'Ujaymi (1724—85), the well-known historian; and Ḥanānyā al-Munīr (1757—1807), the eminent poet, historian and theologian. Many of the Lebanese intellectuals travelled to Europe, mastered its languages, worked in its capitals, and reported to their readers on their findings. But because of the small readership of their publications, the impact of Europe remained restricted. Furthermore, most of the Lebanese intellectuals were Christian, and this limited their impact on the largely Muslim societies of the Arab world. None the less their enthusiasm for the revival of Arabic language and literature was as formidable as that of the Muslims, for they saw its furtherance as an act of national defiance against the Ottoman.

The rest of the Levant also participated in this early revival. Aḥmad Pasha al-Jāzzār, the ruler of Acre, who repelled Napoleon's invasion of Palestine, was a prominent reformer. Most of the leading Levantine intellectuals as well as some Egyptians and Iraqis flocked to Palestine, worked for his court and enjoyed the fruits of his patronage. He was a strong supporter of literature who established a great library and collected hundreds of books and manuscripts. Arabic books had become available in this part of the Arab world in the eighteenth century, for it was to a Syrian from Aleppo[27] in 1712 that the Ottoman Sublime Porte granted the first decree to establish an Arabic printing-press, 86 years before the one that Napoleon brought to Egypt. The designer of types for the Aleppo press was a Lebanese who established another press in al-Shiwayr in 1734 and this was followed by another in Beirut in 1753.[28]

Confrontation with the French Expedition

When Napoleon arrived in Egypt in 1798 the encounter with the West accelerated this revival of Arabic culture and provided it with a new sense of direction. The impact of the French expedition was radically different in scale and influence from the previous limited exchanges with travellers or through visits. It was an encounter through a war and wars are major catalysts of change and transformation. The sensitive spectator and gifted chronicler of this era, 'Abd al-Raḥmān al-Jabarti, describes the powerful impact of the confrontation with Europe upon the Egyptians.[29] His account of his visit, with some of the leading intellectuals of his age, to the cultural and scientific institutions of the French occupation illustrate their amazement at the wonders of European culture, which seemed to them to be *obscurum per obscurius:* "the strangest thing I have ever seen", "the extraordinary ... the unprecedented ... the unfamiliar}; "they have abnormal and special knowledge and perform bizarre experiments the results of which baffle our comprehension"... etc.[30]

Though revealing shock and implicit admiration, and an inarticulate awareness of the cultural gap that had to be bridged, his remarks do not imply any dismissal or disregard. He is even impressed by the arrangements for the prosecution and trial of Sulaymān al-Ḥalabi[31] by a French court in Cairo. This was the reaction not of a layman or an ignorant fanatic, but of an open-minded intellectual whose father had a substantial library and a lively literary salon in which scholars from throughout the Arab world congregated with orientalists and European travellers. However, in his account of the three years of the French occupation in Egypt, one can detect the depth of the relationship the Egyptian intellectuals were beginning to develop with French culture, and the amount of adjustment they felt they had to undergo.

The early sense of wonder at European civilization was mixed with a deep-rooted reluctance to accept a foreign creation. This was largely because all that was new was accompanied by the undesirable fact of French military occupation. Fortunately, the French occupation was short-lived, and as soon as it disappeared, people started to recognize the importance of the ideas to which the expedition had introduced them. From these years dates their recognition of the challenge of Western civilization and the relevance to them of many aspects of its culture: modern empirical science, parliamentary democracy and constitutional government, and, most valuable of all, the awakening of nationalism, which started with Napoleon's proclamation to the Egyptian people when French warships were at the gates of Alexandria.[32] In this proclamation, which appeals specifically to the Egyptian consciousness, one can find an important set of ideas: respect for Egypt as a glorious and distinctive nation combined with the principles of the French Revolution: liberty, equality and fraternity. The proclamation attacked the tyranny of Mameluke rule and the inequality of the feudal system, and introduced parliamentary and constitutional institutions to Egypt. It laid special stress on scientific and rational values.[33]

These concepts remained for a long time the *leitmotiv* of the struggle for independent nationhood in modern Egypt, and were adopted by many others in the Arab world, albeit with minor variations. In Egypt, the struggle commenced directly after Napoleon had conquered Egypt with the first popular revolution in the modern history of the country. The leaders were the *'ulamā'*, traditional intellectuals, and the notables who were influenced by the idea of popular government introduced to them for the first time by the French. When, after this revolution, they shared the rule of the country with the French, they discovered the meaning of democratic rule and this made them more aware of the need for national independence. After the evacuation, they went more urgently about seeking a role for themselves in the government of the country. They imposed their will upon the Sublime Porte and forced the Sultan to take their views into consideration when he appointed the *wali,* or ruler, of Egypt and when he confirmed the system according to which the country would be governed. The leaders of the Egyptian intellectual community clearly appreciated the significance of the political and scientific institutions of the French — the first seeds of Western influence sown in Egypt.[34] The French system not only promised them a say in their country's affairs, but pointed towards an even brighter future.

They conceived of themselves as the spokesmen of public opinion and were determined to fulfil Egypt's aspirations. It is possible that their lack of experience and the wide gap between their ambitions and their abilities caused their early destruction and set the tone of the tragic career of the Egyptian intellectuals.[35] Ironically, it was Muḥammad 'Ali, the very figure who had been called for by these new leaders, who was responsible for their downfall. Shortly after his appointment, the vanguard of Egypt's national and intellectual movement were bought off,[36] exiled,[37] or assassinated.[38] Their confrontation with Muḥammad 'Ali taught them how deeply culture and enlightenment interact with politics, for "in developing countries, the cultural apparatus is usually confined to very small circles and ... the main task of the indigenous intelligentsia is often understood by its members to be the political creation of a national economy and a national state. For them the cultural task and the political struggle are clearly one. From its beginnings, their cultural apparatus is filled with political vision".[39]

The success of Muḥammad 'Ali's programme of reform inside the country and his victorious military campaign abroad created a strong impetus for change. Muḥammad 'Ali's success was attributed to the modernity of his state apparatus, and this encouraged Egyptian and Levantine intellectuals to continue adopting the methods of the French, after the fears and inhibitions of the occupation had receded. This was accepted because the ruler who adopted such foreign methods was not only successful, but had also been duly appointed by the people. In addition, Muḥammad 'Ali's success helped to placate the strong traditional Muslim opposition to the cultural and linguistic reforms of the Lebanese intellectuals, many of whom were suspected of proselytizing. Thus, "one generation after the French expedition, real intellectuals appeared in the Egyptian milieu",[40] as well as in the Levant, intellectuals willing to bear their responsibilities and play their proper role. With their appearance, the original and translated culture, the intellectuals' commodity, grew to occupy a significant place in the general life of the country, and by the end of the 1830s the press, the schools, and the intelligentsia had become important elements in the running of the modern state apparatus which had produced them.

Fortunately, Muḥammad 'Ali, who had destroyed the vanguard of traditional Egyptian intellectuals, paved the way through his radical reform for a new generation of intellectuals. He brought European, mainly Italian and French, experts and advisers to regulate and modernize the country's affairs. He stressed the role of education, opened several schools, and sent many Egyptians to study in Europe. "In terms of education and the beginnings of the scholarly and intellectual milieu in Egypt, the foundation of the printing-press and the School of Languages and Translation were perhaps the two greatest achievements of the Muhammad 'Ali period within Egypt. And this should not detract from the importance of the educational missions overseas".[41] Rifā'ah Rāfi' al-Ṭahṭāwi (1801—73) went to France with these missions as the *imām,* or religious and spiritual guide, of the Egyptian students there. His master, Ḥasan al-'Aṭṭār (1766—1838),[42] having had contact with the cultural institutions of the French expedition, was deeply convinced of the importance of a comprehensive knowledge of European culture and thought. Because he was too old to go, he recommended that his brightest student, al-Ṭahṭāwi, be sent to France.

The Pioneers of Cultural Transition

When al-Ṭahṭāwi returned after five years in France, he played a major role in the cultural life of Egypt, a role more crucial than that of any of the students who had been educated abroad. He alone played "the role of a complete cultural institution, translated and supervised the translation of hundreds of books which introduced to the Egyptians the essence of the progress of European civilization at that time. He also organized and controlled the events of the educational renaissance during Muḥammad 'Ali's era and supervised the translation of the French civil code, which later became the basis of Egyptian law in general".[43] He edited the first cultural periodical in Egypt, *Rawḍat al-Madāris* (1870—73), which allowed those who returned from study abroad to publish their work, spread their ideas and play a significant role in influencing the reading public and changing its social and cultural attitudes. Apart from translations and the journal, his two books, *Takhlīṣ al-Ibrīz fi Talkhīṣ Bārīz*[44] (Summing up Paris, 1834)[45] and *Manāhij al-Albāb al-Miṣriyyah fi Mabāhij al-Ādāb al-'Aṣriyyah*[46] (Egyptian Approaches to Contemporary Literature, 1869), were milestones along the road to modernity. From these two books Egyptians learned, for the first time, about many of the achievements of European thought and literature after they had passed through the filter of traditional Islamic culture. Al-Ṭahṭāwi's admiration for the rationality of occidental culture led him to compare what he had learned in France with Islamic values and synthesise a new approach to both Islamic and European cultures. He applied rational criteria to the selection of what was relevant to the Arab condition in general and to Egypt in particular. He then fused his selection with the major tenets of Islam in a manner that placed Arabic thought on a new and promising path.

This amalgam of comparison and compromise in the original writing of al-Ṭahṭāwi reflects the fact that "at that time men's minds were undergoing the same transformation as their cities and their history. An elite of *'ulamā'* were clear-sighted enough to recognize this. Former members of al-Azhar faced the challenge of progress courageously, as al-Ṭahṭāwi had done, but while answering the appeal of innovation, remained within the classic tradition of al-Azhar".[47] Anyone reading the original works of al-Ṭahṭāwi, either his books or his editorials in his review, will discern that the reaction of Egyptian intellectuals to European culture, which had initially been the naïve astonishment recorded by al-Jabarti, had now reached a phase of relative maturity. Perplexed amazement had turned into diffident comprehension which led in turn to a laborious attempt to combine what was of value in European culture with that which was of value in traditional Arabic culture. The fact that al-Ṭahṭāwi was at pains to reconcile the ideas of the West to Islamic tradition is in itself a testimony to the strength and coherence of Arabic culture before its contact with Europe.

Al-Ṭahṭāwi's counterparts in the Levant were Aḥmad Fāris al-Shidyāq (1809—87) and Francis Marrāsh (1836—73). The Levant, particularly Lebanon and Palestine, experienced the Western impact on its cultural and national identity before Egypt. Jesuit and Orthodox missionary schools, which began in the late seventeenth century, changed the cultural outlook of the Levantine. In the early nineteenth century the advent of the vigorous Protestant missions and the moving of their printing-press from Malta to Beirut in 1834 provided new impetus. At this time, the Christian intellectuals of the Levant were devoting their energy to the reform and revival of the Arabic language as a means of asserting their independence from the Turks. The Levantine Muslims were subjected to reform first during the brief rule of Ibrāhīm Pasha, Muḥammad 'Ali's son, and then under the influence of the Ottoman programmes of reform, *Tanẓimat-i Khayriyyah,* as they were called in the edicts of 1839 and 1856.

Unlike their Egyptian counterparts who embraced the radical reforms of Muḥammad 'Ali, the Levantine Muslims resented and resisted reform because of its strong association with European intervention in the area. The European powers which obtained trade concessions from the Ottoman Porte favoured Christians and other minorities and undermined the position of the Muslim majority. The influx of manufactured goods had a drastic effect on the still largely artisanal economy. Jockeying for power, the Europeans disturbed the delicate equilibrium of the Levantine community, its social harmony and class structure. Coupled with heavy taxation and economic decline, this led to widespread disturbances and anti-Christian riots in Aleppo (1850), Nablus (1856), Mount Lebanon (1859/60) and Damascus (1860). This turbulent decade of anti-Christian riots drove most of the Christian intellectuals of the Levant to Egypt and so confirmed it as the centre of cultural reform and progress. It also played a role in establishing the autonomy of Lebanon, for while Egypt developed its administrative autonomy under Muḥammad 'Ali, Lebanon achieved hers by the *Règlement Organique* of 1864, which detached it politically from the rest of Syria.

Al-Shidyāq was the most prominent of a long Lebanese tradition of Christian scholars combining Arabic and European cultures. He was preceded by such distinguished names as Niqūlā al-Turk (1763—1828), Ilyās Iddah (1741—1828), Buṭrus Karāmah (1774—1851); and accompanied with Nāṣīf al-Yāziji (1800—71), Mārūn al-Naqqāsh (1817—1855) and the Bustānis-Buṭrus (1819—83) and Salīm (1847—84). From an early age, al-Shidyāq distinguished himself by working for the influential *al-Waqā'i' al-Miṣriyyah* in Cairo, running the American Missionaries Press in Malta, visiting London and Paris, participating in the translation of the Bible into Arabic, establishing and editing an influential newspaper, *al-Jawā'ib,* and working for the Bey of Tunis. In Tunis he was converted to Islam, for he realized that conversion was essential to remove any obstacles to his reformative ideas and to gain access to and acceptance by the wider reading public. Although he wrote two influential books on European culture, *al-Sāq 'alā al-Sāq fi ma Huwa al-Fāryāq* (The Life and Adventures of Fāryāq, 1855) and *Kashf al-Mukhabbā 'an Aḥwāl Ūrūbbā* (Revealing the Hidden Side of Europe, 1862), his major achievement was in the field of language. He simplified the language of journalism, purged it of heavy-handed rhetorical devices and ornamentation, and enriched it with new vocabulary.

His contribution to the lucid Arabic translation of the Bible was consolidated by his two books on the Arabic language, *al-Jāsūs 'alā al-Qāmūs* (Inspecting the Dictionary, 1882) and *Sirr al-Layāli fi al-Qalb wa-l-'Ibdāl* (Contemplating Language, 1884), in which he offers modern solutions to many linguistic problems in an attempt to widen the expressive and syntactic scope of the Arabic language in order to respond to the needs of a rapidly changing society. This contribution proved to be vital for the genesis of narrative discourse, for without the linguistic change many other factors would have been impaired. He laid the foundation for emphasizing the communicative function of the language and liberated it from the shackles of tradition. Unlike al-Ṭahṭāwi, whose cultural project was intended to root the modern in the traditional, al-Shidyāq's aim was to open the gates to change with little regard for tradition to the extent that his first book on Europe was rejected for infringing traditional standards and offending public morality. His linguistic reform reflects his great admiration for the literary aspects of the language and his awareness of the vital interaction between language, history and social reality.

Francis Marrāsh, who died prematurely, was a Syrian writer from a distinguished intellectual family.[48] Like many of his counterparts at the time, Marrāsh was an intellectual at the crossroad between tradition and change. At an early age he spent a year (1850) in Paris with his father, an experience which left a strong impression on him and led him to study medicine. In 1866 he returned to Paris to further his medical studies, but his health deteriorated and forced him to return to Aleppo before completing his studies, where he died a few years later. Despite his short life, he wrote productively and left eleven books and numerous articles in most of the leading periodicals of his time.[49] He was the first among the writers of his generation to try his hand at narrative discourse. Marrāsh's *Ghābat al-Ḥaqq* (The Jungle of Justice, 1865) both preceded al-Ṭahṭāwi's work and was part and parcel of Marrāsh's intellectual project. It was also followed by another narrative text, *Durr al-Ṣadaf fi Gharā'ib al-Ṣudaf* (Picturesque Coincidences, 1873), a text which develops many of the narrative characteristics of his earlier work.

Narrative in Marrāsh's work is used to project his reformative ideas into a palpable situation demonstrating their expediency and benefit. Although Marrāsh's narrative structure is clearly of a rudimentary nature, *Ghābat al-Ḥaqq* is an interesting and pioneering work. It uses narrative to debate the validity of the major ideas of his time and exploits its symbolic power. It fuses the rules of reason with the ruses of the heart and social reform with fantasy and allegorical presentation. It also develops the question of the interaction between Arabic and European culture. Instead of the laborious synthesis of al-Ṭahṭāwi and the linguistic accommodation of the new ideas of al-Shidyāq, Marrāsh moved the debate from the concern with the origin of ideas to that of their application and relevance. He shows how the adoption of certain ideas changes the course of events and transforms the life of those concerned, and, more importantly, the dire consequences of resistance to change.

Accelerating the Process of Modernization

The work of these three writers and their contribution to change was supported by what was taking place in the socio-political arena. The short-lived relapse during the khedivate of 'Abbās I and Sa'īd did not stop the expansion of education. "Patriarch Kyrillos IV initiated in 1853 the first important non-governmental efforts to establish indigenous modern schools in Egypt. The smaller Jewish, Armenian, and Greek communities also started their own schools. When Sa'īd died in 1863, there were altogether 59 foreign and non-Islamic schools in the country".[50] Some of these foreign schools, such as the Greek Orthodox school in Cairo, began in the middle of the seventeenth century, but the majority were opened in the nineteenth century.

Ismā'īl, who was himself a member of the third Egyptian mission to Europe,[51] took power in Egypt in 1863. He took the cultural achievements of the first half of the nineteenth century on to new heights when he tried to realize his slogan, primarily a cultural one, that "Egypt should become a part of Europe". In bringing his dream to fruition, Ismā'īl paid great attention to the theatre, the printing-press, education and journalism. The number of Egyptians studying abroad had been reduced to 19 under 'Abbās and 14 under Sa'īd; Ismā'īl increased the number of students to 179. This brought the total number of students who had been educated in Europe from the time of al-Ṭahṭāwi to over 600, a significant number for a nation of five million at the time. If it is borne in mind that "the

Egyptians who had studied in Europe as members of the state's educational missions, or who had been trained in the famous School of Languages in Cairo, undertook the translation of basic works in the various sciences from leading European languages",[52] then the significance of such a large number in educational and cultural terms, and its effect on the life of the country at this stage of its development, can be appreciated.

In addition, Ismā'īl increased the budget for education from only £E6000 under Sa'īd to £E40,000 and then to £E75,000. He reopened all the schools which 'Abbās I had closed, and added a considerable number of new ones. Apart from nine specialized military schools, Ismā'īl established five graduate schools, which later became the nucleus of Cairo University, not to mention countless secondary, primary, and industrial schools. He became a patron of fine art and drama in an era when it was impossible for these arts to flourish without such support. His patronage was not confined to Egypt: he offered Syrian and Lebanese intellectuals sanctuary and support when they were harassed and persecuted in their own countries, particularly after the disturbances of 1860 in Lebanon. He also established the first opera-house the Middle East had ever known. He resurrected the state press, which Sa'īd had given to a friend of his as a present, and encouraged the publication of books and newspapers in general.[53] The number of Arabic newspapers which had appeared in Egypt from the end of the French occupation until the beginning of Ismā'īl's reign had not exceeded six; during Ismā'īl's era, the number of Arabic newspapers and periodicals rose to twenty-seven with another thirty published in European languages.[54]

This enlightened atmosphere developed the basis of an intellectual class, the nucleus of which had come into existence during Muḥammad 'Ali's period. These intellectuals were distinguished by their deep understanding of the flaws of their predecessors and also by a sense of their own role and responsibilities. They wanted to provide the new generation with better opportunities and to stabilize the cultural establishment for them. They therefore paid considerable attention to broadening the base of education as far and as quickly as possible. The lessons of the immediate past had made them aware that they were a vulnerable minority, and they saw an increase in their numbers as their best protection and assurance of their role in society. They also seized the opportunity of Ismā'īl's understanding and appreciation of the importance of cultural stability and sought to institutionalize culture and education. Ismā'īl's reign is generally conceived of as the epoch which "provided the basis for the genesis of a Europeanized Egyptian élite in government, education, and letters. The membership of this élite soon expanded and its knowledge increased appreciably until it provided the leaders of the reform and later nationalist movements of the early twentieth century".[55]

Egyptian intellectuals benefited both from Ismā'īl's cultural reforms and his political innovations, especially from *Majlis al-Shūrā*, the consultative parliamentary council, which had been established by decree in 1866. Initiated as an experiment, or a piece of modern décor, the council gradually became a powerful institution, whose members were conscious of the problems and aspirations of the country. They expressed their concern in *al-Lā'iḥah al-Waṭaniyyah,*[56] the national manifesto, and in the draft of the suggested constitution which they tried to impose on Ismā'īl in order to limit his absolute monarchy in 1879. If these two documents of 1879 are compared with what al-'Aqqad calls the first Egyptian Magna Carta, namely that written by the *'ulamā',* or religious intellectuals, of al-Azhar under the leadership of Shaikh 'Abdullah al-Sharqāwi (1737—1812) in 1795, the extent of the development and maturation that Egyptian thought had undergone during the intervening eight decades becomes evident. The comparison demonstrates also that the ideas which al-Ṭahṭāwi and his generation had disseminated had now become established.

All the cultural and educational reforms of Ismā'īl's epoch were closely linked to the development of economic life in Egypt. It is hard to maintain a steady dissemination of culture and education without a rapid pace of economic growth. The era of cultivated land increased by 1,373,000 feddans (Egyptian acre, approximately 4200 m^2) in only seventeen years.[57] This rate of land development and reclamation has never been equalled since. The fast growth of cultivated land required a partial mechanization of agriculture, with its social and psychological ramifications. The appearance of machines in Egyptian villages played a subtle but vital role in modifying the villagers' outlook and undermining the power of the superstition which controlled certain aspects of their vision and their comprehension of the world. In this respect, Ismā'īl's period was one of quite exceptional growth which amounted to an agrarian revolution. Because "Egyptian agriculture has maintained intimate connexions with both the service and industrial sectors of the country, either through forward linkage as a market, or backward linkage as a source of supply for raw materials, the progress of the agricultural sector has, to a considerable degree, determined secular movements in the output of both services and industry".[58] The expansion in commerce and agriculture and the educational achievements of Ismā'īl's reign changed the social structure of the country, resulting in rapid social mobility and the creation of a large middle class.

There was also another factor which exerted a strong influence upon the life of the city comparable to the impact of machines on the villagers. This was the arrival of foreigners in great numbers to work in the various new institutions established during Ismā'īl's reign. As many as 362,600 foreigners entered the country in a period of only eight years (1857—65),[59] and this level of immigration was maintained. Bearing in mind that the population of Egypt was around five million at the time, that many of the foreigners settled in Egypt created their own social life after their own habits and traditions, and that they enjoyed a high social status in the community, one can appreciate the magnitude of their impact on Egyptian society. The effect was twofold: first, their lifestyle with its exotic ceremonies, rituals, and values influenced the Egyptians; and, second, the privileges they enjoyed awoke the spirit of rebellion and resistance in Egyptians.

At the turn of the twentieth century, this high rate of influx of foreigners persisted: the 90,000 foreign residents of 1880 increased to 112,568 in 1897, 216,576 in 1907 and 260,294 in 1917. By 1907 foreign citizens resident in Egypt constituted 25 per cent of the population of Alexandria and 28 per cent of that of Port Said, although they formed less than 2 per cent of the total population. But more significantly, their share of the national income was over 15 per cent, which made the average income of the foreigner nine times that of the Egyptian.[60] This phenomenon was by no means confined to Egypt. Because of its larger Christian minorities, the Levant, particularly Lebanon and Palestine, had known the influx of missionaries and foreigners for many decades. Since the eighteenth century Lebanon's Maronite clergy had been educated in Rome, and the reformist and modernist policies of Bashīr II (1788?—1840), the emir of Lebanon, encouraged more European educational influence and commercial contacts. In Lebanon, "foreign commercial, educational, and religious influences, rather than internal political and economic reforms, led to the formation of a new literary intelligentsia. What Tanzimat had done in Turkey and what economic change did in Egypt, Western education did in Lebanon."[61] In addition "whole communities were taken under protection. A policy which had been pursued by the French since the seventeenth and the Russians since the late eighteenth century was pursued by them and others more consciously and deliberately in the 1840s and 1850s; it was then that the British government, which had no obvious protégés of its own, established a connection with the Jews in Palestine, some of the Druzes in Lebanon, and the new Protestant churches".[62]

Through his efforts to make "Egypt a part of Europe", Ismā'īl provided the community with much of the infrastructure deemed necessary for a civilized country at that time. Although Egyptian society was ready for and receptive to the founding of these institutions, some of his achievements were exceptional. "The first government girls' school in the Ottoman empire was founded, the 185 elementary schools of 1863 had been increased to 4,685 by 1875. 'Egypt', wrote the Alexandria correspondent of *The Times* in January 1876, 'is a marvellous instance of progress. She has advanced as much in seventy years as many other countries have done in five hundred'".[63] It is agreed that "the reign of Khedive Ismā'īl constituted a decisive epoch in modern Egyptian history in so far as the Egyptians learned to adopt modern European methods in many fields of private and public endeavour. In fact the period 1863—82 was most crucial in the evolution of modern Egypt, for the vast educational and intellectual strides made by Egyptians had interesting and, in many ways, enduring cultural, social, and political consequences".[64]

Ironically, Ismā'īl, the Khedive committed to Europeanizing the country, was deposed in 1879 as a result of interference by the European powers, who felt that he had overstepped the limit in his ambitious programme of modernization. This happened partly because he had incurred a national debt of ninety million Egyptian pounds and also because the European powers, who had become very interested in the area after the opening of the Suez canal in 1869, thought that he had gone too far in his endeavour to Europeanize the country when he encouraged the National Assembly to oppose the ambitions of the European powers themselves in the area. The foundation of the National Assembly was the crucial factor in deciding his removal from power, for it posed a serious threat to the establishment of the colonial economy under the Franco-British "dual control" of the *Caisse de la Dette* created in 1876.[65] The colonial powers, preferring to control a single autocrat than an elected assembly, dealt a decisive blow to the emerging democracy and opened the way to the colonization of the region.

Changes in the Levant and Iraq

This period witnessed similar expansion in educational activities in the Levant. In the 1830s during the rule of Ibrāhīm Pasha, the new style of primary education inaugurated by Muḥammad 'Ali in Egypt was introduced in Syria and Palestine. "The scholastic system introduced by Ibrāhīm, although short-lived, gave a powerful stimulus to national education, particularly among the Muslim community; and the start he gave it was all the more far-reaching as his system aimed deliberately at awakening Arab national consciousness among the pupils".[66] In addition to the primary schools which he established all over Syria, he founded large colleges in Damascus, Aleppo and Antioch. The Damascus college had some 600 pupils while its counterparts in Aleppo and Antioch had around 400 each. Because many of these schools were designed to prepare pupils for the Army, the local notables opened schools to compete with those of Ibrāhīm and provide their children with an alternative to a military career. Thus the active interest in secular education was created which continued after the evacuation of Syria by the Egyptian Army in 1840, gathering strength as the years went by.

In Lebanon the traditional Maronite schools started an ambitious programme of reform, introducing some secular subjects and the study of Arabic language and grammar. This process of reform was accelerated by the advent of missionary education in the nineteenth century. In 1834 the Lazarist fathers opened a men's college at 'Ain-Ṭūrā and the American missionaries, Eli Smith and his wife, established the first school for girls in Beirut. "Beginning in the 1840s schools for girls, orphanages, and other charitable institutions were founded by Sisters of St Joseph of Marseille, Sisters of Nazareth of Lyon and other orders. Beirut, Sidon,

Tyre, Nazareth and other towns were the beneficiaries".[67] The rivalry between various Christian denominations, particularly that between the Jesuits and the Presbyterians, benefited the Levantines, who were at the receiving end of this competition. When the Jesuits established a large school in Ghazīr in 1843, the American Protestants built a larger one in 'Ibyah in 1847. When the latter upgraded theirs and moved it to an important site in Beirut in 1866, renaming it The Syrian Anglican College, which later became the American University of Beirut, the Jesuits followed their example in 1875, upgrading theirs and renaming it Saint Joseph's College. Even within a single denomination the rivalry between various nations served the same purpose. When the British established a girls' school in 1860, the Americans followed suit in 1861, followed by the Germans. Between 1834 and 1860 more than thirty-three such schools were founded by Americans in Syria-Lebanon, attended by approximately 1000 pupils, of whom nearly one-fifth were girls.

This rivalry reached its peak in Palestine where, by 1880, there were more than one hundred schools belonging to eleven different Christian denominations, in addition to ninety-five governmental and local Muslim schools. The Russian and Greek Orthodox Church was particularly active in this part of the Levant in competition with the Roman Catholic and Protestant churches. The rival Church schools taught religion, regular school subjects and their respective foreign language. They even sent their brightest students to further their studies in their respective countries-a fact that played a major role in giving the newly educated Arabs firsthand knowledge of the literature of these countries, which in turn played a decisive role in the genesis of narrative discourse.[68] By the 1870s Jerusalem alone had more than 40 schools belonging to eight different religious denominations, from Judaism to Islam, with the various Christian persuasions, ranging from the Orthodox to the Roman Catholic, Anglican, and Protestant, boasting altogether about 4000 students and over 200 teachers.[69] Nablus had more than 30 schools, and there were others in most Palestinian cities.

At the same time, Iraq enjoyed relative political calm after many years of turbulence caused by the struggle between the Ottomans and the Persians and by the troubled Mameluke rule. In 1868 Midhat Pasha became Iraq's ruler, and in the four years of his reign he initiated an ambitious programme of reform in both the educational and cultural fields. He set in motion a massive programme of agricultural, administrative and infrastructural development. "Clogged-up canals were cleared, roads were opened, and a horse tramway line was started; more surprisingly a savings bank was founded and a Euphrates railway was contemplated".[70] In the few years of his reign Iraq saw its first newspaper, *al-Zawrā'* (1869),[71] thus opening the way for a long and prosperous history of journalism. Among his successors, a few left a mark on the country's development. 'Abd al-Rahman (1875—9) was a vigorous educationalist who expanded the number of schools and reformed their curricula. Sirri Pasha was a patron of culture and literature and eager for the material embellishment of his capital. 'Aṭallah Pasha expanded and modernized education, reformed the judicial system by interlacing it with the Napoleonic code, and encouraged the publication of traditional source books and the printing of manuscripts.

But the major boost to education in Iraq took place during the rule of Nāmiq Pasha (1899—1902), who embarked on an ambitious programme of new schools and established the Baghdad Teachers' Training College in order to provide his schools with the much needed qualified teachers. He opened the first governmental girls' school and laid the foundation for a well-structured educational system. By the end of the Ottoman rule in Iraq in 1917 remarkable progress had been achieved: the number of girls' schools had reached eight and schools for boys approached 200 with approximately 20,000 students. The delay in government activity in the field of education was compensated for by private initiatives and religious education. Because of its ethnic and religious composition, traditional religious education in Iraq, particularly the schools of Najaf and Karbala, continued to dominate the local scene, long after the dwindling of its influence in other parts of the Arab world. Yet this very ethnic and religious diversity was responsible for the advent and proliferation of modern schools in Iraq through Latin and Uniate missionary work among Nestorians, Armenians, Jacobites, and Chaldaeans.

The first missionary schools appeared in Iraq in the eighteenth century, pioneered by the Dominicans and the Uniates. By the middle of the nineteenth century, the increase in their number encouraged the local Christian communities to establish a Chaldaean boarding school in Mosul and another Roman Catholic school in Baghdad. Before the end of the century the number of Christian missionary and local schools had risen to sixteen including two girls' schools. In 1865 the first Jewish school in Baghdad was opened, and the number of Jewish schools continued to increase until it reached fourteen by the end of Ottoman rule. In addition there were Persian, Indian, German and other schools. The number of foreign and private schools had reached sixty-four by 1914 with more than 10,000 students. Most of these schools were not easily accessible to the general Muslim population of the country, who relied mainly on traditional and governmental education, and had to wait until the beginning of the twentieth century to see a sharp increase in the number of schools and the opening of several colleges to further their education.[72]

Printing and the Change in Patronage

Similar rivalry took place in the field of publishing and translation: the Americans moved their printing-press to Beirut in 1834 and started to publish the first parts of the Arabic translation of the Bible in 1847; the French established a new press in 1848 and another one in 1854. The Dominicans established their press in Mosul in 1860 and another one followed in Baghdad. The Levant had had the printing-press since the beginning of the eighteenth century. This was a vital factor in the creation of a new reading public because without printing, reading is restricted to the small number of people who have access to manuscripts. Coinciding with the establishment of the Napoleonic press in Cairo, the Patriarch Athanase IV of Antioch established an Arabic printing-press in Aleppo. A few years later, in 1821, a state-run press was founded in Cairo (Qaṣr al-'Aini, then Būlāq), and it published some 250 books in the first twenty years of its operation. In 1847 a third was established in Jerusalem, and in 1855 a fourth, in Damascus.

It may be useful to compare the nature of the first 248 books printed by the Būlāq press with those of two private libraries from the period: one is that of 'Umar Makram (1755—1822), *Naqīb al-Ashrāf* (Head of the Descendants of the Prophet), and the leading intellectual of his age, and the other is that of Aḥmad Taymūr (1871—1930), the father of Muḥammad and Maḥmūd,[73] and one of the major intellectuals of his time. Both Makram and Taymūr were of similar social background and the composition of their libraries, both donated to the Egyptian National Library, make an interesting contrast. The former died in the year in which the Būlāq press started its production; hence, his library gives an idea of the nature and scope of literature before the advent of the press. Taymūr died in 1930, the year in which this study ends, with the maturing of the new narrative discourse, more than a century after the introduction of the press. The similarity of their social and cultural background makes the difference in the scope and composition of their libraries more indicative of the process of cultural change, because it reduces the variables that may affect the composition of such libraries.

Makram's library consists of 325 books, 270 of which are in manuscript form and 55 in print. All the books are of a classical and traditional nature, and their main concern is theological and linguistic topics. They are marked by an evident lack of originality, for half the books have a title that starts with the word *sharḥ,* "elaboration on" (89 books), *ḥāshiyah,* "explanatory note" (60) or *tafsīr,* "commentary" (22). Although the library has a few books on scientific topics such as logic, philosophy, astronomy, they are of a very rudimentary nature and constitute no more than 1 per cent of the collection.[74]

In the twenty years following Makram's death Cairo's printing-press turned out nearly as many books as he had collected in his lifetime, but they were of a completely different nature. The first 248 books published by the state press during 1822—42 are divided as follows: 45.6% in sciences, military subjects, medicine, etc.; 17.7% in literature and geography; 15.3% in languages; 13.3% in Islamic studies and 8.1% in history.[75] Although it is clear from the titles and subject-matter of these books that an overwhelming number of them were translations and served the direct needs of Muḥammad 'Ali's regime and its civil and military administration, a small portion was produced as a commodity for the emerging book market. Apart from al-Ṭahṭāwi's, the books classified as literature were either anthologies of classical Arabic literature or traditional works written by Ḥasan al-'Aṭṭār and another Azharite, Ibrāhīm Muḥammad al-Bājūri.

The cultural revival during Ismā'īl's reign also affected the publication of books. "Between 1872 and 1878, three hundred thousand copies are said to have been printed, that is as many as between 1821 and 1872. Scientific and technical literature had by far the largest share of the new book production industry devoted to it ... In addition, titles which fell specifically in the Arabic Islamic tradition were now increasingly published. By 1890 about 750 Islamic books have been printed",[76] and by 1919 the total number of printed books was approaching 9000.[77] The eight book-sellers in Cairo in 1835[78] had mushroomed into twenty by the end of Ismā'īl's reign and to more than fifty before the end of the century.

It not surprising, therefore, to find that the number of books in the library of Taymūr was 5548 in the first twelve years of its acquisition, 1901—12; 7068 in 1913; 11,816 in 1923; 12, 773 in 1926 and more than 21,000 in 1930. This massive collection of books deserves a separate study for its significance as an indication of the cultural background of certain intellectuals at the time. The books are classified into seven sections: language, 2390 books; letters, 2675; religion 4956; languages and dictionaries, 3974; history, 4273; bibliographies and pictures, 1268 and miscellaneous sciences, 1708.[79] The importance of Taymūr's library is twofold: it shows the scope of knowledge available to the Arab intellectual in the first decades of this century, which in comparison with that of Makram had undergone monumental change, and it provides an insight into the cultural formation of his two sons, who pioneered the writing of modern narrative discourse. The impressive number of literary books in the library shows a departure from traditional jurisdiction and theology into more literary concerns. Works of traditional narrative occupied a place on the library shelves side-by-side with translated fiction, and books from as far away as India and Europe had found their way into the private library of an Arab intellectual.

Similar developments took place in the Levant. The forty years between 1834 and 1874 witnessed a remarkable increase in the number of printing-presses which exceeded thirty in Lebanon alone and ten in Syria, in addition to numerous others in Palestine. In the period 1892—1909 the Ḥanānyā Press in Jerusalem alone printed 281 books in Arabic and other European languages.[80] These numerous printing-presses published largely religious and educational material, yet their cultural output, mainly poetry, traditional prose and translations, maintained four bookshops in Beirut, and several others in the rest of the Levant. Although the whole region was under Ottoman rule, Arabic language and education were of great importance. The Arabic language cause was championed even by the Christians of the Levant as a means of distinguishing themselves from the occupying Turks. By 1900 the four bookshops had multiplied into more than twenty, and their stock had become more interesting and varied,[81] originating not only in Beirut but also in Baghdad, Cairo, Damascus, Jerusalem, India, Turkey and Europe. But the major production of the press was periodicals, which formed the basis of literary and cultural communication and continued to increase in number, volume and quality throughout the second half of the century.[82]

This cultural and educational renaissance led to the appearance of a new phenomenon: the coexistence of otherwise completely separate types of relationships between the artist and the public. The first was a patronage system in which patrons personally supported culture and formed the public for which it was produced. The Khedival palace in Egypt and the Christian missions in Lebanon were among the generous patrons of arts and letters during this period. The second was the emergence of a bourgeois public: the cultural workman had become an entrepreneur. He earned money through the sale of cultural commodities to an anonymous public. Although Ismā'īl was a benevolent patron and generous supporter of art, he also created the base for, and encouraged, the change towards the second type of relationship. Because of both his patronage and the cultural atmosphere he had created, ambitious writers and journalists from Syria and Lebanon moved to Egypt, where they flourished.

The foundation of four theatres[83] enabled the early dramatic works of Ya'qūb Ṣannū' (1839—1912) to see the light of day and encouraged theatrical companies from the Levant, such as those of Salīm al-Naqqāsh (d. 1884) and Yūsuf al-Khayyāṭ in Lebanon, and Abū Khalīl al-Qabbāni (1833—1902) from Syria, to move to, and even settle in, Egypt to perform their plays and dramatic anecdotes. This attracted new audiences, opened up new horizons and eventually expressed a significant change in both the artistic sensibility and the relationship between artist and public.[84] In 1848 Mārūn al-Naqqāsh (1817—55) presented the first Arabic drama, whose title, *al-Bakhīl,* betrays its relationship to Molière's *L'Avare*. It might seem that a theatrical venture starting with a Molière comedy has little to do with the rise of nationalist consciousness, but Naqqāsh chose the cedar tree as an emblem for his theatre and actors, and this was selected, almost a century later, in 1943, as the emblem of the Lebanese Republic and adorned its flag.

The period was in fact remarkable for theatrical and musical activities: the first Egyptian plays, written by Ya'qūb Ṣannū' and others, were performed,[85] and Egyptian music and singing flourished. During this period, 'Abduh al-Ḥāmūli (1845—1901), Almaẓ (d. 1890?), Yūsuf al-Manyalāwi (1850—1911), Ibrāhīm al-Qabbāni (1852—1927), Muḥammad 'Uthmān (1855—1900), Dāwūd Ḥusni (1871—1937), Muḥammad al-'Aqqād and Kāmil al-Khula'i (1880—1938) started distinct musical trends in which Arabic and Turkish themes and melodies were amalgamated with Egyptian folk music and songs. These trends prepared the ground for the appearance of Salāmah Ḥijāzi (1852—1917) and Dāwūd Ḥusni, who in turn paved the way, towards the beginning of the twentieth century, for the birth of authentic Egyptian music in the achievements of Sayyid Darwīsh (1892—1923). Ismā'īl's epoch also saw the early beginnings of Egyptian painting and fine arts.

It is not surprising that this period also witnessed the first signs of fictional literature, when al-Ṭahṭāwi translated Fénelon's *Aventures de Télémaque* and published it in Arabic in 1867, and when his bright student, Muḥammad'Uthmān Jalāl (1829—98), continued in his master's footsteps and translated Saint-Pierre's *Paul et Virginie* and the *Fables* of La Fontaine, and produced an Arabic adaptation of Molière's *Tartuffe,* mainly in the colloquial language. Around this period also, the first original attempt to compile a work of fiction in Egypt took place when the educational pioneer of Ismā'īl's epoch and the mastermind of most of his cultural accomplishments, 'Ali Mubārak (1823—93), wrote his didactic work, *'Alam al-Dīn,* (1882) and published it in four volumes. As a rudimentary narrative, *'Alam al-Dīn* is similar to Marrāsh's work in style, language, organisation and textual strategies, but it is much larger in scale and narrative ambition. Its didactic overtone is as evident as that of Marrāsh which was written seventeen years earlier, with only marked changes in scope and aim.

Urbanization and New Social Norms

Another factor which contributed to the development of the infrastructure of cultural transition was urbanization and the effect of the urban growth of the nineteenth century on the social norms and class structure. In 1800, 10 per cent of Egypt's population lived in towns of over 10,000, and Cairo had a population of about 250,000.

> In geographical or greater Syria, Aleppo had a population variously estimated at 150,000 to 250,000, and Damascus about 100,000, while Hama, Homs, Jerusalem and Tripoli had 10,000 inhabitants or more. Since the total population of Syria was probably below 1,500,000 this implies an extremely high proportion of population living in towns, 20 percent or more. Figures for Iraq ... indicate a population of 50,000 to 100,000 for Baghdad, and 50,000, or a little less, for each of Mosul, Hilla, and Basra. The total population of Iraq may be estimated to have been under 1,500,000, which again would imply a high degree of urbanization-perhaps as much as 15 per cent.[86]

Yet this already high degree of urbanization increased rapidly throughout the nineteenth century. In Egypt, "Between the censuses of 1882 and 1897 towns with more than 20,000 inhabitants grew by 68 per cent, while the total population grew by less than 43 per cent. By 1897 they comprised 13.6 per cent of Egypt's population. This was the period during which the guilds and slavery almost disappeared, with a few remnants left over for the twentieth century".[87] The growth of the urban centres continued to be higher than that of the rest of the country: in 1907 they constituted 15.2 per cent of the total population, and by 1930 sizeable towns catered for more than 18 per cent of the population. In Syria in

1914 the urban population had reached 1,600,000 or 25 per cent of the total population. In Iraq, Baghdad's population rose to 140,000 in 1904, and to 200,000 in 1930. The urban population of the country as a whole rose to 24 per cent in 1867 and 25 in 1890 and maintained this rate until 1930.

In this period Egypt and the various parts of the Arab world were drawn, "to a greater or lesser extent, into the international network of trade and finance. This entailed the immigration of European businessmen and technicians, the investment of foreign capital, the development of mechanical transport, and the shift from a subsistence to a cash crop agriculture. The introduction of modern hygiene led to a sharp population growth, and foreign competition resulted in the ruin of handicrafts".[88] Although the decline of handicrafts slowed down urban growth in certain artisanal centres, the great increase of seaports more than compensated for this. Seaports were centres of trade and grew rapidly with the economic dependence on cash crop exports. The Egyptian cotton crops grew from 944 cantars in 1821 to 213,585 in 1830, 1,181,888 in 1863, and 2,912,073 in 1882, reaching 8,531,172 in 1929.[89] Because most of this cotton was exported, it stimulated both the growth and prosperity of urban seaports and the economic conditions of the urbanites.

This tremendous growth of urbanization was a result of modernization — the spread of education, social mobility, and the development of the economy. This was accompanied with increasing centralization and bureaucratisation, a rise in national income and the spread of Western-style living, and involved a marked change in the composition of the urban population. Town-dwelling farmers gave way to persons engaged in more truly "urban" occupations. This involved a growth in readership, widened the scope of human experience and extended the potential subject-matter available for the new narrative discourse. The non-industrial character of Egyptian, Syrian and Iraqi urbanization constrained the effect of rapid social change, for it preserved certain modes of rural interaction and hindered the elimination of some social barriers which was needed for a more liberal treatment of social issues, a feature required for the formation of narrative discourse. This type of urbanization produced its own social traits and demands and left its impact on the new reading public and its emerging narrative discourse.

The increased urbanization together with the spread of education provided for the genesis of a new middle class. Before the turn of the century, it had become clear, as Hitti suggests, that

> a new class had appeared, it included the new type of businessmen and Western-educated lawyers, physicians, teachers, and other professionals. It lodged itself as a middle class between the traditional group of government officials, landowners, aristocrats, and ecclesiastics and the underprivileged class of manual labourers and soil tillers. Thus the gap widened between the high and the low, the rich

> and the poor. The wider the gap grew the greater was the source of dissatisfaction. In its early stages this class was recruited from minorities, but it was later augmented from the majority groups and it gathered into its hands the forces of control in the society not excluding the political.[90]

The rise of this middle class was important, for it provided a good many of the spiritual, intellectual and political leaders of the Arab countries in this period. Although there are few reliable statistics related to the growth of the middle class in the nineteenth and early twentieth century,[91] there is ample evidence of other sorts to suggest the rapid growth of this class, particularly in the last decades of the nineteenth and early ones of the twentieth century. Apart from the dissemination of education and the ensuing social mobility, the early industrialization and the economic development led by Ṭal'at Ḥarb in Egypt, for example, would not have been possible without a sizeable middle class. In addition, the concentration of industrial and other economic activities in the city encouraged the growth of the urban middle class. Anwar 'Abd al-Malik provides an analysis of the city dwellers of Egypt in 1917, of whom nearly one million could be classified as middle class.[92]

But the most important outcome of urbanization was the transformation of social values and social norms. Compared with its rural counterpart, the urban space is more liberal and egalitarian and offers wider opportunities for social mobility. It is also seen, by a largely conservative population, as civilized but degenerate, in contrast to the savage but noble rural or nomadic culture. Yet the city is sought as a place of prestige, individual freedom and power. The appearance of cinemas and the development of the film industry, which reached Egypt in 1896, the year after the Lumière brothers showed their *cinématographe* in France, in 1895, offered new modes of social interaction and provided its audience with tangible role-models which played a vital role in the scaling of values and the modifications of social conduct.

Transformation of the Sociocultural Atmosphere

By the beginning of the 1880s, the press, schools, theatres, and libraries[93] had become essential institutions in the life of the new educated class in Egypt and the Levant. The great patron of the arts, Ismā'īl, was deposed and exiled, but his institutions not only attracted the creators of artistic works, but also provided their consumers. The educated class became the reading public of literature and the audience of drama and music. This class' consumption of culture was coupled with its quest for national identity, a concept that played an important role in shaping the new modes of literary discourse which emerged throughout the Arab world at the time. Egypt is a case in point. The concept of national identity was expressed and its significance modified through the intellectuals' exhaustive search for a proper role in the life of the country, and through the struggle against the absolute power of the Khedive and the country's decline into foreign domination brought on by the heavy borrowing of the Khedive. So cultural issues were intermingled with nationalist and patriotic ones in every field of expression.[94]

The deposition of Ismā'īl awakened fears and suspicions of Europe in Egypt for the second time, and sharpened the strength of the national desire to put the new popular slogan, "Egypt for the Egyptians", into practice, especially since Ismā'īl, a strong man, shrewd, forceful and dynamic, a man of vision, was succeeded by his son Tawfiq, a weakling, who turned a blind eye to foreign intervention. In practical terms, this slogan was implemented in two major ways: the first was in a return to the past, to Arabic tradition, at the expense of the open window on Europe. This period witnessed the rise of the school which consciously tried to accommodate some modern ideas in traditional thinking, with Muḥammad 'Abduh (1849—1905) at the helm as the major and most enlightened representative. But it became more and more traditional, especially under his student Rashīd Riḍā (1865—1935).

This coincided with and reflected the awareness of the traditional élite that the new tools of the cultural transition could also be used to further their own goals. They used the press to print their books, and made traditional and Islamic texts part of the book market until, by 1900, their cultural production accounted for the majority of printed books. The acculturation of the traditional intellectuals and the ensuing birth of a coherent class with a different world-view facing similar social and economic conditions played a significant role in determining the new cultural milieu. Although this was evident in the cultural scene in general, its reflection can be seen in the field of narrative literature, for a look through the index of the books published in Arabic during the second half of the last century indicates that the flood of translations, which reached its peak in Ismā'īl's reign, began to ebb in the 1880s, and was replaced by the rise of traditional Arabic books.[95]

The second major implication of the slogan was that the national question with its various social, economic, political, and cultural dimensions occupied a central place in the work and thought of anyone who was capable of participating in public affairs at that time. These ideas were not confined to Egypt; variants appeared in the rest of the Arab world, either concurrently or as a result of exchange of influences. Movement of goods and men necessitated improvement in the means of communication and transport. "Egypt got a railway at a time when even Sweden did not have any."[96] During Ismā'īl's era some 400 bridges were constructed across the Nile, 5000 miles of telegraph lines were put up, the 500 miles of railway built by his predecessors were increased to more than 1100, the Suez canal was completed and opened in 1869, and a national postal service were established. In Syria the French built the Beirut-Damascus highway in 1863, and in 1895 the Beirut-Damascus railway was completed. By 1898 Syria was linked by rail to Constantinople with a line from Aleppo via Damascus to Beersheba in southern Palestine and five branch lines to Iskenderun, Tripoli, Beirut, Haifa and Jaffa, respectively. In the same year the Baghdad railway was planned as a continuation of the Ḥaidar Pasha Konia line, skirting the southern fringe of Anatolia eastward to Mosul and then turning southward to Baghdad to run down to Basra, connecting the two cities to Turkey on the one hand and to Syria and Egypt on the other. Later the Hijaz Railway, which added a further 900 miles, was linked to this network. All of this resulted in the speeding up of travel and therefore the communication of ideas in the western Arab provinces of the Ottoman realm.

The accumulation and interaction of these changes created different modes of existence and distinct types of consciousness. ʻAli Mubārak highlighted the changes that were taking place in his *ʻAlam al-Dīn* when he stated that "the nation now sheds her false ideas, frees herself from worthless conceptions and gets used to the new institutions. Within a short time, all has changed: attitudes, habits, customs, and institutions. This is what happened in Egypt today. Anyone who saw Egypt fifty years ago, and who now sees it again today, will find nothing he knew from former times. He will realize that it has experienced a revolution".[97] In the grip of this transformed sociocultural atmosphere, a new artistic sensibility developed as a result of the articulation of the needs and feelings of a new reading public. The composition of this new reading public and the nature of its sensibility is the concern of the following chapter.

2
The Reading Public and the Change in Artistic Sensibility

Since the turn of the century, Arab writers have been searching for an effective role in their society. Their writing has focused on advancing the cause of progress and heightening awareness of the need for reform among the widest possible reading public. This new readership was different from the traditional Azharite one, both in cultural formation and temperament. Writers' awareness of the importance of their relationship with their readers reached its peak during the crucial confrontation between Egyptian nationalism and Europe which culminated in the British occupation of Egypt in 1882. Out of the first stage of this confrontation and the changes in sensibility brought about by the process of modernity was born a new type of discourse: an embryonic and rudimentary narrative which reflects, and is in a way analogous to, the process of cultural transition outlined in the previous chapter. The conception of this new form is closely linked with the rise of the new reading public and the work of the new cultural institutions, on the one hand, and with a many-sided break with tradition, on the other.

"The innovations of Muḥammad 'Ali ... had had as their primary aim to re-model the fighting services and modernize certain branches of the administration, and had served to introduce the forms and patterns rather than the abstract ideology of European institutions. Practical devices are assimilated more rapidly than ideas",[1] but without the material infrastructure elaborated throughout the nineteenth century, it would have been inconceivable to talk of cultural transition or of any change in the composition of the reading public and its artistic sensibility. The study of the Arabic language of the time shows how it struggled painfully, slowly but consistently, forging new words for new concepts and fresh ideas such as nation, nationalism, society and socialism as well as literary terms such as novel, short story and drama. The protracted struggle with such concepts is closely linked to the gradual change in artistic sensibility, and both were triggered and accompanied by a unique awareness of the emergence of a new reading public.

It is now a platitude that "the gradual extension of the reading class affected the development of the literature addressed to them",[2] because literature is always written with a certain reading public in mind, or at least with an intention to develop one. There is evidence to suggest a considerable expansion of the reading public in the late nineteenth century, but it was still relatively small by today's standards. 'Abdullah Nadīm (1854—96), in an editorial with a revealing title, *"Ṭarīq al-Wuṣūl ilā al-Ra'y al-'Āmm"* (Methods of Reaching Public Opinion), expressed a clear awareness of this expanding public. The Arabic title of this article is ambiguously meaningful for it can be interpreted as encompassing both the method of communication with the public and the means for establishing a national consciousness, a consensus. Nadīm states:

> We are witnessing the spread of intellectual power throughout Egypt. Many Egyptians have furnished themselves with knowledge and literary understanding. Their cultural and literary gatherings, in houses or clubs, proliferate. Their curiosity for news and their fondness for reading and newspapers whatever their language or origin, has broadened and deepened. Moreover, the intellectuals among them are developing their powers of observing, assessing and penetrating the mysteries of European policy and its orientation in the East. In this way Egyptians are becoming worthy of Europeans' respect, and are qualifying to carry out intellectual and administrative tasks ... One cannot deny that we Egyptians are succeeding in this because of contact with European ideas and emulation of Western ideals which reach us through what the papers cite of European news.[3]

In this quotation Nadīm identifies the four factors which affected the origination and composition of this new reading public: education, the rise of national and political consciousness, journalism and the contact with European culture and thought. Each one of these four factors played a significant role both in the emergence of the new reading public and in the shaping of the new artistic and literary sensibility. At the quantitative level they broadened the base of the new reading public(s) by providing it perpetually with new blood and at the same time dissociating it from the previous reading public with its traditional literary inclinations. And at the qualitative level they enriched the cultural and political awareness of the new reader by propagating a fresh set of values and ideas, spreading or even promoting new knowledge, and subsequently creating new outlooks, different cultural needs, and new modes of discourse. Because of the significance of these factors, further brief discussion of each is appropriate, emphasizing the example of Egypt.

Educating the New Reading Public

Secular education,[4] the foundations of which had been laid during Muhammad 'Ali's epoch, continued to develop and evolve during the nineteenth century. This had resulted by the 1880s in a limited spread of literacy; that is not literacy in its sophisticated European sense,[5] but in the sense of a bare capacity to read and write one's mother tongue. The new literates differed radically from the traditional ones educated at the *kuttāb,* or religious or theocentric school, who had pursued their knowledge at the Azhar and other mosque schools. Their numbers increased at a far higher rate than the Azharites until they outnumbered their predecessors and "formed a new educated class to contend with the Azharites till it inherited them".[6] In 1839 there were 11,371 students in the schools opened by Muḥammad 'Ali, as compared with 4760 in the *kuttāb* ones; there were 1331 teachers in Muhammad 'Ali's schools, compared with 752 in the *kuttābs.* In that year the government spent £E46,783.28 on education; this was equivalent to 50 per cent of the whole budget.[7] During Sa'īd's period the number of students in schools only fell to 3308 in 1849, despite Sa'īd's retrogressive policy towards education.[8]

During Ismā'īl's reign, education developed in quantity and quality very quickly indeed until the number of students reached 89,893 in 1873 and 125,735 in 1875.[9] However, the development of secular education, during this period, was not at the expense of theocentric education. Ismā'īl's system of education opened channels of higher education to those who graduated from these traditional schools, so that they could continue their study at the governmental schools. In 1875 the number of *kuttāb* students was 112,047 and it jumped to 137,553 in 1878.[10] These few figures indicate how this vast growth in education provided Egypt's public life with a relatively wide base of literate people and stimulated their desire to play a role in their society. Opening the channels of education to those who started in the traditional educational system was crucial for the vitality of the cultural debate, for the acculturation of the traditional élite with their solid linguistic background helped to synthesise a new literary and cultural outlook.

The expansion in education was not merely one of quantity but also of quality. The reforms affected the standard and orientation of the educational system as a result of two revolutionary events: the promulgation of *Lā'iḥat Rajab 1284,* the Rajab prospectus of November 1867, planned and implemented by the great educational reformer of the period, 'Ali Mubārak, and the recommendations of *Qumisyūn Tanẓīm al-Ma'ārif,*[11] the Commission for the Organization of Education, under the supervision of 'Ali Ibrāhīm, in 1880, which changed educational policies, revamped the curricula, raised educational standards and enhanced the chances of the brightest students to continue their education locally and abroad.

By 1881, the year of the 'Urābi revolution, there were 554,930 literate Egyptians; a great many of them had been educated in secular schools, according to new educational concepts and methods, and introduced to European ideas and ideals. While 91.7 per cent of Egyptians were still illiterate, the 8.3 per cent who were literate were sufficient to provide a considerable base for the reading public.[12] A reasonable number had graduated from the different high schools that later formed the nucleus of Cairo University, and most of those who were sent on educational missions abroad during Muhammad 'Ali's and Ismā'īl's reigns, had returned before the 'Urābi Revolution and become part of the culturally productive intelligentsia.

Their position as members of an educated minority drove those who were literate to think deeply about both their cultural and political roles, and the means of opposing the forces of tradition within the framework of feudal and autocratic systems of government linked to a highly inequitable and rigid social system. To protect themselves as a minority required the broadening of their class and led them to propagate ideas of social and political reform. As Bottomore suggests in his exploration of the role of the élites in society, "In order to carry out successfully their policies of reform they would have to permit, and still more encourage, much greater social mobility, to extend education rapidly, and to make their own elite positions more easily accessible to individuals and groups from the lower strata of society".[13] This fact, coupled with a realization that "the quality of policies depends very much upon the intellectual qualities of those who are engaged in them",[14] was instrumental in making education more generally available.

It was therefore natural that when the country was colonized by the British in 1882 and Cromer[15] attempted to undermine the educational system the élite reacted vigorously. The response was in direct proportion to the attack. After the lion's share of the budget had been spent on education for decades, the amount spent on education during Cromer's time did not exceed 1 per cent of gross revenue. "This was totally inadequate even for a colonial regime, and above all for a country ostensibly being trained gradually and wisely for modern democracy. Fortunately for that country, these very obstacles formed the most effective sort of training",[16] stimulating the Egyptians to challenge the occupation which closed most of the secondary schools and reduced the number of overseas scholarships to only two students in 1905.[17]

The notorious Douglas Dunlop, Cromer's educational architect, with his negative and intellectually inadequate educational policy, had a deplorable effect on cultural life. Dunlop translated into educational policy Cromer's aversion to "educating the Egyptian". Indeed, "Cromer did not regard education as of major importance, he knew much more clearly what he did not want — rebellious Egyptian intellectuals — than what he wanted".[18] To prevent the rise of a rebellious intelligentsia, or rather its formation, Dunlop transformed the well-developed machinery of indigenous education into a mere training system which was intended to produce only clerical automata and subservient civil servants to meet the demands of the "British heads and Egyptian hands" theory of government put forward by the colonizers.

The Egyptian reaction to Cromer's policy of education was as strong as it was because "education was one of the sorest points with the Egyptians, every one of whom accused Cromer of deliberately neglecting education so that he could continue to claim that the Egyptians were incapable of running their own administration".[19] The Egyptians did not confine themselves to mere complaints and accusations, but initiated a counter move and established a remarkable number of private schools. "In 1914 there were 328 foreign private schools teaching 48,000 pupils, and 739 Egyptian ones teaching 99,000. On the initiative of the nationalists, evening schools for adults were established".[20] In 1906 Qāsim Amīn (1865—1908) appealed for the foundation of a national university, and two years later Cairo University was brought into existence entirely as a private enterprise.

After Egypt's independence in 1922, education was restored to the top of the country's priorities, and by 1933 a law made education compulsory for all children between six and twelve years of age. These, and other individual efforts, played a major role in broadening the base of literacy and subsequently widening the reading public. It established a strong bond between the intellectual project and the national one, and demonstrated beyond doubt that education had become a national aim and a means of resisting the occupation. It made the intellectuals' aim of widening the base of their reading public a major part of the national strategies of resistance and created a unity of purpose that made intellectual activities analogous to nationalistic ones.

In Greater Syria the largest share of education remained in the hands of private institutions; up to 1930, there were twice as many children taught in foreign or private schools as in state schools. The expansion in education continued in the French mandated territory of Syria, and by 1930 there were 2439 schools with 218,741 pupils (1145 private with 87,157 pupils, 610 foreign with 57,895 pupils, and 684 state schools with 73,689 pupils). The number of pupils in these schools soon exceeded 10 per cent of the total population of the country at the time. This led to a dramatic increase in literacy which was estimated at the time as 40 per cent of men and 20 per cent of women.

In Lebanon the role of the state in education was small, yet because of intensive foreign educational activities the rate of literacy was slightly higher than in Syria, and by 1930 almost all boys of school age and 30 per cent of girls went to school. In Palestine the percentage was comparable to that of Lebanon despite the interruption suffered during the war years and the restrictive policies of the British.

> The progress of Western education was not an unmixed blessing. Although it raised the cultural standard to a relatively high level ..., in other ways it did harm. It emphasized sectarian divisions and added to them, in a country where their existence was one of the main obstacles to national progress. It became an instrument of political penetration as well as a vehicle of culture; and, more reprehensibly still, it facilitated and sometimes deliberately encouraged the acquisition of political power by the clergy.[21]

This in turn accelerated the tension between certain sectors of society.

In Iraq foreign missionary schools and private education continued their expansion, but the major share of educational development was borne by the traditional educational system. Since the educational revival of Midḥat Pasha with its strong military bent, the local notables encouraged traditional education, which continued to cater for the main Muslim population. It was not until the beginning of the twentieth century that a truly modern educational system emerged in Iraq. This system received a phenomenal boost after the creation of the kingdom of Iraq with the extension of primary education to villages and the development of secondary and higher schools in towns. By 1934 the government had started sending one hundred students a year to European universities, a century after similar steps had been taken by Egypt. But this delay was compensated for by the movement of Iraqi intellectuals to other parts of the Arab world, and the import of cultural products, books and periodicals, from Egypt and the Levant to Iraq.

Education and Women's Emancipation

One of the major by-products of the expansion of modern education was the change in social and cultural attitudes of men and the emancipation of women. Without the education of women their emancipation and active participation in public life would have been inconceivable. The first schools to admit women in the Arab world were those of the foreign communities in Egypt, some of which date from the middle of the seventeenth century. In the early days of Muḥammad 'Ali, Clot-Bey, the architect of Cairo's medical school, created a feminine profession, midwifery. "Training was given in a centre of the school where everything was planned, from the teaching of the alphabet, reading, writing, and arithmetic, to lessons in geography, history, anatomy, and the rudiments of medicine. Only the students were missing. Clot-Bey had to buy twenty-four little Negro girls at the slave market. He freed them and trained them before entrusting them with deliveries in the harem".[22] It was not long before these newly liberated girls were replaced by Egyptian girls in need of a different type of liberation. A few years later, thirty Egyptian girls were admitted to the school of midwifery, and it was not long before the education of women became accepted by the main Muslim sector of the population.

In 1873 Ismā'īl established the first modern governmental girls' school in the Ottoman Empire, Suyūfiyyah Girls' School, with a first intake of 400 girls. In 1875 a second girls school, Qirrābiyyah, was opened. Suyūfiyyah's curriculum combined the basic subjects of any modern school, such as arithmetic, geography, history, Arabic language and religion, with training in practical household crafts, and this set the standard for future schools for some time. The various foreign schools had accepted Egyptian girls, particularly since the Coptic Patriarch Kyrillos IV (1806—61) had established the first Egyptian girls' school in 1858.[23] By 1873 when the first governmental girls' school opened, there were already 3018 girls in the various other schools in Egypt.[24] By the beginning of the twentieth century the girls made up 9 per cent of school pupils, rising rapidly to 14 in 1910, 18 in 1920 and 22 in 1930. In 1927 Cairo University and other institutions of higher education were opened to women. By 1930, 10 per cent of all females were literate, as against 30 of males. Given the almost equal gender distribution of the population, this meant that females constituted one-quarter of the literate population, a percentage that continued to rise thereafter.

The Levant had pioneered the modern education of women since the beginning of the nineteenth century. Private schools for girls had appeared in Lebanon by 1840. In 1861 the British Syrian Mission founded a teachers' training college for girls in Beirut, and the Prussian Deaconesses of Kaiserswerth set up a centre for hospital and orphanage work in Sidon. In 1862 Beirut became the site of another modern school for girls. In 1895 the Orthodox Palestine Society was invited to take responsibility for the girls' school in Damascus. By 1897 the Beirut Orthodox school had grown into five schools with 800 pupils and twenty-three teachers. In 1924 the American University of Beirut became co-educational, opening its door to the graduates of these many girls' schools. In 1930, two of the seven Syrian higher schools for girls had more than 1404 students, many of whom went to the university after their graduation.

In 1858 Tsarina Marya Aleksandrovna built Bait Jala school for Orthodox Arab girls, and after years of growth it was turned in 1886 into a women's teacher training college (WTTC). By then, another had been founded in Nazareth, and in the following year a third was opened in Beirut; all had Russian teachers and headmistresses. The presence of these Russian teachers had considerable influence over the female Arab population. By 1895 Bait Jala WTTC had more than thirty students and its attached primary or 'model' school had more than two hundred.

> Visitors to the school, including the Patriarch of Jerusalem, were astonished by the girls' ability to speak Russian ... Yet there were complaints within the Society[25] that too much money was spent on instilling unnecessarily high standards in the girls' personal lives and that after eight years at the school they were proving reluctant to return to the much lower standard of their village. A minor revolution

> was brought about in the lives of those girls who remained as teachers with the Society. They had graduated from the school at eighteen and by the age of twenty-one were still unmarried in a country where the usual age of marriage was considerably lower.[26]

Their reluctance to go back to the type of life they had led before is symptomatic of a more profound revolution that effected the change in their attitude and outlook.

Iraq was a little behind establishing the first governmental girls' school during the rule of Nāmiq Pasha (1899—1902) with 95 pupils, but the number of schools had increased to eight by 1917 with over 700 girls. Long before the appearance of governmental education, foreign and missionary schools had been educating girls, and by 1914 they had 2163 girls. Yet basic education for women in Iraq remained for a long time under the domination of traditional religious authorities, particularly in the Shi'a-controlled areas. This led to the prevalence of highly conservative views in Iraq concerning the emancipation of women at a time when progressive ideas were spreading in other parts of the Arab world. One year before the publication of Qāsim Amīn's book in Egypt, the Iraqi writer Khayr al-Dīn al-Alūsi wrote his notorious book, *al-Iṣābah fi Man' al-Nisā' min al-Kitābah* (Conclusive Reasons for Opposing the Education of Women, 1898), in which he elaborated the perils of educating women and warned of the ensuing social evils and disintegration of morality. But this attitude was soon changed when the nationalist movement saw education of both males and females as the necessary prelude to liberation.

But in this respect Iraq was more of an exception to the rule; elsewhere the education of women sowed the seeds of their emancipation. Although a number of women had started writing in the 1860s, such as Wardah al-Turk, Wardah al-Yāziji (1838—1924), 'Ā'ishah Taymūr (1840—1902), Hind Nawfal (1859—1920), Zainab Fawwāz (1860—1914), Labībah Hāshim (1880—1947) and Malak Ḥifni Nāṣif (1886—1918), it was the men who first spoke out for women's emancipation. As early as 1870, Salīm al-Bustāni, building on the seminal work of al-Ṭahṭāwi in *Manāhij*,[27] called in his magazine *al-Jinān* for the emancipation of Arab women from the repressive traditional ideas about their role and position in society.[28] He argued that women entrusted with the upbringing of men shape the whole society by their actions and attitudes; thus, it is difficult to hope for free men, when they are brought up by women who are burdened with shackles and prejudice.[29]

A few years later, Qāsim Amīn championed the cause of women in his seminal works: *Taḥrīr al-Mar'ah* (Women's Emancipation, 1899), and *al-Mar'ah al-Jadīdah* (the New Woman, 1901). In 1910 the Iraqi poet Jamīl Ṣidqi al-Zahāwi (1883—1936) published an article in a Cairene newspaper[30] defending women's rights and criticizing the divorce laws. A flood of replies inundated the newspaper, and he lost his job as lecturer in law in Baghdad as a result. The tradition of elaborating the arguments for women's emancipation and rooting them in Islamic law continued with Manṣūr Fahmi's controversial doctoral thesis, which he submitted to the Sorbonne in 1913 on *"La condition des femmes en Islam"*. The strong Azharite hostility and opposition to Fahmi's work was vociferously intimidating and eclipsed anything that Qāsim Amīn had encountered. The author was dismissed from his job as a lecturer in the Egyptian University (later known as Cairo University), subjected to a humiliating campaign and asked to repudiate his own work. He was not forgiven until after his nationalist role in the 1919 revolution and his public disavowal of the book, which remains unpublished in Arabic today. Nevertheless, Fahmi's example soon culminated in *Imra'atunā fi al-Sharī'ah wa-l-Mujtama'* (Women in Islamic Law and Society, 1930) by the Tunisian writer Ṭāhir al-Ḥaddād (1899—1935).

Yet it was the women who took the practical steps in the struggle for their own freedom. Hudā Sha'rāwi (1879—1947), the wife of one of the three founders of the Wafd Party (which was the most popular nationalistic political party for decades), linked the emancipation of women to the liberation of Egypt and put the feminist cause on the nationalist agenda by leading the first Egyptian women's demonstrations in the 1919 revolution. She became president of the Wafdist Women's Central Committee, and in 1923 founded *al-Ittiḥād al-Nisā'i al-Miṣri* (the Egyptian Feminist Union), and launched its journal *l'Égyptienne*. "As the lure of new ideas and invitation to think and act independently attracted the youth, fear of subversion harassed the old. The improved status of women, entailing new temptations and new perils, aroused social opposition".[31] The tension between the two poles of this opposition continued to be vital factors in many sociocultural debates and played a significant role in changing certain aspects of the national ideology.

These changes manifested themselves first and foremost in the family. "By the opening of the twentieth century Western-style education was beginning to challenge the validity of the old scale of values and to wreak havoc on the family institution. Young men and women demanded the privilege of choosing a mate; she or he could be outside the kindred circle. The smaller family unit, the biological, replaced the older extended family. With the disruption of the family unit, time-honoured loyalties and homely virtues were strained to the breaking point".[32] This proved to be one of the major themes of the emerging narrative discourse.

The Awakening of National Consciousness

The second factor which participated in the formation of the new reading public and changed its sensibility was the awakening of political consciousness, which manifested itself first in Muḥammad 'Ali's independent tendencies, and then in the Lebanese autonomy of 1860. This was clearly reflected in the public discourse and the emergence of new concepts of *waṭan* (homeland), *abnā' al-waṭan* (countrymen), and *waṭaniyyah* (patriotism), which started to gain currency in the writings of al-Ṭahṭāwi, al-Yāziji and al-Bustāni after 1860.[33] These were the years of Ottoman *Tanzimat*, or reform, when the autonomy of Lebanon had a tremendous impact on the awakening of national consciousness in Syria and Palestine. The reformative years of Ismā'īl had strengthened the cultural and nationalist spirit and resulted in an active nationalist movement that made the task of his weak successor and the foreign powers behind him extremely difficult.

As early as 1876, *The Times* was talking with some alarm about a "Revolutionary Proclamation in Egypt"[34] and of the formation of a revolutionary cosmopolitan party. By 1880 this revolutionary movement had developed its organs, in the form of Nadīm's first newspaper, and its organisation, which was led by Aḥmad 'Urābi. This was also the time to which George Antonius traces the first organized effort in the Arab national movement to give shape to the ideas of the leading intellectuals and rally their people behind them.

The formation of a secret society was initiated in 1875 by a group of graduates of the Syrian Protestant College in Beirut. It developed branches in Damascus, Tripoli and Sidon, and by 1880 had started to post anonymous placards in the streets. "The main points of their programme were: (1) the grant of independence to Syria in union with the Lebanon; (2) the recognition of Arabic as an official language in the country; (3) the removal of censorship and other restrictions on the freedom of expression and the diffusion of knowledge; (4) the employment of locally-recruited units on local military service only".[35] The demands of the society, which were very similar to those of the Egyptian officers led by 'Urābi, reveal an awareness of the interaction between the two aspects of the cultural life: the nationalist and the literary. Syrian and Lebanese intellectuals articulated the desire to control their destiny after many years of inefficient Ottoman administration and the onslaught of assertive Western capitalism on their economy.[36] But while the Syrian and Lebanese intellectuals limited their activities to secret meetings and placards, their Egyptian counterparts went into open defiance and challenged the power of the Khedive.

The 'Urābi revolution was a unified expression of various rebellious tendencies against both the autocratic monarchy and foreign interference in the country. It focused the anger and indignation felt by Egyptians because of the predicament in which the country found itself as a result of Ismā'īl's heavy borrowing and lavish expenditure. The revolution was defeated by the intervention of the British, and ended with the occupation of the country. Indeed, the British occupation can be seen in one respect as an attempt to thwart the rising nationalist spirit in the area in order to keep it open for foreign intervention. Ironically, it did the opposite. Egypt resented and resisted the British occupation from the very beginning, and laboured, especially under the iron rule of the architect of British policy in Egypt, Cromer, to put an immediate end to it. Unlike that suffered under Muḥammad 'Ali, which put the awakening national consciousness into hibernation, this set-back to the nationalist movement accelerated its rise. Within less than a decade of the occupation, Egypt had ceased to put any faith in Britain's numerous declarations of her intention to withdraw from the country,[37] and had come to realize the deep contradictions between these verbal pledges and the steps Britain was taking to secure her power in Egypt.

The occupation was not to be short or temporary, as had originally been claimed, and Egypt realized that she had to struggle to regain her lost independence and to recover her national character, which the occupying forces were attempting to obliterate. This was a reaction to the severity of the military confrontation, a result of the involvement of several social strata in the events, and an implied declaration that the military defeat of the revolution did not mean the débâcle of the nation or the elimination of the spirit of resistance. The broad base of literacy was also a factor, as was the opposition of Russia and France to the British occupation and the experience gained from an earlier confrontation with the French, in strengthening the will to resist. The pen was the advance guard of this resistance because writers were aware of the evident lack of understanding of the several dimensions of the national question at that time.

The occupation had a disastrous effect on many aspects of Arab life. It guided the region's economy towards an exclusive dependence on agriculture and export,[38] and minimized investment in industry and manpower. In the field of industry, the policy of the occupation in Egypt was to hold up any investment in industry except where this would cater to export requirements.[39] In 1890, it abolished the Egyptian guilds, which were the backbone of local light industry. It also put obstacles in the way of foreign investors who wanted to invest in industrial projects in Egypt. The consequences were the death of local industry and an influx of foreign goods into local markets. In the field of human welfare, the occupation dramatically decreased investment in health and education. Egyptian intellectuals responded to these grave developments by convening a conference, in 1911, under the auspices of Ṭal'at Ḥarb,[40] to discuss the country's economic situation and by forming the famous Committee of Commerce and Industry in 1916.[41] Both the conference and the committee hammered out plans to enable Egyptians to develop their economy and to free it from the grip of imperialist domination.

By the turn of the century, the nationalist question had become a focal point of intellectual activity in the Arab world and had replaced most of the purely intellectual or theological concerns which had previously occupied scholars' attention. The first three decades of the twentieth century proved to be decisive and had far-reaching effects on the course of Arab intellectual and national history. They witnessed the first fully national revolutions in the modern history of both Egypt and Iraq, and in the heat of the dramatic events of these three decades the beginnings of most of the genres of the new narrative discourse in modern Arabic literature were forged.

From the very beginning of this struggle, Egyptians, Iraqis, Syrians, Palestinians and Lebanese were conscious of the interaction between the quest for independence and the reconstruction of their national identity. The two causes came together in the crucible of the struggle against the British and later French occupation, and remained fused throughout this period of continuous strife during which Arabs were compelled to prove to forces alien to their culture and lands that they were worthy of independence, and to refute the occupation's dismissal of them as "incapable of governing themselves". By World War I, the whole Arab area under discussion had fallen under foreign domination and the struggle for independence had become the main platform for the fusion of intellectual and nationalist activity.

Resistance to the occupation was not limited to the economy and education, but manifested itself in other aspects of political and cultural endeavour. 'Abdullah Nadīm and Ibrāhīm al-Muwayliḥi (1846—1906) illustrated in their writing the beginnings of a national awakening and sketched some patriotic ideas which were seized upon and nourished by Muṣṭafā Kāmil in his call for Egyptian patriotism. Kāmil reformulated these ideas in a manner which inspired the younger generation and inflamed their patriotic sentiments. Through his eloquent and zealous speeches, he appealed to the core of Egyptian national consciousness at the time, the students, the educated middle class, and the best elements of the lower classes, to unite and take pride in being Egyptian. "Like other nationalists of this age, Kāmil believed that unity could be based on 'feeling': the sense of belonging to the nation and responsibility for it. Patriotic spirit, *waṭaniyyah,* there lay the secret of European strength and basis of civilization".[42] Despite, or perhaps because of, the simplicity of his ideas, Kāmil played an important role, because, at this time, Egypt badly needed an orator of Kāmil's quality to help restore its self-confidence.[43] He "tried to generate national energy by arousing public interest in politics and directing it in a way which would lead to his goal: through the nation-wide party, the popular manifestation, the student strike".[44] Kāmil's public career was crowned by his active, and crucial, role in the Dinshiwāy case, which brought about the deposition of Cromer in 1907.[45]

It was not mere coincidence that along with the first success, albeit modest, of the nationalist movements, symbolized by the deposition of Cromer, Egyptian political parties emerged. The polarization of nationalist forces during the fierce confrontation with the British demanded some form of institutionalisation to give shape to the varying tendencies and to provide a framework for pursuing the struggle for independence. Six Egyptian political parties were founded in 1907,[46] and the remaining two in 1908.[47] Each party had its own newspaper with its own vision of the national cause. Whether or not the motives behind the genesis of these six major parties were completely sincere and creditable, their appearance in such profusion reflects the richness and diverse self-consciousness of the nationalist movement.

Similar developments of nationalist activity took place in Syria at the time.

> Both the movement of ideas in Syria and the political ferment which it fostered are vividly described in the ...writings of contemporary observers. A French writer who visited Syria in 1882 has left a record of his impressions of the new spirit: "A spirit of independence is abroad. During my stay in Beirut, young Muslims were busy organizing societies to promote the establishment of schools and hospitals and to work for the regeneration of the country. An interesting feature of this activity is its freedom from all taint of sectarianism".[48] ... Another Frenchman who, after extensive travel in North Africa and along the shores of the Red Sea and the Persian Gulf, sailed up the Tigris as far as Baghdad in 1883,[49] found symptoms of unrest in all parts of the Arab world.[50]

The events of the 'Urābi revolution and the revolt of the Mahdi in the Sudan in 1885 inspired many Syrians and Palestinians and led them to work for liberation from both the Turks and the Western powers.

"By the turn of the century the intellectual revival had turned into political unrest, based upon a strong anti-Turkish feeling and a strong sense of the superiority of Arab to Turkish peoples. Al-Kawākibi (1849—1903) was one of the first Arab writers to say that Arabs must take over the leadership of the Muslim world from the corrupt Turks".[51] The nationalist movement in Syria was directed against the Turks, and not the French, who controlled the country only during World War I. 'Abd al-Raḥmam al-Kawākibi was one of the most influential Syrian intellectuals of this period. He was educated at the leading Muslim College of Aleppo, in the non-Western but profoundly humanistic tradition, and pursued a career in journalism and the law. At a young age he edited the newspaper, *Furāt,* and made it the rallying point of nationalism. His radical views, revolutionary outlook, outspoken denunciations of tyranny and bold public stands earned him the wrath of conservatives and later a term in prison and the seizure of his property.

On his release in 1898 he left Syria and went to live in Egypt, as generations of Arab intellectuals had done before him, and continued to live there for the rest of his life, with intervening periods of travel in Africa and Muslim countries. Although his educational and cultural background is similar to those of Afghāni and 'Abduh, his writing is marked by a much sharper sense of social justice. He was a dauntless, open-minded intellectual who practised what he preached and dedicated a great deal of his time to helping the poor and the unfortunate from all groups and creeds. This earned him the name, *Abū-l-Ḍu'afā'* (Father of the Weak), in his home town. Unlike Jamāl al-Dīn al-Afghāni (1838—97) and Muḥammad 'Abduh, he distinguished between the Arab movement and the general Pan-Islamic revival proclaimed by them. His was an Islamic revival which is consciously aware of the special history and the social context of every case, in which the greatness of Islam is demonstrated in its universality as much as in its specificity. He believed that the Arabs were destined to lead the Muslim world, and his views laid the foundation for the ideology of Arab independence.

His daring articles were collected in a book, *Tabā'i' al-Istibdād wa Maṣāri' al-Isti'bād* (The Attributes of Despotism and the End of Tyranny, 1899?) which is still banned in his own country.[52] His book, *Umm al-Qurā* (Mecca, written 1896) is an audacious work of didactic narrative in the tradition of his compatriot, Marrāsh's, early work. It is a profound and comprehensive debate on the state of the Muslim world conducted by twenty-two fictitious characters congregating in Mecca for the pilgrimage. They are deeply concerned about the deterioration of their society, and the bulk of the book uses the technique of documentary presentation to elaborate upon their imaginary proceedings. They conduct numerous meetings and discuss the major issues of the day, formulating a programme for the rejuvenation of the Muslim community. Although the work is overwhelmingly didactic, the sharpness of ideas and the strong sense of humour animate the narrative, endowing it with intensity and vigour.

National sentiments in Syria and Palestine continued to ferment, aided in part by the Egyptian resistance to the British and by Arab intellectual activity in Europe, which gave rise to some influential publications such as the minor classic, *Le Réveil de la nation arabe* (The Awakening of the Arab Nation), published in Paris in 1905 by Najīb 'Āzūri (*c.*1873—1916). The Young Turks' call for reform and their success in ending Sultan Abdül-Ḥamīd's tyranny in 1908 and restoring the 1876 constitution gave a tremendous boost to the Arab nationalist movement. Its impact on the literary movement was as great as on the nationalist one, for in the following years numerous poems and no less than three novels appeared, dealing with the various aspects of this momentous event. The novels were: *Ḥasnā' Sālūnīk* (The Belle of Salonica, 1909) by Labībah Mīkhā'īl Ṣawāyā (1876—1916); *al-Inqilāb al-'Uthmāni* (The Ottoman Coup d'État, 1911) by Jurji Zaydān (1861—1914); and *Bayn 'Arshayn* (Between Two Thrones, 1911) by Farīdah 'Aṭiyyah (1867—1918).[53] Although these three novels are of secondary literary merit, they were of considerable political significance, and the fact that two out of the three authors are female indicates women's involvement in political life.

If women's reaction to the events was literary and cultural, men's response took a more active and direct form. In 1911 a group of Arab students established *al-Jam'iyyah al-'Arabiyyah al-Fatāh* (The Young Arabs' Society), with the aim of working for the independence and progress of the Arabs within a Turco-Arab framework.[54] Two years later, on 18—23 June 1913, the first Arab Conference was held in Paris (with participants from Syria, Lebanon, Palestine and Iraq). This called for the decentralization of the Ottoman Empire, formulated a programme of reform and recommended cooperation with the newly founded *Ḥizb al-Lāmarkaziyyah* (Decentralization Party) in Egypt. This "was greeted with demonstrations of popular fervour not only in the Syrian provinces but also in Iraq. Public meetings were held in Damascus, Aleppo, Acre, Nablus, Baghdad and Basra, and telegrams acclaiming the scheme as being the expression of the universal desire in the Arab provinces poured into Constantinople".[55] A month later the Turkish government concluded an agreement with the conference organizers and conceded their demands. Hopes were raised, only to be dashed by the outbreak of war.

"Except in Egypt it was not until after the imposition of the mandates that nationalist reaction against Western imperialism became pronounced ... Before Arab awakening took a political form it was purely intellectual".[56] The drive for independence, a corollary of the nationalist spirit, did not become a moving force until after World War I. As late as 1913, when the first Arab congress was held in Paris, Arab demands centred on the recognition of Arabic as an official language where it was the mother tongue. Decentralization was the demand at the time and the name of the party which was founded in Egypt in 1912 and had secret branches in Syria and Iraq. Yet the intellectual nature of the nationalist debate did not obscure its political significance. Indeed, from the outset, the intellectual movement was ahead of the political one. For example, long before the Balfour Declaration, Levantine intellectuals were warning their nations of the dangers of the Zionist threat to their countries. Shibli Shumayyil (1860—1917) engaged in a long debate with Najīb Naṣṣār (1862—1948), the editor of *al-Karmil* (Haifa, 1908—33), concerning the danger of the Zionist threat to Palestine as early as 1909.

With World War I came Britain's declaration of a protectorate over Egypt, its promise in 1916 to Sharīf Ḥusain (1856—1931) of Mecca to recognize the independence of the Arab lands in exchange for his revolt against the Turks and support for the British in the war, the infamous Sykes-Picot agreement with the French to divide the Arab lands between Britain and France, and the 1917 Balfour Declaration promising a national home for the Jews in Palestine, a year after it had been promised to the Arabs in the lengthy correspondence between Sharīf Ḥusain and Sir Henry McMahon, the British High Commissioner in Egypt at the time. The apparent contradiction between these agreements and pledges became evident by the end of the war, and a series of troubles began, the ramifications of which continue to afflict the Arab world.

In 1920, by the treaty of Sèvres, the Turks renounced all claims to non-Turkish territory: Hijaz was recognized as independent; Syria and Lebanon were assigned as mandates to the French; and Iraq, Palestine and Trans-Jordan to the British. To the Arabs, the mandate, though ratified later by the the League of Nations,[57] was but another version of the Sykes-Picot agreement of 1916. In Egypt, the Khedive 'Abbās Ḥalīm was deposed, and Ḥusain Kāmil was nominated as the Sultan of Egypt; he was universally dismissed as the puppet of the British. The economic difficulties of the war with the consequent pressure upon daily life brought about a new stage in Egyptians' awareness of their national identity. The war period witnessed two attempts to assassinate the British-appointed Sultan, whose elder brother had refused to take the post from the British. There were also a great number of civil disturbances. When the war came to an end and the time fell due for Britain to fulfil the pledge she had given to withdraw from Egypt, if the latter helped in the war effort, there was more serious civil unrest.

In 1919, on three major occasions, there were nationwide demonstrations in which Egyptians asserted their determination to regain independence for the country. The first was when the nation *en masse* authorized a delegation of Egyptian politicians to present Egypt's case at the peace conference in 1919, with a great demonstration of power, testified to by the rapid collection of hundreds of thousands of signatures legitimating the process of authorization. The second was the general strike and the revolutionary events of March 1919, known as *thawrat tisa'tāsher,* the 1919 revolution, which involved people from every walk of life. The third was the total boycott by the whole nation of the Milner Committee when it came to Egypt, in an attempt to brush aside the authorized delegation and to look for Egyptian substitutes willing to cooperate with the British and turn a blind eye to their protectorate over the country.[58] This clearly expressed, and in some instances violent, national awakening led to the revoking of the protectorate. In 1922 the High Commissioner issued a declaration of Egypt's independence, and, in 1923, as the culmination of Egypt's long search for a political identity, the first Egyptian constitution was promulgated.

Similar developments took place in the rest of the Arab world. In March 1919 massive demonstrations broke out in Palestine to manifest to the American Committee investigating the legitimacy of the British mandate the Palestinians' repudiation of it, and the disturbances continued throughout the year, culminating in the Jerusalem revolt of 1920. On 11 March 1920, a National Congress of Syrian and Palestinian leaders met in Damascus and called for independence, rejected the Balfour Declaration, and declared Fayṣal, the son of Sharīf Ḥusain, King of Syria (including Palestine). Britain and France rejected the decisions of the Congress, Fayṣal was expelled from Syria by French troops, and Britain appointed him King of Iraq in 1921. In the previous year Rashīd 'Āli al-Kilāni led an uprising in Iraq. In 1921 disturbances spread in Jaffa and its suburbs, leading to the imposition of martial law. In Syria, popular dissatisfaction broke into open revolt from 1925 to 1926, in the course of which Damascus was bombarded twice by the French. In 1925, the new French High Commissioner, fifth in a rapid succession, promised a general amnesty and authorized elections. The constituent assembly, elected in April 1928, drafted a constitution which gave no recognition to the French mandate. This constitution was rejected by the French, and a new phase of nationalist struggle commenced and continued until the termination of the French mandate in the complete evacuation of the French from Lebanon and Syria. As for Palestine, the 1920s was a turbulent decade, ending in the Burāq (Wailing Wall) uprising of 1929.

It is clear that the first three decades of the twentieth century is a period in which the national question had become both the major concern of the intelligentsia and the drive behind writers' search for a means of expressing the views and aspirations of their people. The resistance to the colonization of the region played a major role in forging a strong sense of national identity. In the heat of the battle against the British and the French, a different perception of the role of the individual and of that of the nation was shaped. Greater participation in the public debate led to the development of a new reading public and the modification of its national as well as artistic sensibility.

Cultural Societies: A Vision in Search of a Role

The intellectual awareness of embarking on a new age and a new type of thinking led writers to seek support and verification from their peers, and this resulted in the formation of cultural societies and associations. The societies were the modern manifestation of the literary salons of the *Ṣūfi* orders that had provided the previous revival with its debating forums. Each of these societies had a bulletin publishing the new work of its members and popularizing their ideas and endeavours. The active participation of the public in the shaping of their new world had long been heralded by the intelligentsia, who aspired to play a leading role in their society. The new intellectual elite shared a vision of the future of their countries and a dream of disseminating and realizing it. The newly emerging intelligentsia were aware from an early stage that the amplification of this shared vision required the crystallization of its major components on a smaller and more specialized scale before introducing them to the wider public. The elaboration of the various aspects of this vision was responsible for the rise of cultural societies, while the communication of the outcome was behind the proliferation of journalism.

The American missionaries were behind the foundation of the first cultural society in Lebanon, The Society of Arts and Sciences in 1847, which provoked the Jesuits to initiate the Oriental Society in 1850. Both societies had had a predominantly Christian membership, though their activity prompted the foundation of the first truly Arab society in 1852, *al-Jam'iyyah al-Sūriyyah* (the Syrian Literary Society). It had members residing not only in Beirut, Jerusalem or Damascus, as its name suggests, but also in Cairo and Constantinople. Among them one finds Muslims, Christians and Druze bonded together by the very secular nature of their endeavour.[59] Its aims were the dissemination of rational ideas and the promotion of education and publication. It continued its activities for a number of years and gained currency and recognition in a number of cultural centres including Constantinople. The universal nature of this society and its very democratic composition is highly significant. "It was in a secret session of this society held in Beirut in 1868 that a twenty-one year old poet, Ibrāhīm al-Yāziji, recited original verses which, transmitted by word of mouth, incited Arabs to rise against their oppressors, thus sounding the first clarion call to Arab nationalism and independence".[60]

In 1875 the Beirut Secret Society was established. It had some links with the Freemasons and was responsible for the foundation of the influential magazine, *al-Maqtaṭaf.* In 1882 *al-Majma' al-'Ilmi al-Sharqi* (Oriental Scientific Academy) was founded in Beirut and met with strong opposition from the Ottoman authorities. The society of *al-'Ikhā' al-'Arabi* (the Arab Brotherhood) was formed in 1908 with a combination of cultural and political aims. *Al-Muntadā al-Adabi* (the Literary Club), which was established by a group of Arab officials, men of letters and students in Constantinople in 1909 to serve as a meeting place for Arab residents and visitors, has a more cultural and literary orientation. *Al-Qaḥṭāniyyah* (True Arabs) was formed in 1909, a few months after *al-Muntadā al-Adabi,* but was secret, to cater for the political side of the intellectuals' activity. Its founder, 'Azīz al-Miṣri, also founded another secret society, *al-'Ahd* (The Covenant), in 1914. He was one of the most controversial political figures in Arab politics at the time.

Jam'iyyat al-Iṣlāḥ al-'Ām fi Wilāyat Beirut (Beirut Society for Comprehensive Reform) came into existence in 1913. It established *Nadi al-Iṣlāḥ* (Society of Reform), and called for the local autonomy of Lebanon within the constitutional framework of the Ottoman state. The other secret society, *al-Jam'iyyah al-'Arabiyyah al-Fatāh* (Young Arab Society), was established in 1911 by seven Muslim Arabs from greater Syria who were pursuing their studies in Paris. "No other society has played as determining a part in the history of the national movement".[61] Its centre remained Paris for the first two years of its activity, but as soon as its founders graduated and returned home its social and religious base was widened, its membership rose to 200, and it moved to Beirut in 1913 and to Damascus the following year. The Arab Congress held in Paris in 1913 created a Committee of Reform of eighty-six members. A number of these societies played an active role in the Arab revolt of 1916 and were responsible for its enthusiastic reception in Syria and Iraq. In 1920 migrant Syrian and Lebanese intellectuals established *al-Rābiṭah al-Qalamiyyah* (Literary Association), in New York, which played a major literary role in changing the artistic sensibility and was the most influential among more than twenty societies established by Arab intellectuals in the *mahjar.*[62]

In Egypt, cultural societies started in the reign of Ismā'īl with the formation of *Majlis al-Ma'ārif al-Miṣri* (Egyptian Council for Education) in 1859 with the ambitious aim of extending education to every Egyptian village. In 1868 two leading intellectuals, Muḥammad

'Ārif and Ibrāhīm al-Muwailḥi, founded *Jam'iyyat al-Ma'ārif* (the Society of Knowledge) with the aim of raising cultural consciousness, disseminating new ideas, enlightening the reading public, and encouraging translation and publication. In 1871 Shaikh Muḥammad al-Khashshāb al-Falaki established *Jam'iyyat al-Adab* (the Literary Society) with the clear aim of providing the traditional intellectuals with the new cultural media which the secular intellectuals were using effectively to expand their influence. This was followed in 1873 by another society with similar aims, *Jam'iyyat Ruwāq al-Shām* (the Society of the Syrian Hall of Residence at the Azhar) which, as its name suggests, attempted to consolidate the efforts of the Syrian students at the Azhar and emphasized their cultural contribution.

In 1875 Ismā'īl initiated *al-Jam'iyyah al-Jughrāfiyyah al-Khidīwiyyah* (the Khedivial Geographical Society), which became one of the major cultural and scientific projects in the history of modern Egypt. In 1877 Ya'qūb Artin and Sulaymān Abāẓah founded *al-Jam'iyyah al-Sharqiyyah* (Oriental Society) with the aim of replicating the activities of European orientalists,[63] disseminating new ideas, and stimulating public debates and publications. The role of orientalism in influencing certain sections of the cultural movement was evident from that early period, and Arab intellectuals participated regularly in the biannual international Congress of Orientalists at the time. In 1878 two societies, *al-Jam'iyyah al-Khayriyyah al-Islāmiyyah* (the Islamic Philanthropic Society), founded by 'Abdullah Nadīm, and *Jam'iyyah al-Maqāṣid al-Khayriyyah* (the Charitable Society), initiated by Sulṭān Pasha, were established with the declared aim of offsetting the activities of Christian missionaries in the field of education and European influence in Ismā'īl's cultural renaissance.

The early years of the British occupation witnessed a lull in the activities of these societies, but they soon resumed. In 1886 the Levantine intellectuals established *Jam'iyyat al-I'tidāl* (Society of Moderation), modelled on the Syrian Society in Cairo, which attempted to integrate them into the cultural life of Egypt by creating a forum for them to work together with their Egyptian counterparts. In 1892 *Jam'iyyat al-Ta'rīb* (Society of Translation and Adaptation) was founded in Cairo to promote translation and the integration of this new activity into the life of the reading public.[64] The formation of this society is highly significant, for it was founded twenty years before the first society for authors was formed, *Jam'iyyat Ta'līf al-Kutub* (Writers' Association) in 1911. The appearance of a society for translators long before that for authors is a reflection of the nature of historical development in which translation paved the way for the writing and publication of indigenous literary works. In 1898 a group of Azharites and conservative intellectuals formed *Jim'iyyat Iḥyā' al-Kutub al-'Arabiyyah* (Society for the Revival of Arabic Tradition), in order to provide the reader with a literary production to offset the influence of orientalists in this field, which continued to increase until it reached new heights after the foundation of Cairo University in 1908. By the end of the century, Egypt had 160 different societies, among which there were seven literary clubs, numerous theatre associations and thirteen charitable organizations to promote culture and education, five of which were Coptic.[65]

Alexandria was a centre for a number of cultural societies such as *Jam'iyyat al-'Urwat al-Wuthqā* (Society of Divine Bond) in 1891, *Jam'iyyat al-Ibtihāj al-Adabi* (Literary Society) in 1894, *Jam'iyyat al-Taraqqi al-Adabi* (Society for the Progress of Literature) in 1894, *Jam'iyyat al-Sirāj al-Munīr* (Enlightenment Society) in 1895, *Jam'iyyat al-Ittifāq* (Consensus Society) in 1896, and ten other societies for drama and acting with the main purpose of performing plays. Alexandria at the turn of the century was the theatrical capital of the Arab world.[66] By 1914 Egypt had ten major theatre companies, 34 smaller ones and 32 amateur theatre groups performing at one period or another. The emergence of political parties and the congregation of intellectuals around them soon played a significant part in the role of these societies. Yet they continued to appear as a forum for innovative literary movements such as the two famous literary groups of *al-Diwān* and *Apollo*. The foundation of *Majma' al-Lughah al-'Arabiyyah* (Arabic Language Academies) in Damascus and Cairo institutionalized these fora as highly influential, official institutions.

These societies articulated in their aims the new visions of the intellectual élite and attempted, with varying degrees of success, to put them into practice. Many of them were but rudimentary forms of political association, trade union or even political party, but some remained purely cultural and were concerned with the elaboration of new ideas and visions. The societies were the intellectuals' tool in their struggle with recalcitrant interests and traditions both national and foreign. It was the form in which their ideas departed from their abstract form and acquired a palpable existence. Their short life and multitude is indicative of the resilience of the intellectual and their dynamic response both to the oppressive practices of the ruling establishment, and to the changing nature of reality.

Journalism and Cultural Change

Journalism was the first of the new discourses to appear and develop in the Arab world, and within its domain a host of other discourses appeared. It accelerated the cultural transition and played a significant role in the composition of both the new reading public and the narrative discourse which first emerged. The introduction of the printing-press in the eighteenth century and its steady increase throughout the nineteenth had an important but gradual impact on the cultural life of the Arabs. It accelerated the extinction of the system of patronage and rendered the *nussākh,* or manuscript copiers, obsolete, thus playing an important part in breaking up old traditions and establishing new ones. The slow cumulative process of learning was a feature of the pre-printing era; now that the press could execute in one hour what would have taken a team of copyists months, the process of learning, transferring and distributing knowledge was bound to change.

By the end of Ismā'īl's reign newspapers had become one of the principal media, and continued to increase in number and influence after his overthrow. While the number of Arabic newspapers which appeared in Egypt during his reign was twenty-seven, between his deposition in 1879 and the end of the century this number had increased to 310.[67] Ismā'īl also subsidized a number of Syrian and Lebanese periodicals which were widely read in Egypt and/or supported him in his alliance with the Russians against the Turks.[68] A similar rate of increase was achieved in Lebanon while the rest of the Arab world lagged behind.[69] Between the publication of the first Lebanese newspaper in 1858 and 1870, nineteen newspapers appeared, but this number increased tenfold to 196 between 1871 and 1900, though half of them were published in Egypt. This rate of increase continued, for between 1901 and 1930 the number rose to 800.[70] It is true that many of these papers were short-lived, but their very number indicates the growth of journalism and the way in which the press became a vital medium of public communication. It satisfied the hunger of the reading public for adequate information about current events, and it also participated in awakening the national consciousness and helping the individuals to perceive and formulate their role in society.

The official induction of journalism and its monopoly by the state in Egypt at the beginning of its development is in marked contrast with Syria. In 1855 it was to a Syrian, Rizqallah Ḥassūn (1825—80), that the first Arabic language newspaper emerging as a private venture, *Mir'āt al-'Aḥwāl,* owed its appearance, ten years before the publication of the first official Syrian newspaper.[71] Yet Syria had few newspapers in the nineteenth century; and the number did not exceed ten until 1900, growing to eighty-seven newspapers and periodicals by 1914. After the declaration of the Ottoman constitution in 1908, the proliferation of newspapers in Iraq and the Levant experienced a dramatic boost in number and quality. In the early period after its declaration Palestine had more than ninety newspapers, thirty-six based in Jerusalem; and Iraq had more than seventy.[72]

By today's standards, the circulation of newspapers and periodicals in the nineteenth century was extremely low. This was the result of two restrictive factors, the low level of literacy and economic stringency. Less than one-tenth of the population of Egypt, Syria and Iraq was literate until the end of the second decade of the twentieth century, while the rate for Lebanon and Palestine was slightly higher. The great majority of Egyptians were short of the bare necessities of life, for in 1880 the *per capita* income was £E5.14, this rose to £E7.12 in 1894, to £E 7.48 in 1904 and to £E7.56 in 1913.[73] At the same time the prices of books and newspapers was relatively high:[74] the price of a daily newspaper was the equivalent of .25 per cent of the annual *per capita* income, and that of a monthly review or a medium-sized novel amounted to between one and two per cent of the annual *per capita* income, while the subscription for a weekly or a monthly magazine was between 15 and 20 per cent of the *per capita* income.

Despite these restrictive factors, the circulation of newspapers at the time is indicative of a sizeable reading public. Reliable information about newspaper circulation is scarce, but one can derive some indication from statistics about the circulation of sixteen papers in Egypt in 1892 published in Nadīm's magazine *al-Ustādh.*[75] The total circulation of these sixteen papers was 17,492.[76] Five years later, in 1897, *al-Hilāl* stated that "fifteen years ago, in 1882, there were no more than five thousand subscribers to Egyptian newspapers; now they have exceeded twenty thousand. As for the readers, they may reach 200,000 because the copy of the newspaper is usually read by ten or tens of people".[77] There are two additional factors which may support *al-Hilāl*'s statement about the wider readership of each copy: the first is the economic one discussed above, and the second is that towards the end of the nineteenth century there was a degree of political or patriotic polarization represented in most of the important papers, compelling the reader to be content with one paper. In fact, this has remained true for the majority of the Arab reading public up to the present day.

Before the turn of the century, papers had become an indispensable means of communication between writers and readers, a medium which both attracted and influenced authors. Undoubtedly, the writers' awareness of the fact that the papers were not only read, but read aloud to the illiterate, affected their style and treatment of the ideas and subjects which concerned this wide section of the population. Orality, which journalism attempted to eliminate from the language of written discourse, lingered longer than necessary because of the writer's awareness of this phenomenon. Yet the elements of orality in journalistic discourse helped to develop the rudiments of narrative language. Q.D. Leavis wrote about Britain in a comparable period: "The give-and-take of journalism when it took the form of essays written 'in an air of common speech' provided the novelist with the best of all styles, combining the maximum flexibility with complete absence of pretension".[78] In Arabic, this was even more relevant than in English because of the rigidity of prevalent linguistic canons. In other words journalism's influence went beyond the reading public and journalists, and affected literary taste, participated in crystallizing the artistic sensibility, and provided the writer with useful stylistic solutions. Journalism is, indeed, one of the major factors in shaping public taste and morality, and in creating a cultural atmosphere conducive to narrative discourse.

The immediate power of journalism is, in this respect, much greater than that of the book, for it has the means to keep a campaign or an issue going. As much as it can change public taste or promote new writing, it can hinder this change and become a means of reinforcing the *status quo*, and, although the press aided the rise of modern narrative discourse and facilitated its proliferation, it was also responsible for hampering its development. The press was more interested in enhancing its position in society by adopting and defending its public morality than in the promotion of narrative works. As early as 1882, *al-Muqtaṭaf*[79] attacked the reading of fiction on the ground that it spread immorality among the youth, wasted their time, and corrupted their taste. But a few years later it published an article in which it stated that fiction should be permitted on condition that it be didactic, moralistic, and reformative.[80] It then went back again to its original stand and maintained that although a few works of fiction were useful, the majority of both translated and original narrative works were harmful.[81]

Al-Hilāl's stand was a more balanced one, for its editor was a professed novelist, and understood the linguistic interdependence of journalism and the new narrative discourse. He was aware of the danger of misusing the moralistic argument and was keen to disarm the opponents of narrative. Thus, the magazine cautiously promoted fictional works, but, because of the prevailing atmosphere of puritanism, it did not forget to stress both the didactic message of the work and its moralistic and reformative role.[82] In its promotion of narrative works, *al-Hilāl* claimed that *riwāyāt,* a term which was freely used to denote both novels and short stories and can be better rendered as 'narrative', has the highest circulation among books, and that at the turn of the century there was a strong demand for narrative works.[83] The significance of this statement is twofold; it declares that the demand for narrative texts had made itself clearly felt even before the end of the century, and maintains their comparative edge over other texts.[84]

Translation and the Contact with the West

Education in the Arab world in the nineteenth century was the main channel for the dissemination of European culture and thought, especially in state educational institutions which embraced the European cultural outlook virtually without reservation. By the end of the century, the contact with European culture was almost two centuries old in the Levant and nearly a century old in Egypt; thus, many of the new ideas had infiltrated social and cultural life. The contact with Europe was both physical and cultural. Arab intellectuals travelled, studied and worked in Europe, and Europeans flocked to the Arab world. The Lebanese pioneered foreign travel and, after the middle of the nineteenth century, emigration to Europe and the Americas. "Because of their seafaring tradition and Christian background they felt more predisposed to adventure and to feel at home in Europe and America than other Near Easterners. Syria stood next as a source of emigration".[85] They also migrated to Egypt and participated actively in its new cultural institutions.

Wherever they went, they took with them their printing-presses. "A 1929 census lists 3023 Arabic newspapers and periodicals, extant or extinct in the world. Of these 102 were born in North America, 166 in South America and 14 in Great Britain".[86] Many of these found their way back to the Arab reader in the Middle East.

Westerners had run missions and schools, given students grants to study in their respective countries, issued newspapers and periodicals, lived among Arabs, socialized with the élites, taken certain minorities under their protection, developed business interests and popularized their different world-view. This played a decisive role in the transformation of the new reading public's view of both time and space and their perception of themselves. The very intrusive presence of Europeans particularized many of the general ideas about the "other" and forced the Arab "self" to re-identify itself and its world in a new light and with a new set of priorities. A study of the biographies of the leading Arab intellectuals of the nineteenth century, in comparison with their predecessors of the eighteenth, reveals that while those of the eighteenth century saw Constantinople and other Ottoman cities as their ultimate goal and visited or even resided in them for some time in their career, those of the nineteenth aspired to visit European capitals. While Turkish was the main foreign language of Arab intellectuals before the nineteenth century, they gradually neglected its study for French, Russian or English and dissociated themselves from the Ottoman outlook. By the middle of the nineteenth century it had become a cultural imperative to study European languages and live in one or several European cities in order to gain first hand knowledge, not just of Europe, but of the "world".

Those who failed to do so, familiarized themselves with European ideas through extensive reading of translations. The appearance of numerous translations which attracted a wide section of the reading public is strong evidence of the changing needs of this new public and their intellectual élites, on the one hand, and of the acceptance of certain aspects of European culture by its Arabic counterpart, on the other. It is true that translation of works of science, history and other thought influenced the Egyptian public in a broad sense, but what concerns this study is the increasing number of translations of literary works, for these are the works which both participated in crystallizing the new sensibility, and attracted the reading public's attention to the new forms of narrative discourse.

> Translation has been called, by Wilhelm von Humboldt, one of the labours most essential to any literature; partly because it introduces those ignorant of foreign language to forms of arts and humanity which they would never come to know and this is an important gain for any nation; but partly also, and especially, because it widens the capacity of meaning and expression possessed by one's own language. It provides the most important channel through which international influence can flow.[87]

In Egypt and the Levant, literary translation, in particular, played this role from the time of the publication of al-Ṭahṭāwi's translation of Fénelon's *Aventures de Télémaque* onwards. Unlike government-sponsored translations in Egypt, or church and missionary ones in the Levant, literary translations were undertaken without any support or subsidy, as a result of individual initiative and in response to market needs, whether real or perceived. They introduced readers to new literary forms previously unfamiliar to them, but it tackled this task with a certain degree of caution and hesitation at first. Therefore, such works were initially nearer to adaptation than accurate literary translation. Early translators endeavoured to put the foreign literary work into the nearest traditional Arabic form; in other words, to translate not only the language but also the form and some of the narrative strategies as well in order to adapt the translated text to the readers' horizon of expectations. Often translators tried to Egyptianize, or Levantize the events, the characters, the plot and the form. In this way translation and adaptation played a major role in relating the fictional elements and techniques inherent in European literature to the fictional techniques and the familiar narrative strategies of *maqāmat, bābāt,* traditional stories and anecdotes.

While these translations influenced the interests of the reading public and widened the perspective of its cultural concerns, they were also influenced by the disposition and cultural background of their reading public. This was due to the fact that "translations are, in great measure, created by their public, because the average reader wants to find in translation the kind of experience which has become identified with 'poetry' in his reading of his own literature ... The translator who wishes to be read must, in some degree, satisfy that want".[88] It seems that many of the Egyptian and Levantine translators were aware of this fact from the very beginning. They chose works which would satisfy the taste of the avant-garde reader; the result was that most of the translated works, at that time, were of a romantic and sentimental character, full of adventures and surprising events, or took the form of legends and fables which usually ended with didactic judgements and aphorisms. Any scrutiny of the translated fictional works of this period bears this out,[89] and also testifies to the fact that the literary taste of this period was still traditional, although demanding more than the traditional fictional works could offer.

Since the title is the first element of narrative the reader encounters, the titles of translated narrative works were adapted to the canons of tradition. When al-Ṭahṭāwi translated Fénelon's *Aventures de Télémaque,* he altered its style, characters, and action and rendered its title in Arabic in the traditional rhymed form, *Waqā'i' al-Aflāk fi Ḥawādith Tilīmāk.*[90] Between the appearance of al-Ṭahṭāwi's translation in 1867 and the end of the nineteenth century, many translations using the same approach were published. A few examples are sufficient to illustrate the prevalence of this traditionalisation of narrative strategies to facilitate the transition from the old to the new narrative discourse.

Muḥammad 'Uthmān Jalāl translated La Fontaine's *Fables choisies* into Arabic poetry under the rhymed title *al-'Uyūn al-Yawāqiẓ fi al-Ḥikam wa-l-Mawā'iẓ* (1870), and Bernardin de Saint-Pierre's *Paul et Virginie* under the rhymed title *al-Amāni wa-l-Minnah fi Ḥadīth Qabūl wa-Ward Jannah* (1872). He Egyptianized Molière's *Tartuffe* as *al-Shaikh Matlūf* (1873) and finally translated a number of Racine's tragedies under the rhymed title *al-Riwāyāt al-Mufīdah fi 'Ilm al-Tirājīdah* (1878). When Murād Mukhtār translated a narrative text from Turkish, he retitled it *Qiṣṣat Abi-'Ali Ibn Sinā wa-Shaqīqih Abi-l-Ḥārith wa-ma Ḥaṣal minhumā min Nawādir al-'Ajā'ib wa-Shawārid al-Gharā'ib* (1878), which gave it the appearance of a collection of *maqāmāt,* or traditional anecdotes. It seems to have been successful, for it was reprinted again in 1887. Najīb Ḥaddād also translated and adapted Walter Scott's *Tales of the Crusaders* under the Arabic title *Ṣalāḥ al-Dīn,* Corneille's *Le Cid* as *Gharām wa-Intiqām or al-Sayyid,* Hugo's *Hernani* under the Arabic title *Ḥimdān* and his *Les Burgraves* as *Thārāt al-'Arab,* Shakespeare's *Romeo and Juliet* under the title *Shuhadā' al-Gharām*[91] and *Othello* as *Ḥiyal al-Rijāl.* Muḥammad 'Iffat translated Voltaire's *Mérope* as *Tasliyat al-Qulūb fi Riwāyat Mérope* (1889). When literal translation produced a viable Arabic title with traditional resonance, it was adopted as in Ḥaddād's translation of Molière's *L'Avare* as *al-Bakhīl* and Alexandre Dumas' *Les Trois Mousquetaires* as *al-Fursān al-Thalāthah.* The major translators of this era, such as Aḥmad Jalāl, Bishārah Shadīd, 'Abdullah Abū-l-Su'ūd, Muḥammad Qadri and Aḥmad Zaki, followed the same method.

There are, according to Goethe, "two maxims for translators: one demands that the author belonging to some other nation should be brought over to us, so that we can regard him as our own; the other demands of us that we should go across to the stranger and accustom ourselves to his circumstances, his manner of speaking, his peculiarities".[92] Most of the Egyptian and Levantine translators of this early phase followed the first of these maxims, not only because of the restrictions of the prevalent taste, but also because of the somewhat conservative nature of the reading public, who were unfamiliar not only with the substance but also, and this was the main disadvantage, with the form and conventions of the translated works. Knowing that the reading public could not tolerate any attempt to go too far beyond the limits of traditional culture, the translators tried to introduce the public gradually to the new narrative discourse and familiarize them with its conventions. They used rhymed prose, puns, and verbal decorations which had high status in the scale of artistic and literary values of that period as a convenient bridge to bring the reader over to the new work. Some of the translators simplified the plot, characters and a great deal of the action, thinking that the reading public could not follow complicated plots, until some of these early translations resembled modified forms of the traditional Arabic tales and anecdotes.

None the less, these rudimentary translations answered a real need for fresh literature, and prepared the reading public to accept better translations and more important original fictional works. In these primordial translations there is ample evidence of the insurmountable rupture between the demands of the new reading public and the canons of literary tradition. Their textual space had become the battleground for subjugating the language and techniques of traditional narrative to the dictates of the new narrative discourse. In them, the moulding of the new narrative in traditional media of expression demonstrated the power of the old modes as forms of thinking and categories of comprehension. Abstracting the new narrative and approximating it to the nearest general category of traditional narrative showed the inability to comprehend the implications of its particularization. As Locke suggested, "ideas become general by separating them from the circumstances of time and place",[93] and the principle of individuation is that of existence at a particular locus in space and time. It therefore is not a mere coincidence that time and space were the two elements most heavily altered in these translations, for without their alteration the translator had to deal with the complex process of individuation.

From the turn of the century onwards, translators moved steadily but slowly towards the second of the two maxims; towards a more literary translation which conveyed more and more the spirit and characteristics of the original. Thus, gradually, the reading public was introduced to the complex techniques and devices of a different narrative discourse without crutches of traditional rhymed prose and narrative strategies. This does not mean that translations at the turn of the century were free from shortcomings or even completely accurate, for the inaccurate translations continued to flow long after that; perhaps they have never stopped. Nevertheless, they moved on gradually from the stage of adaptation because the reading public had become relatively accustomed to these new publications, and because the success of certain works drove the translators to look for other works by the same author and render them quickly into Arabic,[94] or even to retranslate the successful work when it went out of print.[95] The success of the early translations of al-Ṭahṭāwi, Jalāl, Ḥaddād and others was in itself a guarantee against failure, and encouraged subsequent translators to move closer to the spirit of the original.

The first results of this gradual change in the translators' approach appear in the language of the works translated, which started to dispense with many of the fetters of the traditional, heavily decorated style. The linguistic changes were accelerated by the entry of new translators onto the scene, many of whom (unlike their predecessors, who were well read in both classical and modern cultures) had not been to al-Azhar or any traditional institution before they studied foreign language and culture. They had received all their education in the new civil schools, which could not provide them with a high standard of traditional and literary knowledge. Thus, their style and linguistic tastes were far removed from conservatism, and they relied on their instinctive feel for the language, which was, in some cases, because of their reading and cultural formation, in keeping with the dictates of modern narrative discourse. The language of translated narrative tended to be simple and economical. This was the case with the translations in the Levant, but those in Egypt and Iraq followed suit because of the participation of many Syrian and Lebanese Christians in their cultural life after fleeing from communal strife in their countries.

In general, the new translators' lack of traditional stylistic skill was in the interest of the translations they produced, because it forced them to stick to literal translation and minimize their stylistic interference in the text. Judging the accuracy or the literary value of these translations is beyond the scope of this study, but what concerns us here are two facts: the first is that the trend towards precise literal translation taught translators and readers alike about the specific nature of narrative language and crystallized their ideas about structure, plot, character, and other conventions; the second is that the appearance of many translated novels and short stories reflected the readers' thirst and fondness for the new narrative discourse. Translation not only familiarized them with the conventions of narrative and answered their need for new reading material, but also served as a training ground for would-be writers. It is not surprising that many of the translators of the early period played a pioneering role in writing various forms of narrative. Among many such translators were Khalīl Baydas, Najāti Ṣidqi, Kalthūm Naṣr 'Awdah and Anṭūn Ballān (Palestine); Najīb al-Ḥaddād, Sulaymān al-Bustāni, Faraḥ Anṭūn (1874—1922), Salīm al-Naqqāsh, Niqūlā Ḥaddād (1872—1954), Shibli Mallāṭ, and Nasīb Mash'alāni (Lebanon); Maḥmūd Aḥmad al-Sayyid, Salīm Baṭṭi and Anwar Shā'ūl (Iraq); Muḥammad Kurd 'Ali, Najīb Ṭarrād and Ṭanyūs 'Abduh (Syria); and Ḥāfiẓ Ibrāhīm, 'Abd al-Qādir Ḥamzah and Ṣāliḥ Ḥamdi Ḥammād (Egypt). The constant popularity of translated fictional works motivated many of the leading writers at the time to try their hands at writing fiction.

Unquestionably, the taste and culture of both the reading public and the new generation of translators were reflected in the choice of the works translated. Most of the works were of French origin, French being the first foreign language at that time both in the schools and among the educated class in general. Although this continued to be the case in the Levant, in Egypt the scale shifted gradually after the 1890s towards the English language because of the British occupation.[96] By 1919 there were more than twenty French writers[97] whose work had been translated into Arabic, as compared with only five English writers.[98] Although by the end of the second decade of the twentieth century the majority of the graduates from both secondary and higher schools in the Arab world knew more English than French, the balance in the field of translation continued to favour French literature. By 1930 there were more than 150

French writers available in Arabic translations and no more than fifteen English ones.

The Impact of Russian Literature

The impact of Russian culture and literature on the Arab cultural scene in the last century has been singled out here for detailed discussion because of the vital role it played in the genesis of narrative discourse. As we shall see in the following chapters of this book, Russian literature was adopted by many writers as the model for their literary endeavour. It is therefore necessary to study the history of Russian cultural influence and identify the channels through which it was transmitted. Although Russian contact with the Holy Land and pilgrimage to Jerusalem is centuries old, the first Russian political contact with the Arab world began in 1820 with the establishment of a Russian consulate in Jaffa, the port through which Russian pilgrims entered Palestine. By 1839, when the Jaffa consulate was transferred to Beirut where it became the Russian consulate for Syria and Palestine, the Russians had consulates in Aleppo, Latakia, Sidon, and Alexandria.

"In 1841 the first moves were made which were to lead to the establishment of a permanent Russian presence in Jerusalem — one which continued almost without interruption until 1917".[99] Soon after this date, Porfiri Uspenski arrived in Palestine and started his religious and educational activities to halt the conversion of the Arab Orthodox of Syria and Palestine by the energetic Catholic, Uniate, Anglican and Protestant missions. From the outset, he realized that schools played the decisive role in conversion and directed his attention to the education of the Arabs. He opened a seminary in the Monastery of the Cross in Jerusalem and encouraged the patriarch to set up an Arabic printing-press in the city. By 1853, the Patriarch of Jerusalem had appointed him chairman of a board of guardians for all Palestinian schools, in which he gave the Arab pupils priority over the Greeks. He encouraged the modernization of parish schools, which were no different from the elementary *kuttāb,* sought to establish more advanced ones and sent young Arabs to be educated in Russia. The rivalry between the Greeks, who controlled the Orthodox Church in Greater Syria at the time, and the newcomer Russian Orthodox led the latter to favour the Arabs and to champion their religious and educational cause. In 1854, the aims of his successor, Cyril Naumov, were to provide Arab priests with the opportunity of receiving training in Russia, "the completion of Greek and Arab schools in Jerusalem, the founding of an Arab press, and the printing of service and dogmatic books".[100] By February 1854, several works had been printed, and in the following years he extended Russian activities to Alexandria and Antioch, proceeded to improve the Orthodox churches in Damascus and bought land near Beirut for a Russo-Arab school. In March 1858 the Tsar decreed the foundation of the Palestine Committee,[101] with the vision of a more active role in the religious and educational life of the Arabs.

Following the anti-Christian disturbances of 1860, money was sent by the Tsaritsa and other Russian sources to open schools and ameliorate the situation of the Orthodox Arabs.

In 1864 the Tsar ordered the dissolution of the Committee and replaced it with the Palestinian Commission, which became a department in the Ministry of Foreign Affairs. And in the following year Antonin Kapustin was sent to Palestine to bolster the declining influence of the Russian church there as a result of its rancour against the consulate. He proved to be the best thing that happened to the Russian Orthodox Church in Palestine and expanded its programme of strengthening the respect for Russian efforts among Arab population. In 1866, a large plot of land was bought in Bait Jala with money given by the Tsaritsa, on which the school for Orthodox Arab girls, the first truly Russian school in Palestine, was built. It grew in strength and importance during the following twenty years, and in 1886 it became a women's teacher training college. In 1882 the Orthodox Palestine Society was formed, and the Grand Duke Sergei became its first president. In the following year, the Society appointed an Arab from Damascus, Iskandar Kuzmā, educated at the Moscow Ecclesiastical Academy, to assume responsibility for the Russian system of schools in Syria and Palestine. "The choice proved a happy one and around Kuzmā was to develop the whole system of Russian schools in Palestine. He continued to work for the Society until its dissolution in 1917".[102]

In 1889 the Tsar conferred the title "Imperial" on the Society and transferred to it the responsibilities, affairs and capital of the Palestine Commission upon its closure. This enabled the Society to multiply its branches and enlarge its membership. By 1902 it had forty-three branches in Russia with more than 5000 members. In 1900 there were twenty-three Russian schools in Galilee and Jerusalem alone, and more than fifty in the rest of Syria and Lebanon. "The chief aim of Russian educational policy in Palestine was to ensure at least a primary education for every Orthodox Arab child",[103] a major task given that Orthodoxy was prevalent among 90 per cent of the Christian Arabs of the Levant at the time. The main obstacle to the accomplishment of this task was the lack of qualified teachers, because many of the Arabs who were sent to study in Russia became naturalized and failed to return.

In 1885 a new boarding school, the Nazareth Seminary, was established under the headship of Kuzmā[104] to train the brightest graduates of the other Orthodox schools to teach. Both Arabic and Russian were taught intensively at this school, as well as Greek, arithmetic, geometry, history and geography, but the two latter subjects were Biblical in emphasis. A stream of Russian teachers was attracted by the high salary and came to teach at the school. "Russian was allotted a large share of the timetable and all subjects in the senior classes except Arabic were taught in it. On days when a Russian teacher was on duty the pupils were obliged to speak Russian even among themselves ... Russian was taught to give the boys access to Russian literature, as modern Arabic literature, especially works by Orthodox writers, was almost non-existent".[105] Its women's counterpart, WTTC in Bait Jala, which had a syllabus similar to that of the Nazareth Seminary, was, by 1898, providing the Russian school with one-fifth of the eighty-two women teachers employed by the Society. By 1911, after having graduated some seventy students, the Seminary had provided the Russian schools with forty-two teachers.

In 1895, and as a result of the financial difficulties of Spiridon, the Patriarch of Antioch, the Society was invited to take responsibility for the girls' school in Damascus and for fifteen village schools. The number quickly multiplied, and by 1900 the Society was maintaining forty-one schools in Syria with 5500 pupils. Although the huge expansion strained the facilities, some of these schools, particularly the large ones in the towns and larger villages of Syria and Lebanon, were remembered with affection.

> George Ḥannā [1893—1969] recalls the school he attended in Shoueifat: these schools[106] established a love for Russia in the hearts of the population as they were completely free and as they accepted pupils from all sects of Arab society without preference ... The teaching was free, school books were given free. The teaching of Arabic language was on a higher level than in other foreign schools. All this made the Russian schools the target of pupils whose material situation did not allow them to enter other schools.[107]

The emphasis on the high standard and special care devoted to the teaching of Arabic is also echoed by Nu'aymah,[108] who went to another Russian school. Despite the varied social background of the pupils, the majority of whom came from the lower strata of society, the graduates were provided through education with a chance for social mobility and joined the middle class afterwards.

Russian interest in the area was not confined to Syria and the Holy Land, nor was it only religious and educational. During the reign of Ismā'īl, Count Ignatev, director of the Asiatic Department of the Ministry of Foreign Affairs and later the Ambassador to Constantinople, schemed with the Khedive "to provoke a simultaneous uprising of the Arabs of the Nile and Tigris-Euphrates valleys together with an insurrection of the southern Slavs".[109] Ismā'īl also subsidized a number of newspapers which supported him and favoured the Russians in their conflict with the Sublime Porte. Even before Ismā'īl's era, a hefty tome on the history of Peter the Great, *al-Rawḍ al-Azhar fi Tārīkh Buṭrus al-Akbar*, was translated by Aḥmad 'Ubaid al-Ṭahṭāwi in 1841, attracting the admiration of the Egyptian intellectuals for the Tsar's energy in building his country.

After the British occupation of Egypt in 1882, Russia protested strongly and attempted to limit its duration. A convention was signed in 1887, providing for the withdrawal of British troops within three years.[110] Although not as widely publicized as that of France, Russia's opposition to the British occupation of Egypt, and its sympathy with the Egyptian nationalist movement, particularly after the Russian revolutionary government's publication of the secret Sykes-Picot agreement and Lenin's supportive message to Zaghlūl during the 1919 revolution in Egypt, increased the respect for its culture among the intellectuals. In addition many Arab writers saw several aspects of their experience, hopes and frustrations aptly portrayed in Russian literary narrative.

In addition Russian influence contributed to the rise of nationalism, for, unlike those of the French, American and British missionaries in the area, the Russian interests coincided with those of the nationalists. Russian activities were seen as efforts to protect and preserve the character of the traditionally Orthodox Christian community against the offensive of other Western denominations. By Ottoman law, the Muslim and Jewish communities were closed to the indoctrinating activities of Christian missionaries, and since the onslaught of Western missionaries on the area Catholics, Protestants and Anglicans were busy converting the Orthodox Arabs until the Russians came to their rescue. The Russians came to offer the Arab Orthodox Christians what other missions were offering them, but without exacting from them the expensive price of abandoning their faith. Their activities were therefore perceived as defensive of Orthodox Arabs and not as an assault on their faith or integrity. In his study of the Russian presence in Syria and Palestine, Derek Hopwood states that, "during the latter part of the nineteenth century Arab resentment increased and on several occasions exploded into open revolt. The growth of national feeling, of the desire of the Arabs to assert their independence and their own identity, was fostered by Russia".[111]

This Russian sympathy with the nationalist aspirations of the Arabs, though motivated by Russian interest and discord with the other major powers of the time, endeared the country, and particularly its literature, to the emerging intellectual élite in the Arab world. The fact that some of them read Russian assisted the intellectual movement in its search for a wider knowledge of Russian literature. The testimony of a native Russian who frequented the Arab world in the early years of the twentieth century gives evidence of the fluency of some of the bright graduates of Russian schools in the area. Krachkovski, the Russian orientalist, wrote about his visits to Syria and Lebanon in 1908—10:

> Whenever I arrived in a small village in Lebanon I first of all got to know whether there was a 'madrasa Muskobia' in the neighbourhood. I knew very well that I would not meet Russian teachers who usually lived only in the large towns... Very rarely would you see Arab teachers who had been in Russia... often, however, I met teachers who spoke Russian so freely that I was amazed how they could become so fluent when they had never left their own country. If they did not all speak so easily they all knew and copied the magazine *Niva,* and in the room of each you could see volumes of Turgenev or Chekhov, even

> the recently appearing green fascicles of *Znaniya* and sometimes such literature as was banned in Russia itself.[112]

This testimony is significant for a number of reasons. It indicates that at least some of the graduates of these Russian schools were fluent in Russian and had a sound comprehension of Russian literature. The fact that they had volumes of Turgenev as well as certain literature that was banned in Russia itself demonstrates a high degree of interest in the literature and keenness to keep up with its significant developments, a degree which is difficult to achieve without enhanced awareness of its relevance and a belief that it responds to their real needs.

This is confirmed through the increasing demand for both translations of Russian literature and original Arabic works emulating its narrative strategies. The latter is the subject of the following chapters, and the former deserves a brief mention here. It is worth noting in this context that although some of the translators of French or other European works tried their hand at writing original Arabic narrative, the percentage and the degree of success is much higher, more than double, among those who translated Russian literature.[113] Although a considerable number of the graduates of Russian schools emigrated to America — among them three outstanding graduates of the Seminary, Mīkhā'īl Nu'aymah, 'Abd al-Masīh Ḥaddād and Nasīb 'Arīḍah — they remained faithful to the spirit of Russian literature and contributed to the genesis of narrative discourse.[114] 'Arīḍah, though in America, filled the two magazines, *al-Sā'iḥ,* which he edited with Ḥaddād, and *al-Funūn*, which he edited for five years (1913—18), with translations of Russian narrative works. The writers of the *mahjar*[115] were reading as much Russian as American or other literature, for in these magazines Tolstoy, Lermontov, Turgenev, Pushkin and others were regularly translated.

But the translation of Russian literature was not confined to the *mahjar;* those who remained played a major role in popularizing Russian literature among the new reading public. One of them, Khalīl Baydas (1875—1949), a graduate of Nazareth Seminary and the teacher of Nu'aymah at Biskinta, translated a Russian work every year during the ten years following his graduation in 1893. His wife, Idāl Abū-l-Rūs, a graduate of Bait Jala, also translated some. He published his first translation of Pushkin's *The Captain's Daughter* as *Ibnat al-Qubṭān,* in 1898. When the press was not printing them as fast as he was translating them, he seized the opportunity of the Ottoman constitution of 1908 and obtained permission to publish a magazine, *al-Nafā'is,*[116] which appeared in the same year. It continued until 1923, with an interruption during the war years, and opened the floodgates for the translation of Russian literature. Indeed, it stimulated such translation and participated in shaping the new literary sensibility.

The editorial of its first issue demonstrates an increasing awareness both of the demand for narrative works and of the strong role they played in the life of the reader. Baydas states that

> it has become evident that narrative works in their different forms have an enormous impact on the hearts and minds of their readers. They are considered to be one of the major pillars of modern culture, for they contain valuable messages and insights which illuminate the mind ... We intend therefore to publish literary narrative works and other interesting tales to attract the attention of every enlightened man.[117]

By the time of its closure tens of Russian novels and hundreds of short stories had been translated and published in the magazine, encompassing all the major names in Russian literature at the time from Pushkin and Gogol to Dostoevsky and Gorky. Novels were serialized, and, after their completion, appeared separately, but short stories were rarely collected in book form afterwards. Apart from Baydas and his wife, many of the graduates of the Nazareth Seminary and Bait Jala girls' school translated Russian works. Among the most active were Anṭwān Ballān, Najāti Ṣidqi, Sulaymān Būlus, Ibrāhīm Jābir, Luṭf-allah al-Khūri Ṣarrāf, Kalthūm 'Awdah and Fāris Mudawwar.

The success of *al-Nafā'is* and its popularity among the young intellectuals of the time in Egypt as well as in Greater Syria stimulated the translation of narrative works from other literature and the emergence of original Arabic narrative.[118] Some of these translations of English and German works were translated second-hand from Russian.[119] Some were translated directly from English, French, German and even Greek.[120] In addition, Russian literature had become fashionable in Europe in the early years of the twentieth century, and those who were translating from other European languages fell under its spell and translated it second-hand into Arabic. There is evidence to suggest that other translators of Russian literature in the rest of the Arab world were aware of the work of the *al-Nafā'is* group of translators and sought to avoid duplication and widen the horizon of the reader's choice.

The impact of this literature on the new breed of intellectuals who found little joy in what was available to them in Arabic literature is articulated in the words of one of the eminent graduates of the Seminary, Nu'aymah. "I left Nazareth with joy in my heart. In my head were pictures, ideas, facts and visions which had not been there previously. They were my harvest from the past four years of my life and were a blessed and valuable harvest. They have opened for me the door of a new world".[121] The discovery of this new world and the expression of its ideas, facts and visions were the major preoccupation of the Arab intellectuals after the beginning of the 1880s, and their attempt to give them shape is the subject of the next chapter. But before moving to this chapter, a brief discussion of the new world-view informing this attempt is essential.

The Composition of a New World-View

Inherent in the spread of education, women's emancipation, the rise of nationalism, the expansion of journalism and the popularity of translations is a newly codified system of values and customs; in short, a new world-view. The first elements of this world-view can be traced to the ideas of al-Yāziji, al-Bustāni and al-Ṭahṭāwi in the early decades of the century. Both al-Yāziji and al-Bustāni expressed their thought in brief newspaper articles, but al-Ṭahṭāwi elaborated his in a number of full-length books and thus had the chance to present a coherent set of ideas. He also popularized his views in a widely circulated periodical, and this is the reason for selecting his work to demonstrate the nature of this new set of values at the moment of its inception. The enlightened ideas of al-Ṭahṭāwi in *Manāhij* soon found a wider outlet in his magazine *Rawḍat al-Madāris* (1870—8), which was established at the instigation of 'Ali Mubārak, who vented his ideas in its pages. His main aim in establishing it and entrusting al-Ṭahṭāwi with its editorship was, as he stated in its first issue, "the consolidation of the educational system and the shaping of the minds of the students and their sensibility". Besides Mubārak and al-Ṭahṭāwi, the main writers of this magazine were 'Abdullah Fikri, 'Ali Fahmi Rifā'ah, Maḥmūd al-Falaki, Ṣāliḥ Majdi and 'Abdullah Abū-l-Su'ūd, most of whom were students of al-Ṭahṭāwi or of the educational missions abroad. But it also published articles by some enlightened members of the traditional cultural establishment such as Ḥusain al-Marṣafi, Ḥamzah Fatḥallah and 'Abd al-Hādi Najā al-Ibyāri. Most of these articles produced variations on al-Ṭahṭāwi's major reformative ideas, and popularized the cause of change.

The emergence of the concept of *waṭan* (nation), as opposed to that of *ummah,* or *millah* (the community of the Muslims), is the cornerstone in the changing world-view that led to the genesis of diverse new forms of literary, social and political discourse. Some trace the concept to Napoleon's proclamation of July 1798 and the period of the French expedition;[122] others root it in the writings of al-Ṭahṭāwi and his students.[123] Both groups, however, give al-Ṭahṭāwi a prominent role in promulgating the concept in his two major works, *Takhlīṣ* and *Manāhij.* The assessment of al-Ṭahṭāwi's work is beyond the scope of this study, but his consistent attempt to use Egyptian and Arab history to justify the tenets of the French revolution in *Takhlīṣ* and to consolidate the concepts of patriotism, nationalism, social justice and egalitarian and enlightened rule in *Manāhij* is analogous to the quest of the translators, and later the creative writers, to utilize the strategies of traditional narrative in vindicating the new narrative discourse and endorsing its novel ways. At the heart of both endeavours is the desire to root a new discourse in Arab culture, and to appropriate its tradition and employ it in the service of the new modes of expression.

The very concept of *waṭan* was soon expressed in the title of a newspaper which championed the cause of Egypt against the control of the

Ottoman and supported the Khedive in his leaning towards the Russian as against the Turk.[124] The concept was not confined to Egypt, for al-Yāziji and al-Bustāni had called for it and combined it with the enthronement of the Arabic language, the revival of which was seen as a patriotic task. From the new concept of *waṭan* emanated major ideas and processes of cultural transformation that led to the change in artistic sensibility. The most important of these is the change in the concepts of time and place, for in the heart of the idea of *waṭan* is the establishment of bonds of citizenship, not on an abstract or religious basis as inherent in that of *millah,* but on a specific geographical and historic foundation.

As Ian Watt demonstrates in his study of the rise of the English novel, the change in the concepts of time and space is essential for the genesis of narrative discourse. The particularization of time is one of the functions which narrative discourse purports to achieve. But

> space is the necessary correlative of time. Logically the individual particular case is defined by reference to two co-ordinates, space and time. Psychologically, as Coleridge pointed out, our idea of time is always blended with the idea of space.[125] The two dimensions, indeed, are for many practical purposes inseparable, as is suggested by the fact that the words present and minute can refer to either dimension; while introspection shows that we cannot easily visualise any particular moment of existence without setting it in its spatial context also.[126]

In traditional Arabic literary discourse, place was frequently almost as general and vague as time, while the bonds between co-religious individuals were equally nebulous. The previous forms of literary and artistic expression were largely oral in form; comic or epic in structure. In his explanation of the absence of dramatic literature before the reign of Ismā'īl, 'Awaḍ suggests that a predominantly rural culture, such as the one that prevailed in Egypt and the Levant up to the mid-nineteenth century, produces only comic or epic literature, and that the development of urban culture is crucial to dramatic and other written forms of literary expression.[127] The elements of orality with their built-in transience do not foster solid circumstances of time and place.

In order to change the concepts of time and place in narrative, they have to be changed in reality, and it is rather striking that al-Ṭahṭāwi was aware of this from the outset of his cultural career. His efforts to elaborate the curricula of geography and history and make them the cornerstones of his educational reform have been well studied.[128] For without a strong awareness of the vitality of geographical and historical dimensions of being, it would have been impossible for the cohesive links of nationhood, *waṭan,* to replace the old spiritual or blood bonds with connections of space and time. In the concept of *waṭan* the geographical and historical dimensions supersede, and in certain respects suppress, those of religion. The new ideals of nationhood and political equality corresponded to certain socio-political changes and codified them at the same time. These changes also lay behind a different social conception of the self, and

> of society which at that time was spreading in the public opinion of Egypt. Where man felt himself traditionally belonging to his vocational or class corporation *(ṭā'ifah)* and to his religious community *(millah)*, people started now to talk of fatherland *(waṭan)* and nation *(ummah)*. The rulers looked benevolently on these new words, as they seemed likely to absolve their subjects from loyalty to the Ottoman Empire which represents the Islamic *millah* and to strengthen their moral and legal ties to the Egyptian state.[129]

Without the concept of *waṭan* supplanting that of *millah*, it would have been impossible to perceive the Turks, who share with the Arab the same religion, as being as inimical to their progress and independence as the British or the French, and, more importantly, to forge stronger bonds between the members of the same *waṭan* despite their religious differences. This radical change in the perception of allies and enemies implies a radical transformation of the world order and the traditional scale of values. The wide interest in the archaeological excavations at the time strengthened the rising sense of nationalism, and rooted the new concept of time into the individual as well as the national consciousness.

> The intrusion of new ideas, religious, political, scientific and socio-economic, was bound to generate conflict between the old and the new ... Individual strands of the encroaching culture, rather than the whole are first admitted by the host culture. Once a strand is admitted it invites other strands. The penetrative force of each is normally in inverse proportion to its value: an ideological strand is apt to penetrate faster and farther than a political one, the political faster than the religious. Economic change involves less emotion and consequently less strain than social change, but these involve less emotion and less strain than religious change.[130]

But the potency of these changes required their codification into a separate category capable of favourably contrasting itself with the prevalent tradition, and this was achieved through the adoption of the European perception of the traditional outlook as incarnating a period of *inḥiṭā* (decadence), thus positing the new changes as part of the desirable process of *nahḍah* (renaissance).

The power of the term "decadence" having been coined by European orientalists, thus acquired a certain verve, and it cannot be overlooked, for it played a major role in heralding a new reality. "Culture which had been produced prior to 1821, a year which can be defined as a 'break' in Egyptian cultural history, no longer had the same value as culture emanating from the post-1821 period. As the pre-1821 culture could not be 'measured' by the standard of European culture, the eighteenth century had to be seen as a period of decline, as part of the universal Islamic decadence".[131] The shaping of the new world-view went hand in hand with separating it from the old in a manner that helps to reconstruct the scale of values. Labelling strategies aim to change the perception of both the public and the members of the two opposing camps. The power of the term "decadence" was not purely cultural, but also social and political, affecting all aspects of human experience. Traditional forms of artisanal handicraft were abandoned for mass production; guilds were replaced by industrial schools or professional unions, manuscripts by books, the power of the notables by political parties and the Azhar by *al-Jami'ah al-Ahliyyah* (Cairo University).

Traditional forms did not simply disappear, but the negative value assigned to them by the new world-view helped to defeat, or at least minimize, their obstructing force in the battle between the old and the new. The impact of the categorisation of the traditional culture as "decadent" can be seen in the struggle of the traditional intellectuals to prove that Islamic culture can offer a way forward. In the nineteenth century the tendency among the leading traditional intellectuals, from Nāmiq Kamāl (1840—88) in Turkey, Khayr al-Dīn al Tūnsi (1829—89) in Tunis and Jamāl al-Dīn al-Afghāni in Egypt to Muhammad 'Abduh and his students,[132] was to posit the early period of Islam, an epoch free of any form of decadence, as the counterpoise to the European-based *nahdah.* They lowered the value of *taqlīd,* adopting tradition, and raised that of *ijtihād* (independent judgement), a move that was opposed by the pillars of the traditional establishment. They had overcome that opposition before the end of the century when it had a prominent place in Muḥammad 'Abduh's book *Risālat al-Tawḥīd* (A Treatise on Theology, 1897), and through it entered the syllabus of the Azhar. The success of 'Abduh helped to consolidate the power of the new world-view and vindicated its emphasis on independent judgement and rational thinking.

By the time of Ismā'īl also, the sociocultural atmosphere and the civil conditions of daily existence underwent radical transformations. The urban geography of Cairo and Alexandria was the symbol of the new mode of social existence, for it acted not only as the home of the new middle class, but also as host to the Levantine intellectuals who had fled their inhospitable environment. The very architecture of Ismā'īl's modern city created a different space and reflected or even demanded new modes of social interaction. The wide streets, tree-lined avenues, open plazas, spacious squares, carefully landscaped gardens and public fountains of the *nouvelle ville* created a type of public interaction different in form, tempo and rhythm from that usually practised in the warren of crooked lanes, narrow alleys and culs-de-sac of the old city.[133]

Ismā'īl's epoch was, in fact, remarkable for providing the infrastructure for developing a national and intellectual movement complete with the press, journalism, European ideas about progress and nationalism, developed cities, a sizeable reading public or an educated middle class, and even a rudimentary market economy. The quantification by the market system of the older hierarchical, feudal or metaphysical environment is a prerequisite for any faithful representation or reconstruction of reality through narrative, for such quantification is the essence of any careful mimesis. But more important was the development of a new reading public as a result of his expansive educational and cultural programme. Subsequently this led to the development of new modes of expression to meet the demands of the new sensibility of this era. In addition, the tolerance of the other views and the multiplicity of harmonious elements within a unified framework, which were necessary for the development of narrative discourse, and inherent in the urban setting, can be traced to the fact that Ismā'īl did not close any of the many Syrian or Lebanese newspapers published in Egypt and supporting the Ottoman view against his own, a practice that became widespread only after the British occupation.

The change in artistic sensibility was both triggered and accompanied by a unique phenomenon: the coexistence of otherwise completely separate types of relationships between the artist and the public: a patronage system in which artefacts are produced under the auspices of, and for, a known patron, and a market-based system dependent on the sale of artistic commodities to an anonymous public. This unique combination continued to exist in various guises and forms throughout the development of modern Arabic literature. The former led to the institutionalization of cultural activities under the sponsorship of the ruling establishment generally prevalent in Egypt. The latter encouraged individual entrepreneurs to venture into the field of cultural activity and provide outlets for cultural artefacts in general and for those denied a market by the state in particular, and this was until a few decades ago the case with the rest of the Levant.

The tragic sectarian events of Lebanon in 1860, which drove many intellectuals to migrate to Egypt, and the 'Urābi revolution in Egypt in 1881, which ended with the banishment of its leaders, heightened the intellectuals' sense of both time and space. The particularization of time and space is as vital for the concept of representational narrative as that of quanitification, for "the principle of individuation", which is seen by Watt as the main factor in the rise of fiction, is defined as follows:

> Time is an essential category in another related but more external approach to the problem of defining the individuality of any object. The principle of individuation accepted by Locke was that of existence at a particular locus in space and time: since ideas become general by separating from them the circumstances of time and place, so they become particular only when both these circumstances are specified. In the same way the characters of the novel can only be individualised if they are set in a background of particularised time and place.[134]

In 1861 Lebanon became autonomous, and both its autonomy and its strong historic affinities with Europe enabled it to play a more active role in the cultural revival of the area. Its autonomy provided for relative stability and encouraged missionaries to embark on numerous educational projects, enhancing the interaction with Western culture and emphasizing the study of Arabic language and culture in opposition to the domination of Turkish.

The ideas of the French Revolution acquired a clear social slant through the role of the French followers of Saint-Simon who flocked to Egypt after their difficulties in France and worked for the governments of Muḥammad 'Ali and Ismā'īl.[135] Their activities provided some of the early abstract ideas which influenced al-Jabarti and his generation with a practical programme for change. They influenced some of the Egyptian intellectuals with their utopian socialist ideals and their passion for the spread of education. Their ideas concerning the blending of theocratic government with rational and technocratic practice appealed to the Egyptian intellectuals because of their suitability for Egyptian society. Their call for equality and their dream of harmonious cooperation of all people against nature struck a chord with many intellectuals at an early stage of their development. Their enthusiasm for artistic education and for the foundation of a school of fine arts soon came to fruition, though their idea of art for art's sake did not find much support. Enfantin, one of the leading Saint-Simonists in Egypt, introduced Muḥammad Maẓhar, a member of the first educational mission and a lecturer at the School of Engineering, to Auguste Comte, who in turn introduced him to John Stuart Mill. Maẓhar was the route through which Comte's altered version of certain aspects of Saint-Simonist thinking, particularly that of the separation of religion and the state, reached Egypt and influenced al-Ṭahṭāwi.

This important concept of the separation of religion and the state, expounded hesitantly by al-Ṭahṭāwi in *Manāhij,* and elaborated by a number of his successors, such as 'Uthmān Ghālib, 'Abdullah Nadīm, Farīd Wajdi and Ṭanṭāwi Jawhari, reached its fullest expression with 'Ali 'Abd al-Rāziq (1888—1966) in his seminal book *al-Islām wa-'Uṣūl al-Ḥukm* (Islam and the Principles of Authority, 1925). 'Abd al-Rāziq's rational argument and lucid articulation of the logic of a new system of rule brought on him the wrath of the traditional establishment. It is true that the process of change was bringing many of the bright members of the traditional establishment nearer to the centre of the new world-view, but the leading figures of the new traditional élite, such as 'Abduh, Riḍā or Shakīb Arslān (1869—1946) were careful not to go as far as 'Abd al-Rāziq and Ṭaha Ḥusain (1889—1973). Indeed, Ḥusain went as far as 'Abd al-Rāziq in his radical thinking, and caused a major cultural and political crisis when he published his influential book, *Fi al-Shi'r al-Jāhili* (On Pre-Islamic Poetry, 1926), in the following year. Less controversial, but no less important are the ideas of the *al-Dīwān* school and of Mikhā'īl Nu'aymah in his seminal book, *al-Ghirbāl* (The Sieve, 1923).[136]

The New Reading Public and Its Sensibility

The formation of a new reading public as well as the shaping of its new experience are necessary preludes to the emergence of a new literary discourse capable of codifying this experience. The new public was radically different, both in nature and composition, from its traditional predecessor, and its needs were a major factor in the development of new modes of narrative discourse. The new public played a remarkable role in the modification of the literary scene, and encouraged the early attempts at fictional writing. The radical difference between this new reading public and its predecessor was its preference for a closer link with reality and tangible facts, as a reaction to the traditional taste for illusion and fantasy. The past generations' perception of literature and the religious nature of their culture had led them to appreciate the pun, rhymed prose, and heavy verbal decoration in the language of literature; the peculiar, imaginary, extravagant, and irrational in its events and plots; and the heroic and fabulous in characterization. So it was inevitable that the writers became attached to abstract generalizations, and concentrated on provoking the readers' emotions and, at best, stimulating their imagination.

The new reading public came to expect in narrative discourse a dramatization of aspects of concrete reality known to them in their new urban setting, and a rational or logical progression of thought and action. This translated itself, in literary terms, into a growing interest in simple and direct language; also, with the changing pattern of education, many readers were less well qualified than their predecessors to enjoy or even fully understand the more sophisticated conventions of classical imagery. The factors which participated in the formation of the new reading public played a significant role in the shaping of this public's world-view and changed the artistic sensibility and literary canons. The new scientific knowledge which formed a basic part of the educational curricula and the rise of rationalism had dislodged their attachment to heroic myths and fables, and predisposed them to sympathize with personal and individual experiences in literature. This was obviously part of a growing self-consciousness, a feeling for self-criticism and self-understanding, which led them to seek in art a more realistic picture of life.

Like the traditional reading public, the new one was still conservative in its view of morality, not only because the change of moral values is a very slow process, but also because of the strong religious sentiments which prevailed among them. But unlike the previous reading public, whose aesthetic and literary values were forged in the *sūq*[137] (market-place), where poets contended and the rhetorical value of the work and the oratorical skills displayed in its delivery could prevail over other more subtle aesthetic features, the new reading public, which came into existence in the era of the printing-press, derived their pleasure from the printed word and formed their aesthetics according to the individualistic reception of its subtle and rational values. The change from orally based and inspired aesthetics to written ones involved a change in tone and presentation, for the text was no longer addressing a collective audience as a whole, but was expounding to the individual reader its own equally individual point of view. It had to shape a different kind of rhetoric capable of absorbing the new mode of experience and reflecting the new perception of both the self and the world. So it was to be expected that writers should embark on a period of experimentation, as they worked to fulfil the needs of this new public and to look for new modes of discourse to express their aspirations.

Philip Hitti equates the change in the language of culture at the time to that of the great Abbasid revival.

> In response to the new stimuli, however, a radical change in outlook came out, necessitating a change in language. And Arabic again did it! Precisely a thousand years earlier the language of the *Qur'ān* and poetry responded to the challenge of philosophical and scientific translation from Greek and yielded adequate material. Confronted with a parallel problem, modern European tongues had no alternative but to resort to Greek and Latin to express modern scientific concepts. But Arabic, too proud to borrow except terms phonetically harmonious and morphologically assimilable, offered from its tri-consonantal verb roots the raw material from which new words could be coined to convey with precision up-to-date concepts in science, philosophy and arts. Without undue strain it served as a hospitable host to a myriad of new thoughts that sought admission into the minds of its users. Arab minds, like other minds, once stretched by new ideas refused to recoil to old dimensions.[138]

There is ample evidence to suggest that by the last two decades of the last century the steady growth of the reading public and the popularity of narrative discourse in either its traditional or its modern translated form paved the way for the rise of fiction. More importantly, there is also strong evidence that the growing sense of individualism and the development of a clear sense of national identity had altered the very nature of the experience of life, and, more significantly, the individual's perception of it and made it more conducive to narrative.

This more than anything else gave rise to the early embryonic forms of short narrative, for the changing perception of the living experience generated a new mode of expression which proved crucial in developing the early works in this genre. The authors of these early works were aware of a need to tell the stories of everyday life, not to record its tedious details but to endow it with a dimension of temporal continuity, extend the scope of human experience, and exchange experiences by the very act of telling them. The primacy of this urge to tell a story over any preconception of the form suitable for expressing it is demonstrated by the fact that the early pioneers who played a major role in delineating the area of experience most conducive to narrative treatment did not even canonize the changed nature of their writing by a change in nomenclature; for in Arabic the specific use of the terms "short story" or "novel" was not fully established until the 1920s.

3
A Modern Narrative Discourse in Embryo

At the genesis of a literary genre, writers who participate more effectively in its formulation are not necessarily those who make it their business intentionally to develop a new genre, but rather those who are more aware of the needs of the emergent reading public and receptive to its vision. This is because literary genres emerge more as an answer to a wide range of cultural needs and less as a result of a deliberate attempt to renovate existing modes of discourse or to introduce new cultural products. The latter may widen the scope of an existing genre or at best realize some of its unrealized potential, but they rarely give rise to new genres. Since genres, as Jauss demonstrated, are necessary for the process of understanding, their rise is linked to the schism in artistic sensibility associated with the generation of a new world-view and a fresh way of expressing and consequently understanding it. They are new mechanisms for comprehending, shaping and responding to reality.

In response to the new stimuli, new modes of discourse started to emerge. The last decades of the nineteenth century witnessed a tough competition between many literary discourses all trying to satisfy readers' demand for narrative fiction. The plethora of cultural responses to the transformation of reality and the changing world-view indicated a state of constant search for a new literary discourse capable of absorbing the changes and assimilating its most representative features into a new discursive field. As far as narrative discourse is concerned, it is possible to identify a number of attempts to probe the various narrative prospects and their ability to satisfy the needs of the new reading public. The needs of the public were as imperceptible and equivocal as the nature of the writers' search, for the public knew more about what they did not want than what they wished to read.

The new critical discourse of the period was trying with some competence to identify the negative aspects of traditional literature, but had little success in articulating the characteristics of the new one.[1] The publishers of the last decades of the nineteenth century were busy reprinting a variety of narrative texts,[2] while the writers of the same period were either reproducing or modifying traditional narrative discourse in response to the emerging critical discourse, or adapting European examples. The relationship between variable and constant structural elements that come to light in the radical historical change which swept over Arabic culture at that time can be established only from a diachronic perspective; hence the linear and consecutive ordering of materials in this study.

Oral, Traditional and Translated Narrative

The common denominator in the interactive processes of cultural transition (which included the emergence of a new reading public, the change in artistic sensibility and the shaping of a different world-view) is the shift from the general to the particular and from the abstract to the concrete; that is from the inconclusive to the definite. The manifestation of this complex transformation in the field of literary narrative is seen in the move from oral to written modes of presentation, and from collective creation to the individual author. The Arab world had experienced many forms of narrative over the centuries, and there is ample evidence that this tradition continued well into the nineteenth century. Lane[3] and other European travellers to the Arab world give us accounts of the public recitation of romances as a form of "attractive and rational entertainment", animated by a skilful narrator in a "half narrative and half dramatic" mode of expression.

This was a common practice in many cafés in major Arab cities where rhapsodes who specialized in particular cycles of romances or epics were considered valuable assets.[4] The romances of *'Antar*[5], *Bani Hilāl* (The Tribe of Hilāl), *Saif Ibn Dhi-Yazan, 'Ali al-Zaibaq* and *Dhāt al-Himmah* (A Woman of Great Resolve) were among the most popular. Even smaller towns and villages, as Ṭaha Ḥusain demonstrates in his famous autobiography,[6] have enjoyed their share of these oral epics. Najīb Maḥfūẓ (b. 1911) tells us that this was the first form of narrative he discovered in his childhood, and that the practice survived in Cairo cafés well into the end of the 1930s, when it was superseded by the radio.[7] The eventual death of this form of oral literature coincided with the maturing of the written narrative discourse on the one hand, and the arrival of a new form of entertainment on the other. It is interesting to note that the argument Maḥfūz uses against the continuation of the reciting is as follows: "We know all the stories you tell by heart and we don't need to run through them again".[8]

There was a boredom with the old stories, and a desire for new ones. The problem with folk and epic narrative is that the audience knows the story by heart. Other forms of traditional narrative which share this quality with oral literature are those of *The Arabian Nights,* which, despite their literary value, were banished by moralistic crusaders and conservative literary taste to the margin of popular and cultural interest. Collectively created oral literature has to be consumed collectively, but the new modes of urban existence required a more individualistic and private literary consumption. This was behind two different but complementary phenomena: one was the popularity of the translation and adaptation of European literary narrative, and the other was the revitalization of the *maqāmah* and the reprinting of traditional narrative.

At the turn of the century there were hundreds of full-length books of translated European narrative, mostly novels,[9] and more than 10,000 shorter pieces, published in Arabic newspapers and periodicals.[10] From the very beginning of journalism, translated short stories appeared in Khalīl al-Khūri's *Ḥadīqat al-Akhbār* (1858) and in Rizqallah Ḥassūn's *al-Nafathāt* (1867), in which he translated a large number of Kryloff's *Russian Fables.* By the end of the century most of the newspapers and magazines were publishing translated fiction, including those which had expressed some initial reservations.[11] No less than fifteen periodicals specialized in narrative fiction, including *Silsilat al-Fukāhāt* (Beirut 1884), *Muntakhabāt al-Riwāyāt* (Cairo 1894), *Silsilat al-Riwāyāt* (Cairo 1899), *al-Riwāyāt al-Shahriyyah* (Cairo 1901), *Musāmarāt al-Nadīm* (Cairo 1903), *Musāmarāt al-Sha'b* (Cairo 1905), *al-Fukāhāt al-'Aṣriyyah* (Cairo 1908), *al-Nafā'is* (Jerusalem 1908), *Silsilat al-Riwāyāt al-'Uthmāniyyh* (Tanta 1908), *Ḥadīqat al-Riwāyāt* (Cairo 1908), *Al-Rāwi* (Cairo 1909), *al-Riwāyāt al-Jadīdah* (Cairo 1909), *al-Musāmarāt al-Usbū'iyyah* (Alexandria 1909), *al-Samīr* (Cairo 1911), *Musāmarāt al-Mulūk* (Alexandria 1912) and *al-Riwāyāt al-Kubrā* (Cairo 1914).

Translation has to be widely read before an indigenous narrative writing appears, for it is easier to accept a translated text that runs against the established norms of literary taste than a native one.[12] The very foreignness of the translated text facilitates its acceptance and reduces the reader's rejection of its different ways. It helps to suspend temporarily local norms with regard to the reception of literary texts. This is more easily accomplished when, as was the case in Arabic literature, the translated text is a completely new type and does not infringe the conventions of well-established genera. But once accepted into the culture, foreign texts can exercise significant influence in modifying the prevalent literary taste, changing artistic sensibility and, more importantly, establishing conditions conducive to the acceptance of a new discourse, and stimulating the reader's demand for it. We have seen the effect of this on the pioneers of translation, such as al-Ṭahṭāwi and his student Jalāl. In fact, Jalāl's translations played an important role in reconciling the old with the new, not only because his translations were more adaptations than translations,[13] but also because he used the colloquial language in his dialogues.[14]

In his studies of the early Arabic narrative and drama,[15] Najm demonstrated that after a long period of translating, the translators moved to a freer adaptation in order to integrate the story and the characters in the local scene. In drama, hundreds of plays were translated before adaptation took place, and, similarly in the field of narrative fiction, where after some alteration from the translator some plays appeared as novels. With a few exceptions, most of the translators were very relaxed about their work. One of the most prolific, Ṭanyūs 'Abduh, was reputed to read a chapter of the original novel or short story and then put the text aside and rendered it, or rather what he remembered of it, freely into Arabic.[16] The reading market was thus inundated with narrative texts, many of which bore little resemblance to the original. Yet they were still asking for more, because many of the new readers were not satisfied with indigenous narrative at that period.

The Revitalization of the *Maqāmah*

The sociocultural changes that took place throughout the nineteenth century created demands for new modes of writing and challenged the monopoly of scholastic and theological concerns over the process of literary and intellectual production. The production of this type of writing has also played a part in its own downfall, for it has long been characterized by a decadent intellectuality, lack of originality, isolation from public concerns, preoccupation with trivia, and an exaggerated sense of complacency. The traditional élite recognized the nature of the problem and responded to it by utilizing fully the new mode of cultural production, the press. They started printing their work and began to bring the treasures of classical Arabic literature to the attention of the new reading public. In 1870 over 90 per cent of the books printed in Arabic and classified as literature were of a classical and traditional nature. This decreased to 80 per cent by 1885 and to 64 per cent by 1900, and it continued to recede until it dwindled to a mere 17 per cent by 1950.

The traditional élite's large share of the literary production in the early period was not due to their prolific output, for many of the printed books were anthologies of classical literature or printing of classical manuscripts, but to their influence on, even control of, the literary establishment. The reversal of fortune indicated both the rise of a new literary élite and the acceptance by the older one of the changing literary demands. This acceptance manifested itself in the printing of traditional narrative texts and in the revival of the *maqāmah* form. The *maqāmah* had emerged earlier as part of what Gran called the cultural revival of the late eighteenth century,[17] and by the second half of the nineteenth century it had become clear that it was the best tool available to the traditional literary establishment for responding to the steadily growing demand for narrative texts. The printing and reprinting of translations led the old intellectual élite to print traditional narrative texts to satisfy the readers' need and save them from the iniquitous influence of translation. The reprinting of popular and folk works of traditional narrative overcame the lack of a collective audience and made them available for private reading, but it did not change the mode of their experience or presentation.

Apart from the printing of many of the popular romances and folk epics, the following books of traditional narrative appeared during the last century: *Maqāmāt al-Suyūṭi* (1858), *Maqāmāt al-Ḥarīri* (1859),[18] *Maqāmāt al-Rāzi* (1865), *Kalīlah wa-Dimnah* (1868), *Aṭwāq al-Dhahab* (1876), *Maqāmāt al-Wardi* (1882), *Nawādir Juḥā* (1883), *Maṣāri' al-'Ushshāq* (1883), *Maqāmāt Ibn al-Mu'aẓẓam* (1885), *Alf Laylah wa-Laylah* (1887),[19] *Maqāmāt al-Hamadhāni* (1889), *al-Faraj ba'd al-Shiddah* (1891), *al-Maqāmah al-Sundusiyyah* (1891), *al-Maqāmāt al-Luzūmiyyah* (1892), *Maqāmāt al-Zamakhshari* (1894), *Maqāmāt al-Tilmisāni* (1894) and many other similar books. But the major change in the attitude of the pillars of the traditional literary establishment was their active involvement in the production of new narrative texts in response to readers' demand. Since the only model they knew and valued was that of the *maqāmah,* they all wrote their new *maqāmāt* with an intensity of production unparalleled since the *maqāmāt* of Badī' al-Zamān al-Hamadhāni (968—1008), written in 990. The nineteenth century alone witnessed the writing and publication of more *maqāmāt* than in the preceding 800 years.

There was hardly any significant writer of talent who did not try his hand at *maqāmah* writing. The writing of *maqāmāt* started as early as 1800 with Ḥasan al-'Aṭṭār's *Maqāmāt fi Dukhūl al-Faransāwiyyīn ilā al-Diyār al-Miṣriyyah* (*Maqāmāt* on the Entry of the French into Egypt),[20] which Gran calls "an important forerunner of modern literary realism".[21] Then came the *maqāmāt* of Muḥammad al-Ḥifni al-Mahdi (1737—1815), one of the leading Azharites in Egypt during the French expedition; Aḥmad 'Abd al-Laṭīf al-Barbīr (1747—1818) an Egyptian who lived in Damascus; and Ḥanāniyā al-Munīr, a Lebanese abbot who was one of the leading clerics of the Shawair monastery. Some of Mahdi's *maqāmāt* whose full manuscript was curiously entitled *Tuḥfat al-Mustayqiẓ al-Ānis fi Nuzhat al-Mustanīm al-Nā'is wa Maqāmāt al-Bīmāristān* (The Present of the Joyous Awakener for the Delight of the Somnolent Sleeper and the Hospital Maqāmāt) was translated into French by J. Marcel as *Contes du Cheykh el-Mohdy.*[22]

The floodgates had been opened and every major figure of the Levantine renaissance wrote his own *maqāmāt,* such as Nuqūla al-Turk, Nāṣīf al-Yaziji, Ibrāhīm al-Aḥdab (1826—91), Yūsuf al-Hāni (d. 1885), and Manṣūr al-Himish al-Ghazri, Muḥammad al-Jazā'iri and Ta'ūfīlis Anṭūn al-Ḥalabi (1836—98). In Iraq, a number of traditional intellectuals such as Abū-l-Barakāt and Abū-l-Fawz al-Suwaydi (d. 1830), Ḥasan 'Abd al-Bāqi, Khalīl Biktāsh[23] and Abū-l-Thanā' Maḥmūd al-Alūsi (1802—54) wrote them.[24] In Egypt, the tradition continued with 'Abdullah Fikri (1834—90), Maḥmūd Ḥusni, Muḥammad Sharīf, Ḥasan Tawfīq al-'Idil (1862—1905) and others.[25] Before the end of the century more than twenty books of the genre were in print as well as more than seventy other books of traditional narrative.[26] Other Levantines wrote variations on the theme, such as Jibrā'īl al-Mukhalla' (1801—51), Anṭūn Ṣaqqāl (1824—85), Amīn Shumayyil (1828—97), Najīb al-Ḥaddād (1867—99), Salīm Jiddi (1870—95), Salīm al-Naqqāsh (d.1884), Yūḥannā Ibkāryūs (d. 1889) and Yūsuf al-Bustāni (d. 1896). In addition, the traditional narrative encompassed some of the Coptic works, particularly *'Iqd al-Anfās* (Neckless of Souls, 1881), a cycle of sacred stories by Wahbah Tādurus, an abbot at the monastery of St. Barmūs.

Most of the *maqāmāt* and other traditionally orientated works of narrative which were published at the time did little to improve the standing of this type of narrative in the quest for a new narrative discourse. Their emergence confirmed the readers' need for narrative, but this type of narrative failed to satisfy their need. Only a few works distinguished themselves in this domain, of which two deserve a particular mention here: the first is al-Yāziji's *Majma' al-Baḥrain* (Confluence of the Two Seas, 1856) for its educational and nationalistic value and for his innovative intention, because, as his title indicates, he aspired to achieve the confluence of the sea of tradition with that of modern forms and concerns. The second is Fikri's *al-Maqāmah al-Fikriyyah al-Saniyyah fi al-Mamlakah al-Baṭiniyyah* (Fikri's Spiritual Explorations, 1872) for its linguistic elegance, classical style and impressive traditional structure, and also for its innovative intention of rooting the world of a translated text in the domain of traditional narrative.

All the intellectuals of the period were aware of the popularity of narrative, for in 1881 Muḥammad 'Abduh, the prominent member of the traditional establishment at the time, published an article about the most readable types of books and included narrative at the top of the list.[27] The three most popular categories of books among the readers were those of history, moral essays and narrative which he called *rūmāniyyāt* and among which he included such works as *Kalīlah wa-Dimnah, Fākihat al-Nudamā', Murzūbān Nāmah* and *Télémaque*. The inclusion of traditional works of classical Arabic narrative side by side with translated ones in 'Abduh's article (which drew the attention of the reader to another translated work of narrative that was serialized in *Al-Ahrām*),[28] disclosed the very general nature of the understanding of narrative at the time. But more indicative was the bundling together of narrative with history and moral essays. Many Arab writers sought for a long time to fuse the three interests into one discourse in which narrative was blended with history and a strong moral message. This encumbered narrative discourse for many years with a strong didacticism and a desire to root the characters and the action in historical settings. It also attracted many writers to it who used it only as a vehicle for moral or historical interest.

The Emergence of Indigenous Narrative

It is no mere coincidence that embryonic fiction appeared in Egypt in 1881, a year marked by political fervour and a remarkable awakening of the national consciousness, culminating in the 'Urābi revolution. It was also the year when the Secret Society in Beirut through its anonymous placards called for independence, the recognition of Arabic as an official language, and the removal of the censorship and other restrictions on the freedom of expression and the diffusion of knowledge. The emergence of indigenous narrative discourse in Arabic literature is historically connected with the growth of an awareness of a national identity, and the need to express and communicate this awareness. It is also linked to the various social and cultural changes, outlined in the previous chapters, which led to the disintegration of patronage and the rise of a new reading public.This radical change in the relationship between the creators of culture and the recipients of their products started during the last decade of Ismā'īl's reign, not only because of the emergence of an educated class and a new reading public, but also because of the disintegration of the old sensibility and the incipient conflict between the artists' views and morality and those of their patrons.[29]

The real beginning of the new narrative discourse started with Nadīm in his independent magazine, which relied mainly on the support of the reading public. Early and less efficacious examples of indigenous narrative appeared during Ismā'īl's reign in a magazine that enjoyed the backing of his patronage. Salīm al-Bustāni's *al-Jinān* (1870) was the first Arab magazine to devote considerable attention to narrative fiction, for its editor was himself one of the pioneers of the genre. Like previous magazines, *al-Jinān* published translations of narrative works, mostly from French with a few works from Italian and English, but, unlike any before it, its editor, Salīm al-Bustāni, and other members of his family,[30] published original works of rudimentary narrative. In the first issue Salīm al-Bustāni published a short narrative text, "*Ramyah min Ghayr Ram*"[31] (An Unintended Shot), and a long one, "*al-Huyām fī Jinān al-Shām*"[32] (Love in the Syrian Paradise), and continued to publish them intermittently. They proved to be both popular and influential, for they set the pattern for narrative writing, particularly among Levantine writers, for years to come.

Salīm al-Bustāni is an important pioneer in this field, because after a long apprenticeship with his father, Buṭrus al-Bustāni, he became aware that his task was not to emulate his father's achievements but to develop them further. He started by translating and adapting French narrative works and soon realized the need to create indigenous narrative free from the manacles of the *maqāmah*. His long historical stories[33] with their interest in Arabic and Islamic history were the influence behind the series of historical novels which his compatriot, Jurji Zaydān (1861—1914), started twenty years later and continued throughout the rest of his career. They have also inspired the work of two Syrian contemporaries, Nu'mān al-Qasāṭili (1854—1920) and Shukri al-'Asali (1868—1916), who published some of their work in his magazine. But his most significant contribution was in his narrative work, which endeavoured to explore the various aspects of social reality at the time, and played a role in the preparation of the new narrative discourse.

His most recurring theme was that of the incompatibility of marriage and the difficulty of attaining congenial relationship between couples without radical changes in social customs and conditions. In *"Najīb wa-Laṭīfah"*[34] he argued that the ideal man alone cannot provide the marriage with harmony and happiness as long as the woman is lacking in everything except money, while in *"Ghānim wa-Amīnah"*[35] he proposed the opposite case in which the woman is ideal, but without a matching man the marriage cannot properly function. In *"Zifāf Farīd"*[36] (Farīd's Wedding) he elaborates the disastrous effect of this incompatibility when the man, who is the provider of the family, encounters serious social and economic problems. The theme in these narrative works is rarely elaborated through the action or characterization, but mostly through authorial intrusion in the form of didactic statements. Despite the rudimentary nature of his narrative it is clear that it was generated by a strong sense of changing social perceptions and reflects a period of transition from the old to the new world-view during which the relationship of the sexes was perceived in a radically different manner.

Many of his longer works of narrative — particularly *Asmā'*[37], *Bint al-'Aṣr*[38] (A Woman of the Age), and *Fātinah*[39] — treated the same theme in the context of wider ideas of social reform. The last two (*Salmā*[40] and *Sāmiyah*[41]) modified the theme by widening its horizon and blending it with some patriotic and allegorical elements. At this stage of its development, the writers of narrative did not differentiate between various genres of narrative, and most of them wrote long and short works without an awareness of any generic characteristics. This lack of discrimination was in harmony with their perception of narrative as a tool for social reform and didactic messages. They used the term *riwāyah*, a narrated story, to refer arbitrarily to the novel, the novella, the short story and drama. At the time the term *riwāyah* was more acceptable in the Levant than in Egypt, where the term *fuṣūl* performed the same general function. A number of al-Bustāni's contemporaries, including his sister Alīs, Sa'īd al-Bustāni (d. 1901), Nasīb Mish'alāni and others, wrote similar works.

Al-Bustāni's work suffers from authorial intrusion and interruption of the narrative to elaborate moral messages or compare the predicament of the characters with what might have happened to them had society adopted certain European ideals. The lack of the use of dialogue and a complete reliance on telling with very little showing is another flaw which affected his narrative. From traditional narrative he develops the technique of the pairing of characters in a manner that provides each protagonist with his or her own antagonist. This could have provided his characters with a certain vitality, but the inadequacy of his characterization, his failure to motivate the action convincingly, and his constant resort to chances and unexpected events weakened his narrative. Al-Bustāni was mainly a social reformer who resorted to narrative in order to create a springboard for social preaching in an attractive context. He even declared that the aim of writing narrative was "to demonstrate our faults and the defects of others and lay them bare for ourselves and others to see through the writing of narrative, and to explain the negative and positive aspects of life by the description of the individuals whose stories we relate".[42]

The preponderance of moral and didactic elements had two complementary functions; it justified the reading of narrative on moral grounds in face of certain attacks by the traditional establishment, and it provided the author with opportunities to inject the text with both traditional morality and classical stylistic features. The contention with tradition was prominent at the time, for although "the rise of narrative literature in Egypt is linked to the growth of its middle class ... whose knowledge of the literary tradition was almost nil, the writers were very aware of this literary tradition and keen to win the recognition of the representatives of this tradition",[43] that is to say, the literary establishment rather than their new reading public.

When 'Ali Mubārak wrote his heavily didactic and structurally rudimentary narrative work, *'Alam al-Dīn*, in 1879, he gave the manuscript to 'Abdullah Fikri to "trim it and improve its style",[44] or, in other words, give it a touch of conventionalism to merit the approval of the literary establishment. He admitted in its introduction that his main goal was a pedagogic one and that he had resorted to the narrative form because of its popularity.[45] Apart from Mubārak's testimony, there is ample evidence to indicate the rising demand for fiction. But it was not until Nadīm's works appeared in 1881 that this demand was fulfilled by original writing which endeavoured to mirror the life and problems of those who demanded more narrative literature.

Nadīm: The Qualification of the New Writer

Nadīm was the only writer of his time able to assimilate and express the needs of the new reading public, almost completely outside the bounds of tradition. More than any of his contemporaries, he had the relevant sensitivity combined with the widest experience of life: experience which had equipped him with a deep social and political conscience. He described that life in his own words:

> I learned from the *'ulamā'*, associated with writers, and mixed with princes and governors. I took up my quarters with notables and men of industry. I lived with craftsmen and the fellaheen. I recognized how each category of people was steeped in ignorance and came to know what causes them pain and suffering and became acquainted with their hopes and dreams. I rubbed shoulders with many of the Europeanized Arabs, and discovered the impact of occidental ideas upon their characters. I associated with many of the distinguished educated Arabs who studied in the West and returned to occupy high and prominent posts. I knew numerous Europeans and explored their ideas and views, whether meritorious or objectionable, about people from Arab lands. I accompanied eminent merchants, and was able to decipher the rationale of their behaviour in commerce and politics. I mixed with sundry persons from different walks of life, different races, nations, and religions. I studied the holy books of various religions, the books of wisdom, history, and literature. I became addicted to reading newspapers. I was appointed a civil servant in the Egyptian government for a considerable period of time, and practised commerce and agriculture at other periods. I served thought and ideas by teaching for a while, and also by speaking in public and editing papers at other times.[46]

This is as much a description of the extremely broad life that Nadīm lived as an outline of the education needed to enable writers to perceive the realistic mode of discourse and qualify them to develop the response to the demands of the new reading public.

The conscious highlighting of a wide variety of firsthand experience was an emphasis on their vitality and their role in purging the new discourse from abstract notions and shallow, speculative, second-hand knowledge. The new narrative discourse had to be born from a real knowledge and intimate observations. Nadīm's varied experience allowed him to travel all over the country and to move between different social and cultural strata of society. Nadīm's broad experience enabled him, both consciously and intuitively, to assimilate various aspects of Egyptian life and explore its undercurrents. It provided him with a feel for the rhythm of this life and enabled him to put his experience and profound knowledge of Egyptian society to good use. His selection of a category of experience or a group of individuals would not be dictated by limitations and scarcity but informed by richness and abundance.

Nadīm's talent and insight enabled him to discover the literary discourse which was capable of expressing these experiences and, at the same time, answering the reading public's demand for new forms. Apart from this firsthand knowledge of his country and its people, Nadīm's own education made him aware of many of the different strands which were to converge in the art of of Arabic narrative. He started life with a traditional religious education at al-Anwar Mosque, a replica of al-Azhar, in Alexandria, and was later influenced by the reforming and patriotic ideas of al-Afghāni, whose regular meetings in a Cairo café he attended for years. He was also influenced by European culture through translations and by the Europeans with whom he came into contact. (Alexandria at that time had a large European community.)

Nadīm started his literary career in the early 1870s. It was a period of significant educational and cultural achievement and, at the same time, of severe hardship for the Egyptian masses. They paid very dearly both for the country's rapid development, and for Ismā'īl's self-indulgence, his extravagantly expensive tastes, and his excessive spending on luxuries. Without Nadīm's writings, the other side of Ismā'īl's reign, and the extent of the hardship and suffering which many Egyptians, especially the peasants, endured would not have been accurately and impressively revealed. The fact that he worked under Ismā'īl's autocratic rule, and held highly critical views of it, was responsible for many changes of fortune in Nadīm's career. Although the details of the ups and downs of Nadīm's life are not this study's concern, they indicate the nature of the conflicting atmosphere — social and political as well as artistic — in which creative writers lived at that time.

Nadīm was a gifted orator and a talented poet who wrote his poetry in the Egyptian colloquial language. He was thoroughly familiar with classical Arabic culture and acquainted himself with European thought and literature. Expertise in both classical Arabic and colloquial Egyptian and ability to use them creatively and deftly are also major qualifications for the development of the new narrative discourse. Nadīm's fluency in both linguistic media and his insight into the poetry of the colloquial with its close affinity to everyday life enabled him to forge the new language required for realistic representation. What helped him even more in developing such a language was the fact that he turned from literature and political oratory to journalism, a medium which provided him with a means of communication to the wider reading public, and exerted a necessary, and useful discipline on his polemical and literary style. In his career as a journalist he edited three weekly magazines: first *al-Tankīt wa-l-Tabkīt,*[47] then *al-Ṭā'if,*[48] and finally *al-Ustādh.*[49]

He started his journalistic career with *Tankīt,* whose title (Banter and Rebuke) clearly indicates its biting and humorous nature, for satirical journals can play a vital role in periods of transition, as Schücking observes in his study of the changing literary taste.

> The revolution of taste extended to the satirical journals. In place of the polite stereotyped exaggerations that had been regarded as comic in the past, there now came 'true stories' mainly in the form of letters addressed to the periodicals. It was possible to object that a story is no more comic for being true, but with the reader's increased sense for the real this condition did at least add to the attraction of the story.[50]

The humorous nature of these journals liberated them from the shackles of strict adherence to traditional taste, and, more importantly, helped to deflect the resistance to their new ideas, by catching the readers off guard. Nadīm was aware from the outset that he had to write the narrative and literature suitable for the urban condition and new social experiences, and that the humorous mode of discourse was the most appropriate vehicle for this aim.

Nadīm's experience led him to appreciate the importance of speaking to and writing for the new middle class, which had emerged during the first eight decades of the nineteenth century. Right from the beginning of his journalistic career, Nadīm tried to construct a new style through which his ideas and convictions could reach a wide range of readers. This involved intensive experimentation, because he had come to realize, as he travelled about the country, that the language and the medium used in conveying the teaching of someone like al-Afghāni reached only a few well-educated individuals. So the quest for a new style and fresh mode of discourse was a fundamental part of his conception of the journalism he wanted to establish — the journalism of a literary man. The first, promotional issue of his first weekly, *Tankīt*, which he distributed free with the daily *al-Maḥrūsah,* gave an indication of the nature of his target reading public. In the first editorial he outlined some of the characteristics of his new style while introducing the magazine to the reader:

> I am urged by a sense of duty and patriotism and by love and care for you, *ayyuhā al-nāṭiq bi-l-ḍād,* O speaker of the Arab tongue, to introduce this simple journal. It is a literary and reformative magazine which introduces wisdom, literary anecdotes, proverbs, jokes, and other entertaining and useful items to you in clear and simple language, which does not earn the derision of the learned nor compel the simple man to seek help in order to comprehend it. It describes incidents and events in an attractive and pleasing way capable of touching the heart and soul. Even when some pieces seem ostensibly improper they will reveal valuable meaning if you scrutinize them. Its simple appearance is intended to tell you that there is a splendid beauty beneath it. There is wit and humour beneath its satire and slander, and rebuke behind its praise and adulation. It shuns verbal embellishments, avoids figurative adornment and refrains from attracting attention to the eloquence of its editor, for it resorts to familiar language and everyday concerns. It will not induce you to seek the help of a dictionary or a learned elucidator ... Do not disown it before examining what it tells you in the light of our present reality, and do not think that its jokes slight our people or ridicule their deeds. They are only sighs of regret at the contrast between our present condition and our glorious past.[51]

In this editorial Nadīm not only introduced a new magazine, but also a new language for dealing with reality. He spoke of suggestive, inspiring but simple and plain language, stripped of its traditional rhetoric and ornamentations. It was to be an economical and functional language that deliberately refrained from attracting attention to itself or to its writer, and its aim was to convey various layers of meaning.

This was a valid remark, for the language of the period was full of grotesque verbal decoration. Inherent in Nadīm's concept of language, and running counter to the canons of tradition, is a new perception of the role of the writer and a clear attempt to stress the literary text rather than the author. Without this prioritizing of the text over the author, it would have been impossible to perceive the literary work as an autonomous and complete entity. In describing the mode of presentation, he outlined two main principles, on attractive and subtle presentation which may involve more meaning than it ostensibly suggests, and verisimilitude, or faithful representation of external reality, because he knew that "the reader is only interested in what touches his own daily life".[52] Yet faithful representation is not photographic but involves stimulating, contrasting and imaginative elements and what modern criticism calls irony and allegory.

He emphasized the use of wit and comic elements in creating an entertaining text and charging the work with passion — he describes some of the pieces as "passionate sighs" to provoke an emotional response. What has been written about the development of the English narrative decades earlier, that "the new literary balance of power, then, probably tended to favour ease of entertainment at the expense of obedience to traditional critical standards, and it is certain that this change of emphasis was an essential permissive factor for the achievements of Defoe and Richardson",[53] was equally true for Nadīm. Yet Nadīm was more conventional than his British counterparts, for he did not relinquish the use of the didactic, which had been the main function of literature up to that time.

Language and the New Sensibility

The new characteristics of the style outlined in Nadīm's editorial took precedence over his acknowledgment of conventional values in literature at the time. They represented the beginning of a new concept of writing and betray a sensitivity to the potentials of the new medium which was capable of masking many of the writer's personal views and feelings. It was as if Nadīm was aware of the fact that the printing-press provided a literary medium much less constrained by the censorship of public attitudes than the stage, and that this was intrinsically better suited to the communication of private feelings and views. He was certainly aware of what had happened to Ṣannū' when he had affronted social attitudes in his plays. However, it was difficult for a writer to sustain a meaningful relationship with a reader who was nourished on didactic and mundane writing. In fact, most of the fictional work which Nadīm introduced in his magazine featured a strongly didactic tone. Its reformative aim was too explicit, and therefore it cannot be considered as anything but the mere embryo of fictional discourse. That said, it must be seen in context, as a product of an era when the writer was considered primarily as a teacher of morals, and didacticism and instruction through allegory were the major justifications for literature.

In dealing with these early works, the use of the term "short story" is avoided, because it is difficult to treat any of them as anything more than narrative discourse in embryo. But the reading public's favourable response to Nadīm's new narrative discourse proved that the reader of the late nineteenth century both needed and enjoyed these works which modified the old and combined it with new. Nadīm was the first to understand the nature and needs of the new reading public. He was the first to attempt to capture the new sensibility of the period and to devise a form capable of assimilating the various aspects of this sensibility. It was straightforward enough to embrace the unsophisticated views and lives of the new reading public, simple enough not to arouse their aversion, and stylistically flamboyant enough to be tolerated by the literary establishment. The ingenuity of Nadīm's achievements in this field has led one critic to declare that he "was a man before his time, a stranger in his age; he abandoned the rhymed prose and verbal decoration from the very beginning of his literary career ... and liberated his style from their shackles, while others continued to use them for decades to come".[54]

In fact, Nadīm himself was fully aware of what he was doing, and defined his approach, in the first issue of *Tankīt,* when he described the nature of his magazine:

> We do not want it to be embellished with metaphors and metonymy, or ornamented with allusion and equivocation, or to be vainglorious with the grandioseness in its style and eloquent sentences, or to show off the richness of its knowledge and the sharpness of its intelligence. But we want it to talk to you in an intimate tone, to use the language which we are accustomed to hear, and to introduce topics with which we are familiar. It should not require you to look up a word in the dictionary of al-Fayrūzabādi ... It will not need an interpreter to explain its subjects or a sheikh to simplify its meanings. But it will keep you company as a friend who talks to you about what concerns you, or a servant in your house who only asks for what he knows you can grant him, or an entertainer who tells you the things that amuse you.[55]

These were Nadīm's declared aims from the very beginning: an intimate tone, and a form of writing which dealt with familiar topics and issues which interested the reading public, a new mode of discourse which treated what the literary establishment looked upon as unliterary subjects — everyday issues, matters which were considered inimical to literature and looked down on.

The intimate tone was not a mere linguistic issue but an expression of the writer's desire to produce what purported to be an authentic account of the experience of individuals. In practice, Nadīm went even beyond this statement, which was considered extreme for that period, adapting prose style to give an air of authenticity, and using the vernacular in a great deal of his writing, especially in his narrative sketches. He relied on it entirely in writing dialogue even when he was writing the narrative in his own simple, formal language. This is significant when it is seen in the light of Nadīm's call for the importance of language in the preservation of national identity, and his campaign under the slogan *"iḍā'at al-lughah taslīm li-l-dhāt"*[56] (neglecting language jeopardizes national identity), urging readers to uphold it in the face of the incursion of foreign languages.

Evidence that Nadīm's attitude to language responded to the real needs of the public was demonstrated in the public's reaction to his unexpected announcement, at a later stage, that he would cease using colloquial Egyptian in his magazine in the interest of the literary language. His readership showered his magazine with letters asking him to continue, and finally persuaded him to change his mind and resume using the vernacular in his narrative episodes. The most persuasive argument for the resumption of writing in the colloquial was put forward in a letter signed by a group of Azharites who considered themselves the legitimate defenders of language and tradition.[57] After arguing convincingly that the audience for his *fuṣūl tahdhībiyyah* (narrative sketches or moral tales) was much wider than simply those who were literate, the letter went on to demonstrate that the nature of the issues and the topics discussed in his magazine demanded the highest possible degree of clarity and sensitivity to enable those who were illiterate to grasp their meaning, a clarity which was only attainable through the use of the colloquial. It is remarkable that the letter condoned the break with the accepted canons of prose style, regarding it, not as incidental, but rather as the price the writer had to pay in order to achieve immediacy and verisimilitude.

The letter also stresses the importance of the narrative sketches and their tremendous effect on the audience: "Your didactic narrative sketches have achieved what sermons and other forms of discourse failed to accomplish".[58] The emphasis on the narrative sketches shows that these items were much appreciated by their audience, as well as attracting the attention of other writers. The popularity of this form of discourse encouraged and inspired a few amateurs to try their hand at the form.[59] What did Nadīm introduce in these narrative sketches to make them so significant, and what was the artistic quality of this new form of discourse?

Although Nadīm was aware that both the content and the style of his writing were radically different from the common modes of discourse at the time, he did not realize that, with his narrative sketches, he was paving the way for a new literary discourse. He adopted his different style through an overwhelming desire to reform his community and improve their lives. This new writing was a product of Nadīm's keen sensitivity and creativity which brought together the most representative social phenomena of his time. It was, most of all, the result of Nadīm's efforts to popularize a number of problematic national issues and to simplify many of the intellectually complex issues on which his master al-Afghāni had preached. Least of all was it a consequence of a conscious attempt to create a new literary form, or a gratuitous search for a new mode of discourse.

During the initial stage of *Tankīt* Nadīm was not able to suggest a proper name for this literary genre of narrative which he was bringing to fruition. However, in the face of some criticism, he called it *fuṣūl tahdhībiyyah*,[60] and maintained the name as a generic term during the later period of *al-Ustādh,* when it became more didactic. It is natural that Nadīm and others after him who played a major role in delineating the area of experience most conducive to narrative treatment and the language suitable for its portrayal, had difficulty in codifying the changing nature of their writing. This was also the case with the pioneers of the English novel, who "did not even canonize the changing nature of their fiction by a change in nomenclature".[61] The use of the term "novel" in English literature was only established decades after the publication of the early novels. In Arabic, the specific use of the literary terms *qiṣṣah qaṣīrah* (short story), *riwāyah* (novel), and *masraḥiyyah* (play), denoting various genres of narrative discourse were not fully established until the 1920s. Until then, the term *riwāyah,* which meant anything that was related by a narrator, an event or even a play, was used indiscriminately to describe all forms of narrative and drama.

Nadīm refrained from the use of the term *riwāyah,* which had been used by al-Ṭahṭāwi, Jalāl and al-Bustāni, as he was aware of the ambiguity surrounding the traditional connotation of the term (which was widely used in classical Arabic), and also because of his desire to break with the old forms of narrative. He saw "realism" or authentic representation of "intimate" scenes and experience, as the defining characteristic which set his work apart from previous narrative writing, which was marred by exaggeration and imagination. He was aware that he was not writing what until then was conceived of as *riwāyah,* an imaginary tale, but a different mode of discourse. This claimed to intimate a type of knowledge that was no longer derived from direct experience but was still subject to what Walter Benjamin calls "prompt verifiability",[62] supplementing experience rather than supplanting it.

The Early Narrative Sketches

Although Nadīm was not fully aware of the innovative nature of his own narrative, he was conscious of the power of metaphor and allegory from the very beginning. He was also aware of the reforming aims and didactic function of his work. Didacticism combined with a deep concern for the issues of daily life lay behind the rapid success of the magazine.[63] In the first issue of *Tankīt,* Nadīm published five of his new allegorical or didactic narrative sketches dealing with a variety of topics, and continued publishing them until the end of September when the national question began to take up most of the space.[64] Most of these narrative sketches were rudimentary in style and conception, yet they were highly significant because they set the tone and delineated the main thematic area of the early modes of narrative discourse. They focused on middle-class characters and scenes, and were characterized by their strident, often simplistic, didactic tone.

The five narrative sketches in the first issue varied in theme and technique and demonstrated the width and breadth of Nadīm's scope and talent. In *"Majlis Ṭibbi 'alā Muṣāb bil-Afranji"*[65] (Medical Consultation for a Syphilis Patient), he tells, through a fine allegorical structure, the story of an upstanding, cultured, handsome young man, who enjoys the respect and affection of the people around him. A crafty swindler, who pretends to be learned and devout, sneaks into his life and tempts him into sinful actions until he is infected with *al-dā' al-afranji,* the European disease: i.e. syphilis. The healthy, good-looking protagonist becomes sick and deformed, and the doctors diagnose his illness, prescribe medicine, and advise strongly against any further association with the swindler and his ilk. Using this allegorical structure, Nadīm attempted to demonstrate the evils of Europeanization, indicating that surrendering to temptations associated with foreign culture was particularly harmful when it was accompanied by the relinquishment of learning, and characterized by a slavish imitation of that culture. But he assured the reader, challengingly, that it was not too late, and that a cure was still possible, provided that quick measures were taken. The interpretation of the allegory was all too evident. Egypt was in a critical situation at the time; it had incurred debts and loans at exorbitant rates of interest, often as high as 20 per cent,[66] and was suffering from the shock of modernization and its temptations.

In *"'Arabi Tafarnaj"*[67] (An Arab Becomes Westernized), Nadīm treated another aspect of the same theme, attacking the ingratitude of some of the Egyptians who, having been sent to study abroad, returned to deny the rightful claims of their society over them and looked down upon its traditions and norms of conduct. Nadīm presents his protagonist, Zi'aiṭ, at the moment of his return from Europe, speaking a strange mixture of Arabic and French, and rejecting his parents' simple way of life. The dialogue between him and his parents, Mi'aiṭ and Mi'aikah, is lively and humorous showing convincingly how Zi'aiṭ's haughty attempts to mock his parents' way of life alienates him from his surroundings. In the end he is unable to contribute to the progress of his society or even to adjust to his milieu. His knowledge gained in the West seems meaningless, bearing out what C. Wright Mills observes in his sociological study on the élite: "Knowledge that is not communicated has a way of turning the mind sour, of being obscured, and finally of being forgotten. For the sake of the integrity of the discoverer, his discovery must be effectively communicated".[68] Nadīm argued persuasively for the importance of this effective communication which the new educated class could not attain without respect for, and understanding of, the social ethos and traditions of the recipient culture.

"Sahrat al-Anṭā'"[69] (Smoking Party) introduced a new theme which, like that of the conflict between oriental and occidental culture, or tradition and modernity, remained at the centre of Arabic narrative discourse for many years to come; that is, the attack on those who sought refuge in narcotics and alcohol. He ridiculed them, criticized their escapism, and depicted the consequences of their behaviour upon society. He demonstrated how their addiction to drugs or drinking drained their resources and diverted their attention from serious matters, as they became exhausted and sterile members of their society. A significant feature of this narrative sketch and other similar pieces on this subject[70] is that Nadīm eschewed the use of the usual religious argument which prohibited alcohol and condemned stupefying drugs, and argued the case purely on social and economic grounds. He also emphasized the enlightening and preventive role of education, and he often went out of his way to advise and explain how much such wasted money and talent could have achieved for the country if they had been channelled in the right direction

In *"Muḥtāj Jāhil fi Yad Muḥtāl Ṭāmi'"*[71] (An Ignorant Needy in the Hands of a Greedy Crook), he introduced his third major theme: the social disparity between the classes and the suffering of the poor. He exposed the usurious transactions of foreigners and their exploitation of the peasants, to whom they lent money at an extortionate rate of interest. He demonstrated a great concern for the suffering of the poor in general, and the peasants in particular, to whom he addressed various provocative pieces of writing in most of the issues of his short-lived magazine.[72] The last narrative sketch in this issue was *"Ghiflat al-Taqlīd"*[73] (The Pitfalls of Emulation), which presented a funny and eccentric character not so much for the message that could be drawn from his actions but for the comic effect of his peculiar ideas. It was a theme which proved attractive to later writers. The detailed account of the character's peculiarities and the text's fascination with his actions were intended to equate the new discourse with reality and demonstrate its ability to mirror life's strangest features.

The themes treated in these five pieces recurred in many others, particularly that of the narcotics and alcohol which appeared in no fewer than six other sketches.[74] One of these six sketches, *al-Mazzah al-Muṭaharrah*[75] (Cleansed Snacks), borders on the erotic and is clearly ahead of its time in its open treatment of sex. But new themes kept emerging, especially that of the drive against superstition. In a number of his works,[76] as well as in works by others published in response to his campaigning style,[77] Nadīm tried to expose those who exploited religion to achieve their own, often immoral, ends. This theme was one of the few which elicited immediate response from other writers, and it became an effective tool in discrediting the old intellectual élite. But Nadīm's treatment of the theme was part of his drive to change the attitude of his readers and create in them a rational way of thinking.

A related theme was that of the drive against apathy and inaction. In *"Nahāyat al-Balādah"* (The End of Paralysis),[78] he used a powerful and highly entertaining allegory to illustrate the disastrous consequence of a fatalistic approach to life, both personally and nationally. The narrative in this humorous sketch is about a lily-livered hero, and Nadīm uses the recurring cycle of events to make the point instead of the conventional resort to authorial commentary. The strong attack on folk wisdom is fair and courageous, but the final comment of the thief is rather heavy-handed and shows a lack of understanding of the importance of convincing characterization. Another sketch on this theme is *"al-Dhi'āb Ḥawl al-Asad"*[79] (Wolves Around the Lion), which uses the animal fable, a familiar narrative genre in Arabic for centuries, to illustrate the problems of the country at large, focusing on social disparity, and reflecting the country's gloomy present in contrast to her splendid past.

The issues of *Tankīt* contained a number of letters to the editor, some objecting to the harshness of his criticism, some supporting his position with additional examples, and some complaining about the treatment they had received in his narrative sketches.[80] The letters demonstrated the reading public's acceptance of these narrative sketches, not as fiction but as a reflection of reality and even as its accurate portrayal. Hence the occurrence of arguments about the accuracy of certain information, including the price of drinks in certain cafés, or whether the author meant a specific group of people in a specific café. Some even argued that a story was partially correct except that the ending did not take place in the real situation as described.[81] Nadīm's reply to some of these letters focused on the concept of plausibility as opposed to photographic presentation of reality. He assured the readers that although he wrote only about his experience and what he knew, he also avoided any direct reference to particular situations or recognizable locations in order not to embarrass or offend specific people, for it is more effective to get advice through the other, and not by mocking or ridiculing the self.[82]

Exploration of Further Grounds

In most of his early narrative sketches, Nadīm fluctuated between imaginative literary treatment of the theme and unsophisticated didacticism, but many of them demonstrate that

> Nadīm has discovered a great and important fact, that is, teaching through narrative. He puts advice in a shape of a story and examples in the form of humorous sketches. He relates social defects through the characters of his fictional works. And when he realizes that the fictional style is more attractive, effective in disparagement, and rationally acceptable, he commits himself to it.[83]

Although narrative elements were developed as tools to sharpen the effectiveness of his writing and to demonstrate their connection with reality, they acquired a presence of their own and attracted readers and would-be writers at the same time.

Nadīm showed a clear awareness of the effectiveness of this literary form, because when he resumed writing after the failure of the 'Urābi revolution and his long years in hiding and in disguise, he continued to experiment in the same style in his final magazine *al-Ustādh.*[84] He not only preserved the form, but also repeated many of the themes and the character types he had developed in his first magazine. The main subject was the rapid, radical change that had taken place in Egyptian society as a result of the influence of European culture and the subsequent British occupation. The effects of this change upon society and on human character were intensified and its negative aspects accentuated by the arrival of the British. Nadīm, an ardent opponent of the British occupation, directed his sarcastic wit and sharp tongue against the detrimental European influence on Egyptian society. Although in the second stage of his writing he continued to be a social critic with even more vehemence, he resorted to more obscure allegory to evade censorship, which intensified under the British.

In the second stage, Nadīm continued his earlier campaign against drunkenness but with a different slant. In a series of dialogues between *"Ḥanīfah wa-Laṭīfah"*[85] or *"Laṭīfah wa-Dimyānah"*,[86] he illustrates the torment and suffering of deserted wives and the effects of their dissolute, drunken husbands' behaviour upon their lives and their families. He intensified his attack on the Europeans who exploited the ignorance and the weakness of Egyptians who were imitating them blindly. He showed how such Egyptians were dazzled by the tinsel of the least worthy aspects of European civilization, without assimilating its more valuable accomplishments or paying them the attention they deserved. He attempted at this stage to treat his previous theme from a different angle, through the wives, and to reduce the directness of his didactic tone. He also broadened the scope of his theme by dealing with other common addictions. In *"Zubaidah wa-Nabawiyyah"*,[87] he portrayed hashish addiction and its grave consequences, and in *"Madrasat al-Banīn"*[88] (Boys' School), gambling and its destructive effects. In all these narrative sketches, Nadīm touched upon various dimensions of the conflict between oriental and occidental cultures and its manifestation in everyday life.

Apart from his recapitulation of old themes in the second stage, Nadīm introduced some new subjects. In a series of fictional dialogues, *"Madrasat al-Banāt"*[89] (Girls' School), which contained lengthy discussions between different generations of women,[90] Nadīm underlined the importance of women's emancipation and education, albeit in a limited way. He expounded the kind of education he considered suitable for women in this period of Egypt's evolution, and described the inner life of the Egyptian woman, her role and social status, and the type of problems which she faced. He also gave an interesting account of domestic life, displaying an insight into the questions of housekeeping and the household at the time, and discussed various aspects of the family life of a middle-class Egyptian household. He enabled the reader to know, for the first time through a literary discourse, what was expected from a woman, how a man behaved in his home, and what the recurring anxieties of the Egyptian middle-class urban family were at the turn of the century. Although he concentrated on both the life and problems of urban women, he was particularly concerned with the problems of social and cultural transition which rural women faced when they moved to the city.

In a similar series of fictional dialogues, *"Madrasat al-Banīn"*, he satirized Europeanized Egyptians who were unable to reconcile the two cultures constructively, and subsequently failed to contribute to their country's progress when it was badly needed. He raised a number of subsidiary subjects in this series of dialogues: the condition of Egyptian industry in its early stage, and the fact that Egyptians were not supporting it enough; the importance of investing Egyptian money, wasted on drinking and gambling, in new industries; and the need to reclaim unused land. In *"Sa'īd wa-Bakhītah"*,[91] he treated the problem of manpower wasted in trivial domestic work and suggested that it should be directed to reclaim land or trained to work in the factories which should be built with the money the comfortably off spent on extravagance.

In *"al-Murāfa'ah al-Waṭaniyyah"*[92] (the Patriotic Defence), he put the responsibility for the country's social, economic, cultural and even moral deterioration on the educated class and urged them to save their country from foreign domination and the abyss of backwardness into which it had fallen. He called upon Egyptians to stop being lazy and apathetic, and urged them to be more involved in what concerned their oppressed country. In *"'Imārah wa-Zanāti"*,[93] he pointed out the folly of the rivalry and hostility among Egyptians which has led them to economic and spiritual ruin, and emphasized that the foreigners and colonialists were the only people who benefited from such a situation.

Elements of the new Narrative Discourse

In his treatment of this variety of subjects and themes, Nadīm succeeded in devising a tone and a mode of discourse capable of accommodating traditional puritanism and satisfying the increasing demand for new narrative discourse among the reading public. He also brought together two hitherto separate reading publics: newspaper readers and the more allusive reader of folk literature. In fact, Nadīm's embryonic narrative discourse owes a great deal both to folk literature and to journalism. Of a comparable period in English literature history, Q.D. Leavis remarks that such rudimentary narrative was, "the product of journalism in an age when no distinction existed between journalism and literature, when journalism that set out to amuse"[94] had to establish for itself a role in the life of the society. It drew simultaneously upon folk literature and oral tradition and tried to replace them with a form morally acceptable to the literary establishment. Nadīm had to intensify the moral tone of his work to earn the approval of those who dictated the canons of taste.

Some of Nadīm's works come very close to a rudimentary form of short story; others were further from it. All of them use, with varying degrees of success, some narrative elements. Because Nadīm was neither fully aware of the embryonic narrative form in his hands, nor consciously aiming at writing stories or even revitalizing the neglected form of the *maqāmah,* he failed to develop these narrative elements fully or guide them towards maturity. Nevertheless, some of these fictional elements are artistically more mature in the early works than in the later ones. This is because Nadīm's major concern at first was to reach and attract the new reading public, by expressing their problems and touching upon social and national questions which concerned them. He did this in an effective and appealing manner through the use of concrete detail and recognizable characters.

He realized that dramatic and imaginative presentation of such issues was more effective in influencing the reader's views and opinions than the rhetorical method of direct sermons and simplistic didacticism. In his new narrative presentation, Nadīm never contemplated diminishing the didactic tone, because for him the message was always more important than the medium. He intuitively discovered the importance of his medium and its suitability for the questions he wanted to raise, yet he was not in a position to devote more attention to it, nor was he aware of the contradictions between traditional and modern elements in his writing. However, the lucid, simple prose of Nadīm, based on contemporary speech rather than the bookish style of his predecessors, succeeded in attracting a wide reading public. This new and simple style was in sharp contrast with the dominant stylistic values of the time, and was a significant step towards the creation of a language suitable for effective narrative presentation.

Yet these remarkable linguistic changes are not sufficient in themselves to qualify Nadīm as a pioneer of the modern Arabic narrative. However, Nadīm introduced to Arabic literature certain elements which were fundamental for the genesis of narrative discourse. The first element was the dialogue, which played a leading part in giving Nadīm's work its narrative character. The dialogue fluctuated between two patterns. In most cases it was opaque and unsuggestive as a didactic, and occasionally trite conversation,[95] but sometimes it became a poetic and allusive artistic medium capable of crystallizing the narrative situation and of exploring the social, psychological, and cultural make-up of the characters.[96] Nadīm used the vernacular in most of his dialogues, and where he was successful he revealed its poetic and allusive power as a language rich with imagery and abundant in compact expressive idioms.

But whatever his degree of success in using dialogue, dialogue on its own is not sufficient to maintain a narrative structure. Therefore, Nadīm used a number of other devices to sustain his dialogue and to strengthen the fictional plausibility of his writing. He used a rudimentary form of narrative to summarize the action or to give a rapid account of events. In a few cases he used this type of narrative to offer his reader a general description of the setting, to isolate some aspects of the situation, or to delineate certain features of the character.[97] In general, he failed to employ his narrative to create a reasonable plot, and consequently did not furnish his work with the elements of anticipation and suspense needed to encourage the reader. This failure to use the narrative effectively, despite his partial success in the use of dialogue, affected the characterization in Nadīm's work. Despite his innovation in the realm of narrative language and dialogue, Nadīm's characterization remained in the grip of traditional narrative strategies. Most of his characters are merely types representing professions, social classes, human behaviour in general, or abstract ideals, and their narrative predecessors can be found in the one-dimensional characters of the *maqāmah.*

Nadīm's use of allegory lay in his desire to confront certain social and political problems without defying censorship or laying himself open to the attacks of the pro-British press.[98] Although there is strong evidence that Nadīm was familiar with the allegorical methods used in certain Arabic classics such as *Kalīlah wa-Dimnah* and *The Arabian Nights,* his allegories fail to attain the artistic quality of these traditional works. Yet some of them[99] are artistically successful in that they operate at different levels of interpretation and combine this subtlety with satire and fine sense of humour. Nadīm was also influenced by the traditional narrative genre, *maqāmah,* in his use of a subsidiary character to advise the protagonist, become his confidant, or comment on the main action. The simplistic didactic tone of this somewhat superfluous character was not only tediously explicit but indicated the writer's lack of confidence in his readers' ability to comprehend the narrative. It also betrayed his lack of understanding of the freedoms and limitations of this new narrative discourse, for the unnecessary comments of this extraneous figure, explaining the clearest of issues, destroy the artistic quality of these otherwise coherent narrative sketches.

In general, Nadīm did not appreciate that the fictional form has many essential components: character, plot, setting, dialogue, gradual progression of the action, and authorial comments and attitudes, and that each deserves special consideration and demands an awareness of its natural limitations. He allocated the lion's share of his attention to direct comments and didacticism, and this naturally was achieved at the expense of the other factors. In this respect, Nadīm failed to grasp the subtle difference between the tone of an orator who speaks aloud to an audience and that of a creative writer who seeks to communicate with his reader in an intimate and private manner, and to make his work an extension of the individual's life or experience. This failure to realize the difference between oral narration, a form that dominated the world of popular entertainment at the time, and written narrative jeopardized both the effect and the structure of his work.

This lack in artistic skill was made up in part by Nadīm's sensitivity to, and deep experience of, human character in general and Egyptian social ailments in particular. This enabled him, in a number of cases, to introduce lively situations and to create a number of convincing characters who had never before appeared in modern Arabic literature; in particular, the distressed and neglected housewife, who was the archetypal character in many of his fictional sketches and episodes.[100] She was fated to endure the unbearable coarseness of her drunken husband and to wait patiently for him to be cured of his vice. For the first time, such female characters were portrayed realistically with little stylistic embellishment; they were depicted as compliant yet despairing, and he demonstrated how individual sufferings and anxieties were closely linked to, and often reflected, the general issues and problems of the country. The central place of women in Nadīm's fictional work did not escape the attention of his contemporaries.[101]

Despite their rudimentary artistic nature, their unsophisticated didacticism, their recourse to stereotypes, their lack of variety, and their failure, by and large, to integrate their abstract generalizations into a detailed observation of the particulars of life, Nadīm's narrative works were of great importance. For, in spite of his poor knowledge of the principles of narrative form and structure, he sowed the seeds of a new narrative discourse and prepared the ground for the growth of modern Arabic literature. Its major components — characterization, narrative, dialogue, realistic presentation, concern for the issues of daily life, etc. — are, present in his works. The rudimentary nature of Nadīm's narrative sketches was largely due to the transitional nature of the new narrative discourse. Having not yet established its literary conventions, it had to rely on those of the traditional narrative and compromise some of its principles in order to communicate with readers and win them over to the new genre. The positive reception the reading public gave to these works proves how genuine the need was for a new literary discourse. Nadīm was not consciously creating a new literary genre, but searching for an effective means of communication with his readers in order to raise their national consciousness. This confirms the link that existed between the emergence of the new narrative discourse and the enhancing of national awareness.

Nadīm pointed the way for Arab writers towards a new literary discourse, demarcating the area of major concern. He failed to deliver any mature and coherent examples of the writing that his earlier works promised, because he did not succeed in achieving a complete break with the conventions and modes of expression of traditional prose writing, a break necessary for the birth of new literary sensibilities and new modes of discourse. He had the talent and insight to discover the need for a new form and sensibility, but lacked both the courage to meet the exigencies of the difficult and pioneering task of creating the new literary form, and the means to liberate his writing from the constraints of traditional prose.

Nevertheless, the extent of the reading public's response to his literary endeavour demonstrated the emergence of a new artistic sensibility among the reading public, and at the same time, the urgent need to satisfy its demands. His concern was with everyday activities and issues, the small talk of housewives and their affairs, the domestic scene in middle-class homes, the hardships of the peasants, the simple discussions of ordinary people about their problems and the various themes which touched upon the country's major problems. This drew the attention of a number of Arab writers to the treasures which were buried, before their very eyes, in life's everyday affairs, a source which they had always thought of as unworthy of literary consideration. The narrative discourse of Nadīm is in itself a literary expression of the awareness that the new class, which appeared as a result of various factors elaborated in the previous chapters, required a new literary mode of discourse. Nadīm also provided the new narrative discourse with the elements which enabled it to gain entry into wider literary and social acceptability. Narrative writing was not a respectable activity, but he justified its existence by using it as a vehicle for two highly respectable ends: social reform and patriotic concerns.

The Rejuvenation of the *Maqāmah*

The period which extended from the closing of *al-Ustādh,* the banishment of Nadīm, and his death,[102] to the national revolution of March 1919, witnessed the attempts of writers in Egypt and in other parts of the Arab world to develop the embryonic narrative form, and so complete the task begun by Nadīm. These attempts took two main forms: the rejuvenation of the *maqāmah* in a somewhat modified and modern form using contemporary themes, and the evolution of Nadīm's brisk oratorical style with its rudimentary narrative elements. The former differs from the early revival of the *maqāmah* in its more realistic bent and in its endeavour to liberate the traditional genre from its archaic style and prototypical concerns. It was an attempt to rejuvenate the outmoded genre by injecting it with a vigorous sense of individuality, intimacy, realism and interest in current and domestic concerns. It is important when discussing these new forms of *maqāmah* to bear in mind how the deformation of old structures leads to the formation of new ones. The changing functional relation of art to society enhances the process of the formation of new structures by discrediting the old ones and intensifying the demand for the new.

The earliest endeavour was by Aḥmad Fāris al-Shidyāq in the four *maqāmāt* included in his remarkable autobiographical work, *al-Sāq 'alā al-Sāq fi ma Huwa al-Fāryāq* (The Life and Adventures of Fāryāq, 1855). In his study of Shidyāq, Najm considers him to have been the greatest wasted narrative talent in the period of the literary renaissance.[103] This is true to a certain extent, for in his autobiographical account of his life, as well as in the four *maqāmāt* included in the book, he demonstrated that he had the aptitude for storytelling and an eye for significant details. His four *maqāmāt* developed the genre of *maqāmah* into a narrative essay with strong social themes and took it beyond its traditional, stultified style. Unlike their predecessors, they paid attention to the drawing and motivation of secondary characters, who rarely received any consideration in the traditional genre, which concentrated only on the two major characters: the protagonist and the narrator. This provided them with a heightened degree of plausibility and brought their themes to life. Apart from the first *maqāmah* with its linguistic over-indulgence, the other three *maqāmāt, Muq'adah, Muqīmah* and *Mamshiyyah,* dealt with various aspects of the domestic scene and the issues of marriage, celibacy and the selection of women for marriage and their desirable treatment. They treated their themes in a humorous and sarcastic manner and succeeded in integrating some realistic and individualistic concerns into the traditional form. They also represented the first conscious attempt to widen the horizon of the genre by including sarcastic and critical remarks about many of the shortcomings of the *maqāmah* form.

In addition to these four *maqāmāt*, parts of his autobiography and some of his sketches in his periodical, *al-Jawā'ib,* offer the reader further confirmation of Shidyāq's talent for narrative discourse. Indeed, Najm sees them as "almost constituting a decent basis for short stories that were marred by excessive linguistic adroitness and constant digression which disturbed their unity of impression".[104] In many of these texts Shidyāq succeeded in creating interesting characters and paved the way for the development of convincing and multi-dimensional characterization. This was clearly noticeable in the sarcastic portrayal of the protagonist of *"Intikāsah Khāfiyah wa-'Imāmah Wāqiyah"* (Subtle Relapse Under a Protective Turban),[105] the juxtaposition of human qualities in *"Shurūr wa-Ṭanbūr"* (Shurūr and Ṭanbūr),[106] the description of gluttony in *"Ṭa'ām wa-Iltihām"* (Devouring Food),[107] the comic action of *"Ḥimār Nahhāq wa-Safar wa-Ikhfāq"* (A Braying Donkey)[108] and *"Ighḍāb Shawāfin wa-Inshāb Barāthin"* (Anger and Aggression),[109] and finally in the apt characterization of *"Qiṣṣat Qissīs"* (The Story of a Priest).[110] The last-named dealt with Christian clergy in the manner encountered in Nadīm's narrative sketches about corrupt religious figures.

'Ali Mubārak's *'Alam al-Dīn* can also be seen as a canny attempt to rejuvenate the form of the *maqāmah* through an autobiographical narrative that adopts the basic structure of the genre. As in the *maqāmah* form, the narrator, 'Alam al-Dīn, is coupled with his son, Burhān al-Dīn, and an English tourist who wishes to study Arabic in a journey of discovery. He called its 125 episodes *musāmarāt,* which is synonymous with the term *maqāmāt,* and emphasized the moral and didactic elements from the outset. He did not hesitate to declare in the preface his didactic intentions:

> I have realized that the readers are inclined to reading epic tales, narrative fiction and entertaining works, rather than works on pure

> scientific or practical concerns. The latter works breed boredom and lead the readers to shun them, particularly when they are busy or tired and require entertainment or relief ... This persuaded me to write this useful book in a form of attractive narrative to entice the reader to absorb its useful information and instructions which have been collected from many Arabic and foreign books in arts and sciences ... I wrote my book in the form of a journey of a learned Egyptian and an Englishman in order to have the opportunity to compare our circumstances with those of the West.[111]

The reformative and informative aims of Mubārak were given prominence over the narrative concerns of the text. The book is mainly a testimony to the popularity of narrative and the failure of those who conceived of it only as a vehicle to advance a cause.

Another attempt to broaden the horizon of the *maqāmah* genre at the time can be found in 'Ā'ishah Taymūr's *Natā'ij al-Aḥwāl fi al-Aqwāl wa-l-Af'āl* (Ramifications of Words and Deeds, 1888) and *Mir'āt al-Ta'ammul fi al-Umūr* (Contemplating Matters, 1893). In these two works she blended elements of the traditional linguistic elegance of the *maqāmah* with others from translated narrative works, particularly al-Ṭahṭāwi's translation of *Télémaque*. She coined a new term for her narrative, *uḥdūthah,* which implies her interest was more in action than in characterization, and declared from the beginning that her intention was to entertain the reader, console those who underwent similar experiences and enable them to articulate their feelings.[112] Although she kept the rhyming title which was customary in the period, she simplified the language of traditional narrative, while not getting rid of its verbal ornamentations.

Her contribution to the formation of a new narrative discourse is twofold. She broke with the structural framework of the *maqāmah* and adopted instead one derived mainly from translated narrative in general, and from al-Ṭahṭāwi's translation of *Télémaque* in particular. This established a new perception of narrative structure in which indigenous concerns can be adequately served by the use of a hybrid narrative structure which draws simultaneously on translations, the *maqāmah* and *The Arabian Nights*. She also presented the first consciously feminist attempt to invert the stereotypical male perspective, for, despite being clearly influenced by certain structural features of al-Ṭahṭāwi's translation of *Télémaque,* she inverted his male purview by making men the source of evil in her text instead of women.[113] The evil nymph in *Télémaque*, Calypso, is replaced by the two male characters, Dishnām and Ghaddūr, while women are depicted positively throughout. In addition, her concern with nationalist and political issues as well as with the theme of social justice provides her narrative with relevance.

Nadīm was also a pioneer of the first form with his work *al-Masāmīr* (1894);[114] literally "The Nails", but with the meaning of "spurs and prods" by extension, not to mention the pun on Mubārak's *musāmarāt.*

The work consists of nine *maqāmāt,* called in the book *masāmīr,* and borrows the main structural framework of the *maqāmah* form, for it has a narrator, al-Sharīf Abū-Hāshim, who tells about the deeds and adventures of its main hero, al-Shaikh Madyan Abū-l-Qāsim. The nine *masāmīr* are marked by their powerful characterization, acerbity, humour, and imaginativeness. However, the contemporary elements and realistic details which relate the work to the social milieu are very weak. Nadīm wrote this work in Constantinople after being banished from Egypt, and therefore far from his daily scene. In addition, because its main character is a satirical presentation of a non-Egyptian, Abū al-Hudā al-Ṣayyādi (1849—1909),[115] and the whole work is a travesty of life in and around the court of the Ottoman Sultan (Abdül-Hamid), Nadīm selected the traditional form of the *maqāmah* for this work and refrained from writing it in his innovative narrative discourse. The *maqāmah* suited the satirical and allegorical mode of the work, on the one hand; and showed Nadīm's awareness of the vital interaction between form and content, on the other.

Although theological matters and personal lampoon were the main concerns of Nadīm's *maqāmāt,* or, as he preferred to call them in their new sarcastic and prodding form, *masāmīr* (goads or spurs), they also included criticism of social and contemporary issues. Religious hypocrisy and social dissimulation are among the important themes of these *masāmīr* which were to recur in future works, especially those using the *maqāmah* form. The general theme of *al-Masāmīr*, the attack on religious hypocrites and pretentious piety, was also one of the themes which was to become popular with later writers. In *al-Masāmīr*, Nadīm developed his early characterization to a more coherent stage and demonstrated his skilful use of sarcasm and humour to enhance both the immediate impact of the work and its allegorical implications.

Two years after Nadīm's death, Muḥammad al-Muwailiḥi (1868—1930) published his connected series of modern *maqāmāt* under two titles: *Fatrah min al-Zaman* (A Certain Time) or *Ḥadīth 'Īsā Ibn Hishām*[116] (The Stories of 'Īsā Ibn Hisham). The duouble title reflects the dual nature of the project and its attempt to integrate two different discourses into one text. The former title reveals, with its clear temporal implication, the desire to deal with a particular time and to explore certain aspects of the "individuation of time". The latter is taken verbatum from the *maqāmāt* of al-Hamadhāni and appeals to the traditional set of narrative conventions. Al-Muwailiḥi was clearly influenced by Nadīm's fictional sketches and the innovations in the *maqāmah* form which he had introduced in *al-Masāmīr.*[117] Al-Muwailiḥi's work, which is considered by many scholars and critics to be the authentic debut of modern narrative discourse in Arabic literature,[118] deals mainly with the ramifications of social and cultural changes over a period of time, and touches upon many of the issues and problems which Nadīm had treated before. It tackles various dimensions of the cultural conflict between the Middle East and

Europe,[119] the decadence of the Egyptian rich and their apathy,[120] and the way in which the bright lights of the city tempt and corrupt wealthy villagers and waste their money.[121]

Although many of Nadīm's themes can be found in al-Muwailiḥi's work, the narrative quality of *Ḥadīth 'Īsā Ibn Hishām* is superior to that of Nadīm's works, and its episodic structure becomes an integral part of its content. The sketches are structured so as to further the action and this creates a certain unity of form, so that the work is, strictly speaking, outside the domain of short narrative genres.[122] Some classify it as a novel, one heralding the rise of the novel in modern Arabic literature. As far as the genesis of modern narrative discourse is concerned, it plays an important role in consolidating the relationship between literature and everyday issues on the one hand, and in developing and popularizing fictional writing on the other. It altered the nature of the stereotypical hero of the *maqāmah* and brought him a step closer to the individual hero of modern narrative.

Attracted by the success of his son's *maqāmāt,* which were serialized in his magazine *Miṣbāḥ al-Sharq* in 1898, Ibrāhīm al-Muwailiḥi (1845—1906) started in the following year to publish a similar series of modern *maqāmāt* entitled *Ḥadīth Mūsā Ibn 'Iṣām (*The Stories of Mūsā Ibn Isam) or *Mir'āt al-'Ālam* (The Mirror of the World).[123] However, al-Muwailiḥi the father was prevented by the censor from publishing his work after a few issues, because of its mordant social criticism and its strong anti-British tone; the work attacked the British and their protégé institutions with sharp satire and sarcastic humour. Al-Muwailiḥi's modern *maqāmāt,* as their title suggests, are an attempt to portray the world around him through its characters and explore the most significant issues. Compared to the *maqāmāt* of al-Muwailiḥi the son, they are marked by a stronger social and political awareness and weaker sense of artistic structure.

The fact that the author was prevented from publishing the rest of his *maqāmāt* points to two important considerations. The first is that the rejuvenated traditional form of *maqāmah* was beginning to have a real impact upon the reading public. This influence must have been more significant than other forms of discourse, because the author was prevented only from publishing his creative work (modern *maqāmāt*) without being prohibited from writing altogether. The second is that the revival of the old form was closely linked with the need to express new social, political, and cultural realities, and, as a result, the narrative discourse's treatment of controversial social and political issues inevitably led to confrontation with authority. The unfinished *maqāmāt* of al-Muwailiḥi the father, though less artistically dexterous than those of his son, are no less significant in their contribution to the genesis of the new narrative discourse. They enhanced the sense of the political and established themselves as a powerful discourse capable of challenging the establishment.

The modern *maqāmāt* continued to deal with everyday and national issues in various allegorical forms. In 1901, after trying his hand at some forms of historical narrative,[124] Aḥmad Shawqi (1868—1932) published his allegorical *maqāmāt* under the title *Shayṭān Bintā'ūr* (Bintā'ūr's Muse), in which he followed the structural framework of the genre and blended it with elements of animal fables, the two main characters of his *maqāmāt* being an eagle and a hoopoe. In 1906 Ḥāfiẓ Ibrāhīm (1871—1932) published *Layāli Saṭīḥ* (Saṭīḥ's Nights), which were more coherent and artistically mature *maqāmāt* than those of Shawqi. It is useful to compare Ḥāfiẓ's modern *maqāmāt* only with those of al-Muwailiḥi the son, for although the two works belong to, or at least are based on, the traditional narrative genre of *maqāmah* and remain artistically close to their rudiments in structure and in style, they are distinguished by their increasing emphasis on contemporary social questions. Ḥāfiẓ's modern *maqāmāt* in some instances make less use of verbal decoration than al-Muwailiḥi's, but characterization in them is less mature, despite the fact that they come closer to everyday concerns.

However, the modern *maqāmāt* that came closest to the rudiments of the new narrative discourse were those of Muhammad Luṭfi Jum'ah (1884—1953) in *Fi Buyūt al-Nās* (In Other People's Homes, 1904), *Fi Wādi al-Humūm* (In the Valley of Vexation, 1905), and *Layāli al-Rūḥ al-Ḥā'ir* (The Nights of the Troubled Soul, 1912). They not only demonstrated the author's desire to continue writing and developing his technique within the framework of the new form, but also, as seen in his introduction to his second book, displayed a high degree of awareness of the nature of his task. He conceived of the art of fiction as being divided into two main trends, *al-ḥaqīqi* (the realistic) and *al-khayāli* (the fantastic); the former that of Balzac and Zola, and the latter that of Scott and Dumas.[125] His declared intention was to model his work on those who wrote their fiction *'alā asās al-ḥaqīqah* (according to realistic criteria).[126] The rest of his introduction was devoted to the nature of his theme, *inqadh al-mar'ah min al-suqūṭ* (saving women from abuse), which he handles in a manner that suggests that women's emancipation was one of the burning issues of the period.[127] He stated that he was endeavouring to adopt a more comprehensive social approach in dealing with this question, an approach which he attributed to Tolstoy.[128]

But before dealing with the significance of Jum'ah's break with the form of the *maqāmah,* two important factors should be considered: the writer's awareness of the various types of European narrative, and his production of romantic discourse despite his stated intention of writing in a realistic vein. Both factors refer to the nature of the cultural milieu in which the early attempts to shape the new narrative discourse in Arabic literature took place. Jum'ah's awareness of certain aspects of European literature was not unique, nor did it result from his activity as a translator, but it was a reflection of the general interests of the intellectuals of this period. The existence of translated material and widespread interest in the achievements of European literature had the effect of making both readers and writers receptive to European literature.

Around the turn of the century, literary criticism played a significant role in sharpening the perception of European literature and developing writers' perception of their own and European works. In 1897, Najīb al-Ḥaddād (1867—99), an outstanding Lebanese journalist and accomplished translator, published his seminal article, *"Muqābalah bayn al-Shi'r al-'Arabi wa-l-Shi'r al-Afranji"*[129] (A Comparison between Arabic and Western Poetry), which was harshly critical of Arabic poetry and full of praise for its European counterpart. In 1904, the Palestinian scholar Rawḥi al-Khālidi (1864—1914) published his book *Tārikh 'Ilm al-Adab 'Ind al-Ifrinj wa-l-'Arab* (The History of Literature in Arabic and European Traditions),[130] in which he familiarized the reader with French literature, particularly with the work of Victor Hugo, whose centenary celebrations he attended in France.[131] He presented French literature in the wider context of European literature, namely Russian and English. One of the most significant aspects of this book is his elaboration of the orientalists' criticism of both the content and the form of the *maqāmāt,* which helped to provide his contemporaries with a fresh outlook on this form.[132] In the same year, Sulaymān al-Bustāni (1856—1925) published an extensive introduction to his translation of Homer's *Iliad,* in which he continued the tradition of commenting on various aspects of European literature, so sharpening would-be writers' awareness of the literary potential before them.

All these activities enhanced Jum'ah's and his readers' awareness of European literature and of the orientalists' criticism of the *maqāmah* form. Yet, even in its maturest form in his third book, *Layāli al-Rūḥ al-Ḥā'ir,* Jum'ah's writing is a world away from any realistic form of discourse. It may best be classed as romantic, appearing within and sharing the sensibility of what Shukri 'Ayyad terms "the period of romantic explosion in Arabic literature".[133] Jum'ah influenced the romantic writers who followed him by setting the tone and defining the thematic ground. His concern with social injustice, enveloped as it was in sentimentality and exaggerated bewailing of the lot of the destitute, was to become a standard motif in many romantic short stories for years to come. His second major theme, the torment of love, also became a favourite theme. His romantic characteristics were most evident in his presentation of themes which stressed, and even exaggerated, the emotions and sentiments at the expense of social factors, and emphasized the role of imagination both in writing and in life.

Romanticism is generally associated with the revolt against old forms,[134] and it is not unreasonable to link Jum'ah's romantic content and representation with his attempt to release his writing from the form of the *maqāmah,* for Jum'ah's works were clearly influenced by the modern *maqāmāt* of Shawqi and Ḥāfiẓ,[135] but they were also marked by their sustained movement away from the *maqāmah,* so much so that in certain pieces in his last collection the major elements of the *maqāmah* technique had been eliminated.[136] Even the maturest of these pieces, or *layāli* (nights), as he calls them (probably after *The Arabian Nights*), are still too rudimentary and incoherent to be termed short stories, yet some critics call them short stories[137] on the grounds that they are free from the undesirable stylistic elements peculiar to the *maqāmah*. Some of Jum'ah's works — such as *"Narjis al-'Amyā'"*, (Narjis the Blind)[138] and *"Ṣadīqi 'Ali"* (My Friend Ali)[139] — could be seen as constituting the final steps on the road from the rejuvenated *maqāmah* to the short story, but they are still far from being short stories.

Their language is weighed down by the heavy verbal decoration of the *maqāmah* and they have not benefited from the precedent set by Nadīm, who used dialogue both to enhance the characterization and to convey a sense of reality. They retain the device of the outside narrator and the linking together of the various episodes, rather than their separation into autonomous fictional texts. However, their use of narrative is superior to what went before and prepares the ground for the realization of the short story as a complete form in itself. The works of Muḥammad Luṭfi Jum'ah, especially those of his third collection, lead us on from the embryonic discourse evolved by Nadīm within the tradition of the *maqāmah* and represent the first attempts to build upon Nadīm's fictional endeavours outside this tradition. One of Jum'ah's significant achievements was that he replaced Nadīm's didacticism with sentimental and emotional undercurrents.

The Romantic Break with the Past

The romantic and sentimental sensibility in this period had a strong influence on Jum'ah, leading him to write a romantic discourse when he had intended to produce a realistic one. In his account of the development of Arab history, Hitti remarks that "the intuitive, imaginative element in European romanticism rather than the rationalist element in its literature was the one congenial to Arab borrowers. French literature, a Mediterranean product, exercised a larger measure of fascination for Arab writers than 'cold' Anglo-Saxon literature".[140] This romantic sentiment held sway for a long time among Arab intellectual circles, culminating in the early years of this century, according to another scholar of the period, Shukri 'Ayyād.

'Ayyād points out that in the four years 1906—9, Jibrān Khalīl Jibrān (1883—1931) published *'Arā'is al-Murūj* (The Brides of the Meadow, 1906) and *al-Arwāḥ al-Mutamrridah* (Rebellious Souls, 1908), Muṣṭafā Luṭfi al-Manfalūṭi (1872—1924) started to publish his highly influential and sentimental pieces in *al-Mu'ayyad* in 1907[141] and 'Abd al-Raḥmān Shukri (1886—1958) published his first collection of romantic poems in 1909. Romanticism involves a break with traditional form, and those who were sensitive to such changes and to the needs of the new reading public began to develop certain aspects of the Arabic narrative discourse. The writers built on the achievements of their predecessors and familiarized their readers with some narrative conventions necessary for its reception. On the crest of this romantic wave Arabic narrative discourse broke with most of the traditional elements of narration and consolidated the basic characteristics of the new discourse.

This break with the past took place simultaneously in Lebanon, the *mahjar*, Iraq and Egypt, while the Palestinian attempt of this period moved instead towards a more realistic discourse. Numerous writers cultivated romantic traits in their narrative discourse, and a few are worthy of discussion: a female writer from Lebanon, a male one from the *mahjar* and two groups from Iraq and Egypt.

The break with tradition was appropriately initiated by a woman writer, Labībah Hāshim (1880—1947), whose appearance on the literary scene constituted a radical departure from the traditional hegemony of men. She was born in Lebanon and spent her early years in Beirut, but then moved to Egypt where she was taught by Ibrāhīm al-Yāziji (1847—1906), the editor of *al-Ḍiyā'*. She contributed original and translated works of fiction to his magazine from 1898. After his death, she edited a successful magazine, *Fatāt al-Sharq* (1906—39), in which she continued her translations and original writing. In 1914 she became the secretary of the Egyptian Women's Association established by Hudā Sha'rāwi, and played an active role in the women's movement. She published a number of short narrative pieces in various periodicals and a longer one, *Qalb al-Rajul* (Man's Heart, 1904). She was one of the prototypes of the 'new woman', widely travelled. She taught at Cairo University (1911—12), worked as an inspector of education in Damascus (1919—21) and then went to Chile and edited an Arabic magazine in Santiago, *al-Sharq wa-l-Gharb* (1923—4). She later returned to Cairo and resumed working for her *Fatāt al-Sharq*.

From the publication of her very first story, *Ḥasanāt al-Ḥubb* (Decorum of Love) in *al-Ḍiyā'*,[142] her narrative was free from traditional elements and had its frame of reference in the translations of the time and not in the *maqāmah*. She continued writing sporadically in *al-Ḍiyā'*[143] and in her magazine and later collected her contributions in book form. Most of her short narrative pieces were more of a summary of longer ones than short stories in the real sense of the term. They tell elaborate and sentimental love stories that start with love at first sight, that are then plagued with obstacles that hinder the consummation of that love, and that are packed with unexpected turns of events. They take the reader to exotic places such as the mansions of Istanbul, the battlefields in the Sudan, and the royal palace of Persia. They normally end happily, for they aim to entertain and please the women who constituted the majority of her readers. Indeed, the main role of her stories was to popularize narrative among the women readers and familiarize them with its conventions.

Her stories were of great significance for they introduced the reader to a new concept of narrative plot that required resolution through a denouement, and shifted the emphasis from the character to the action. This shift was vital in terms of the break with traditional narrative genres, for it highlighted the process of the particularization of place and time, and not a stereotypical individual. Although Hāshim lacked talent, her journalistic skills, simple language and ability to tell a story and sustain a relatively complicated plot made her the pioneer of a trend of simplistic narrative.

Like Hāshim, Jibrān did not attempt to reproduce the form of the *maqāmah* in a new guise, but was genuinely experimenting with a new form of narrative discourse. He had been exposed to European narrative in translation and in the original language after his departure to the United States, but was moved by a genuine need to communicate ideas, rather than experiment with the creation of the Arabic short story. Although Jibrān was writing his works in the *mahjar* (abroad), their setting was his home in Mount Lebanon and their impact was immediately felt throughout the Arab world and particularly in the Levant. He is considered by many critics[144] to be the greatest romantic of the Levant.

His early short narrative pieces, which were called *riwāyāt*[145] or *ḥikāyāt*[146] by his friend, the editor of *al-Mahjar* newspaper, attempt to "illustrate the sentiments of the various strata of society from the beggar to the prince, and from the blasphemous to the saintly".[147] But they end up exaggerating these sentiments and creating a highly romanticized view of the suffering of the poor and the torment of love. Jibrān linked these themes to the lack of freedom and social and political oppression, including those practised by men against women. Like Nadīm, his view of women is generally positive, compared with his view of men, and his attack on the Christian religious establishment and its clergy echoes those of Nadīm on hypocritical sheikhs. Again, like Nadīm, he realized that the changing perception of self required a new approach to both reality and literature and a fresh language to express the change.

In the first story in his first collection, *"Ramād al-Ajyāl wa-l-Nār al-Khālidah"* (Old Ashes and Eternal Fire),[148] Jibrān attempted to root the new narrative discourse in the historical and spiritual consciousness of his readers. He placed the first part of his love story in the ruins of a Phoenician temple of 116 B.C. and placed its second part 2000 years later, in 1890, with the reincarnation of the two lovers and the fulfilment of the prophecy of the ancient goddess to reunite them. The story posits a new foundation for the relationship between the sexes, one not based on the hackneyed and corrupt social practices, which are castigated in his stories, but on love and historical and spiritual bonds. Jibrān was aware of the importance of elaborating the substitute before challenging present practices. This theme was developed in two stories of the second collection, *"Wardah al-Hāni"*[149] and *"Maḍja' al-'Arūs"* (The Resting-place of the Bride).[150] The former was a strong attack on arranged marriage and the latter was an exploration of the consequence of prudish social conventions on the new generation who were endeavouring to build their relationship on understanding and love. In all the stories on this theme, Jibrān presented love as a virtuous and natural sentiment almost inviolable and always associated with beauty and happiness, while social conventions were invariably portrayed as restricting and obstructive.

In "*Martā al-Bāniyyah*" (Marta of Bān),[151] he introduced a new theme, the conflict between the country and the city, a theme which proved to be popular with later writers. Marta, the beautiful and pure shepherdess from an equally enchanting Lebanese village, Bān, is seduced by a strange man from Beirut, who leads her to her destruction. The story is in two parts: the first is full of romantic adulation of the country and the serene and innocent life of Marta among its fields; the second, which takes place six years later, finds her on the verge of death in the slums of Beirut with her misbegotten five-year-old son selling flowers to support his dying mother. The contrast between the two sections of the story is very evident, yet the author rarely lets his narrative speak for itself and constantly comments on it.

Jibrān's last major thematic contribution to the romantic explosion was the theme of social justice and the corruption of the religious institutions. In "*Yūḥannā al-Majnūn*" (John the Fool)[152] and "*Khalīl al-Kāfir*" (Khalil the Heretic),[153] he directed his attack against the pillars of the religious institution and revealed its unholy coalition with the political establishment. The first tells how its hero was badly wronged by the last people one would have expected to exploit and victimize others — the monks of the monastery. It accentuated the contrast between the wealth of the Lebanese monasteries and the destitution of ordinary Christians, and demonstrates how such wealth was accumulated through the cruelty of the abbots and the violation of the very essence of Christianity. The story suggests an analogy between its protagonist and his namesake, John the Baptist, and how no one listened to his screams in the wilderness. The second repeats the situation but ends not with its hero screaming in the wilderness, but organizing the poor against both the corrupt religious institutions and the political ruler of the district. It can also be read as a re-enactment of the story of Christ, for it is laden with Biblical allusions.

All Jibrān's themes recurred throughout his writing and some of them became popular with the readers and writers. Although his narrative is still rudimentary and lacks vigour and coherence, it is more sophisticated than that of Nadīm and shows a deeper understanding of the progression of action, functional description and characterization. This generates a stronger sense of credibility. Yet his didactic aims are as simplistic, overt and obtrusive as those of his predecessors. His narrative is long-winded, and his language is highly emotive and loaded with religious connotations. Jibrān used narrative as a herald of change whose main task was to remove the obstacles to change and reveal the hypocrisy of established social and spiritual practices, showing how they violated the basic teachings of Christianity.

The Dream as a Narrative Discourse

In Iraq, there was a group of writers[154] whom ʻAbd al-Ilāh Aḥmad, the foremost scholar of Iraqi narrative discourse, calls *kuttāb al-ru'yā* (the writers of dreams or the visionary discourse).[155] They experimented with narrative modes of discourse, remaining independent of the traditional form of the *maqāmah*. Their writing was laden with romantic tendencies. They started writing in the influential magazine, *Tanwīr al-Afkār*, in 1909 and continued until 1921, also contributing to other publications.[156] Like Nadīm's fictional episodes, it seems that the new form captured the imagination of young writers, who experimented with it with varying degrees of success. Although al-Muwailiḥi used the dream as a literary device in his *Ḥadīth ʻĪsā ibn Hishām*, the Iraqi narrative form seems to be unconnected with this experiment.[157] It has been suggested, however, that al-Muwailiḥi's use of the dream as a justification for certain aspects of his narrative was strengthened by Maʻrūf al-Ruṣāfī's translation, published in Iraq in 1909, of a long, and at the time, influential narrative text written by the Turkish writer Nāmiq Kamāl and entitled *Riwāyat al-Ru'yā* (The Visionary Novel).[158]

This assumption is supported by the strong similarity between the themes of Kamāl's text and that of the early "visionary dreams" written by a number of those writers. Like Nadīm's episodes, "the visionary dreams" were highly didactic with a clear moral message concerned with the nationalistic issues of the day. From the first *ru'yā* (visionary dream), *"Ru'yā al-ʻArabiyyah"* (An Arab Dream),[159] it is clear that the elements that went into the making of this narrative discourse are a blend of traditional literary values and nationalistic dreams. The dream starts with a scene reminiscent of *The Arabian Nights* in which the dreamer finds himself in a palatial, magical tent with a woman radiating beauty and wisdom. The writer suspends the narrative temporarily in order to parade his skills in portraying her beauty and erudition and relating her to the great women of the past, from the Virgin Mary to the wives of the Prophet Muḥammad, in a manner which demonstrates his mastery of the traditional literary canon. When he asks in rhyming prose for her identity, the answer, which provides another opportunity for flight into stylistic elegance, is *al-ʻArabiyyah*, best translated as the spirit of Arabism, referring to the neglected Arabic language as much as to the desired unity of the Arab people.

The ideas which emerged from most of the "visionary dreams" were a clear reflection of those in Kamāl's book and of the intellectual debates which were being conducted throughout the Arab world after the promulgation of the Ottoman Constitution of 1908. But the optimism of this first *ru'yā* soon receded, and the subsequent texts, particularly those written after the advent of the British, were filled with gloom and despondency. Some of them even retreated from public issues and moved to more individualistic concerns, or treated sensitive political questions by resorting to allegory and symbols.[160] The "visionary dreams" that came close to the new narrative discourse were those of 'Aṭā' Amīn, particularly in his later work as when he ascertains at the end of "*Ru'yā Ṣādiqah*" (A Dream Come True) that "everything related in this story of events, description and prayers is realistic without any segment of imagination".[161] His use of the term *qiṣṣah* (story), indicates his awareness that the dream is merely a technical device and that what he is writing is a "realistic" discourse portraying reality, and not a product of his imagination, as the word *ru'yā* may suggest.

From his *ru'yā* and the few stories published in 'Abd al-Ilāh Aḥmad's anthology,[162] it seems that 'Aṭā' Amīn was the most important pioneer of Iraqi narrative. He was aware right from the start that he was producing narrative and realized the difference between long and short narrative texts. In "*Waqfah 'alā Diyālā*" (A Stop by the River Diyālā),[163] "*Lawḥah min Alwāḥ al-Dahr*" (A Sketch of Destiny)[164] and "*'Āqibat al-Ḥayāh*" (Ramifications of Life),[165] he used sound narrative techniques, including the development of imploding symbols, and demonstrated a mature understanding of narrative and plot. In his latest *ru'yā,* he even moved from the feigned first-person narrative and conducted the whole work in third-person, and even the rare second-person, narrative. He also developed a relatively simple narrative language liberated from the heavy verbal decorations which continued to burden most of the work in this style.

The significance of Amīn's work is that he did not confine himself to the "visionary dream" but was aware that the resort to the dream was principally a device to introduce the reader to the structure of narrative. Unlike other writers whose dreams contained imaginary scenes redolent of the atmosphere of *The Arabian Nights,* he intended to reproduce reality and aspired to create a sense of plausibility. Yet his work remained largely within the domain of romantic sensibility which was linked strongly with nationalist issues. Like those of Hāshim before him, many of his works appear to be summaries of longer ones. Indeed, his *ru'yā*, "*Waqfah 'alā Diyālā*", was taken up seven years later as the basis for a novel by another Iraqi writer.[166]

Despite their name, the "visionary dreams" can be read as a commentary on the present rather than a blueprint for the future. Their main concerns were the social problems facing the country, the disunity of its people, the oppressive nature of its ruling establishment, the importance of education and female emancipation, and pride in the country's past as an inspiration for its future. The "dreams" were deeply concerned with thorny social and nationalistic matters. They combined elements from the *maqāmah* (at the beginning, stylistic; later, thematic), using narrative as a mask for their attack on the political establishment and British policies. The style of the "visionary dream" was merely a device to justify dealing with the relevant issues of the day as well as an attempt to evade the censor.

The Iraqi writers of this narrative mode of discourse resorted to the dream as a narrative device. The delay in the appearance of an indigenous narrative production in Iraq, thirty years after its emergence in Egypt and the Levant, indicates both an impasse in its cultural development at the time, and the reading public's lack of familiarity with other narrative discourses. The dream is something that is simply narrated in everyday life and the reader is clearly acquainted with its conventions. The problem arising from the use of this genre as a rudimentary literary discourse was the conflict between the suggestive and fantastic nature of the dream and the obtrusive and didactic qualities of the discourse that used it. This became apparent in the disjunction between first-person narrative and the tendency for authorial intrusion and direct comments.

The Sentimental Slant of the Romantic

The Egyptian writers of the first decade of this century succeeded in popularizing the romantic tone by intensifying its sentimental aspects and directing its didacticism to appeal to the reader's heart. Two years before Jum'ah wrote his third collection, *Layāli al-Rūḥ al-Ḥā'ir*, the didactic and reformative elements which he had eradicated from his work were all too evident in the works of Ṣāliḥ Ḥamdi Ḥammād (1863—1913) especially in his collection *Aḥsan al-Qaṣaṣ* (The Best of Stories, 1910),[167] and in the early fictional pieces of Muṣṭafā Luṭfi al-Manfalūṭi in *al-Naẓarāt* (Contemplations, vol. I, 1910 and vol. II, 1912). Al-Manfalūṭi's didacticism faded gradually to make way for the increasingly pervasive sentimentality of *al-'Abarāt* (Tearful Lessons, 1915).[168] The success of *al-'Abarāt* was, perhaps, one of the major inspirations for Muṣṭafā Ṣādiq al-Rāfi'i (1880—1937) in his strikingly similar fictional sketches in *al-Masākīn* (The Poor, 1917); sketches which, like many of al-Manfalūṭi's, rely mainly on their elegance of style and their emotive and contemplative power, and not on their characterization or narrative merits.

The works of Ḥammād, al-Manfalūṭi, and al-Rāfi'i are closer to what 'Ayyād calls the "fictional essay"[169] than the proper short story, yet they gain their special importance from their writers' partial awareness of some of the principles of narrative, and their endeavour to satisfy, or at least sustain, the reading public's need for narrative fiction. The three writers' point of departure was identical to that of Nadīm: to play a reformative role in the life of their society and guide their compatriots along the right path, or, as al-Manfalūṭi puts it, "to write for the people not to please them but to reform them".[170] The readers they were aiming at were not the élite or the intellectuals, but the public at large: the intelligent common reader.[171] The three writers were aware of the fact that they were struggling with a new medium, through which they wanted to deliver their reformative and didactic message. For them, as for Nadīm before them, the message remained separate from the medium; in other words, the didactic aims and fictional characteristics are mixed together without being synthesized into a convincing whole.

Ḥammād gives priority to his reformative aims, and "insists on explicating the message of the story and emphasizing its didactic aim at the beginning of every one of his short or long fictional works".[172] He, moreover, describes one of his short narrative works as "a contemporary literary essay which includes an imaginary story and a moral sermon",[173] a discription which demonstrates the degree of confusion regarding the nature of the new form of discourse, and indicates the writer's longing to make his writing both attractive and useful.

Ḥammād, the least famous of the three but probably the most socially respectable of them,[174] did not possess the stylistic ability of the other two, an ability which was highly regarded and thought of as synonymous with literary aptitude at the time. He even admits that his work lacks the skill of an able and experienced writer,[175] yet the very lack of this stylistic ability makes his narrative artistically more mature than that of the other two. And this, coupled with the fact that in some of his works, he succeeds in "creating a unity of time, a unity of action, and also a unity of impression",[176] gives his narrative work credibility and importance, despite his obtrusive interference in the action and the rudimentary structure of his works. He also manages to dispense completely with the link between the various fictional pieces in his book — which al-Rāfi'i, for instance, retains — and is, in fact, the first to draw a line between short and long fictional forms.

In his customary prologue to one of his short narrative works, "*min al-Faqr ilā al-Ghinā*" (From Rags to Riches),[177] he gives a glimpse of his theoretical understanding of the nature of fictional writing when he says:

> I have compiled this short work of narrative without exceeding, in what it contains of description, the limit of useful abridgement. I have not attempted to make its imaginary actions seem peculiar or surprising. For if they lack the skilfulness of the brilliant writer of fiction who is capable of adorning them with artistic ornaments, they are still worthy of careful reading, especially by the youth, for what they contain of economic instructions [*sic*] and social advice.[178]

In these opening lines of the brief prologue, Ḥammād conveys a degree of understanding of some principles of narrative discourse. The first principle is that there is an important distinction to be made between the three forms of narrative (he refers to the other two in various places in his collection): *al-riwāyah al-ṣaghīrah* (short story), *al-riwāyah* (novella), and *al-riwāyah al-ṭawīlah* (novel). The line between *al-riwāyah* and *al-riwāyah al-ṭawīlah* is quite blurred, but that between them and *al-riwāyah al-ṣaghīrah* is somewhat clearer. For him, *al-riwāyah al-ṣaghīrah* is characterized by its precision and shortness, but he confuses precision with abridgement; and this affects his comprehension of the nature of these short works of narrative, which he sees as summaries of longer works. However, the conception of a laconic style and concentration of the subject-matter as inherent characteristics of short works of narrative discourse is, in itself, a demonstration of a greater understanding of aspects of fictional art.

The second principle of narrative discourse is that there is a need to approximate reality, to be closer to the probable and the realistic, and to shun improbable and surprising events — an idea which echoes Jum'ah's call for *madhhab al-ḥaqīqah.* The third principle is the existence of an ability termed *mahārah riwā'iyyah* (fictional skill), of which the author confesses, in feigned modesty, his lack, and therefore tries to compensate his readers by offering them economic advice and social and moral counsel. The recognition of this skill implies that the art of fiction is an independent form of discourse and that its limits and techniques are not yet established in Arabic literature. The fourth and last significant principle to be drawn from this brief introduction is that the kind of reading public which the writer is concerned about and hopes to reach is the younger generation and not the traditional reading public. This, coupled with al-Manfalūṭi's remark on the intelligent common reader, indicates an awareness by writers of the type of readers they were aiming at.

But when one compares the theoretical framework derived from Ḥammād's prologues with the few short narrative works he wrote, it is clear that Ḥammād's theoretical understanding of the nature of narrative was far ahead of his actual ability to express it. Nevertheless, his characterization, especially in *"fi al-Rīf"* (In the Country),[179] is more mature and convincing than that of any of his predecessors or contemporaries. Although he wrote only four short fictional works, he uses a variety of themes: the problems caused by social disparities, the consequences of emotional anger, the conflict between Arab and European culture, the heedless imitation of foreign fashions, and tormented love in a closed social milieu.

He tries to create an illusion of reality by using the initials of the names of characters and places; one of his short works is even entitled "*S. Bey*",[180] with the implication that he is telling real stories and is, therefore, obliged to conceal the identity of his characters and locations. But his attempt to create an illusion of reality in his works is not borne out by a more profound, underlying realism in his writing. He was clearly influenced by romantic writing and French romanticism in particular.[181] Like most of his contemporaries, his understanding of the nature of romanticism leads him to exaggerate the role of sentiment and emotion and overlook the importance to romanticism of the revolt against tradition in order to free narrative language from hackneyed usage and increase its ability to express a wide variety of feelings and everyday issues.

Al-Manfalūṭi's short narrative works are a clear demonstration of this simplistic understanding of romanticism, particularly those in *al-'Abarāt* which he subtitled *riwāyāt qaṣīrah* (short fictions). Al-Manfalūṭi's temperament and his stylistic taste are in harmony with the exaggerated emotions expressed, for they provide him with an opportunity to employ his linguistic skills. He pays considerable attention to the stylistic aspects of his work, and he is, in a peculiar way, skilful in arousing emotion. But, as far as his few fictional works are concerned, this stylistic gift does not save them from serious shortcomings. In fact, his stylistic merits, in themselves the subject of much controversy,[182] have done his fictional work more harm than good. He is often carried away in a display of style for its own sake, with the result that certain elements of his subject-matter are exaggerated at the expense of others. Al-Manfalūṭi is, in this respect, a frustrated romantic poet who failed to fulfil himself in poetry and endeavoured, therefore, to channel his poetic talent into prose fiction.[183] The type of prose writing which al-Manfalūṭi would have probably excelled in — that is, the style of 'Abdullah Fikri and Ḥifni Nāṣif (1856—1918) — had gone out of vogue, and he therefore had to try his hand at the more fashionable fictional essay.

Both by temperament and by education, al-Manfalūṭi — an outstanding student of Muḥammad 'Abduh — was not made for narrative writing; the traditional streak in him was far too powerful to accommodate the new sensibility. Yet his impact on readers and would-be writers was extremely powerful. One of the would-be writers of that time, Yaḥyā Ḥaqqi, has provided us with a vivid testimony of al-Manfalūṭi's influence on his generation. "Al-Manfalūṭi was the most cherished writer among my generation. His magic was irresistible and his impact on us was great."[184] This wide impact is the subject of an interesting study of his work, which suggests that he posited sadness and frustration as an appealing ideology for the disenchanted new readers and intellectuals. He sublimated the grief of the noble failure in realizing neither the individual project nor the nationalist one.[185]

Even the *Diwān* group, who attacked al-Manfalūṭi and dismissed his writing, acknowledged his influence and popularity. Al-'Aqqād suggested that he was responding to a genuine need among the new reading public, and though he denied his impact on discerning readers and confined it to the least educated sector of the reading public, yet he admitted that this sector is the majority and al-Manfalūṭi's writing satisfied a genuine need in them.

> It is necessary to say that those who benefit from his writing and sympathize with it are more numerous and in need of education and culture than those who do not benefit from or sympathize with it. His views on morality and sentiments are admittedly more beneficial and easily accessible to them than anything else. It may be the best emotional and cultural nourishment for them, for they are really in need of al-Manfalūṭi, and had this Manfalūṭi whom they know and cherish not appeared for them, they would have needed another Manfalūṭi to satisfy their needs.[186]

Yet despite his skilful expression of the central sentiments of the period and his ability to respond to the needs of the wider reading public,[187] his narrative language was still incongruous with the sensibility of the new discourse. Some of his contemporaries realized the conflict between the two contradicting sensibilities in his writing. In an article on *al-'Abarāt* published in the first issue of *al-Sufūr*[188] and signed by the first name "'Ali", the author points out this conflict when he criticizes al-Manfalūṭi's narrative works because of their incoherent structure and simplistic didacticism, and stresses the distinction between the didacticism of the reformative essay and the narrative or creative work. The manner in which he referred to this distinction suggests that, at least among a certain class of discerning intellectuals, this was an accented distinction. After dealing with the incoherent structure of these works "'Ali" continues:

> If al-Manfalūṭi's fictional talent had been equal to his skill as an ingenious prose writer, he would have been able to integrate the didactic and elaborate theoretical views into the realistic details of his narrative work. By doing so the attraction of his beautiful style might have made up for the incorrectness of his views and crudeness of his didacticism. The promulgation of ideas and views in the form of mere rhetorical discussions is a hackneyed method which the worst writers can master. If al-Manfalūṭi fails to harmonize fiction and didactic prose writing, he should turn to other forms of discourse where his puns and eloquence of style may conceal the reactionary attitude of his reformative principles.[189]

In these criticisms one can recognize the disintegration of the old literary sensibility and a clear awareness, on the part of the critic and other writers of the younger generation, of the inability of the old canon to respond to the changing reality and its new literary demands.[190] Stylistic skills which were once highly regarded and even revered as a major literary attribute were now being questioned or even repudiated. Instead, the main criterion of literary value has become the integration of the various components of the literary text in a harmonious manner. There was also the recognition of the distinction between separate reformative essays and narrative fiction, and the emergence of a stated convention that narrative work could no longer tolerate the sort of abstract arguments featured in the "*mabāḥith*" (investigative essays), as "'Ali" calls them.

Nevertheless, writers persisted in mixing the two different literary forms without succeeding in integrating them. The juxtaposition and sometimes the amalgamation of the two forms, which is a main feature of al-Manfalūṭi's narrative attempts,[191] continued to appear throughout al-Rāfi'i's narrative pieces in *al-Masākīn,* perhaps with the exception of his most mature piece "*Miskīnah ... Miskīnah*" (A Pathetic Woman).[192] Like al-Manfalūṭi's, al-Rāfi'i's perception of literature was traditionally orientated, and therefore most of what has been said about al-Manfalūṭi applies to al-Rāfi'i, including the attempt to channel a frustrated poetic talent into prose writing.[193] However, al-Rāfi'i wrote mainly to teach and to impress his reader, and although he did not exaggerate the sentimental aspects of his writing as much as al-Manfalūṭi, he paid considerable attention to his style and juxtaposed narrative with contemplative essays in his work, especially in *"Saḥq al-Lu'lu'"* (Pulverizing the Pearl).[194] Like al-Manfalūṭi, his writing betrays a shallowness of mind and little knowledge, for, outside the sphere of traditional verbal ornamentation, he makes crucial mistakes in developing his narrative and displays hackneyed and reactionary views.

He is at his most vulnerable when he deals with sophisticated feelings or with the ramifications of the process of social change (*"Saḥq al-Lu'lu'"*), and he is at his best when his main theme is quite in harmony with traditional thinking and views (*"Miskīnah ... Miskīnah"*). In fact, this narrative piece — *"Miskīnah ... Miskīnah"* — comes closer than anything written by Ḥammād and al-Manfalūṭi to the proper form of the short story. It deals with the theme of social disparity by illustrating the suffering of a poor woman who begs a rich woman to help her when she is starving. In the first half of his work, the two women seem to be personifications of two ideas, or cardboard characters fated to play their parts in a simplistic game of polarization of ideas in which the author goes through a tedious dialogue on poverty and richness. But in the second half, when the author tries to introduce an element of fate, he abandons the theoretical argument and attempts to develop his ideas through action and characterization. The work starts to progress in a manner which ironically mocks most of what had been said in the "learned" debate on richness and poverty. The action turns full circle, and the poor woman who had been the object of sorrow and sympathy is now in a position to feel sorry for the rich woman, who is suffering because of the death of her beloved only daughter.

The title of the story is an utterance of both ridicule and sympathy which is used throughout the story with different shades of meaning and implications by the two opposing characters, a technical device which indicates a certain skill in narrative writing, for it is carefully used both to widen the scope of the meaning and develop the characterization. Yet the rest of the narrative does not live up to this skilful artistic use of phrases for it is packed with dysfunctional rhetoric and burdened with heavy stylistic embellishments. The excessive verbal decoration and its inherent tautology is in conflict with the economic language of narrative, and this in turn affects the characterization. Instead of participating in the progression of the action and the development of characterization, the dialogue becomes a means of suspending them in order to prove the writer's cleverness in debating two simple contradictions. The social and cultural, as well as the psychological, differences between the two characters fade, and the dialogue — written in elegant *fuṣḥā* (literary Arabic) — turns into an exercise in which the writer's language and logic are substituted for those of the characters.

The concentration on rhetorical elements, in both al-Manfalūṭi's and al-Rāfi'i's work, is associated with the flatness of description and overlooks the role of the setting in developing the action and creating a sense of reality. The writers are not aware of the importance of the particularization of time and space in the process of individuation. But the circular structure of *"Miskīnah ... Miskīnah"* and the way in which the action is made to progress so that the views and expectations of the antagonist are mocked, and the protagonist is avenged, is in itself a remarkable achievement at this stage in the development of Arabic narrative discourse. When the action turns full circle, the two characters exchange positions, but the poor woman does not seize the opportunity to take revenge; instead, she prays for the rich woman.

The author, who is obviously unaware of his narrative achievements, does not leave the irony to speak for itself, but ends his work with a verse from the Qur'ān to serve as a simplistic comment on the action, and so spoils the dramatic effect of the situation. In retrospect, the work loses a great deal of its validity and becomes a mere explanation of the sacred lines, a demonstration of their greatness and correctness. What seemed a form of cosmic irony capable of generating meaning and charging the title with ironic implications is rendered, by the emotional and religious power of the Qur'ānic verse, a mere demonstration of the validity of the scripture. The extrinsic nature of the verse, its belonging to a different body of text, prevents this authorial intrusion from presenting the situation as an act of divine justice.

However, this work presents its critic with a unique form of the "intentional fallacy",[195] for it haphazardly accomplishes, on the narrative level, far more than it was intended to. It indicates that the new mode of writing had penetrated the work of many literary figures, and that readers' enthusiastic response to certain types of narrative discourse was now on its way to establishing new literary conventions. The works of Ḥammād and al-Manfalūṭi imply an awareness of these conventions despite their relative failure in putting them into practice. A great deal of their failure is due to the fact that, unlike Nadīm, their awareness of the national identity, their experience of its aspirations, and their sense of time and place were not strong enough to give their writing spirit and a sense of purpose.

The writers of the romantic sensibility contributed, each in his or her own way, to the development of the conventions of short narrative forms. They helped to popularize the form, liberate it from the conventions of the *maqāmah,* stimulate demand for it and encourage a number of new writers to experiment with its potential. They did not come up with a mature and coherent short story because they failed to recognize the most significant achievement of their predecessor, Nadīm, that is his ability to adapt simple, economic language to the needs of fiction. Their dysfunctional rhetoric and highly ornate language suited neither their themes nor their medium. Excessive verbal decoration affects the characterization and renders most of the description flat, abstract and lacking in the ability to provide the narrative with its temporal and spatial aspects.

Despite their failure on the formal plane, these works demonstrated two major facts: the demand for narrative was steadily rising, and the changing literary sensibility was able to attract followers among the traditional intellectuals such as al-Manfalūṭi and al-Rāfi'i. As for the general reading public, the works of Jibrān and al-Manfalūṭi were the most influential. They confined themselves to the task of reforming rather than inspiring their readers as Nadīm tried to do. Therefore their works are of a more compromising nature, and, despite their appeal to the reading public, they failed to deliver the form which Nadīm's embryonic fictional writing promised. Nevertheless, these writers were confident that their works played a desired and valuable role in their society, and in spite of their shortcomings, they prepared the ground for the more mature and coherent modes of narrative discourse which were forged in the struggle for independence and national identity.

Muṣṭafā 'Abd al-Rāziq: A Neglected Pioneer

Another prominent Egyptian writer of this early period was the significant but now completely neglected Muṣṭafā 'Abd al-Rāziq (1885–1947), whose house was the most influential, innovative and progressive literary salon in Egypt during the first half of this century. He was the son of a prominent and well-established Egyptian family from Bahnasā in Upper Egypt. His father Ḥasan 'Abd al-Rāziq was the representative of the county of al-Minyā in the first consultative national assembly established during the reign of Ismā'īl, though he was known for his criticism of the Khedive. He continued to be active in politics long after Ismā'īl's abdication, as a member of the assembly and as one of the main founders of *Ḥizb al-Ummah,* which later became *Ḥizb al-Aḥrār al-Dustūriyyīn* (the Liberal Constitutional Party), and was one of the active proponents of the call for Egyptian nationalism. Muṣṭafā studied at al-Azhar where he attended Muḥammad 'Abduh's classes and became one of his most bright and faithful students. 'Abduh was also a friend of his father and one of the major inspirations in his life.

After 'Abduh's resignation from al-Azhar and his subsequent death in 1905, Muṣṭafā worked with some of 'Abduh's faithful students and colleagues to fulfil his ideas of reforming al-Azhar, and, particularly, of establishing a modern school for *al-Qaḍā' al-Shar'i* (Jurisprudence and Islamic Law). Their effort was successful and the school was founded in 1907. Upon his graduation from al-Azhar in the following year, Muṣṭafā was appointed a teacher in the newly established school. But after one year, and because of his active involvement in the rebellious Azharite movement,[196] he resigned his post and went to further his studies in France in 1909, where he attended Durkheim's classes on sociology at the Sorbonne for one year. He then moved to Lyon to teach Arabic and study the history of philosophy, French literature and Islamic philosophy until he returned to Egypt in 1914 after the outbreak of World War I.

As soon as he returned, he started publishing his articles ar d fictitious diaries[197] in *al-Jarīdah,* and after its closure, he worked with a group of young writers to establish a new magazine. He was one of the energetic members, if not the driving force, behind the founding of *al-Sufūr* and was among its regular contributors from the first issue.[198] With his strong support and guidance, *al-Sufūr* attained respectability and continued to be a tireless crusader for the cause of literary innovation and progress. Six months after the inauguration of *al-Sufūr*, he was appointed secretary to the governing body of al-Azhar despite stern opposition, mainly because of his association with *al-Sufūr*. It is noteworthy that while he occupied this influential position at al-Azhar, the bastion of traditionalism, Muṣṭafā continued to write his innovative articles and narrative texts.

He published critical essays and narrative pieces in *al-Sufūr* and did not collect them in any of his subsequent publications. This is probably because Muṣṭafā 'Abd al-Rāziq was a leading intellectual and was appointed a few years later Professor of Islamic Philosophy at Cairo University. In 1938 he was the first Azharite to become Minister of Religious Endowments in the government of Muḥammad Maḥmūd, and this made it even more difficult for him either to continue writing fiction, or even collect his previous work in this genre. Writing narrative fiction was not yet a respectable profession; hence the significance of the work of one of the pillars of the establishment at the time. Although both al-Manfalūṭi and al-Rāfi'i were of traditional background, Muṣṭafā 'Abd al-Rāziq's role was more significant in this respect, because he occupied a much higher position in the social and political hierarchy, and his opinion carried, as a result, more weight. He also was more open to the new ideas and literary ideals than any of the others, and his style was simpler and more suitable to narrative presentation, for he combined the strength of a classicist with the lucid and economic language of the new intellectual élite.

Muṣṭafā 'Abd al-Rāziq started writing his narrative pieces at the time of al-Rāfi'i, and there is ample evidence to suggest that he enjoyed the support of the reading public at the time, even more than the latter, especially among the readers of narrative fiction. A reader expressed this in a letter published in *al-Sufūr* in which she lamented the absence of Muṣṭafā's narrative which acted as a substitute for her lack of rich social life. She confirmed that the love life and emotional endeavours of his characters solaced her and provided her with a tenderness which her life did not allow her to experience.[199] The significance of this rare letter from a reader, and a female one as well, is that it confirms that the reading public of narrative discourse was aware of the power of narrative and its ability to replace direct experience. This confirms Benjamin's observation that narrative gave rise to a desire for a form of knowledge that would no longer be guaranteed by the life experience of its propounder, but would instead be understandable in itself and subject to "prompt verifiability".[200]

In his first narrative piece, "*'Ibrah ba'd Ibtisām*"[201] (A Lesson and a Smile), Muṣṭafā 'Abd al-Rāziq presents a narrative sketch, not of a character, but of an action from the cherished past that was evoked in the mind of the narrator many years later when he passes by the same road that witnessed his first Platonic love. This theme of Platonic love reappears in a number of other pieces, and its treatment is marked in many of them by the deliberate effort to invent excuses for dealing with such a theme. It is either a memory from the distant past of something which took place in the forest of a clearly European, or at least foreign, country, as in "*min Tadhkār al-Māḍi*"[202] (A Memory from the Past), or a story and a love poem which the author found in a discarded piece of paper in the street, and hesitated to pick it up out of hypochondriac fears, as in "*Ṣaḥīfah fi al-Ṭarīq*"[203] (A Piece of Paper in the Road). His presentation of this theme is always rendered retrospectively with the added effect of nostalgia, and this enhances the impact and coherence of the work internally and spares the author any direct intrusion or exaggeration of sentiments.

In addition to the theme of Platonic love, 'Abd al-Rāziq meditates on the appearance of grey hair in one's head as a significant junction in life in "*Ḥasrah 'alā al-Shabāb*"[204] (Sorrow for Youth). He also deals with a number of prevalent social ills, as in "*Ḥādithah Faẓī'ah*"[205] (A Tragedy), which could have been written by al-Manfalūṭi, except for its more controlled emotions and less florid style. In this vivid narrative sketch, the contrast between poverty and wealth is played up, and the reader is persuaded to ponder over the ironies of the situation. The sketch points to both the injustice of the social system and the failure of the government to provide its citizens with the minimum of social or health care. The argumentative nature of the piece affects its narrative presentation, but its vivid portrayal of the situation and its resort to irony saves it from becoming a mere didactic essay.

But the pieces of his narrative writing nearest to a more coherent narrative structure are "*Ḥubb al-Nisā' wa-Ḥubb al-Māl*"[206] (Love of Women and Money) and "*'Abd al-'Alīm*".[207] In the former the comic presentation of the action and its anecdotal tone enhance the narrative effect. The character is presented in a simple but convincing manner, and the didactic message recedes to the background, leaving the action to speak for itself. The latter is his maturest narrative sketch despite the complexity of its theme, which would have lured another writer to indulge in lengthy didacticism. The sketch deals with the sensitive issue of the cultural gap in its various manifestations and presents its hero in a balanced and sensitive manner. The gap between the moral and cultural background of 'Abd al-'Alīm and that of the two British women he meets aboard the ship corresponds to the one between him and his "polished" and elegant compatriot who volunteers to save him from an embarrassing situation. The author is keen to demonstrate that the gap between various scales of values within the same culture is more disabling than that between different and opposing ones. For if the latter results from different customs and logic, the former emerges from the failure of ethical and moral criteria.

In these works Muṣṭafā 'Abd al-Rāziq plays a significant role in the propagation of the new narrative discourse and the dissemination of ideas contributing to the reader's acceptance of its new modes of expression. His major achievement is in simplifying the language of narrative and introducing a fresh style marked by the competence of the traditionalist and the economy of the language of narrative. He purged the narrative writing at the time of the exaggerated sentimentality fostered by the popularity of the romantic writers, by introducing a subdued sense of objectivity and emphasizing the verisimilitude in the presentation of action, setting and characters. Because he wrote both essays and narrative fiction, he restricted the high didactic tone to his essays and allowed the narrative to communicate his message to the reader with a minimum of authorial intrusion. This and the prominence of his social stature gained both popularity and respectability for the new narrative discourse, and earned him a place among its pioneers.

The Herald of Realistic Narrative

Among all the pioneers of narrative writing of this early period, the Palestinian writer Khalīl Baydas played the most significant role in the genesis of the new narrative discourse. From the outset of his literary career, he opened the eyes of the readers and writers alike to Russian literature. A graduate of Nazareth Russian Seminary, Baydas went on to study in Russia and returned to teach in the Russian schools of Palestine and Lebanon. His activity in the translation and promotion of Russian literature has been discussed in Chapter 2,[208] and we shall confine ourselves here to his original creative writing. From a very early age Baydas was fascinated and inspired by the life and work of the great Russian poet Alexander Pushkin (1799—1837), and he tried to play an equivalent role in the life of his own society. His reading of Pushkin's work and biography led him to value the role of publishing a magazine in order to promote his own work and encourage the young writers to follow suit.

Like Pushkin who published the journal *Sovremennik* (The Contemporary, 1836), Baydas started his magazine *al-Nafā'is* in 1908,[209] ten years after the publication of his Arabic translation of Pushkin's *The Captain's Daughter,* whose portrayal of the life of the Russian peasants touched a raw nerve in Baydas. Written at the peak of Pushkin's maturity and dealing with Pugachev's uprising against the Empress Catherine, *The Captain's Daughter* (1832) set an example of narrative excellence, particularly in dealing with an oppressed and marginalized group of people. It is the love story of Marya, the daughter of Captain Mirnoff, and young Grinyev, who is sent to fight for the Tsarina against the rebellious Cossacks. It is also the story of the interaction between human destiny and the people's destiny, narrated by an unbiased eyewitness who sympathizes with Pugachev as an embodiment of the people's strength and talent but who remains faithful to his own duty as a member of the gentry. The spiritual dilemma of Grinyev, split between his obligation to the state and his sympathy with the poor, captivated the young Arab intellectuals, who were themselves torn between their moral duties towards the poor and their allegiance to the establishment. Baydas also was struck by what another Palestinian writer, Najāti Ṣidqi,[210] describes as "Pushkin's profound understanding of Russian society, his deep knowledge of various parts of his country and her history, his close scrutiny of the interaction between the different classes of the Russian community and his ability to educate himself constantly and to the highest of standards."[211]

He started his magazine after the promulgation of the Ottoman Constitution. In the ensuing optimism, Baydas aspired to play Pushkin's role in Arabic culture and to use literature not to preach to his people but to sharpen their consciousness and refine their sentiments. Unlike his forerunners, who understood literature in didactic terms, Baydas' perception of literature and its social role was more sophisticated. His involvement in the translation of Russian literature for many years before the publication of his magazine and the creation of his own original work provided him with extensive training in this respect. The prevalence of didacticism in Arabic narrative was the direct outcome of the writers' yearning to play a reformative role in their society and their desire to support and even accelerate the process of social progress. Russian literature with its predominant sense of social and political commitment and its subtle, but powerful, moral messages provided the Arab writer with the ideal solution.

Baydas was the first to draw upon the rich reservoir of Russian literature which ignited the imagination of the young and aspiring Arab intellectual. Nu'aymah, one of Baydas' students, articulated this feeling:

> When I read Russian literature and grasp its philosophy, I cannot but compare it with our own literature. Oh, my God, what a wide gulf between the two! What a literary darkness envelops our existence! We focus on life's husk and fail to mull over its import. My poor country, even international luminaries like Tolstoy did not yet dissipate the darkness of your night.[212]

When Nu'aimah was voicing this indictment in his Russian Seminary in Poltava, Baydas was busy dispelling the literary darkness by the publication of his magazine studded with the works of Russian literary stars. When he translated Alexei Tolstoy's historical novel *Prince Serebriany* (1863) to serialize in his magazine, he changed its title to *Ahwāl al-Istibdād* (The Ordeal of Tyranny) and declared in its introduction that he "had omitted, changed, altered and reorganized parts of the text in order to suit the Arab reader".[213] His changes reflect his conception of narrative and his awareness of the reader's need to master its conventions gradually.

Nevertheless, his active participation in the reorganization of translated narrative was Baydas' first stage of writing one. He was the first Palestinian writer to start with a conscious intention of producing short stories when he edited his influential magazine, *al-Nafā'is al-'Aṣriyyah* (1908—14, 1919—23),[214] and devoted it almost entirely to the publication of short and long narrative texts. As an active translator from, and even into,[215] Russian,[216] he soon learned the technique and turned to writing his own novels and short stories which were clearly influenced by his translation of Russian literature.[217] He was aware of the nature of narrative and its popularity with the reading public, as is revealed in his introduction to the first issue of his magazine. "It is clear that fiction ... is one of the pillars of modern culture ... for which every enlightened reader is avidly longing".[218]

Yet, when he started writing his own short stories he demonstrated that there was a wide gulf between theoretical awareness of the nature of narrative discourse and its realization. His theoretical awareness can be deduced from his several introductions to the novels serialized in his magazine and from his introduction to his sole collection of stories, *Masāriḥ al-Adhhān* (The Theatres of the Mind), in which he declares that the "truly artistic narrative is distinguished by its perceptive intention and literary inclinations. It strives to glorify probity and deplore vice, to refine ethics, enlighten minds, sanctify hearts and rectify conduct."[219] Here one finds a different approach to literature, which still acknowledges its active role in the education of the reader, but sees this role in fresh terms free from insolent didacticism. Implicit in this approach is a different method of representing both reality and issues in narrative discourse and a mature understanding of the role of the writer which liberates his narrative text from direct authorial intrusion and employs the mimetic argument to enhance the reader's involvement in his work. Both the author's declared aim and the title of his collection are far from mimetic justification of literature, and bring the argument closer to the dialectics of text and context.

The realization of these mature intentions in his original narrative works, though far from delivering what they promised, succeeded in taking the new narrative discourse into a new direction. His writing offered new themes and presentation and sharpened their impact by their close association with Russian literature. When his magazine was closed, he collected thirty-two of his short stories in *Masāriḥ al-Adhhān*, and subtitled them "a collection of literary artistic fiction exploring real life". The emphasis in the subtitle is as much on the literary and artistic qualities of his work as on its verisimilitude, but the title itself is more true to the nature of the collection than its subtitle. For it is, as the Arabic word *masāriḥ*[220] indicates, an intellectual exploration of the form of the short story as much as a reasoned investigation of the range of issues it can fathom.

In some of his stories he debates the difference between fact and fiction,[221] in others he uses a mythological,[222] historic,[223] philosophical,[224] pedagogical,[225] symbolic[226] or even social[227] framework.[228] But most of his admirable formal experimentation was marred by authorial intrusion in the narrative, redundant moral messages, feeble characterization and the excessive use of chance and surprise. Yet his work is marked by its keen interest in the particularization of time and space, and by its strong tendency towards a more plausible representation of reality. He emphasized the connection between his narrative and reality, and confirmed within the text its verisimilitude, but this was mainly an attempt to draw within the text the rules of its reception. He often starts his stories with verbs such as *ḥadath* (it happened), *rawā* (someone related), *waqa'* (it took place) in order to give them an air of authentic reporting on real events and experiences. As one of his critics states, "Baydas was not interested in rarity, curiosity or novelty but in truth and reality. He did not hesitate to sacrifice rarity, curiosity or novelty for true representation when he feared that they might jeopardize the realistic effect or enfeeble the story's plausibility".[229]

Realistic representation was perceived as essential for concern with the inherent injustice of the class system and preoccupation with middle-class affairs. The aspiration of the newly educated middle class for a simple, but just and enlightened, life occupies a central place in his work. He was the first to understand that the short story was the literary genre most conducive to the portrayal of marginalized social groups and sensitive forlorn individuals. In this respect his work was well ahead of its time, and this may explain the fact that his stories which appeared first in his magazine in its early days had to wait until 1924 to be published in book form, not in Palestine but in Egypt where both Baydas and Russian literature had a big following.

The common denominator in all these attempts to create a new narrative discourse is their awareness of the emergence of a new reading public with new literary needs, and their quest to legitimize the new discourse and justify its existence and relevance. There is a certain analogy between the infrastructure of cultural transition and the emergence of these new types of narrative discourse which in a way constituted a form of infrastructure of narrative discourse. The emphasis on Nadīm stems from his endeavour to satisfy the readers' need, without resorting to the by then established approach of validating the new discourse by rooting it in Arabic history, by writing *maqāmah* or by adaptation from European literature. These were the three recognized areas, but Nadīm established a different one. The elaboration of a new discourse which derives its validity from its relevance to readers' daily concerns and roots itself in reality and not in traditional or borrowed literary canons warranted many responses. Most of the succeeding endeavours appear to be in one way or another a rejoinder to this new discourse and an attempt to appropriate its themes and at least some of its narrative strategies.

The responses spanned the whole range, from distancing oneself from the past and rejuvenating the *maqāmah* to the romantic, sentimental and realistic narrative. Such responses did not confine themselves to short narrative forms, but pervaded the whole range of narrative ranging from the lyrical to the dramatic. This was the period in which early attempts were made at rooting Arabic drama and the Arabic novel in the historical consciousness of the Arab by adopting historical themes and using the new genres to revive readers' sense of their own history and identity. There are certain analogies between the attempt of the writers of the new narrative discourse and those of drama, and even within the narrative discourse between those who wrote short narrative pieces and those who wrote longer ones; indeed, most of them wrote both. If the writers of short narrative works sought to root their endeavour in the Arabic literary tradition by rejuvenating the form of the *maqāmah*, those of the longer ones tried to accomplish a similar effect by resorting to Arab history.

Many of the early attempts to develop an indigenous Arabic novel went along this path from the work of Salīm al-Bustāni to that of Jurji Zaydān, Ya'qūb Ṣarrūf (1852—1927), 'Abd al-Ḥamīd al-Zahrāwi (1854—1916), Zaynab Fawwāz, Farīdah 'Aṭiyyah, Niqūlā Ḥaddād, Faraḥ Anṭūn, 'Abd al-Masīḥ Anṭāki (1874—1922), and others.[230] But other writers relied on certain elements of romantic representation such as Jibrān, Aḥmad Shawqi, Maḥmūd Khayrat, Muḥammad Ḥusain Haykal (1888—1956) and Sulaymān Fayḍi al-Mūṣili.[231] In addition many of the writers discussed in this chapter also wrote novels in which they replicated on a larger scale what they achieved in their shorter works.

Similar developments took place in the field of Arabic drama when the early pioneers dramatized certain traditional tales from *The Arabian Nights* or folk epics or even religious stories. Among them were Mārūn al-Naqqāsh, Aḥmad Abū-Khalīl al-Qabbāni, Maḥmūd Wāṣif and 'Ali Anwar.[232] Other playwrights of the same period resorted to Arab history including Khalīl al-Yāziji (1856—89), Ibrāhīm Ramzi (1884—1949), Aḥmad Shawqi, Anṭūn al-Jumayyil (1883—1948), Muḥammad 'Abd al-Muṭṭalib (1871—1931) and Faraḥ Anṭūn.[233] But some were concerned with social issues including Ya'qūb Ṣannū', Zaynab Fawwāz, Ismā'īl 'Āṣim, Khalīl Kāmil, Nakhlah Qilfāṭ, Faraḥ Anṭūn and Ibrāhīm Ramzi.[234] Both the novel and drama flourished in this period, and by 1915 there were no fewer than 900 dramatic pieces, some translations but mostly originals available in Arabic.[235]

4
The Quest for National Identity and the Birth of Narrative Genres

The new narrative discourse rapidly came of age with a clear demarcation between its various genres in the cultural climate engendered by the fervent quest for national and political identity. There were major revolts against colonial domination in the area (the 1919 revolution in Egypt, the 1920 revolutions in Iraq and Palestine, and the 1920 and 1922 uprisings in Syria). These revolts were both a product and a precipitator of a keen sense of national identity and were closely linked to the rise of the modern Arabic short story. This was not only because the national and political fervour inspired Arab intellectuals to create art worthy of their countries' ambitious aspirations, but also because the new forms of literature, as well as other forms of expression, were evolved to fulfil a need for an art form which would reflect the consciousness of a distinctive national identity.

The fact that the new narrative genres were conceived in the atmosphere of the patriotic struggle left its distinct mark on both their form and their content. However, the relationship between the new art forms and the national and political awakening was not unidirectional, for just as the national awakening had a seminal impact on the cultural and spiritual life of the Arabs, the cultural renaissance in turn made a valuable contribution to the national and patriotic movement. In other words, both the nationalist sentiment which swept the Arab lands throughout the second decade of the twentieth century and the emergence of new cultural and artistic movements are demonstrations, on two different levels, of the Arabs' yearning to prove their distinctive identity.

Nationalism and New Artistic Endeavour

It is not surprising that the period round the 1919 revolution in Egypt witnessed a vigorous movement to revitalize its material and spiritual life. Unlike the reviving measures taken by Muḥammad 'Ali and Ismā'īl, this movement did not come from above, but sprang from beneath and surged up within the country against the will of the ruling establishment. It was a movement to express the new awareness of a national identity, to shape the dreams and aspirations of the nation, and to purge Egypt of the distortions which had resulted from the occupation. This new movement, in itself a manifestation of the growing national consciousness, aimed at creating a "national literature" to express the "national character" through new media, and to recover the authentic face of Egypt, which had been obfuscated by dependency and occupation.

It expressed itself in the cry "*miṣr lil-miṣriyyīn*" (Egypt for the Egyptians), and in the wave of the revival of various art forms which sought to articulate the collective consciousness of the nation and shape its new world-view. Sayyid Darwīsh captured the mood of the revolutionary events in his music, and continued, after the tide had turned away from it, to create songs and melodies inspired by folkloric subjects and nationalist themes. His music expressed the difficulties endured by the peasants, the working classes and the lower strata of society, transcending their suffering through beautiful melodies and incorporating political observations and patriotic sentiments into his evocations of their daily concerns and mixing major nationalist themes with individual concerns.

Maḥmūd Mukhtār (1891—1938) with his sculpture and Maḥmūd Sa'īd, Aḥmad Ṣabri, Yūsuf Kāmil, and Rāghib 'Ayyād with their painting attempted to revitalize the country's major and most ancient arts, not by recording the glory of the rulers and their magnificent deeds, but by endeavouring to reveal the beauty incarnate in the body of the Egyptian woman with her characteristic gestures.[1] The theatre also witnessed a great revival: many theatrical companies flourished[2] and dramatic performance came of age through the works of 'Azīz 'Īd, 'Ali al-Kassār, Jūrj Abyaḍ (1880—1959), Yūsuf Wahbi, and Najīb al-Riḥāni (1891—1949). Most of the works of these men of the theatre, all of whom ran their own companies, tried to root drama in the social and national life of the country. Similar developments, albeit on a smaller scale, were taking place in Iraq and the Levant.

The cultural leadership passed during the latter half of the nineteenth century from the traditional religious leaders to those who brought together traditional and European cultures. At the beginning of the twentieth century it was taken over by those with a secular education and a fair knowledge and experience of European culture such as Qāsim Amīn, Aḥmad Luṭfi al-Sayyid (1872—1963), Waliyy al-Dīn Yakan (1873—1921), Amīn al-Rāfi'i (1886—1927), Muḥammad Ḥusain Haykal and others. This transference of the cultural leadership was accompanied by the growing importance of Levantine intellectuals who had come to Egypt earlier, and by the beginning of this century had become an important part of the cultural life and of the cultural establishment.[3] The change in the cultural leadership was indicative of a more profound change in literary sensibilities and in the needs of the new reading public, which had a different cultural orientation from the old one which enjoyed traditional literary works.

The accumulation of these changes, which played a vital role in the development of narrative discourse, demonstrated itself in a powerful manner several years later, after the new literary values and concepts had became common currency in literary circles. After the 1919 revolution, a few years after their first being coined in newspaper articles, these literary concepts were widely publicized, as if they had been born out of revolutionary ebullience. In 1921, 'Abbās Maḥmud al-'Aqqād (1889—1963) and Ibrāhīm 'Abd al-Qādir al-Māzini (1889—1949) published their important book *al-Dīwān*. Five years later Ṭaha Ḥusain, who had come back from France in the year of the revolution, shocked the literary community to the core when he published his seminal, and, at the time, highly controversial, work, *Fi al-Shi'r al-Jāhili* (On Pre-Islamic Poetry, 1926). In the following year Salāmah Mūsā (1888—1958) published *al-Yawm wa-l-Ghad* (The Present and the Future, 1927), and Muḥammad Ḥusain Haykal published a series of articles on *"al-Fann al-Miṣri"* (Egyptian Art),[4] calling for a national art and literature which had a distinctive identity, and which was able to express the anxieties and shape the aspirations of the "national character".

Common to all these works was an unprecedentedly rational approach to their subject, and a new value judgement formed on the basis of the world-view which had been taking shape throughout the previous decades. The idea that deep human experience was essential to any work of art gained ground, while the notions which identify literary standards with reference to paronomasia, and grandiloquent expressions of various kinds fell into disrepute *(al-Dīwān)*. The rational and critical approach to literature, which questions and scrutinizes every aspect of the data under discussion in order to reach solid and reliable results, dispensed with many old values and ideas and violated some taboos *(Fi al-Shi'r al-Jāhili)*. The call for new forms of literary discourse based on a new understanding of the function of literary work and an assimilation of the valuable achievements of European culture replaced the old conceptions concerning the verbal nature of literature *(al-Yawm wa-l-Ghad)*.

The Emergence of the Short Story

The dissemination of these ideas helped to mature the early attempts to create a new narrative discourse which, as we have seen, managed to break with the traditional forms almost completely before the 1919 revolution, and endeavoured to create new forms responsive to the needs of the reading public. It also helped to eliminate crude didacticism and accelerated the decline of elements of pure entertainment in fictional writing. Although some writers can take more credit than others for bringing about these changes, the shaping of the new literary sensibility and the creation of new literary forms was very much a collective effort which continued to evolve throughout the second and third decades of the twentieth century until it reached its acme, as far as the emergence of the short story is concerned, in the works of *Jamā'at al-Madrasah al-Ḥadīthah* (the New School). However, this collective effort would have been much more difficult without the encouragement of a responsive reading public, and without the attempts of the earlier writers from al-Bustāni to al-Rāfi'i.

The appearance of the short story as a distinctive genre of narrative, which tends, by its very nature, to express a state of defeat and trace the elements of failure and depression in human experience,[5] was delayed for some years until it found a favourable climate in the state of frustration which came in the wake of the destruction of the revolutionary spirit of 1919. The ruthless manner in which the British put down the revolution, and the imperfect independence (shackled by the notorious four reservations of 1922), caused serious cracks to appear in the *Wafd* Party, which had stood effectively for national unity before that. This in turn resulted in a great deal of frustration and dismay, and in this atmosphere of frustration and despair the Arabic short story was born and matured throughout the third decade of the twentieth century.[6]

This decade witnessed serious endeavours by numerous writers to create coherent short stories which sought to avoid the compromises and shortcomings of previous attempts. These writers were more conscious of the nature and limits of the literary form they wanted to perfect than were their predecessors, and were also equipped with a fair knowledge of the theoretical aspects of their work. This self-conscious awareness is one of the major distinctions between the attempts to create a new literary discourse dealt with in the previous chapter and those discussed here and in the following two chapters: not only did it provide the necessary break with the traditional form needed for the emergence of a new literary genre, but it also put in a new perspective the attempt to satisfy the demands of the new reading public and to create a national literature capable of expressing the anxieties and soul-searching of the Arabs at the time.

However, the pioneering nature of the new attempts is reflected both in the wide gap between the young writers' theoretical understanding of the literary genres they wanted to bring into being and their actual attempts to put this understanding into practice, and in the fact that the desire of some of them to become worthy of their pioneering task led them to divide their activity among various new genres[7] without paying enough attention to the artistic quality of their writing. Unlike their predecessors, the writers of the early decades of this century were aware of some of the unique characteristics of the various narrative genres they were aspiring to create. Their awareness that they were breaking new ground encouraged them to preface their creative work with elaborate critical introductions, in which they tried to establish a bridge between the reading public and their work; in other words, to familiarize the reader with the conventions of these new forms and demonstrate the usefulness and necessity of fiction.

Almost without exception, every young writer at that time tried his hand at the short story. Even some of those who were never well-known as short-story writers, such as Salāmah Mūsā,[8] al-'Aqqād[9] and Haykal,[10] published occasional stories. The young writers who paid considerable attention to the writing and development of the short story in this crucial decade of its history were as follows: Muḥammad Taymūr (1892—1921), Yūsuf Iskandar, Zakariyy Jazārīn, Maḥmūd Taymūr (1894—1973), Ḥasan Maḥmūd, Sa'īd 'Abduh, 'Abd al-Ḥamīd Salīm, Ḥusain Su'ūdi Iskandar, Kāmil Kīlāni, and the group of writers who called themselves *Jamā'at al-Madrasah al-Ḥadīthah*[11] in Egypt. In the same period, Maḥmūd Aḥmad al-Sayyid (1901—37), Sulaymān Fayḍi, Anwar Shā'ūl (b. 1904), 'Abd al-Wahhāb al-Amīn, Yūsuf Mattā, Shālūm Darwīsh and Luṭfi Bakr Ṣidqi were producing stories in Iraq.

All the countries of the Levant witnessed the production of many types of literary discourse during the early decades of the twentieth century. Many of the Levantine writers writing in the *mahjar* were using the new form to cement the bonds between their new reality and the country they had left behind. Among them were 'Abd al-Masīḥ Ḥaddād (1881—1950) and Mīkhā'īl Nu'aymah (1889—1978). In addition, the most talented Syrian writers of this period, 'Īsā (189?—1922) and Shiḥātah 'Ubaid (189?—1961), moved to Egypt and produced their work there. Yet there were other Syrian writers working in Damascus such as Ṣubḥi Abū-Ghanīmah, Liyān Dīrāni (b. 1909), 'Ali Khilqi (1911—84), Fu'ād al-Shāyib and 'Ali al-Ṭanṭāwi. In Palestine there were Aḥmad Shākir al-Karmi (1894—1927), Muḥammd 'Azzah Darwazah (1898—1984), Jamīl al-Baḥari, Isḥāq Mūsā al-Ḥusaini (1904—91), Najāti Ṣidqi and Maḥmūd Sayf al-Dīn al-Īrāni (1914—74).

Obviously, neither all those mentioned, nor every work they produced, deserves detailed and close consideration, for there is a great deal of repetition in the themes and artistic accomplishments of these works. Therefore, one needs to select the most significant writers and their most important work in order to elucidate the progression of the new narrative discourse, in form and content, at this early stage of its development. The work of Muḥammad Taymūr is discussed here as representative of the work of the Egyptian writers of this early period who had set out to write short stories and had had a relatively clear theoretical comprehension of their project. The works of 'Īsā and Shiḥātah 'Ubaid demonstrate the bond between the Levantine cultural movement and its Egyptian counterpart, and how Levantine intellectuals were clearly integrated in a unified literary movement. Mīkhā'īl Nu'aymah and 'Abd al-Masīḥ Ḥaddād are selected as representative of the *mahjar* dimension of Levantine literature and the significant contribution of its writers to the development of narrative discourse, and Maḥmūd Aḥmad al-Sayyid as representative of the most mature work of the Iraqi writers of the period. In fact, these writers were the most eminent names among the many writers who were trying to develop their work simultaneously and with limited awareness of each other's work. They were responding to the change in literary sensibility and the demands of the new reading public more than to each other's work.

It is rather striking that all the five writers[12] who made the most important contribution to the early development of the Arabic short story in Egypt, and wrote what can be described as authentic and indigenous examples of it, were descendants of non-Egyptians. Although they were born in Cairo, they were the offspring (sons and grandsons) of immigrants from Turkey, Albania, the Peloponnese and Syria who had settled in Egypt. Being the descendants of families which were not deeply embedded in Egyptian society set them apart from the community to some extent and made them benevolently curious about the workings of it.

Their unique situation as partly foreign Egyptian citizens provided them with both the sensitivity of a foreign observer and the intimacy of a close relation. They were perhaps instinctively overcoming any unease they may have felt by rooting themselves more deeply in the basic structure of Egyptian society. In an indirect endeavour to embed themselves in the life of the community, and to assure themselves of their genuine Egyptian identity, they attempted to become the eloquent voice of Egypt, to express its dreams and anxieties, and to give it a distinctive national identity in literary terms. The deliberateness of this endeavour left its mark upon their writing, and continued to influence the Arabic short story for some time until the emergence of a new generation of skilled Egyptian writers who had no need to advertise their identity in this way.

Muḥammad Taymūr's Pioneering Work

Among these five writers, Muḥammad Taymūr was the first to publish short narrative works which came very close to the short-story form, and critical essays in which he tried to pave the way for new literary discourses in general, and the short story in particular. After three years in France he returned in 1914, full of enthusiasm for the creation of a new Egyptian theatre, and an appropriate form of expression for the short story, the novel and literary criticism. He divided his energy over all these fields, without favouring one at the expense of the others; though, under the influence of his contemporary and colleague Muḥammad 'Abd al-Raḥīm Lāshīn,[13] he gave the theatre special attention.[14] Because he distributed his energies among several literary forms without being properly armed with the vast cultural background necessary for sustaining such wide interests, his short career as a writer[15] is characterized by its inconsistency. Relatively mature short stories stand alongside naïve and incoherent efforts, and the standard of his work in the different media varies considerably.

Taymūr was convinced that literary independence was inseparable from political independence, and he therefore devoted a whole article[16] to illustrating the importance of national unity as a valuable step towards this goal. He urged his compatriots to accept that "the Egyptian people have a common history which unites them ... they form a unified living nation which should fulfil its duties and enjoy its rights. It is the sacred duty of every individual in the country to realize that he is an Egyptian and to devote his life entirely to Egypt's interests".[17] In another article,[18] he demonstrated the close connection between the emergence of Egyptian nationalism and the revolutionary events of March 1919 which made plain the unity that existed in the nation. In a third article,[19] he carried the argument further by saying that emergent Egyptian nationalism would be in danger without a literary movement to provide it with a tongue to express its cause. "The country which lacks a literary movement is like a body without a heart which cannot feel or comprehend. Therefore it is a must for every nation to have this literary movement".[20]

With all the zeal of a youth in his twenties who had read some French literature, and wished to create similar work for his country, the ambitious Muḥammad Taymūr started to write and publish short stories in the weekly experimental magazine *al-Sufūr* under the general title *"mā Tarāh al-'Uyūn"*.[21] This comprehensive title ("What the Eye Can See") reflects the ambition of these rudimentary fictional pieces, which was no less than to sum up the dilemmas of the Egyptian nation and to come as close as possible to a frank illustration of reality in society. Although his ambition far outstripped his capacity to realize his dreams, he was more conscious than his predecessors of the limits and potentialities of the literary form he was advocating.

Unlike the preceding writers whose narrative achievements were somehow incidental to their reformative goals, Taymūr's prime aim was to create a new literary discourse and establish it outside the domain of the conventional literary canon. It is interesting that Muḥammad Taymūr, who was brought up in a conventional educational and literary atmosphere, and whose father, Aḥmad Taymūr, was among the pillars of the traditional literary establishment, was the first to start the complete and conscious break with conventional literature. His awareness of the shortcomings of conventional literary practices and desire to break new ground were the highlights of his artistic endeavour.

This is not surprising, because, since the time of al-Jabarti and al-'Aṭṭār, the enlightened among the traditional intellectuals had recognized the value and importance of modern and European knowledge and education. Thus, it was natural that, after providing him with a solid base of traditional education, Aḥmad Taymūr should send his son,

Muḥammad, to France to read law. Muḥammad Taymūr's upbringing in a literary atmosphere[22] played an important role in directing his attention to French literature and drama while he was studying law. He took up literature as his hobby, and this gave his work an amateurish touch and reflected at the same time the general attitude of Egyptian society to literature.

When he began to publish his short stories in *al-Sufūr,* he repeatedly drew the reader's attention to the fact that what he was publishing under the general title *"mā Tarāh al-'Uyūn"* was in reality "several independent stories on different subjects, each one complete in itself and having no connection either with the preceding or with the following one".[23] Taymūr did so in an endeavour, on the one hand, to negate any vagueness that might be suggested by the overall title and, on the other, to affirm the independence of each story and eliminate any link with the episodic structure of the *maqāmah* form. He was also aware, as the title of his collection suggests, that realistic presentation was necessary to consolidate the independence of the new literary genre he was attempting.[24]

The Gap Between Theory and Practice

Although he did not write any elaborate articles on the art of narrative fiction, his profound essays on the theatre[25] betray a relatively mature and advanced understanding of artistic matters. This mature understanding reflects itself in Taymūr's work in the field of fiction, which was, by any standard, a secondary activity for him, and in which, therefore, his amateurish attitude to literature demonstrates itself very clearly. A brief critical examination of his adaptation of Maupassant's short story "Moonlight" reveals both the extent of his comprehension of the nature and limitations of this newly emerging narrative genre and his amateur attitude to literature.

He prefaced his adaptation with a few lines of introduction, saying that he had "changed the characters, the time, the location, and the subject of the original story, thus Egyptianizing everything in it to the extent that nothing remains from the original but the spirit of the author [i.e. Maupassant]. The adapter has followed Tolstoy's approach in the stories he has taken from Maupassant".[26] Although this introduction suggests that Taymūr is thoroughly familiar with the short stories of both Maupassant and Tolstoy, his actual adaptation of Maupassant's splendid story[27] shows that he understood the meaning of the story only at a fairly crude level and was insensitive to the underlying subtleties of meaning and the organic relationship between texture and structure in the original story.

He overlooked the most important level of meaning and structure in Maupassant's story — the metaphorical structure — in which the ostensible message of the story is subjected to an ironic scrutiny implicit in the way the story is worked out. This ironic scrutiny, which enriches the story and widens the scope of its implications, is achieved by the use of certain delicate religious images, allusions, and keywords which penetrate the action and act as pivots for its progression. The denouement of Maupassant's story comes as a meaningful act of recognition which demonstrates the radical change in the Abbé's attitude towards love by a complete reversal of his perception of himself, for he feels that he is intruding on the love scene and entering a world in which he is as much an alien as the devil in paradise.

The irony is twofold; the abbot becomes as much an alien figure as Satan, and the military implication of his name, which is alluded to in the first line of the story, is ironically reversed by his final retreat. Although Maupassant's "story is essentially a plot, it is not without design. The early sample of the Abbé's reasoning is repeated at the end with its startling new conclusion that God *must permit love* ... The design and the tone reinforce in various subtle ways the irony of the plot. The strength of this little story lies in the way all these elements cooperate to achieve its comic effect".[28] The Abbé, who had been too pure to accept the nuns of his convent as his spiritual equals, is finally seen as having profaned the temple of love.

Unfortunately, Taymūr does not appear to have discovered that the strength of Maupassant's story lies in the irony and the comic elements which reveal to the reader the very depths of the human character. In other words, he fails to realize that details and events in this story are means of characterization, and that this poetic and sophisticated characterization, rather than the plot, is the major technique of the story. Although he retains most of the action and characters of the original story, he is unable to retain the comic irony or the dialectical relationships between the various levels of meaning. He even overlooks the minute details of the action which do so much to enrich the plot and widen the horizon of its human implications.

His minor modifications of the plot demonstrate this very clearly, for in order to Egyptianize the situation he makes the abbot a traditionally devout Muslim father and the niece of the original story becomes his daughter. The father's piety lacks the logical dimension and the rational process of reasoning which informs the abbot's conduct, and which is the decisive factor in the transformation of the abbot's attitude to both women and love. Moreover, the irony and the comic reversal of the image of the abbot to that of Satan are eliminated. In this way Maupassant's story of the abbot's spiritual education turns, in Taymūr's hands, into a feeble love story with a happy ending, and the long section on the sublimation of nature and the harmony between its beauty and love, an essential component of the original story and vital for the motivation of the reversal of the abbot's action, becomes a redundant part of Taymūr's story.

Although Taymūr tries, through the title which he selected for his adaptation, *"Rabbi li-man Khalaqt Hadhā al-Na'īm"* (Lord! For Whom didst Thou Create this Paradise?), to capture part of the abbot's reasoning process, it seems in his version a mark of intrusive, even faulty, reasoning. This is not only because of the lack of any reference to the father's rationality and the absence of any hint that his piety has an inherent logical dimension, but also because of the lack of consistency in the portrayal of the father's transformation in the light of both his regressive views and his conduct in the early part of the story. The father's accidental witnessing of the puritanical love scene in which his daughter is involved when he is walking in the garden unable to sleep is in direct contrast with both the premeditated confrontation between the abbot and the lovers in Maupassant's story, and the father's previous reaction to his daughter's challenge to his will in Taymūr's adaptation.

The father's conciliatory attitude is additionally incongruous in Taymūr's version, coming as it does just when he has been portrayed as suffering from nerve-racking insomnia. Perhaps the daughter-parent relationship which Taymūr has established between the two characters justifies the father's mild reaction and the happy ending of the story, but he hastily introduces an element of class conflict (by making the lover of the rich daughter a poor young man), an element which very much affects the plausibility of the ending.

His shortcomings in understanding the structural interrelationship between the elements which go to make up a work of narrative have also left their mark on his original short stories. In most cases, Taymūr's short stories appear to be mere "instant sketches in which he records his immediate feelings or reactions when his eyes catch sight of one of life's contradictions, or of a comic character, regardless of their suitability for narrative treatment. Sometimes they create a fictional situation, while often they fail to possess any narrative quality, and like most beginners' works they are not free from crude didacticism".[29] However, it was extremely difficult to avoid didacticism at this early stage in the development of the new narrative discourse, for to abandon the pedagogic role was almost impossible without finding another justification for literature.

In this respect, Taymūr's pioneering role is remarkable, because he defined literature as having a definite nationalistic and spiritual function — to become the heart and the conscience of the nation.[30] He liberated writers from their conventional concepts, he advocated freedom of expression and experimentation in creative literature, and, by setting an example to them through his articles, he led them to conceive of themselves as creative.[31] With regard to form, his works were more mature than those of his predecessors, but his themes and subjects covered the same ground as those of his predecessors in general and Nadīm in particular. He also adopted Nadīm's point of departure and his perspectives in dealing with many of these themes, thus contributing to the development of a distinct "discursive field".

The plausibility of his themes and the validity of many of his views and moral arguments refer to and rely on a scheme of moral values existing outside them; so the more concrete and explicit this scheme was, the more effective were his themes. However, this reliance on a fixed and stable external system of moral and social values is a weak point in Taymūr's stories, because the era during which he wrote them was one of great social mobility and rapid change in these values. But he managed to modify the direct didacticism of his predecessors, and freed his works from the prevailing sentimentality of the period to a remarkable extent, given the nature of his language, which was heavily influenced by traditional stylistics and hence prone to exaggeration and sentimentality.

Thematic and Artistic Contribution

Like Nadīm and al-Muwailiḥi, Taymūr dealt with the disadvantages of addiction to spirits and drugs and illustrated the harmful effects of such bad habits upon the community in general and on the coherence of the family in particular, as in "*'Aṭfat al ... Manzil Raqam 22*"[32] (House 22 in ... Alley). He demonstrated also how drug addiction and alcoholism could swallow up the wealth of the few Egyptian rich in "*Bayt al-Karam*"[33] (A House of Generosity), and how such habits could handicap a talented Egyptian and jeopardize his future, in the lengthy unfinished story "*al-Shabāb al-Ḍā'i'*"[34] (Lost Youth). Like Nadīm and al-Muwailiḥi, he rebuked the rich for wasting their money on useless extravagances instead of investing it in a manner more profitable both to them and to their country, in "*Bayt al-Karam*" and "*al-'Āshiq al-Maftūn bi-l-Rutab wa-l-Nayāshīn*"[35] (A Lover of Titles and Decorations).

He also ridiculed those who had been taken in by the false brilliance of Western civilization, and were infatuated with certain aspects of European conduct, disdaining their own society and tradition, in "*Ramaḍān fī Qahwat Matātyā*"[36] (Ramadan in Matatya Café), "*Sirr min Asrār Ta'akhkhur al-Miṣriyyīn*"[37] (One of the Causes of the Egyptians' Backwardness), and "*Rayyān yā Fijl*"[38] (Fresh Radish). In these three narrative sketches he underlined the importance of Egyptian solidarity in sustaining national identity and inspiring the individual. In one of his artistically most significant stories,[39] "*fī al-Qiṭār*"[40] (On the Train), he repeats, in an almost identical manner, Nadīm's complaints about the crushing poverty, terrible suffering, and generally bad conditions of the Egyptian peasants.

Although he does not go far beyond Nadīm's themes and subjects in these stories, in his artistic treatment of these old issues he represents a considerable advance. In "*fī al-Qiṭār*" his repetition of Nadīm's theme is compensated for by both his maturer artistic presentation and the integration of the perspective through which he treats the various dimensions of his theme. Moreover, he also tries on occasion to break new thematic ground: in "*Ṣuffārat al-'Īd*"[41] (Christmas Toys) he sheds light on the deprivation, poor conditions and lack of security from which orphans suffer in a world that offers them no guarantee of a decent life. In these two stories, and in the general section entitled "*Khawāṭir*"[42]

(Reflections), Taymūr demonstrates a fondness for depicting social contradictions and for seizing upon ironic aspects of people's behaviour and paradoxical situations.

But his treatment of these ironies remains superficial and is designed solely to provide him with an opportunity to deliver eloquent counsel or sarcastic comment on social mores.[43] Yet this in itself is a step towards liberating narrative discourse from didacticism and direct authorial intrusion, for it is indicative of the writer's awareness that his moral message has to be structurally integrated in the text, and that advice needs to be part of the action. Taymūr also attacks the double standard of morality of the traditional sheikhs — a subject popular with succeeding authors — and their method of teaching by rote, in *"Dars fi Kuttāb"*[44] (A Lesson in a Traditional School). In some cases, in the pieces entitled *"Khawaṭir"*, the details of his narrative sketches are impressively sensitive in contrast to the flat didactic remarks he makes upon them. Besides destroying the narrative effect of these pieces, many of these remarks manifest a certain shallowness of experience and lack of insight into human character.

"Ṣuffārat al-'Īd" is one of his best works, for despite a shade of sentimentality,[45] it is a high point in Taymūr's achievements in the field of the short story both in form and in content. The story picks a significant moment in the life of its protagonist,'Ali, who is an impoverished orphan living in a poor quarter in Cairo; outside this moment, on the morning of the *'Īd* (the Muslim equivalent of Christmas), 'Ali's life is almost indistinguishable from those of the rest of the poor boys in the quarter. But the morning of the *'Īd* brings all the intangible elements of his deprivation into focus: unlike the rest of the children, he does not receive the new clothes, sweets and toys given at the time of the feast to all other children of his age, nor does he have the money to buy sweets or a whistle like theirs. Against a background of the rhythm and rituals of long-established customs in the quarter, and through the traditional games the children play on such an occasion, the writer develops his story by interweaving the main action with elements derived from the daily life of the quarter's inhabitants. This widens the horizons of the story, creates certain parallels between the world of children and that of adults, and foreshadows certain future events.

The gradual and causal progression of the action depends on the restatement of the theme with new details and through various forms of coextension, and the use of similarity and contrast as structural elements. The similarity between the orphan 'Ali and a brawler of the quarter suggests the kind of future which the protagonist can expect, while the contrast between him and the well-bred children deepens the reader's understanding of his suffering. The sensitively drawn contradiction between the tones of joy that are struck and the torment of sadness and isolation that is evoked contributes to both the smooth progression of the action and the development of the characterization.

In this story characteristics common to Taymūr's short stories in general can be observed taking shape. One such characteristic is his keen interest in the description of the scene, something completely neglected by his predecessors. But he sometimes goes too far in his detailed description of the setting, mentioning the names of real places, streets, cafés, bars, etc., apparently to convince the reader of the authenticity of his narrative account and also to act as a substitute for the lack of what Booth calls the artificial authority of the author over the reader, who is invited to accept unquestioningly all the facts and information the writer provides.[46]

As a result of his relatively wide experience of writing for the theatre, he has a tendency to emphasize the setting of the scene, but he fails to bring his virtuosity in dramatic dialogue to his short stories. Unlike Nadīm's vivid and spontaneous dialogue written in the vernacular, his dialogue, written, in general, in simple literary Arabic (*fuṣḥā*), is often flat and incapable of conveying the social, cultural and psychological features of the characters. On several occasions, the author's direct remarks spoil the subtle narrative effect which the action or the characters have created, a fault inherited from the writers who preceded him.

Nevertheless, Taymūr achieved what most of the preceding writers not only failed to achieve, but did not even perceive the need for: he made a complete break with the conventions of traditional prose writing and storytelling. He was unprecedentedly independent of the literary conventions which might have interfered with his primary intention to create a new narrative discourse. For he realized that the divorce from the traditional modes of discourse and the conventions of previous fictional techniques was as important as the accentuation of the characteristics of the new discourse. Both his awareness of the requirements of this pioneering task and his readiness and ability to implement them were much more comprehensive than those of his predecessors. Thus, in some of his more mature works, there is a clear conflict between the author's loyalty to literal truth and his faithfulness to the requirements of the new literary form: a constant attempt to integrate his views of reality with his conception of the new genre.

His break with the literary conventions was not a mere rebellion against tradition, but the product of a genuine need to find an appropriate means of expression for the new ideas and visions, which in turn resulted in a clear shift in emphasis. In order to accentuate the shift in emphasis, he paid greater attention to the role of description in his narrative, producing not only a detailed and somewhat theatrical description of the location but also an elaborate, and sometimes suggestive, account of the characters' appearance. Indeed, he was aware of the need to introduce his characters to the reader before and during their participation in the action. In his characterization, he was a true pioneer in his use of similarity and antithesis as a structural device to suggest the circular nature of the action, and the relationship of the particular events he was portraying. This was a significant change both in emphasis and in the comprehension of the form, for it developed the role of characterization and confirmed the ability of the short story to treat complex issues.

Some of his new techniques were part of this shift in emphasis; for example, the ambitious use of letters[47] and diaries[48] are an artistic means of broadening the scope of the narrative, and his emphasis on irony, particularly in his narrative sketches, reveals the depth of certain amusing or contradictory situations. However, Taymūr's techniques were a means of implementing the task which the title of his collection tries to formulate: to put before the reader everything his eyes have seen, in narrative form. But all he was capable of achieving in his short literary career was to make his accounts appear both objective and causal, yet he was not capable of expressing the dreams and questions of Egyptians in their search for a national identity, a goal which some of his contemporaries tried, perhaps more successfully, to attain.

Nu'aymah and the *Mahjar* Experience

Mīkhā'īl Nu'aymah from Lebanon and 'Abd al-Masīḥ Ḥaddād from Syria serve the double function of representing the work of the Lebanese and Syrian writers in this early period and that of the Arab writers who emigrated to the Americas at the same time. It is significant that the most mature attempts of Levantine authors to write narrative discourse at the time took place in the *mahjar,* for nothing was written at home to match the coherence and maturity of the works written in the *mahjar.* This is true as much for short narrative works by Nu'aymah and Ḥaddād as for longer works such as Jibrān's novel, *al-Ajniḥah al-Mutakassirah* (Broken Wings, 1912). The emergence of the Levantine new narrative discourse in the *mahjar* is analogous to the phenomenon of the descendants of non-Egyptians making the major contribution to the development of narrative fiction in Egypt at the time.

In the *mahjar* the rupture was both cultural and geographical. Being Christian, their education in missionary schools introduced them to Arabic language and culture, emphasized the link between it and Islam, and thus liberated them from its traditional grip. The geographical rupture created a crisis of identity, which was intensified by their failure to dissolve into the melting pot, or rather by their resistance to such dissolution. The life in the *mahjar* provided the Levantine writers with the two operative factors in the Egyptian phenomenon: the distance from the subject-matter necessary for its objective presentation in narrative, and the desire to use the authentication of the new literary discourse as a means of bolstering a less than secure sense of identity.

The strong sense of nostalgia and yearning for the homeland acted as a substitute for the fervent quest for national and political identity which was associated with the rise of narrative discourse in Egypt. The new narrative discourse both enhanced the Levantine expatriate community's sense of identity and boosted the confidence of the country that they left behind. In this respect their narrative discourse had two parallel functions: to assure those who had been left behind that the expatriation of their élite was both temporary and undertaken for the good of the country, and to act as an expression of the country's desire to enhance its national and international standing. It is rather ironic that the new discourse which served genuine national needs had to emerge in the *mahjar,* but it is probable that the birth of the new discourse away from home facilitatied its liberation from the shackles of traditional literary canons, and enabled it to establish its own language and conventions more freely.

Like those of Jibrān before them, Nu'aymah's and Ḥaddād's bodies were in the *mahjar,* but their hearts and souls were still in the homeland they had left behind. This qualified them to represent the work of writers who did not leave Lebanon, e.g. Mārūn 'Abbūd (1886—1962), or Syria, e.g. Ṣubḥi Abū-Ghanīmah, Liyān Dīrāni and 'Ali Khalqi, and probably failed to attain the same artistic quality for that reason. The work of the writers who remained in the Levant was hampered by compliance with the rules of the traditional literary canon and its idiosyncratic resistance to change. Another source of the maturity found in the early work of Nu'aymah and Ḥaddād was their firsthand knowledge of Russian literature and their ability to benefit from its literary and thematic achievements.

Nu'aymah was the first among these writers to publish his short stories in the *mahjar* journals such as *al-Sā'iḥ,* which appeared in New York in 1912, while *al-Funūn* appeared in 1913. The former was edited by Nasīb 'Arīḍah (1887—1940) and the latter by 'Abd al-Masīḥ Ḥaddād himself. Both editors knew him since they had all studied together in the Nazareth Seminary. His first story *"Sanatuhā al-Jadīdah"* (Her New Year) appeared as early as 1914, and he continued to publish them until 1925, though his first collection, *Kān mā Kān* (It has Happened),[49] which contained these early stories, did not appear until 1937. The early date of the publication of his first short story has led some critics to suggest that Nu'aymah was the first Arab writer to produce fairly mature short stories, even before Muḥammad Taymūr.[50] The problem with this view is that it gives too much importance to a difference of three years between the publication of Nu'aymah's first story and that of Taymūr, and ignores the fact that the impact of Taymūr's work on his contemporaries was more immediate and much greater than that of Nu'aymah. The publication of Nu'aymah's first story may have preceded that of Taymūr,[51] but the fact that Nu'aymah republished his early stories in Beirut in a literary magazine, *Alf Laylah,* when he returned to Lebanon in 1932 indicates that they were scarcely known to the literary circles.

Unlike his compatriots in the *mahjar,* Nu'aymah maintained strong ties with Lebanon, and his solid knowledge of its reality is clearly reflected in his early short stories. These stories compare favourably with the most mature works of the early pioneers of the genre and are marked by their understanding of the nature of artistic experience and the techniques of its presentation. Like Baydas before him, Nu'aymah was fluent in Russian, and his firsthand knowledge of Russian literature was acquired during his years of study at the Seminary of Poltava (1906—11). As he tells us in his informative autobiography, he came top of his class at the Nazareth Seminary and as a result was sent to Russia to study. The five years he spent there had a seminal impact on him and introduced him to Russia's intellectual life and literature. He was enchanted by the works of Gogol, Turgenev, Dostoevsky, Tolstoy, Chekhov and Gorky, and lamented that Arab intellectuals were not more acquainted with their wonderful work.[52] In addition, his contemporary, the eminent critic Ismā'īl Adham (1911—40), elaborated the nature of the impact of Russian literature on Nu'aymah's work,[53] and demonstrated the awareness of the cultural movement at the time of the importance of this influence.

By the time he returned to Lebanon after he had completed his study in Russia, his two elder brothers had immigrated to the United States and settled in Walla Walla in Washington state. He soon followed them and continued his studies at the University of Washington (1912—16), from which he obtained two degrees in literature and law. Although he wrote all his work which falls within the period of this study in the United States, he did this under the spell of the Russian literature that he aspired to emulate. From his first story *"Sanatuhā al-Jadīdah"*, and throughout Nu'aymah's early work the influence of Russian literature is evident in both the structure and the choice of subjects and characters. The recognition of spiritual power as an active force in everyday life, a salient feature in the classics of Russian literature, is conspicuous in his stories. The sublimation of simple events and the unconscious deeds of simple people into acts of divine providence, another feature of Russian literature, governs the progression of Nu'aymah's narrative text.

Another effect of the Russian influence on Nu'aymah's work was his interest in probing the inner psyche of characters and elaborating the personal and social implications of their actions. Indeed, the main part of his stories is devoted to the exploration of the inner conflict of characters in Dostoevskyan fashion. This is clear in his first story, *"Sanatuhā al-Jadīdah"*,[54] in which the struggle of man against his unjust fate is interwoven with spiritual and psychological elements. The story presents its protagonist, Buṭrus al-Nāqūs, the head of his village community, in the prolonged moment of waiting for the birth of his eighth child. After seven successive girls he is desperately hoping for a boy to carry the family name and inherit the banners of his authority. The obsession with the son which made him try eight times gradually takes over in a well-orchestrated crescendo, blinding the protagonist to any human or parental feelings and leading him to kill the newborn daughter, by burying her alive in the pine forest. Afterwards he bribes the midwife to declare to the village on the following morning that the child was a stillborn boy.

In a truly Russian style, the story presents its protagonist in a sympathetic and understanding manner, for instead of simplistic indictment there is a sincere attempt to fathom his inner psyche and probe his motivations. He is presented as the descendant of a long history of adherence to village values and upholding of its tradition, and his family is singled out as the only family of the village that has refused to pay *jizyat Kūlumbūs* (Columbus tax),[55] a sign of its standing and nationalism. His desire for a boy is also seen not as a selfish quest for immortality, but as a social or even nationalist need to maintain the continuity of this tradition. The equation of the desired boy with the icon of Christ and the newborn girl with a stillborn boy reveals the inner logic of the action and fuses the fatalistic with the social. The birth of a boy is seen as another manifestation of the Saviour to save the protagonist spiritually as well as socially, and the setting of the action on the eve of the new year enhances this interpretation.

The second story, *"al-'Āqir"*[56] (The Barren), is a mature and well-structured work, but it suffers from the writer's desire to explain the obvious in advocating social justice, a corollary of the lack of narrative conventions. The action and characterization deliver the story's message in a more effective manner than that of the thinly disguised authorial remarks. It deals with an ideal couple, 'Azīz and Jamīlah, whose marriage was made in heaven and who started their life happily and lovingly, but when the years have gone by without Jamīlah's becoming pregnant, their life is spoilt by the interference of 'Azīz's mother and her attempt to get Jamīlah treated, first by doctors and then by quacks, but to no avail. Calmness and happiness disappear and the life of the couple turns into an inferno in which the true nature of both characters is revealed; 'Azīz as an insolent male chauvinist who puts all blame on her, and Jamīlah as a sensitive female who has sensed all along that her husband was the sterile one. When she can take no more abuse, she sleeps with another man and becomes pregnant, and this transforms both 'Azīz and his family, who suddenly bend over backwards to please her. Instead of being relieved, she cannot go through with the pregnancy and commits suicide, leaving a letter in which she explains everything to her husband.

Apart from this lengthy letter (one-quarter of the text) which brings to the story direct authorial comment and elements of sentimentality, the story is a remarkably mature piece of narrative in which the author substitutes showing for telling and narrative for description. He introduces his characters artistically and economically and makes full use of every detail in the introduction to motivate their action and elucidate their conduct. Although the action spans ten years, the story avoids any lengthy account of events by focusing on selected turning-points in its characters' development, leaving the action to speak for itself. This endows the text with a suggestive power of narrative and enables the story to transmit various messages. In addition to its criticism of established social mores and manners, it is mainly a powerful plea for the liberation of women and for reasonable and equal treatment of the two sexes. As in the previous story society places all the blame on women, often for no fault of their own, but, unlike it, this story places the blame on men and contrasts their cruel behaviour with the women's suffering.

Like Taymūr, Nu'aymah was driven by the feeling of the pioneer who had to plough as much virgin land as possible. Thus, he did not repeat any of his themes and endeavoured to explore a new theme and a new area of experience in every story. In *"al-Zakhīrah"*[57] (The Holy Relic) he mocks superstition and shows the dire consequences of the belief in the power of a talisman. He does so without any preaching and through the effective use of sarcasm and humour. This enables the story to sublimate this ordinary topic into the realm of the conflict between fantasy and reality, with the inevitable result of the character preferring the former to the latter.

In *"Sa'ādat al-Baik"*[58] (His Excellency the Bey) he demonstrates the impact of rapid social change and the misery of its victims. His treatment of this subject circumvents the pitfalls of sentimentality which encumbered the work of his predecessors by resorting to irony and comic presentation. He also uses the technique of mirroring the tribulations of the protagonist in another character who empathizes with him, but the sympathizing one is no less of a victim of the old social mores than the one of the title. The comic irony of the title character's behaviour is enhanced by the total acceptance by the owner of the restaurant of the protagonist's pretence.

In *"Shūrti"*[59] (The Short One) he uses one of the favourite techniques of the early narrative works, that of the diary, to record his experience during World War I as a soldier in the Allied forces. This enables him to resort to first-person narrative and to filter the war experience through the perception of a sensitive individual. Another story in which he uses first-person narrative is *"Sā'at al-Kūkū"*[60] (The Cuckoo Clock), but through resorting to the letter technique this time and not a diary. The letter seems an unlikely vehicle for such an elaborate narrative structure in which the narrative voice changes twice during the story, as does the narrative time. The story, nevertheless, is chronologically the last of the six stories in the collection, yet it is one of the least mature pieces, despite its important theme, or probably because of it.

The importance of its theme and its closeness to Nu'aymah's personal beliefs resulted in its use as a vehicle for many messages. Its first half is dedicated to the elaboration of the vital role of adherence to the motherland and rejecting the calls for forsaking it in order to achieve some material gain, while the second half, which ostensibly attempts to demonstrate the validity of the first, is mainly interested in the conflict between the city and the country, in the romantic variation of this theme encountered before in the work of Jibrān. But, because it tries to elevate the theme into a higher level in which the conflict between America and Lebanon intensifies the original one between the city and the country, it succeeds in disclosing the extent of the destructive impact of the expatriation on the country and on the life of those left behind. The story's attempt to deal with many themes is reflected in its crowded structure and its many turns of events, some of which are triggered by contrived coincidences. But this is always achieved in Nu'aymah's work without sacrificing close affinity with reality or infringing on the mimetic nature of the text.

Ḥaddād and the Stories of Expatriation

The theme of Nu'aymah's last story is in fact the best introduction to the work of Ḥaddād whose collection was appropriately entitled: *Ḥikāyāt al-Mahjar* (Tales of Expatriation, 1920). Ḥaddād, a Syrian from Ḥimṣ, was a colleague of Nu'aymah and 'Arīḍah[61] at the Nazareth Seminary in 1904, but he left after only one year at the Seminary and emigrated to New York where he soon established himself. In 1912 he founded his biweekly, *al-Sā'iḥ* (whose first issue appeared on 23 April 1912), and by 1920 it had become the organ of the newly formed *al-Rābiṭah al-Qalamiyyah*[62] (Literary Association), an influential literary group whose aims were the promotion of the new literary and artistic sensibility and the creation of a fresh current of ideas and literary concepts to facilitate the transition from the old to the new. Although Ḥaddād became the editor of the association's journal, he was not one of the makers of its beliefs and visions, but rather an enthusiastic follower who attempted to implement them.[63]

The formation of the Literary Association was in fact the culmination of the constant efforts of a group of intellectual expatriate Levantines to establish new forms of literary discourse, efforts which began with the publication of *al-Sā'iḥ* in 1912 and *al-Funūn* in 1913. Although the association was established in New York, Nu'aymah denied any influence of American literature on the group[64] and confirmed that the major literary influence on its writers, particularly those who wrote narrative, was Russian literature.[65] The main cultural influence on Ḥaddād was naturally Russian and although he published his collection long before Nu'aymah's, he was clearly influenced by him. He started writing his short stories at the same time as Nu'aymah, and published them in his journal as well as in other Levantine periodicals before collecting them in his only collection.

From the outset, Ḥaddād declared that his intention was to portray the life of Syrian expatriates as they knew and experienced it without any interference in the arrangements of facts and events, and to present "an exact copy of scenes from the life in expatriation".[66] Indeed, his works, which vary a great deal in length and structure, are generally marked by their photographic reflection of realistic or even naturalistic details. In an interview he admitted that all the characters and most of the events depicted in his collection reflected real people he had met in America and actual events he or others had experienced.[67] Although he had a clear concept of accurate and faithful representation, when it came to the literary term describing his stories he fluctuated between *ḥikāyah* (tale), which he used in his titles, and *qiṣṣah ṣaghīrah* (little story), which he uses in his introduction. It is clear that the former term preceded the latter, for this was the term used when he started serializing them in *al-Sā'iḥ*. By the time he prepared them to appear in book form several years later the term *qiṣṣah ṣaghīrah* and even *qiṣṣah qaṣīrah* (short story), had gained currency.

Ḥaddād's stories, though written concurrently with those of Nu'aymah, are more rudimentary and less sophisticated. They fluctuate between the humorous sketch and the summary of a longer narrative work, and none of them attain the artistic qualities of Nu'aymah's. However he published them in book form long before Nu'aymah, probably because of his position as editor of *al-Sā'iḥ,* and, as a result, played a significant role in influencing his contemporaries by their faithful representation of reality and their light sense of humour. Some of his stories deal with the problems which the Arab expatriate faces in his new life away from home; others are merely humorous sketches or vignettes of situations generated by the cultural gap between the expatriate's home culture and that of the new home. The main themes of his stories are the disparity between expectations and reality, and the hardship of life away from the protection of home. His expatriates experience difficult cultural adjustments particularly related to ethical values and the relationship between the sexes, and they nostalgically yearn for the world they left behind.

The conflict between the expatriate's old world and his new life is reflected in the minutest details.

> Riding donkeys to the river, strolling in the dusty and muddy valleys, and napping among the meadows in the afternoon away from the blazing sun is ... for the Syrian native sweeter than walking in Broadway with its streets crowded with cars, stores and shoppers, with passers-by looking around, fearing for their security and searching for the exit to take them safely away from the maddening crowd. The hut made of adobe and old thatch in the midst of vineyards is more satisfying than sleeping in a New York flat completely deprived of sunshine. Gazing from the window of a simple Syrian house into the limitless open space for miles with its meadows and rustic landscape is more beautiful than the Woolworth skyscraper with its fifty-eight stories. Wearing the Syrian attire which allows its wearer to sit cross-legged, recline or stretch relaxedly without feeling that there is always something pressing against his thighs and legs is much nicer than these horrid trousers.[68]

The raw photographic representation of reality is clearly reflected in his "*Ḥikāyat al-Amal wa-l-Alam*"[69] (Tale of Hope and Pain) which spans ten years of the life of a Syrian émigré and is highly representative of the rest of his collection. It depicts the life and tribulations of a simple Syrian, Abū-Ḥannā, who brought his wife and his newborn son, Ḥannā, to America, dreaming that he could sweep up buckets full of gold from its streets. Instead he leads a miserable existence, unable to support the steady stream of children his wife regularly produces. They take turns delivering them to the orphanage, claiming that they are orphans. The children receive an American upbringing and a decent education, while their parents continue to eke out a living. By the time the parents manage to regulate their lives and earn a sufficient income, the orphanages discover their trick and return their children, by then five, to live with them.

The arrival of the symbolically orphaned children disturbs the life of the couple and shatters the family's peace and the rest of their dream. Not only do the children put a tremendous strain on their budget, but they are also total strangers. They speak only English while their father can barely manage in this foreign tongue, and their habits and tastes are completely American. They criticize their parents' ways and tastes, demand a different diet and reject their father's favourite food. The mother accommodates them at the expense of her husband and life in their household becomes a domestic inferno, forcing Abū-Ḥannā to desert his home. The use of the orphanage trick serves a number of purposes, for while it ostensibly highlights the hardship of the parents and the difficulty of expatriation, it heightens the intensity of the cultural and generational gap. It also accentuates the expatriate's sense of alienation by making him foreign even in his own home and among his own children, and demonstrates that the children are, at least culturally, orphans.

The naming strategy in the piece also acts as a narrative device to widen its implication. The parents are both given names relating to that of their son, Ḥannā; hence, Abū-Ḥannā is the father of Ḥannā, and Umm-Ḥannā is the mother of Ḥannā. *Ḥannā,* the Arabic equivalent of *John,* stands in Levantine culture for any Christian, and the text's suppression of the actual names of the parents is a deliberate attempt to enhance the story's ability to sum up the problems of Syrian expatriates and make the Ḥannās stand for the expatriate family *par excellence*. By relating the whole family to the name of the son, and not of the father, as is the tradition in Arab culture, the story suggests that expatriation involves a denial of both the actual father and the fatherland; it is a symbolic act of patricide. This is reinforced at the end of the story by the banishment of the father and his return to the state of loss which he experienced after his arrival in America.

The story ends with Abū-Ḥannā wandering in the park where he meets a friend from his village back home, the same friend who put him up and helped him upon his arrival ten years ago. The circular structure also accentuates the state of loss and the lack of any real progress in the expatriate's position after ten years of suffering and tribulation. The importance of relating the suffering to the dreams in the title of the story is further enhanced by the circularity of the narrative. The dreams of the Syrian expatriates in Ḥaddād's stories reflect not so much their hardship in America as the life they have left behind. Most of his characters led a gloomy existence in their country of origin and their dreams are but the reflection of everything they lacked there. This was what made them attractive to the reading public in Syria and the rest of the Levant. The positive contribution of his work is that it does not idolize or romanticize the past, but treats this nostalgia with humour and sarcasm. His work is generally inferior to that of Nu'aymah, but it succeeded in extending the scope of the readership of narrative fiction both in the *mahjar* and at home.

The Brothers 'Īsā and Shiḥātah 'Ubaid

'Īsā 'Ubaid was a contemporary of Muḥammad Taymūr, but it is not known whether there was any significant contact between them.[70] Like Taymūr, he died prematurely in his twenties, and during his short but fecund literary life, tried his hand at drama, the novel, the short story, and literary criticism. Unlike Taymūr, his works have been neglected, and have remained so for many years. There was no interest in republishing[71] or posthumously publishing his writing and as a result many of his works have been lost;[72] therefore any assessment of his achievements must remain incomplete. Although his brother Shiḥātah 'Ubaid was also a short-story writer, and, indeed, published one collection during 'Īsā's lifetime, after 'Īsā's death, he chose self-exile in a simple job in Cairo and cut himself off from a deaf society, which was unwilling at this early stage of its development to show appreciation for this pioneering man of letters.

There is also evidence to suggest that the 'Ubaids, the sons of a Syrian emigrant family, were not as comfortably off as the Taymūrs; hence, unlike Maḥmūd Taymūr, who posthumously published the collected works of his brother in three sizeable volumes,[73] Shiḥātah was unable to do homage to his brother in the same manner. It was Yahḥyā Ḥaqqi who discovered 'Īsā 'Ubaid and his brother and introduced their work to literary circles at the beginning of the 1960s, and called for their reconsideration.[74] Since then his two published collections and his brother's one have been reprinted, and a few articles about their work have appeared. Although it is not known if 'Īsā was the older or the younger of the two brothers, he was obviously the more prolific of the two.[75] He was also both more talented and more intellectual than his brother, and so Shiḥātah seems to have been very much under the influence of 'Īsā to the extent that his literary world is like an extension of his brother's, although he was not without talent or distinction himself. It seems also that 'Īsā was Shiḥātah's major source of inspiration, for after his premature death, Shiḥātah gave up writing and abandoned literary life altogether.

'Īsā published two collections of short stories, *Iḥsān Hānim* (Her Ladyship Ihsan, 1921) and *Thurayyā* (1922), and Shiḥātah published only one, *Dars Mu'lim* (A Hard Lesson, 1922). Both of them prefaced their books with lengthy, elaborate introductions, in which they stated the need for a new form of literature. They were relatively unknown to the literary and public life of that period,[76] and, apart from a few pieces, they did not publish their short stories first in periodicals and newspapers, as most of their predecessors and contemporaries had done. 'Īsā published one or two articles in *al-Sufūr,*[77] but there is no evidence that either he or his brother had close connections with the wide group of young writers gathered round *al-Sufūr.*

However, this relative isolation did not mean that they were uninvolved in the central issues of nationalist activities at that time. Their comparative lack of direct and intensive involvement in public affairs was compensated for by their putting praise for Sa'd Zaghlūl and the 1919 revolution into their characters' mouths.[78] Regardless of the limitations imposed by the dictates of their art, they did not hesitate to call for the independence of Egypt in their short stories. Furthermore, 'Īsā prefaced his first collection with an unusually lengthy dedication of this, his literary debut, to Sa'd Zaghlūl, in which he clearly linked the new literature with the patriotic awakening and the growing national aspirations.[79] The brand of nationalism prevalent in their writing is marked by its rational outlook and its emphasis on the bonds of nationhood transcending any tribal or sectarian connections. It is a nationalism permeated with liberal and progressive sentiments and sees literature as a means of shaping and articulating national identity.

From the dedication of his first collection, and from the careful and detailed introductions to his two collections, it is obvious that he attached much importance to the organic connection and close interaction between the movement for the independence of the country and the crystallization of its national art, the shaping of a distinctive national identity and the creation of the characteristic traits of Egyptian literature. He strongly believed that "renaissance usually comes in the wake of revolution and as its natural consequence. The spirit of renaissance shall penetrate every aspect of our political, social and literary life".[80]

In *"Kalimah 'an al-Fann wa-l-Adab al-Ḥadīth fi Miṣr"*[81] (A Word on Modern Art and Literature in Egypt), in his introduction to his first collection, 'Īsā 'Ubaid endeavoured to make himself the herald of this coming renaissance in literature and started preaching it. He carefully and minutely depicted and analysed the defects and shortcomings of the newborn Arabic narrative. He summed up the most fatal of these shortcomings as follows:

> Apart from the lack of creative imagination, inadequate observation, and the absence of analysis, there is the weakness of description and illustrative ability. The description of the setting from which the characters emerge is one of the most important requirements of fictional art, because it has a tremendous effect on forming their characteristics and feelings. Furthermore, the vivid narrative and the use of accurate realistic description have a strong impact on the reader, for they convince him of the truthfulness of the story and of its relevance to real life.[82]

In his summary of the shortcomings of Arabic fiction, 'Īsā 'Ubaid not only put his finger on the essential defects of that new literary genre at the time, but also revealed a clear and strikingly mature understanding of the art of fiction. His brief reference to the lack of creative imagination is directly followed by his remark on insufficient observation, to cancel any misunderstanding of his references to imagination. He clearly links imagination with reality and criticizes al-Manfalūṭi for associating imagination with idealism and sentimentality.[83] He believed that the tendency to idealize reality would impede the development of new literature,[84] and he therefore called upon his fellow writers to eschew these faults and to establish the literature of the future on a solid "basis of accurate observation and profound understanding of the psychological aspects of the character which describes life as it is, without any exaggeration or diminution: life in its absolute and naked truth, for this is the essence of *madhhab al-ḥaqā'iq:* realism".[85]

But the striking element in his account of the shortcomings of modern Arabic narrative was his conception of description — which he sometimes calls *al-waṣf* (description) and often *al-taṣwīr* (depiction or illustration) — that is to say, narrative. He sees it as a technique of both presentation and characterization, for it is the writer's means of achieving a convincing verisimilitude and sustaining the reader's interest. It is also the tool by which the writer creates characters and integrates them socially, culturally and psychologically, into the appropriate setting at the same time. This complete and multidimensional integration of characters cannot be attained, in 'Īsā's view, without a reasonable command of psychology in general and psychoanalysis in particular.[86] He therefore urged creative writers to acquire a greater knowledge of psychology to enable them to fathom the innermost depths of human character.[87]

This mature understanding of both the function of description and the importance of appreciation of the character's psyche is blended with a touch of naturalism. He prevails on his fellow writers to investigate the influence of heredity upon the origin and behaviour of their characters, and to analyse the factors in the characters' environment which contribute to the formation of their problems. Although he uses the word *realism* in its Arabic transliterated form as an equivalent of his *madhhab al-ḥaqā'iq,* indicating that the Arabic term he uses is a translation of the Western concept of literary realism, his explanation or understanding of the term is closer to naturalism than realism. This amalgam of naturalistic and realistic elements which went into the making of 'Ubaid's *madhhab al-ḥaqā'iq* continued to colour the Arabic concept of realism for many years to come.

As for the artistic tools which enable the writer to eschew these shortcomings and to come closer to reality and to a deeper comprehension of character, he thought that the "narrative discourse has no limitation: no special style or general rules. It embraces all styles and tools, as long as it sticks to reality, accurate observation, and psychoanalysis ... it can use the form of epistles ..., of diaries, confessions, or dialogues".[88] All these forms and others were suitable for telling a story as long as they were used with the right approach and aided with sufficient knowledge and experience of both the subject and, more important, the character. For the writer's task, according to 'Īsā's concept of art, was neither to describe imaginary nature, nor to embellish reality. Yet his repeated emphasis on a deeper understanding of the characters' motivation and background stopped him short of adopting a simple photographic or naturalistic reproduction of reality.[89]

In his introduction, 'Īsā 'Ubaid also discusses in depth, for the first time in modern Arabic literature, the artistic questions concerning the language of fiction, and touched upon various aesthetic aspects of narrative discourse.[90] He advocated an artistic language which was both effective and suggestive, a language capable of sustaining more than one level of meaning, yet still faithful to truth and reality.[91] He also discussed the language of dialogues from the point of view of the realist, and criticized Muḥammad Taymūr's solution in this respect.[92] He admitted that requirements of *realism* dictated the use of the vernacular, but he did not want Egyptian literature to sever its bonds with standard Arabic language and literature, and therefore suggested a compromise: writing the dialogue in a simple *fuṣḥā* amalgamated, when necessary, with some colloquial words and coloured with an identifiable local or parochial touch. Through this compromise, narrative discourse could achieve the required verisimilitude without sacrificing its role in serving Arabic language or abandoning its links with both tradition and a rich literary heritage; by maintaining this balance he could participate in creating modern Arabic literature capable of expressing a distinctive national character.[93]

Echoes of all these ideas are found in Shiḥātah's introduction to his only collection, in which he almost repeated many of his brother's views. For he called for the adoption of realistic representation,[94] and criticized the idealization of both nature and reality.[95] He also emphasized the need for detailed study of a character and deep exploration of the psyche,[96] and did not forget to mention the significance of heredity and its influence on a character's idiosyncrasies.[97] Like 'Īsā, he focused his attention on character rather than action and considered it the cornerstone of any work of fiction.[98] He also reiterated the importance of creating new literature, and stressed the interaction between modern genres of narrative discourse and the growing awareness of the specific characteristics of the emergent national identity. He echoed many of 'Īsā's ideas on narrative techniques and on the vital role of a reasonable knowledge of psychoanalysis for developing convincing characterization.

The ideas which both 'Īsā and Shiḥātah 'Ubaid introduce to Arabic literature give the reader some insight into their culture and artistic orientation. It is clear that they were strongly influenced by French literature.[99] This is apparent not only because they mention Balzac, Karr,

Flaubert, the Goncourts, Daudet, Zola, Maupassant, and Rolland in their introductions and allude to French literary schools, such as romanticism, realism, and idealism,[100] but also from their treatment of concepts of artistic truth and their emphasis on the need for accurate exploration of the characters' environment, on the vitality of verisimilitude, and on the importance of vivid description. Their treatment of these artistic and aesthetic concepts is an amalgam of realistic and naturalistic ideas side by side with fragments from Taine's theory of literary criticism and his ideas about the effect of environment on character. They also manifest a fair knowledge of psychology in general and psychoanalysis in particular, alluding to the role of the subconscious in various neuroses.

Real People in Plausible Situations

But whatever the origin of their ideas may be, they present a radical change in literary thinking and introduce a new approach to creative literature: an approach based on knowledge, study and considerable experience of the subject and character. Armed with this new approach to literature and with this reasonably coherent blend of cultural ideas, 'Īsā and Shiḥātah 'Ubaid attempted to express the anxieties and aspirations of the "Egyptian character" in this early stage of its modern history. Even such fine and intelligent theorists as these would have required tremendous artistic ingenuity to realize all these ambitious ideas without any real previous tradition in the field. For when it came to practice, their work was more or less "a mere exercise in preconceived concepts"[101] which restricted the freedom of the writers and affected the vitality of their writing.

They became prisoners of the principles which they themselves had established, even putting some of their theoretical convictions into the mouths of their fictional characters, or inserting them into the narrative regardless of their appropriateness.[102] Even they could not avoid the pitfalls of the very artistic and aesthetic defects which they had so severely criticized. Nevertheless, their works are a great step forward in the formation of a coherent and mature indigenous short story, and their writings are distinguished by their racy descriptions and coherent, simple narrative. They were sensitive to the significance of that gradual progression of action in the short story which Kenneth Burke has called syllogistic progression.[103] They cleverly turned their weakness in the language and traditions of classical Arabic into an advantage by using simple *fuṣḥā* embellished with the *shawām*[104] (Levantine) dialect, giving their style a singular linguistic character.

They were aware, in theory and practice, more than any of their predecessors, of the role of characterization in narrative discourse and the significance of analytical and contemplative elements. In addition, their perception of the interrelationship between the emergence of a distinctive national identity and the genesis of new indigenous modes of discourse enabled them to widen the scope of the themes which the Arabic short story had treated. This was closely linked to their endeavour to push the structural framework of the short story through stages of progressively greater coherence and maturity and so enable it to surpass the limitations of the narrative sketch. With their choice of themes they broke new ground, not only by dealing with some aspects of Egyptian rural life,[105] but also through their treatment of new issues in the life of the urban middle class. They were particularly fond of depicting the rituals of family life and the customs which lingered on but were soon to fade away.

Their stories were unprecedented in their attempt to illustrate authentic relationships between the two sexes and explore the hidden world of Egyptian family life in general and among Christians in particular.[106] Their stories were also the first to reveal different dimensions of the daily life of middle-class women in Egypt, and to touch upon various aspects of female emancipation, a theme which proved to be popular among the succeeding short-story writers. For, before them, women were presented in narrative texts through the eyes of their men, and were not allowed to speak for themselves and express their own views and feelings including their own views of men's behaviour and attitudes. They were keen to present real people in credible situations, and allow their characters to speak for themselves and present the situation as they experienced it. In this respect, as well as in many others, 'Īsā and Shiḥātah 'Ubaid were remarkable innovators whose works merit close and detailed consideration.

Their central theme is the incompatibility of the partners of marriages which take place in a closed social atmosphere, of arranged marriages in particular, and the grave consequences of such marriages on the coherence of the Egyptian family,[107] a subject which was also treated by their contemporary Ḥasan Maḥmūd. In their treatment of this theme, they were the heralds of women's emancipation in Arabic literature, for the women in their stories are much more cultured, sensitive and sensible than the men. They attract the largest share of the readers' sympathy, but they are far from being simply modern versions of Nadīm's ill-treated women who patiently endure the brutality of their drunken and drug-addicted husbands. The 'Ubaids' female characters are portrayed as victims of antiquated convention, and are, in a certain sense, ahead of their time. Their selection of educated women as heroines provided them with an opportunity to demonstrate how the education of women had changed their perception of themselves and their role in a society which was still operating according to the old roles and customs of the era before female education.

Their female characters are sensitive and perceptive, yet trapped rather than liberated by their knowledge and vision, and so find solace in reading poetry and fiction. In fact, one of them criticizes Haykal's novel *Zaynab* as sentimental and unrealistic, because the heroine's feelings, even given that they are exaggerated, are incompatible with the cultural and social level of the character.[108] Another is fond of the music of Sayyid

Darwīsh on purely aesthetic grounds, and plays works by European composers on the piano,[109] while the others, as the heroines of *"al-Bā'inah"*[110] (Dowry), *"Ma'sāt Qarawiyyah"*[111] (A Tragedy of a Village Woman) and *"Mudhakkirāt Ḥikmat Hānim"*,[112] long to overcome their monotonous lives and to rise above their unsatisfactory surroundings. In general, the women in their stories are faithful to their husbands and sincere in their feelings, in contrast to their mendacious husbands, as in *"al-Ikhlāṣ"*[113] (Sincerity), *"Maw'id Gharām"*,[114] (Love Appointment) and *"Iḥsān Hānim"*.

Nevertheless, there are some unfaithful wives, as in *"al-Ghīrah"*[115] (Jealousy), *"al-Naẓ'ah al-Nisā'iyyah"*[116] (Feminine Nature) and *"al-Bā'inah"*, but the authors justify their behaviour in a manner which puts the largest share of blame on their men, and suggest that they commit their adulteries in mitigating circumstances.[117] For their men not only treat them badly and see them as sex objects, but the men are also lacking in sensitivity and are culturally inferior. Indeed, the men commit adultery and indulge in a life of sin without the slightest feeling of remorse,[118] and therefore command less respect, in the 'Ubaids' world. However, the contrast between the portraits of the men and women in the 'Ubaids' works serves to accentuate further the virtues of their female characters. Some variations on these gracious female characters were to appear in Ḥasan Maḥmūd's short stories, such as *"Ḥayāt al-Zahr"*[119] (The Life of Flowers), *"Khārij al-Insāniyyah"*[120] (Outside Humanity), and *"al-Zawjah al-Āthimah"*[121] (the Sinful Wife).

'Īsā and Shiḥātah 'Ubaid were the first to introduce themes of sex and sexual relations into the modern Arabic short story, and use them as a dynamic means of characterization on the one hand, and as a focal point for their study of human personality on the other. Sex in their stories is not in any way an instrument of titillation, but a means of discovery about human nature and an expression of an attitude towards both the character and the world: a manifestation of temperaments and sensual desires which often defy the individual's rational ability to control them (*"al-Bā'inah"* and *"Ma'sāt Qarawiyyah'*). It is also an integral part of their call for closer ties with reality, though they sometimes express it in a crudely symbolic manner.[122]

In their treatment of this theme, they present the reader with the most coherent illustration of the criteria of female beauty in Egypt during the early decades of this century, not only through the way their characters appreciate female beauty, but also through their own depiction of women. It was a more or less feudal set of standards, which placed the fairest-skinned, plumpest woman with fair silky hair in the highest place, a woman to be owned and enjoyed rather than a companion with whom to share one's life (*"Iḥsān Hānim"* and *"Mudhakkirāt Ḥikmat Hānim"*). However, neither of the 'Ubaid brothers[123] appears to have felt that this ideal woman, so obviously not the common Egyptian woman, contradicts in any way their call for Egyptianization, realism, female emancipation, or nationalism.

Seen from a purely Egyptian perspective, this ideal of female beauty is not only out of step with these writers' enlightened liberal ideas, not only in contrast to the views expressed by their women characters and the aspirations of these women, but it also runs counter to the nationalistic sentiments expressed in their stories and their adulation of the country's natural and historical glory. It conforms to the class hierarchy in which the well-fed, fair-skinned Turco-Circassian women were the women of the ruling cliques, in marked contrast to the dark and slender Egyptian peasant. But, seen from a Syrian perspective, it may be taken as a reflection of their Levantine background, and as a realistic description of the women they actually knew in their social surroundings. Taking into consideration other social details, we may see that their female ideal is a result of their adherence to the portrayal of what they knew and experienced in order to enhance their realistic presentation.

Literary Symbols and a Sense of Structure

With the exception of Ḥasan Maḥmūd's short story *"Bint al-Mā'"*[124] in which he used fine symbolism in his portrayal of unrequited love and its attendant suffering, Shiḥātah 'Ubaid's *"Bayn Ghazālatayn"* (Between Two Gazelles),[125] is the first, and only, mature attempt at allegory in modern Arabic narrative. This short story treats polygamy by studying the behaviour of two gazelles in the private garden of a lonely, eccentric, rich man. Like Ḥasan Maḥmūd's, his allegory is too direct, his allusions are too obvious, and, hence, its artistic merits sink under the ponderous explanations and repetition by which he intends to make sure that the story's message is delivered. His brother, 'Īsā, was also the first Arab short story writer to "use an external symbol to reinforce the action and widen the scope of its implications".[126]

The technique of using a parallel symbolic action to illustrate certain aspects of the main action and adumbrate coming events is not only a valuable contribution to the artistic development of the Arabic narrative at the time, but also a clear demonstration of a reasonably sophisticated awareness of the technique of constructing a modern literary work. The striking feature of 'Īsā 'Ubaid's use of this external symbol is that the author controls his symbol, integrates it into both the main action and the setting, and employs it in a realistic manner. *"Ma'sāt Qarawiyyah"*,[127] the story in which he uses this technical device, is, in general, a revealing and interesting story: it is the first modern Arabic story to be set entirely in a rural atmosphere and it presents a view of women different from the one portrayed in most of the urban-based stories of the 'Ubaid brothers.

The story is composed of eight sections: in the first, the writer introduces the background of his story in a manner which intends to capture the rhythm of life in the village. This scene which depicts the village waking up shortly after dawn is a remarkable allusion to the forthcoming tragedy which progresses beneath the calm surface of events. In this scene the author introduces, in a deliberately casual manner, the crows and the kites which will participate in the future development of the action. The people, the birds, the water-wheel, the trees and the landscape form the canvas upon which the artist develops his theme, for they are not a mere background to the action, but somehow participate in its progression. Halfway through this first section, the reader is introduced to the village *imām*, or religious leader, and hears his interpretation of the disaster inflicted on the peasants by the cotton-worm. During the *imām*'s talk with the peasants the reader gains an insight into the family background of the protagonist, Muḥammad, the present state of his mind, and his economic situation. Before this section comes to a close, the author drops a hint about the antagonist which both arouses the reader's interest and prepares for a smooth transition to the second section.

Although the second section seems, at first glance, to be an immediate continuation of the first, it takes place a few months later, during which period the cotton has matured and become ready for harvesting and the seeds sown in the first section start to bear fruit. This section gives more details about the antagonist and introduces the heroine, Fāṭimah, a beautiful peasant girl who was in love with her cousin Muḥammad, and whose heart is now turning to Fakhri, the antagonist, the son of the feudal landlord. It also intimates that the change in her emotions has coincided with the economic misfortunes of Muḥammad, who has lost his cotton harvest to the cotton-worm, and with it his hope of being able to ask for his cousin's hand.

The third section is entirely devoted to Fakhri's background and his role in directing Fāṭimah's attention away from her cousin. As the first section provides the reader with an insight into Muḥammad's family background through a brief reference to the fact that his father had been executed for murdering a villager in revenge, so this section reinforces notions of the effect of heredity and environment on the character by alluding to the adulteries of the feudal landlord's promiscuous wife. In addition, Fakhri is an urbanized young man whose life in Cairo has provided him with experience in handling women and contaminated his feelings and attitudes towards them, making him ruthless and lustful. This creates an element of contrast and similarity in the action, for he and Fāṭimah are driven towards each other by completely different motives, but deep down their motives share certain selfish qualities. His interest in her is purely sensual, while she is innocently and hopelessly in love with him.

Sections four and five accentuate the elements of contrast while advancing the action; the former is devoted to an analysis of Fakhri's psyche and the origin of his carnal attitude towards women, and the latter concentrates on Fāṭimah's feelings and the conflict between her old emotions towards her cousin and the new overwhelming attraction to Fakhri. It also situates this conflict at night to link it to the fearful aspects of nature and darkness: towards the end of section five Muḥammad appears in the dark, unable to sleep, and this view of him seems to suggest that he is receding from her sphere of interest, adumbrates certain elements of suffering and darkness, and prepares for a smooth transition to the following section.

In the sixth section, the confrontation between Muḥammad and Fāṭimah takes place, in a manner which confirms his doubts and substantiates the village's whispering about her relationship with Fakhri. It also develops the action further by solving Fāṭimah's internal conflict; this in turn releases her from hesitation and adumbrates a further development in her relationship with Fakhri, who has left the village for Cairo. His absence inflames Fāṭimah's emotions and arouses her jealousy, especially since he has told her about Cairo's voluptuous women and his previous adventures with them. So, when Fakhri returns, in the seventh section, he finds Fāṭimah inflamed with jealousy on his behalf and no longer involved with Muḥammad. As an experienced womanizer, he feels that the moment has come to strike, and as soon as he starts his attack, she willingly surrenders. Here, 'Īsā 'Ubaid introduces his parallel symbolic action, both to suggest that intercourse took place and to comment on the action. When they start kissing in the field, he moves smoothly to depict a kite preying on a small chick which it takes to a mulberry tree and devours under the eyes of the anxious crow. The chick continues to cry out while the crow watches in rage and impotence, until the kite has devoured its prey, given the crow a contemptuous look, and flown away.

But Fakhri is not as lucky as the kite, for while he is having his way with Fāṭimah in the field, the final section of the story explores Muḥammad's feelings and thoughts since he has realized the changes in Fāṭimah's emotions. His thoughts lead him to believe that Fakhri is the major cause of his unhappiness, so he goes home, picks up his rifle and returns to the field. There he confronts Fakhri and shoots and wounds him. The shooting brings Fāṭimah's family to the field and the scene that confronts them suggests to both Fāṭimah's father and elder brother that Muḥammad's conduct is a respectable deed that avenges their injured honour. So her brother, who does not want to look less manly or courageous than his cousin, suggests that Fāṭimah must be killed. Complying with the time-honoured village conventions, the father gives Muḥammad, as her suitor, the final word in the matter, and he spontaneously approves his cousin's idea. A few days later the police recover the mutilated body of a young woman from the river and are unable to identify her, while the reader is told that Fakhri's wound was not fatal, and the whole episode did not affect him very much.

This story, dated November 1918, is the first Arabic short story to manifest a clear sense of structure and an awareness both of the syllogistic progression of the action and the careful development of the characters. It is also the most successful attempt to put the ideas and theoretical framework laid out in the 'Ubaids' introductions into practice, with minimum affectation. It manages to integrate not only the setting, but also the comments about heredity into the action in a functional and natural manner. It displays a remarkable ability to motivate the characters and to integrate their incentives into the action, for although it mentions certain elements which strengthen the characters' motivations indirectly, it carefully eschews the introduction of any substantial impulse which is not evidently linked to the main action.

Even in the case of the cotton disaster and the gloomy atmosphere which hangs over Muḥammad's business, it succeeds in employing the cotton as a time marker, a setting, an important crop, a whole world of associations which envelops various dimensions of the action and generates the story's internal memory and time structure. As for the relationship with reality, the story shows a mature understanding of this question, for it not only illustrates reality in a plausible manner, but also employs certain aspects of the realistic scene in a symbolic fashion in order to widen the implications of the action. It is also noteworthy for its balanced use of the author's knowledge of psychology to substantiate the characterization and develop a more convincing interaction among the characters.

In other stories, 'Īsā and Shiḥātah 'Ubaid tried, often in a deliberate or even pretentious way, to employ their knowledge of psychology in the interests of their stories, but their remarks on the psychology of the characters and their pseudo-psychoanalysis of them rise to the surface of the works[128] to suggest a conscious, sometimes exhibitionist, effort to attract attention to their writings by the use of such jargon.[129] In some instances, they interrupt the narrative with notes on the importance of psychoanalysis and its vital role in unveiling the inner motives of the character.[130] However, 'Īsā, and on some occasions Shiḥātah, links his remarks to a basic notion which penetrates his stories and gives them a certain element of depth and plausibility: this is his notion that for each gain, either material or moral, characters attain there is a proportional loss elsewhere, as if there were a delicate cosmic balance controlling the interaction between loss and gain. Hence the conflict in their stories involves, at one level of interpretation, an endeavour to restore this critical balance between loss and gain.

The heroine of *"Anā Lak"*[131] sacrifices her image of the ideal man she wants to marry in order to secure her shaky future and to obtain a husband before it is too late. Ḥikmat the heroine of *"Mudhakkirāt Ḥikmat Hānim"* sacrifices her happiness to relieve her mother from worry and anxiety. The Levantine emigrant family in *"al-Bā'inah"* attain the wealth they need in order to secure a large dowry and a respectable marriage for their daughter, but through this the daughter loses her honour because of the project which brought them the money — the bar.[132] However, this idea of balance, of compensation, in 'Īsā's and Shiḥātah's works does not give philosophical or intellectual depth to them, for it seems on several occasions to be no more than a device to accentuate the irony and conflict rather than a cosmic view penetrating the action and adding an element of absurdity to the situation.

Yet its consistency throughout various stories may suggest an abortive endeavour to create this philosophical perspective, which fails because of the incoherence of the overall artistic treatment. Although their general understanding of the limitations and principles of the art of fiction was far ahead of that of any of their predecessors and contemporaries, they often failed to appreciate the subtle differences between the structure of the short story and that of longer narrative genres. Indeed, some of their works[133] appear to be synopses of novels rather than balanced, structured short stories.[134] This is perhaps due to their attempt to include too many issues in one work and to use the story both as a vehicle to deliver ideas and information and as a means of conveying human and artistic experience.

An obvious example of this is their endeavour to use their stories to express their patriotic views and sentiments; thus, 'Īsā devoted a great deal of "*Mudhakkirāt Ḥikmat Hānim*" to the glorification of the 1919 revolution through an enthusiastic account of its events. Shiḥātah also illustrates in "*al-Ṣalāh*"[135] (Prayer) the vigour of the patriotic urge, and how it inspired both the artist and the audience.[136] Nevertheless, they were very much aware of the importance of convincing characterization, and succeeded in going beyond the two-dimensional characters which their predecessors had created. They also succeeded in developing certain technical devices previously unknown in Arabic narrative and in promoting a fresh current of interesting ideas relevant to the development of narrative discourse.

Unlike Muḥammad Taymūr, who used description as mere padding, they were aware that description was an integral part of both the characterization and the progression of the action. Accordingly, they linked the descriptive details to the emotional state of the character and the general mood of the action in order to create a certain degree of unity of impression. They also developed the technique of using realistic details in a symbolic and suggestive manner, and attempted to solve the artistic problems concerning the language of fiction in general and that of the dialogue in particular. 'Īsā had a strong influence on his brother, and although some critics suggest that Shiḥātah's works are, artistically, even more coherent than 'Īsā's,[137] it is difficult to substantiate this view.

Al-Sayyid: The Return to Russian Literary Influence

The pendulum which started with French literary influence on Taymūr swung to the Russian end of the spectrum with Nu'aymah, returned to the French with the 'Ubaids, and went back again to Russian literary influence with the arrival of the Iraqi writer Maḥmūd Aḥmad al-Sayyid,[138] the most talented Iraqi writer of his generation. He was strongly influenced by Russian literature and critical of those who departed from the faithful representation of their social reality.[139] He had read many of the Western narrative texts, particularly Russian texts in their Turkish translation, and had translated some from Turkish translations into Arabic. In 1925 he published an abridged version of Tolstoy's *Resurrection*,[140] and praised the realism of the great Russian writers such as Gogol, Turgenev, Dostoevsky, Tolstoy, Chekhov, Gorky and Artzybashev, claiming that adopting their method was the only way forward for Iraqi literature.[141]

He explained that what fascinated him and many writers of his generation in Russian literature was that in it they found characters akin to themselves, feelings and aspirations they experienced, and social situations similar to their own. But the most compelling characteristic of this literature was its preoccupation with the quest for freedom and an active desire to destroy corrupt and decaying conventions; its call for radical changes in society. In addition, he noted that Russian and other oriental literatures suited the Arab temperament and were close to Arab taste and psyche.[142] "Unlike the stories of feeble imagination, implausible coincidences, excessive sentimentality and false feelings ... Russian literature is concerned with the life of the people and presents it in realistic manner to demonstrate its strength and expose its weakness so that reformers know where to direct their efforts. I therefore call upon our writers to write this type of narrative".[143]

Al-Sayyid was also one of the most widely read of his fellow writers and followed closely the literary development of his contemporaries, particularly those in Egypt. The Taymūrs, particularly Maḥmūd, to whom he dedicated a number of his stories, Qāsim Amīn, Ṭaha Ḥusain, Salāmah Mūsā, 'Abbās Maḥmūd al-'Aqqād and Shibli Shumayyil were the the greatest influences on his literary career. He was aware of the narrative endeavour of the Taymūrs in particular and aspired to reproduce it in Iraq. He also knew of al-'Aqqād and al-Māzini's attack on al-Manfalūṭi and the literature of sentimentality. His attack on sentimentality and his emphasis on the close affinity between narrative and reality and its usefulness in the battle for reform may have been motivated by the desire to clear the reputation of narrative fiction in Iraq. For in the early days of Iraqi narrative, a fierce campaign was waged against narrative fiction, accusing the writers in highly emotive language of propagating immorality and sin.[144]

When al-Sayyid published his early stories which subsequently appeared in his first collection, *al-Nakabāt* (Disasters, 1922), he failed to avoid the pitfalls of sentimentality and packed his stories with unexpected events. He used them to catalogue his travels to Turkey (*"Ṣaḥīfah Sawdā' fi Tārīkh Aswad"*[145] [A Black Page from a Gloomy History]), India,[146] and France (*"al-Ṣu'ūd al-Hā'il"*[147] [the Great Ascent]), and generally to give vent to his sense of disillusionment and his frustrated desire to rebel against corrupt and unjust social conditions.[148] The stories of this first collection were obviously written before his proper acquaintance with Russian literature. They are more summaries of longer works than proper short stories, and they suffer from authorial intervention, particularly in *"Nāṣiḥ al-Qawm"*[149] (The People's Adviser), in which this intrusion becomes intolerable and ruins the story. It turns the story into a series of cautions and suggestions reminiscent of the early attempts of the genre.

Yet, despite their rudimentary nature, these stories are of great significance for the genesis of the new narrative discourse in Iraq. They introduce readers to the major themes of the genre and related narrative fiction to their major concerns. They deal with the main themes of the embryonic stage of narrative discourse, particularly that of alcoholism and its impact on family life as in *"Abṭāl al-Khamrah"*[150] (The Heroes of Alcohol), in a manner reminiscent of Nadīm's work. But they also introduce other themes such that of the self-appointed reformer who tries to change society and succeeds only in complicating his own situation, as in *"Nāṣiḥ al-Qawm"*[151] and *"Saṭrān min Ḥikāyah"*[152] (A Couple of Lines from the Tale). These stories are partially saved by their sense of humour and irony.

In the year following the publication of this collection, al-Sayyid stopped writing narrative in objection to the sloppy and unrealistic style of narrative that prevailed at that time, and also to enhance his literary status by writing more respectable essays. Narrative discourse had still not been integrated into literary life, and lacked respectability. This was a time in which Haykal, operating in the more open and culturally prosperous Egypt, had refrained only ten years before from using his own name on the title-page of his novel *Zaynab,* fearing that this might jeopardize his literary and political career. The literary essay was a highly respectable form, and al-Sayyid resorted to this form to express his ideas. If one's judgement of al-Sayyid were based only on the first collection, he would not have deserved special attention in a study on the genesis of narrative discourse. But luckily, five years later, he returned to writing narrative and published a long narrative work (*Jalāl Khālid,* 1928) and two more collections of short stories: *al-Ṭalā'i'* (Trendsetters, 1929) and *Fi Sā' min al-Zaman* (Once Upon a Time, 1935).

In a letter to his friend Maḥmūd al-'Abṭah, about his second collection *al-Ṭalā'i',* he states:

> These narrative pieces are merely *trendsetters* and a vanguard for the Iraqi realistic narrative literature which I intend to establish. I am on the horns of a dilemma, torn between hope and despair, because I am aware of the insurmountable obstacles, and most of all of the absence of social and intellectual freedom and the scarcity of readers.[153]

Here one sees the maturity of al-Sayyid's critical idiom, for he uses more accurate and precise literary terms such as *adab qaṣaṣi wāqi'i* (realistic narrative literature) than those used by the 'Ubaids, for example. He even became much more careful with the use of the term *qiṣṣah* (narrative) after his wide reading of Russian literature and was content to describe his work in the last two collections with the more modest term, *ṣuwar 'irāqiyyah* (Iraqi vignettes).

Yet, one of the leading literary magazines of the time, *al-Ḥadīth,* describes his story, *"Inqilāb"*[154] (Transformation), as "an accomplished Iraqi short story written in the vein of Russian narrative with its analytical and realistic representation, in which the author depicts a real slice of the domestic life of the Baghdadi family".[155] In another story, *"Sakrān"*[156] (Drunk), al-Sayyid himself refers in its introductory remark to writing it under the influence of Russian literature and to his attempt to replicate in it the work of Chekhov and Tolstoy.[157] In his admirable study of the Iraqi narrative, 'Abd al-Ilāh Aḥmad identifies three major influences on al-Sayyid's work in his second phase: Russian literature, Turkish narrative with its humour and biting social criticism, and the early work of the Egyptian writer Maḥmūd Taymūr[158] with his realistic characterization and concern for the life of the poor.[159]

The stories of his second, *al-Ṭalā'i',* and third, *Fi Sā' min al-Zaman,* collections have common themes and modes of narrative presentation. In his third collection, he included four stories from his second, rewriting three of them and changing their titles,[160] and republishing a fourth one without any modifications.[161] There are also six other stories which he published in various periodicals but refrained from including in his two collections. The exclusion is in itself a sign of discrimination and application of artistic criteria in compiling the collections.[162] The rewriting of a number of his stories, as well as a section from his long narrative work *Jalāl Khālid* in short-story form,[163] was indicative of his awareness of the need to improve his narrative discourse and to purge it of direct photographic rendering, sentimentality and authorial intrusion.

In two of these stories[164] the process of rewriting reveals his recognition of the significance of the temporal arrangement of his narrative and the restructuring of the action. In the second version he abandons the consecutive order of events and resorts to the technique of flashback in order to contrast the past with the present and dispose of unnecessary commentary. But, because a number of these stories have strong autobiographical elements in them, it was difficult to purge them completely of any direct authorial intrusion. This is obviously so because of al-Sayyid's desire to use his narrative as a vehicle for other reformative or patriotic messages. Like the 'Ubaids, he was keen on airing his nationalist sentiments against the Turkish and the British. His longer narrative text, *Jalāl Khālid,* deals entirely with the Iraqi patriotic question, while *"al-Ṭālib al-Ṭarīd"*[165] (The Suspended Student) and *"Abū-Jāsim"*[166] deal with certain aspects of the Iraqi rejection of Ottoman rule.

In *"Al-Amal al-Muḥaṭṭam"*[167] (Broken Dream) and *"Mujāhidūn"*,[168] he portrays the desire of the Iraqi youth to rid their country of the British occupation together with their eagerness to play a more active role in its running and development. He clearly believed that the cause of progress was inseparable from that of liberation and independence. In these stories there are some faint echoes of Maḥmūd Taymūr's stories concerning the frustration of aspiring young artists and writers in a society oblivious to their endeavour. The other recurring theme in al-Sayyid's work is the difficulty, almost impossibility, of love in the closed and highly conservative Iraqi society. In such an atmosphere any move can be interpreted wrongly, thus ending the love affair before it even begins, as in *"Jimāḥ Hawā"*[169] (Unrestrained Passion) and *"al-Dhikrā"*[170] (Memory).

A corollary to this theme is the depiction of the deplorable life in prostitution, for when healthy sexual relationships are denied, unhealthy ones thrive. One in every four[171] of his stories deals with some aspect of this theme. In *"Risālat Hajr"*[172] (It's Over), *"'Ātikah"*[173] and *"A wa-Tasharīn"*[174] (Are You a Night Owl?), he treats the various conditions that lead to the prostitution of women, and how the inhuman position of prostitutes is reflected in the way they treat their men. But he avoids slipping into the sentimentality which was customary in dealing with such a theme at the time. In *"Ṭālib Effendi"*[175] he demonstrates how the prostitution of men is even worse, because it is associated with compromising the nation's interest and helping its enemy.

But his best narrative texts are those which he consciously produced under the influence of Russian literature. In these few texts he attempts to represent real characters in plausible situations and avoids any reformative or moral claims. In *"Inqilāb"* he depicts a simple character from the lower strata of Iraqi society in a simple everyday situation. A man returns to the familiar chaos of his home and finds that his wife has cooked fish, which he hates, has an argument with her, leaves the house and goes to eat in a restaurant. During his meal he goes through his private diary and tears it up, and with each torn page he ponders over certain aspects of his life until he realizes his mistakes. The shredding of the pages of his diary punctuates the more significant act of tearing his own life apart, and prompts the realization that he is responsible for his own suffering. Al-Sayyid was able through careful characterization and attention to detail to illuminate the transformation in his character and to motivate the psychological denouement. In the light of the psychological transition, the details which he has subtly elaborated suddenly come to life and charge the situation with various possibilities. This is also the case in *"Sakrān"* where the sympathetic rendering of the character reveals both his weakness and strength and offers the reader an insight into his anxieties.

In *"Baddāy al-Fāyiz"*[176] he reaches the culmination of his narrative skill, successfully motivating the action and creating a humane and sensitive character. Unlike the rest of his stories, which are all based in the city, this one takes place in a rural setting. The young peasants are all working together to repair a dam on the river Euphrates in order to save the village from imminent flood. When the tribal chief hits Baddāy for his neglect, he rebels in a manner that threatens the chief's authority. Angered by this, the chief berates Baddāy for not avenging his brother's death. Although he had been waiting until the village has overcome the menace of the flood, this accusation of cowardice is the greatest insult for a tribal man, and he can wait no longer. He rushes to avenge his brother and get Jassām, the man acused of killing him. When he crosses the river to the village of his enemy, and aims his gun at him, a part of the embankment collapses and everyone hastens to repair the damage and save the whole village from the flood. Baddāy forgets his vengeance and magnanimously joins in the effort to save his enemy's village. When the task is completed, he returns to his village without retaliating for his brother's death. Jassām's village knows the story and offers a proper compensation for the death of his brother in accordance with tribal tradition.

The story demonstrates how individual action is collectively conditioned and how the process of this conditioning is subtly controlled. It is a study in the intricate interaction between the individual psyche and the collective mind through which al-Sayyid endeavours to criticize certain tribal mores and uphold others. Yet it elaborates the sophistication of the tribal scale of values and how it places the collective security of the village above the settling of scores by an individual. Baddāy's adherence to the dictates of moral values leads to his final victory and to the elimination of the cycle of revenge. His surname, al-Fāyiz (the victorious), heralds this final outcome in both the village battle against nature and his individual battle for avenging his brother's blood. The point of view in the story shifts constantly between that of the individual, Baddāy, and the collective, the tribe, and this heightens the tension and charges the action with various layers of meaning. This enables al-Sayyid to turn a simple story of an individual into a story of a whole culture and of man in his struggle against a harsh environment.

Although this chapter has discussed only the short narrative works of these six pioneers, they all, except Ḥaddād, also produced longer works which contributed to the development of the new narrative discourse. Taymūr wrote an uncompleted novel and a number of plays, Nu'aymah wrote both novels[177] and plays,[178] 'Īsā 'Ubaid wrote a short novel and a number of plays[179] and al-Sayyid published three novels.[180] Their work in the other genres is very similar to that in the genre of the short story discussed here, and there is no doubt that these six pioneers (Taymūr, Nu'aymah, Ḥaddād, the 'Ubaids and al-Sayyid) sowed the seeds of the mature short story in modern Arabic literature by attempting to disseminate fresh ideas concerning its function and technique, and by putting these ideas into practice. Although their contribution to the shaping of the new genre is valuable and beyond question, their works still suffer from certain defects and shortcomings, as one might expect from pioneers in a field which has no previous tradition.

They were indeed aware of the pioneering nature of their work and of both the difficulty and importance of breaking with traditional conventions of prose writing within which the establishment of new modes of discourse was almost impossible. But they failed to carry this task to its natural end; hence, their works suffer from the shortcomings associated with beginning a major task without having either the insight to follow through its natural course of development or the ability to see all the basic elements involved in its execution. They threw off the shackles inherited from conventional prose writing, but failed to achieve the transition from the traditional mode of storytelling to narrative discourse with its new conventions and outlook. They also failed to realize the host of subtle changes and intangible elements associated with this transition, because they did not discover that traditional prose writing, especially that associated with storytelling, had various inherent characteristics of the oral exchange of experiences. One of these characteristics which their works retained, and which can be linked to a host of other features, is the convention that a story be useful.

For storytellers know that in order to be listened to, their stories must contain "openly or covertly, something useful. The usefulness may, in one case, consist of a moral; in another, of some practical advice; in a third, of a proverb or maxim. In every case the storyteller is a man who has counsel for his reader ... After all, counsel is less an answer to a question than a proposal concerning the continuation of a story which is just unfolding".[181] Each of these six pioneers was much concerned about the usefulness of his work; that is, its usefulness to a reading public attuned to the direct and loud voice of the orator. This left its mark both on the structure of the work and on its theme, as well as on the writer's approach to reality, which is seen as the source of counsel. Ironically, this approach to reality was adopted at a time when, as Walter Benjamin argues, the art of storytelling was reaching its end "because the epic side of truth, wisdom, was dying out. This however is a concomitant symptom of the secular productive forces of history, a concomitant that has quite gradually removed ... narrative from the realm of living speech".[182]

Benjamin's point is particularly valid in the case of modern Arabic literature, because the secular, productive forces of history[183] were combined with a conscious desire for further development and modernization. However, Benjamin argues that "the earliest symptom of a process whose end is the decline of storytelling is the rise of the novel at the beginning of modern times ... The storyteller takes what he tells from experience — his own or that reported by others. And he in turn makes it the experience of those who are listening to his tale".[184] Although our six writers were, both theoretically and in practice, heralding the end of the storyteller and the rise of the creative writer of narrative fiction, they continued to suggest, both directly and by allusion, that they spoke from experience and that what they preached bore a strong resemblance to reality. So they overlooked the Aristotelian maxim that "the function of the poet is not to relate what happened but what is possible according to the law of probability or necessity",[185] and endeavoured to fill their works with a great deal of factual material. As a result, their stories are burdened with irrelevant data which affected the general tone of their work. They did not appear to recognize that, in a certain sense, "to write a novel [or a short story] means to carry the incommensurable to extremes in the representation of human life",[186] without sacrificing the overall credibility of the work in question. They also did not realize that the very essence of the mimetic argument was in constant conflict with their creative endeavour to be more active and effective in their societies.

Indeed, most of the recurring shortcomings in the works of these pioneers stemmed from their inability to realize the scope of the transition from storytelling to narrative writing. For it is true that they gave description a major role in their writing, but on the whole they failed to realize the subtle difference between narrative and description,[187] and, consequently, they described where they should have narrated. Despite all its accuracy and virtuosity, the description in their stories was mere padding in many cases, not integrable with other elements of the artistic structure. They realized the importance of vivid characterization, but indulged verisimilitude at the expense of artistic truth. As Maupassant, whom they quoted and admired, says, "To make true, then, one must give a complete illusion of truth by following the ordinary logic of events and not by slavishly transcribing them in the haphazard way they come".[188]

But the first concern of these six pioneers was to transfer as much reality as possible to their stories without applying the principle of *mutatis mutandis* to their external realistic data which requires subjecting them to rigorous artistic selectivity and textual transformation to suit the mode of narrative presentation. The application of this principle would certainly have heightened the concreteness, plausibility, topicality, and impact of their narrative achievements. Indeed, they had a ready excuse in that their fervent desire to create a fictional picture for the totality of Arab life with all its questions and aspirations was a scheme too ambitious to be expressed in only a very few stories.

It is true that if we were to apply rigorous criticism to the works of these six pioneers, none of them would emerge as being particularly impressive. But they must be seen in their historical perspective, for in this perspective alone can their merits be appreciated. They achieved a radical change in the style, technique and sphere of subject-matter of prose writing and laid a solid foundation for the creation of a new discursive field. They reduced the influence of political and moral factors, and distinguished the task of the creative writer from that of politician, moral preacher, or social reformer without cutting the writer off from the general affairs of society. They had inherited from Nadīm the roles of observer and critic of society, but unlike him, they preferred to stand aloof from more practical and direct forms of involvement. By creating a literary mirror which reflected the Arab eagerness to forge a distinctive national identity, they participated indirectly in the evolution of their society, and hence played an effective role in its social and political life in the wider sense. This enabled them to create some archetypal characters and situations which continued to appear in the Arabic short story throughout its development.

They also linked modern Arabic literature with the life of the urban middle classes, and, at the same time, directed attention towards rural life with its simple people and tragic or pastoral scenes. They were particularly fond of revealing the contradiction between the miserable life endured by their characters and the supreme human qualities which they possessed, as if they were presenting the case for their people or a plea for better conditions. Their short stories endeavoured to cover many themes, among which the following are noteworthy: the attempt of individuals to achieve personal salvation, thereby revealing the contradictions between the self's illusions and reality; the suffering entailed in the struggle to attain a better life or to achieve personal happiness; social inequality and the problems of class disparity; the heroic endeavour of individuals to overcome their gloomy present by finding an alternative to harsh deprivation or by transcending their frustrations; and, above all, the presentation of the subtle elements of fascination and splendour in the inner life and everyday rituals of an Arab family and especially its core character — the woman — who had been long absent from literature.

They also contributed, in their various ways, to the shaping of the new artistic sensibility and the dissemination of the new aesthetics, and developed the artistic techniques which modern narrative writers need in their work. They asked the fundamental questions about the nature of narrative, the language of dialogue, the writer's stand *vis-à-vis* reality, the technique of convincing characterization, the interaction between art and reality, the function of description in narrative and in granting the reader a sense of reality, and the importance of gradualizing the progression of the plot and interweaving it with the characterization process. They raised substantial questions about all these topics which long remained at the heart of the debate among writers of narrative discourse, and attracted succeeding generations either to try to find answers to these controversial problems or to reformulate the questions in different ways. However one regards their thematic and technical accomplishments, they put the Arabic short story on the right path to maturity and authenticity.

5
Narrative Genres in Search of an Identity
Maḥmūd Taymūr

By the end of the third decade of this century, the works of Maḥmūd Taymūr (1894-1973) and Maḥmūd Ṭāhir Lāshīn (1894-1954) had brought the stage of the genesis of the indigenous Arabic short story in particular and Arabic narrative discourse in general to an end. In their short stories and novels these two writers were the most talented and dedicated among all those who wrote narrative at the time, and this is the reason for singling them out for a detailed discussion of their work until 1930. Although Taymūr's work is of a lower calibre than that of Lāshīn, it was, ironically, the more directly influential both in Egypt and in the rest of the Arab world.[1] This was probably due to the fact that Taymūr's work was less sophisticated and did not demand a great degree of understanding of narrative complexity from his reader. As a result, his work attracted the attention of the reader and appealed to many would-be writers.

The nature, features, limitations and basic conventions of the new literary genre had become relatively clear and capable of intelligible definition in their own terms. This enabled Lāshīn, towards the end of the 1920s, to disregard the fairly well-established assumption that creative writers should preface their collections of short stories with elaborate introductions aimed at familiarizing the reading public with the writers' devices and techniques, and involving an explanation of their methods and beliefs, and a justification of the need for his new work and of its social or moral function. From the beginning, Lāshīn was content with his role as a creative writer and refrained from writing prefatory notes. He gave this task to the prominent literary figures of the period,[2] or to one of his close friends.[3] If the readers still needed a bridge to give them access to works of fiction, this was no longer considered to be the creative writer's task, but that of the critic.

Introducing a New Narrative Discourse

Taymūr approached this sensitive question differently, took some time to follow Lāshīn's example, and did not do so until his fourth and subsequent collections. Although he was in touch with the *al-Madrasah al-Ḥadīthah* group and published some of his short stories[4] in their journal *al-Fajr,* under the pseudonym *Mūbāsān al-Miṣri* (the Egyptian Maupassant), he was, unlike Lāshīn, not integrated into their literary movement. As a result, he lacked the confidence which Lāshīn had gained from being a member of a literary movement, and felt the need to provide his first three collections with elaborate introductions, one of which, fifty pages long, attempted to cover the vast history of narrative forms from Homer's epics to the modern age.[5] These superfluous introductions can be explained by Taymūr's relative isolation; the strong influence of his elder brother Muḥammad on him; and his literary upbringing at the hands of his father, surrounded by classical and traditional culture.

In his introductions, Taymūr tried to refight battles which had been competently and successfully fought before. He asserted, unnecessarily, the interrelationship between the emergence of modern fiction and the rise of Egyptian nationalism,[6] the independence of the short story as a complete work of art,[7] the importance of a realistic attitude in dealing with fictional material in order to keep the writer as close as possible to the truth,[8] the moral and didactic function of fiction,[9] the writer's need for a vast cultural background particularly in European literature,[10] and the need to abandon adaptation from Western works because of its deforming effect and its inferiority to original creative writing which reflected the features of authentic Egyptian life[11] — all ideas he had inherited from his immediate predecessors, and usefully synthesized into a coherent set of literary conventions. However, Taymūr was rather over-optimistic in predicting, in his first collection, that the short story would soon be the only heir to all the forms of narrative discourse,[12] a statement which he himself came to regret and corrected two years later.[13]

From the very beginning of his career as a short-story writer, Taymūr realized the vital importance of knowing and assimilating European culture. Between 1924 and 1930 he travelled to Europe three times, and spent two years in Switzerland on one of these trips. He admitted that, apart from improving his command of foreign languages and introducing him on a large scale to European writing,[14] these three journeys had a seminal impact upon his understanding of both art and man.[15] He was particularly influenced by the works of Maupassant,[16] Tolstoy, Turgenev and Chekhov.[17] However, he did not penetrate beneath the surface of these writers' works, and could fathom neither the depths of Maupassant's ironies, contradictory characters and the dramatic events of his plots, nor the spiritual adventure and tragic human suffering portrayed in Russian literature.

This was not a result of Taymūr's lack of literary insight or artistic understanding, but a natural consequence of the absence of mature critical discourse and established conventions for the reception of narrative discourse and the decoding of its techniques and strategies. The pioneers of narrative discourse were also pioneers in the process of decoding European narrative and in using their experience to encode their own narrative discourse along similar lines. The lack of systematic study of literature, combined with Taymūr's relative isolation, resulted in his failure to penetrate beneath the surface of the classics of European narrative which he was avidly reading. Integration into an active literary group saved Lāshīn from a similar fate and provided him with the fruits of the collective endeavour of the *al-Madrasah al-Ḥadīthah* group and their ability to complement and enrich each other's understanding.

In contrast to his predecessors, Taymūr introduced quite modest theoretical views in terms of his conceptual framework, but, quantitatively, his was a rich practical achievement. From 1925 to 1930 he wrote and published four collections of short stories[18] and one novel accompanied by a short story.[19] Also, all the short stories published in his fifth collection *Abū-'Ali 'Āmil Artist* (1934) had appeared in newspapers and periodicals before the close of the third decade of this century. Thus, Taymūr was the most productive of the short-story writers during the 1920s. Yet his fictional world remained narrow, his themes were limited, and there was a lack of variety in his characterization. At this stage, his writing neither covered a wider range of subjects nor was more profound than that of preceding authors who had published only one or two collections. But the continuous flow of his works played an important role in familiarizing the reading public with the new literary genre and its conventions. Unlike the two 'Ubaids, who could not publish all their works, Taymūr's family's literary reputation and wealth helped him to publish almost everything he wrote, indiscriminately.

Revisiting Old Themes

In many of his stories, Taymūr concentrated on the themes and questions which his elder brother Muḥammad had briefly treated — the theme of the neglected and depressed wife,[20] and that of the frivolous person who wastes his money and damages his health through shameless sensual behaviour.[21] In many of his stories which deal with the second theme, Taymūr treated his reckless protagonists with a blend of moral harshness and ridicule, regardless of the principle that writers should sympathize with, or at least be neutral towards, their characters. He explained the cause of their fall without real understanding of their motives, and, in loud, moralistic tones, he mocked his irresponsible characters and censured their behaviour.

Needless to say, this technique affected the maturity and coherence of his stories because, instead of leaving the characterization and action to speak for themselves, he preached to the reader without properly integrating his moral perspective into the structure of the work as a whole. This not only weakened his stories, but was also responsible for the existence of a double standard of morality in many of them. It vitiated even further both the artistic quality of the stories and the validity of his moral arguments, for one cannot sacrifice the form without the content withering away. Yet the stories which deal with these two themes were not completely wasted. They echoed real feelings and social questions and endeavoured to dramatize some of the common problems of that period. Because the moral message was badly needed to legitimate the new narrative discourse and justify its relevance to society, the critics of the period, with few exceptions,[22] praised these works and turned a blind eye to their artistic weakness.

None the less, Taymūr was more successful in dealing with the third theme, which he took from his elder brother Muḥammad[23] and his predecessor, Ḥasan Maḥmūd;[24] that is, the theme of the corruption of traditional religious sheikhs, against whom he launched a strong attack in numerous short stories.The common stand of these three authors, soon to be joined by Lāshīn, reflected the deep-rooted struggle between the new generation of Arab intellectuals with their rationalism and enlightenment, and the older generation with its traditional beliefs and metaphysical leanings. In their quest for intellectual leadership, the new *Effendis* (graduates of the new educational system as opposed to the sheikhs who graduated from the old theocentric one) could no longer tolerate the exaggerated respect which the sheikhs enjoyed among the general public. They believed that this status was unjustified and went to the other extreme of denying the sheikhs their very right of existence. These stories were designed to illustrate that the sheikhs' respectable *jubbas* (traditional dress of the sheikhs) concealed swindlers, egoists, charlatans and liars, and that behind the mask of piety, devoutness and learning were cruel, ignorant, licentious and, very often, mad people.

The title stories of Taymūr's first three collections — *al-Shaikh Jum'ah,*[25] *'Amm Mitwalli,*[26] and *al-Shaikh Sayyid al-'Abīṭ*[27] — tell of how mere illiterate laymen become, by accident, blessed and venerable sheikhs. Other stories depict these supposedly learned, religious figures behaving in a foolish and often ridiculous manner, as in *"al-Qalam al-Abanūs"*[28] (The Fountain Pen); or treating their children and families with stupidity, cruelty, and ignorance, as in *"Mashrū' Kafāfī Afandi"* and *"al-Shayṭān"*[29] (Satan). We see how one sheikh swindles simple people by offering them false advice, or by twisting the sacred scripture to suit his purpose;[30] how another plots to cheat a husband out of his wife, and, when the husband becomes irritated, uses the ignorant mob to silence him.[31] Another sheikh betrays his closest friend, also a sheikh, without an iota of guilt or hesitation, by seducing his young wife and ruining his family life; the duped sheikh is no better than his deceiver, for he has betrayed the trust and sacrifices of his previous wife and taken a new wife over her.[32] Yet another example describes the cruelty of a sheikh who enjoys torturing a poor wretch to the brink of death.[33]

In these various examples Taymūr tries to reveal the falseness of this social class which enjoyed a respectable reputation among the general public. He employed his stories to subvert and destruct their social status. Taymūr's attitude towards the sheikhs was calculated: he refrained from introducing any sheikh in his stories in a way which might attract sympathy or appreciation. All this, despite the fact that Taymūr himself was brought up in an atmosphere of classical learning, culturally under the influence of his father and his fellow sheikhs, who were the cream of the period's intellectuals.[34]

If Maḥmūd Taymūr inherited the themes of the neglected and depressed wives, frivolous youth, and traditionalist sheikhs from his elder brother Muḥammad, he took from 'Īsā and Shiḥātah 'Ubaid their favourite subject: inequality and incompatibility within marriage and their drastic effect on the coherence of the family. In Taymūr's work, this distorted form of marriage leads to moral collapse and family disintegration. It ends with divorce and women being forced, through economic pressures, into prostitution (*"al-Usṭā Shiḥātah Yuṭālib bi-Ujratih"*), or a state of moral disaster (*"Mashrū' Kafāfi Afandi"*). Unlike 'Īsā 'Ubaid, who strongly defends his cultured and sensitive heroines as victims of unjust circumstances, Taymūr treats his women as simultaneously perpetrators and victims without defending their views or having a bias towards them. This is not due to artistic subjectivity, but rather demonstrates a deep lack of understanding of their problems and viewpoint.

In *"Shahr al-'Asal Ba'd al-Arba'īn"*[35] (Honeymoon After Forty), he blames both hero and heroine equally, and depicts the lustfulness of a woman who deceives her husband. In *"Jaḥīm Imra'ah"*[36] (A Woman's Inferno), he places the burden of the blame on the heroine and gives credit to the man who stands up against her sexual eccentricity. In *"Man Fāt Qadīmah Tāh"*, he depicts the grave effect of a generation gap between marriage partners on the stability of their family, and on the characteristic idiosyncrasies of the younger partner. In most of these stories Taymūr adopts a traditional, if not reactionary, stand as regards the woman's cause, without realizing that he was imitating those sheikhs whom he so severely attacked.

Experimenting with New Themes

As well as these variations on themes inherited from previous writers, Taymūr presents two other major themes: the effects of a bad upbringing, and the anxieties of young artists and writers in a world which denies them any right or role. He makes his characterization more sensitive and breaks new ground not only by dealing with unfamiliar aspects of Egyptian rural life, but also by abandoning exhortation and didacticism and concentrating on the more literary and poetic elements of writing. In dealing with the difficult first theme, Taymūr relies heavily on the simplistic pedagogic theory of the essential role of domestic upbringing in the life of every human being, in order to compensate for his lack of a genuine and more comprehensive approach to the development of the individual and the understanding of personality. His point of departure is the assumption that a stern upbringing produces feeble and ill-mannered individuals and leads to corruption.

In *"Wāsiṭat Ta'āruf"*, it is clear that the strict upbringing of the hero is responsible for his resorting to prostitutes. In *"Shahr al-'Asal Ba'd al-Arba'īn"* the sternness of I'tidāl's mother and her fanaticism in depriving her daughter of even the most innocent fun provoke I'tidāl to seize the first opportunity to deceive her husband. In *"Fatāt al-Jīrān"*[37] (The Neighbour's Daughter) the rigorous attitude of the mother and her false accusation against her son of flirting with the daughter of their next-door neighbour, incites the son, who has barely reached the age of puberty, to become entangled in an adolescent love affair he never contemplated. The general outline of this story resembles Muḥammad Taymūr's short story *"Kān Ṭiflā fa-Ṣār Shābbā"*[38] (He is No Longer a Boy), which treated the same subject. The plot of both stories concerns a relationship between an inexperienced young man and a more experienced woman. While Muḥammad termed his work a sketch, Maḥmūd claimed that his was a short story, despite the fact that both remain at the surface level of the irony in the situation without exploring its deeper layers.

In *"Ab wa-Ibn"*[39] (Father and Son), the treatment of the serious effect of a bad upbringing is too obvious and brings the story to the brink of melodrama, when the son explodes under pressure from his rigorous father and kills him in an uncontrolled moment of rage. The important theme of patricide is mechanically treated and the complexity of the conflicting emotions involved in the situation is reduced to a simplistic cause and effect. The feeble characterization is clearly exposed when the action reaches the moment of crucial confrontation and the author introduces an element of chance to compensate for the lack of action motivation. There are, however, certain elements of social motivation, but in the absence of psychological probing of characters and events, such motivation fails to substantiate the enormity of the act. A few years later, Taymūr realized the weakness of his plot and rewrote the story under the title *"Kabsh al-Fidā'"*[40] (The Sacrificial Lamb), replacing the patricide with the killing of the father's favourite pet.

The second theme is the predicament of young writers and artists in a society which turns a deaf ear to their activities and ambitions. His elder brother Muḥammad Taymūr had dealt with this subject in his unfinished story *"al-Shabāb al-Ḍā'i'"*[41] (Wasted Youth), but Maḥmūd Taymūr treats it extensively and from various points of view. He approaches the subject from a witty and sarcastic perspective, as a result of which the didactic and sentimental elements fade out. Yet his treatment of this theme is far removed from the subtlety of comic effect with its far-reaching ramifications found, for instance, in Maupassant's short stories. It lacks the touch of a competent writer capable of heightening the narrative structure and employing technical devices in widening the scope of vision in the work. There is a small but highly significant difference between the comic effect which springs from the inner structure of a literary work, and sarcastic or witty remarks which float on the surface.

Taymūr, without much experience behind him, failed, at least in this early stage, to recognize this subtle difference, and to integrate the comic irony into the characterization or interweave it with the details of the situation. In *"Hiya al-Ḥayāh"*[42] (This is Life), he introduces a theatre devotee who is full of hope and enthusiasm about the world of drama and wants to be a dramatist but who is without any practical ability or future prospects in the theatre. In *"al-Waẓīfah Akhīrā"*, he satirizes a character who prepares himself to be a serious writer, but ends his life as a scullion in a nightclub of ill repute. The story entitled *"al-Thālūth al-Muqaddas"*[43] (Holy Trinity) associates art with lunacy, and the behaviour of its three main characters, all of whom are professed artists, with aberration and eccentricity. Despite the story's repetitiveness and structural weakness which make it seem more a synopsis of a novelette than a proper short story, its climax, when the three characters open their so-called Academy of Letters and Arts, is remarkable for its vivid narrative style and a rich comic flavour.

"Abū-'Ali 'Āmil Artist"[44] (Abu Ali Pretending to be an Artist) also shows artistic impulses coexisting with aberration and mental derangement; however, the story fails because of its stark obviousness, its use of spasmodic, incoherent events to convey a sense of reality, and its inability to engage the reader's sympathy for the main character. The association of art with lunacy in the story is too crude to suggest any philosophical background or romantic tendencies, and cannot be linked with the notion of an unconscious element in the inventive process.[45] The witty remarks are too direct and clumsy, despite the author's success in outlining the exhibitionist tendencies of his character. *"Salīm Afandi al-Ṭālib al-Adīb"*[46] (Salīm the Student/Writer) is perhaps the author's maturest short story dealing with this theme. Although Taymūr retains in it superfluous elements of wit and sarcasm, he creates a relatively coherent plot and knows how far to go with the action, where to advance with the characters, and when to introduce the denouement. None the less,

the story relies heavily on a series of coincidences and on some hackneyed notions about journalists and journalism.

In the last group of stories, Taymūr sets out to illustrate certain aspects of human nature. The stories of this group fluctuate between two categories: the fictional sketch simplifying certain conspicuous character traits, and the mature short story which strives for a deeper exploration of the inner life of forlorn and defeated individuals, and seeks to reveal the contradictions between illusion and reality in their lives. Among the stories of the first category are most of those discussed above, in which he isolates peculiar elements and comic external contradictions in his characters' lives or personalities. Additions to this category are other stories such as *"al-Sitt Tawaddud"*[47] (Mrs Tawaddud), which depicts the cupidity of a lonely old woman who sponges on her neighbours for meals and entertainment despite her relative wealth and *"Yuḥfaẓ fi al-Būsṭah"*[48] (*Poste Restante*), the story of a comfortably-off young man who sends perfumed love letters to himself, pretending to his friends that they are written by beautiful girls, in order to prove that he is the playboy of his quarter.

In the same superficial manner *"Hiya al-Ḥayāh"* depicts a character who preaches socialism, the first time that such a character had appeared in modern Arabic literature. The socialist was depicted as a novelty and as a promoter of fresh ways of thinking that shocked and surprised a stagnant society. This was the early 1920s when such ideas were innovative and highly provocative in the Arab world. Several other characters are introduced, at this early stage of Taymūr's literary career, for the sole reason that they possess elements of eccentricity or uniqueness.[49] This sarcastic emphasis on the peculiarities in the human character jeopardizes the artistic quality of these stories and has an adverse effect on their credibility.

In the second category referred to above, he attempts to unravel the inner life of his characters, and so the risk of superficiality decreases and the story becomes artistically more coherent. In *"Abū Darsh"*, the writer weaves a web of causes for the dramatic fall of his hero, who is left alone, helpless and hopeless after the destruction of his old world. In *"al-Rajul al-Marīḍ"*[50] (The Sick Man) he gains the reader's sympathy for his old paralytic hero who lives in hope, waiting for the return of his only son, whom he has sent abroad to be educated. In *"Qaswat al-Shabāb"*[51] (The Cruelty of Youth), *"Budūr"*[52] (Budur), and *"Infijār"*[53] (Explosion), the writer treats three different pairs of lovers and explores their ways of escaping social pressure to express their emotions. He succeeds in showing how their method of escaping this pressure and challenging social taboos leaves its distinct marks on relationships and their development. In *"Ṣ ābiḥah"*[54] (Sabiha) he illustrates how a crime is provoked by a milieu which deprives the individual of the opportunity to express and fulfil his feelings of love.

In all these stories there is a feeling that Taymūr has become aware of the importance of coherent characterization and of the integration of character into both the setting and the action. He pays some attention to the characters' social and cultural background and takes their motives into consideration. Yet he fails to develop in these character studies an integrated artistic world with its own inner logic and laws. His main concern is to describe the parochial features of certain human types as a means of providing the stories with definable Egyptian features. In this he was reacting to the spread of adaptation and trying to establish in modern Arabic literature a sense of originality and authenticity. For him, authenticity was synonymous with the local and parochial, not as means to the human and the universal but as ultimate ends in themselves. So most of these stories fail to go beyond the limited horizon of the parochial and are artistically weak.

The Culmination of his Early Career

None the less, there is one exception, *"al-'Awdah"*[55] (Return), a story which is the culmination of Taymūr's achievements during this stage of his literary career, and of this group of stories in particular. It is a story of an old grandmother who lives alone in the village with her grandson, whose father has left him and gone to the city some years before. The boy, whom she calls *al-Ghāli,* the precious one, becomes the focus of her attention and provides her life with a meaning and a sense of purpose. One day the father returns from the city to take the boy to work as a servant there, but the grandmother refuses to let him go. The father coaxes her into giving him the child, and convinces her that this is the only path for the boy's happiness and progress. She finally agrees on condition that he send the boy to visit her occasionally. She prepares new clothes and cakes for the boy, but when he leaves she loses her reason for existence and her life becomes meaningless. After a few days she makes the absent boy the centre of her life again by preparing his favourite food for him and sending it regularly to the city.

The father does not keep his promise and years go by without her seeing the boy. The waiting becomes the central activity in her life, and she never ceases to send him gifts and to ask when he is coming back to visit her. It dominates her life to the extent that she loses her sense of time; while ageing herself, she nourishes a fixed image of the boy as he was when he left. When she is told that he is coming to visit her after ten years of absence, she makes a new *jallābiyyah* (long peasant dress) for him, prepares an inviting meal and buys a toy. But instead of the docile child, she finds a youth who does not pay any attention to her conversation or consider her feelings, and goes to flirt with the pretty young girls of the village. Only then does she realize that when he left her for the city her precious boy had gone for ever and she bursts into tears.

In this mature, well-written story, the influence of the Chekhovian approach to the short story is evident, and "the unity of character takes precedence over the old unities of time, place and action".[56] The story condenses, sensitively and skilfully, more than ten years of its heroine's life in a long moment of waiting, and succeeds in depicting its main character both as a totally credible individual and an archetype of the Egyptian mother. In this story, Taymūr achieves, for the first time, a sensitive balance between the various elements of narrative, and creates a convincing human character, a mature fictional situation rich in its texture, structure and conflict, and a short story worth reading. He also abandons his loud moral tone and didacticism and exploits the irony of the situation to touch upon the conflicts between village and city on one level and between illusion and reality on another. The denouement of the story transforms the meal, toy and new clothes from symbols of celebration and fulfilment to mere remnants of a dead era and the outward manifestation of shattered illusions, underlining the contradictions between the innocent world of childhood and the roughness of adolescence.

These are the broad outlines and main themes of the narrative world which Taymūr created in his early writings, up to the beginning of the 1930s, and they remained at the core of his world for three more decades, forming the axis of his achievements throughout his long career as a writer of short stories, novels and plays.[57] He treated these same themes and constantly rewrote his early stories in modified, though not always more coherent, versions, or from new perspectives. His settings, subjects and characters remained practically the same and his characters continued to be variations on members of those strata of Egyptian society with whom he had dealt since the beginning of his career. Because his point of departure in dealing with these themes and human types did not alter radically, a close examination of the artistic questions of these early collections is needed.

The important point here is that Taymūr's conscious desire to root the new narrative discourse in Egyptian literary life was not accompanied by a deep insight or clear understanding of man or social life. His upper-class background left its mark on his work, for, instead of capitalizing on his intimate knowledge of Turco-Circassian upper-class scenes, he opted to treat the life of the poor and the middle class, which he experienced only as an outsider. In Egypt at the time, social intercourse between the upper and lower classes was extremely limited, and Taymūr ventured into a world that was relatively unknown to him. Yet Taymūr's avoidance of the themes, characters and settings of the upper class was not accidental, for he was aware that for the new narrative discourse to take root it had to be integrated in the life of those who formed the basis of the new reading public. It was also at this time that writers were calling for the creation of *adab qawmi* (a national literature), and it was clearly inappropriate that the life and scenes of the Turco-Circassian community should form the basis of such literature.

Taymūr's selection of his themes and characters was ideologically motivated by his keen desire to play a leading role in the changing culture.

It is rather ironic that, in order to remain in their prominent place at the helm, the upper-class intellectuals had to concern themselves with the life of the poor and middle-class issues. The separation of Taymūr from the life, language and imagery of the people whose literary tradition he was sharing is the source of his literary weakness. Despite his honourable intentions, Taymūr approached many of his themes and characters from the point of view of an outside observer and failed to penetrate the outer shell of his human type or to delve into the essential questions of the period. Rather than examining certain problems or situations in depth, he touched quickly, and often superficially, upon available materials, themes, human patterns and stereotyped situations around him.

He covered a wide range of themes and situations, dealing with various urban scenes of school and childhood, young dilettanti, adolescent emotional experience, civil servants, and occasionally the relatively well-to-do. He also recorded all that he could comprehend of the rural life which he had observed in his summer visits to the country, and all that he had grasped from the world of the traditional sheikhs which surrounded his father. He was also fascinated by certain eccentric characters from the poor quarters of Cairo. When he describes peasants or characters from the poorer strata of society, he is indulgent, sometimes kind, and sometimes fearful; at best, he reinforces the myth of the "good fellah". He does not pay profound attention to the values of the villagers' lives or manifest a comprehension of the significance of the everyday rituals which reflect the central meaning of their existence. The characters whom he presents exist in a cardboard village, and never come alive.[58] When he depicts characters with whom he can identify, exhibiting violence, morbid sexuality, and drug addiction, he comes nearer to the surface and is less controlled by form. In all these fields of human experience, Taymūr offers his reader information about human life rather than illuminating his rational or emotional experience of life in Egypt at that time. His stories, in spite of their technical control, are often expressions of his reaction to society, not whole works of art, capable of discovering reality about society or the situation. There are certain features of locality in many of his works, but they fail to transcend their parochial limits to become something of more national or universal significance.

This is so despite the fact that Taymūr included in these collections what he considered to be the maturest of his works at the time. Apart from the several pieces of sentimental lyrical free verse (published in *al-Sufūr* in 1916 and 1917), he had written and published many other stories, in newspapers and periodicals, and declined to republish them in his collections.[59] He rewrote some of his stories before collecting them in book form,[60] or at least altered some and provided others with various modifications and improvements.[61] In some stories he made use of his knowledge of French and English short stories and took them as models, but did not resort to overt plagiarism.[62] At this early stage of his career as a short story writer, Taymūr's main problem was not a lack of enthusiasm for rendering authentic the Arabic short story, but a poverty of human experience and an inability to make his narrative account of an event or a character capable of generating various layers of meaning.

Artistic and Conceptual Qualities

However, his works broadened and heightened the artistic and conceptual qualities of the Arabic short story which he had inherited from his predecessors. His works placed some emphasis on the artistic elements already mentioned in the previous chapter and deepened the reader's understanding of them, introducing some new factors as well. Because of his awareness of the importance of improving and rewriting what he had written, his works attracted the attention of the critics, who appreciated his vivid descriptions, a feature which suggested to them elements of modernism and realism.[63] In spite of the positive tone of this rudimentary criticism, description in some of Taymūr's works is only loosely related to the plot and could easily have been eliminated. It had, as Nazīh al-Ḥakīm correctly perceived, a tendency to concentrate on the physical, implying that "the psychology of any character is subjugated to his or her physiological structure; Taymūr therefore illustrates at first the external traits of his protagonists: their gestures, clothes, way of life; then he narrates the story of this character, a story of a moving body while you, the reader, have to provide it with a suitable soul".[64]

Nazīh al-Ḥakīm made this rather perceptive remark in 1944, not in the early 1920s when Taymūr was writing his early work. Al-Ḥakīm's remark is indicative of the rapid maturity of both critical and narrative discourse in Arabic literature, but it is easier to be wise after the event, and particularly after the accumulation of the mature work of many other writers, primarily those of Lāshīn, Yaḥyā Ḥaqqi (b. 1905) and Maḥmūd al-Badawi (1908-85). Taymūr was breaking new ground and his awareness of the vitality of description is in itself a considerable achievement. However, he concentrated on the physical aspects of the character and failed to see through the external features and gestures of people to their innermost traits, so endowing the story with motionless, photographic images. But he did this to establish accuracy of description and to purge narrative discourse of the high-handed tone of the moralistic preachers.

However, this understated description affects characterization, and impairs his portrayal of fully rounded characters. It is ironic that this was the state of characterization in the work of a writer who devoted most of his fiction to character types, and who gave all his early collections of short stories the names of human characters as titles. One critic of his early collections noticed that his works "are more like studies in characters than mere storyettes [*sic*]";[65] another supported this argument by saying that "Taymūr's early works are mere literary portraits: they record one of life's paradoxes, depict eccentric characters, or seize a person in a comic situation. All the stories' only merit lies in mentioning

Egyptian proper names of people and places".[66] Taymūr does not treat his characters with the objectivity, or at least the distance, proper to an artist, but from the point of view of an ethical reformer who praises the good and censures the evil. This was so because Taymūr seemed to adopt "a view that has long been popular and is still very common among lay readers. Imaginative literature can be justified if it communicates historical, philosophical, or moral truths in a lively and pleasing manner".[67]

At this early stage of the development of narrative discourse, and because of the lack of narrative conventions, the author was not prepared to become each character, like an actor in each of his parts, creating their whole idiom and thought process. Instead of partaking of his characters' feelings and dramatizing them through language, Taymūr stood outside the character as an onlooker, observing and judging. He was quite prepared to insult his characters directly throughout the narrative, a strange phenomenon, of which there are many examples. In *"Shahr al-'Asal Ba'd al-Arba'īn"*, he describes his protagonist as follows: "Mr Taha is one of those people whom one could correctly put in the category of the imbecile and the evil. He has a sluggish stupid mind and a vulgar soul".[68] In *"Ab wa-Ibn"*, after describing the physical features of the son, he adds that "he is ill-natured, with a disgusting natural disposition, and his way of life is extremely foul".[69]

In the same manner, al-Ḥājj Fayrūz is depicted as "reckless and frivolous by nature, heedless, ill-natured and with a tendency to commit sins and crimes".[70] Rif'at Afandi[71] is described as "a chatterbox and a fool and notorious for his cruelty and stubbornness".[72] When he dies, his death does not soften the author's stand against him; on the contrary, it provides him with an opportunity to comment that "he died as a victim of his own ignorance, foolishness and illbreeding".[73] On occasion Taymūr uses wit and humour to make his attitude to his characters appear more dispassionate. But this humorous element, although it dramatizes the clash between the character's illusion and reality, in a way which was new to the Arabic short story, did not achieve the delicate, powerful balance of sophisticated irony. However, in a few cases, he did forge an artistic irony between the character's illusions and actual reality, an attainment which contributed to the improvement and maturation of the Arabic short story.

None the less, Taymūr's emphasis on stories based on characters, especially forlorn, injured and defeated figures, was a step forward in the development of the Arabic short story. For this in itself was a discovery of the right ground, even if he failed to raise any real flag over the new-found land. Despite all their defects, his stories succeed in decreasing the story's reliance on a "preamble in which the writer tells us how he came into possession of the facts",[74] and in paving the way for dispensing with it altogether. Although his stories diminish the repetitive role of this preamble, they are still dependent on a simplified form of the introductory statement which aims to convince the reader of the author's omniscience, and to enable the story to create an illusion of reality. This was a feature which he had inherited from the works of 'Īsā and Shiḥātah 'Ubaid, and could not abandon completely because his reader was not yet familiar with the conventions of the new literary genre. He retains these brief opening statements to justify filling his stories with detailed realistic, or rather naturalistic, information about his subject.

Despite this he did not contribute dramatically to the capacity of the Egyptian short story to convey reality, because, after abandoning lengthy preambles, he showed no aptitude for mastering "the technique of informing by means of suggestion or implication".[75] He imparts details about the action, the narrative conflict, or the character mostly through direct statements which are less effective in generating meaning than the subtleties of a work of art. Art communicates its meaning through imagery of various kinds and subtle devices which convey profound meaning both quantitatively and qualitatively.

The Problematic Language of Narrative

The artistic question round which Taymūr's stories revolved was that concerning the language of fiction, its nature, scope and limitations. This was an important question dictated by the changing sensibility and by the writers' need to attract a wider reading public to the new narrative discourse, a need which conflicted with the dominant literary taste on the one hand and the technical demands and aesthetic necessities of the new literary forms on the other. Confidently, Taymūr declared (in the preface to his first collection) that

> the dialogue must be written in the vernacular, the natural language of the speaker. It is much closer to reality. If the story aspires to be Egyptian, the dialogue should be in Egyptian dialect, because the dialect varies with the differences in social class and cultural background, and every social stratum has its own colloquialisms. The writer must take this into consideration throughout his fictional work and must not confuse the different styles of speech.[76]

But two years later, and with similar confidence, he abandoned this concept in favour of its absolute opposite:

> I was fully convinced initially that the dialogue in short stories must be written in the colloquial in order to come closer to reality. I have changed my views after practical experience proved them wrong. The gap between the two languages[77] does exist, and when the formal and the colloquial are juxtaposed, the one for description and the other for conversation, the incongruity between them is marked and shocks the reader as he moves from one linguistic level to another. Thus the writer must write the entire story, narrative and dialogue, in one language — literary Arabic.[78]

The consequence of this new belief was that Taymūr deserted more lively language for the sake of a bookish style in both narrative and dialogue, but, inevitably, some colloquialisms lingered on after this definitive statement.

The whole question of language was, in fact, the subject of a lengthy controversy among the writers and the critics of the 1920s. Although a few writers praised Taymūr's new conservative stand,[79] many of the younger generation criticized it. Ḥusain Fawzi, a young writer and critic, was in favour of Taymūr's original view, and expressed the opinion of the young writers of the time that their duty was to put natural expressions in the mouths of their characters, not bombastic formal speech.[80] Salāmah Mūsā also supported Fawzi's argument, and questioned how a simple Egyptian mother could lament her dead son or lull her child in formal phrases.[81] Neither Taymūr, in either of his opposing stands, nor his critics could advance the argument beyond this limited sphere and discuss the technical and aesthetic ramifications of either alternative. But the failure to recognize this in their theoretical discussion does not mean that Taymūr and other talented writers of his generation did not occasionally show a certain intuitive understanding of these ramifications.

They also apparently failed to realize that "the short story writer's problem of language is the need for a speech which combines suggestion with compression".[82] They all dealt with the question of language largely from the static position of the traditional view of prose language and not from the dynamic position of a recognition of the aesthetic and structural function of language in a creative work of narrative. Their gaze was constantly fixed on the salient traits of traditional prose, and this was often achieved at the expense of the linguistic needs of narrative discourse. Not one of them discovered intellectually that language in a creative work is not a prosaic vehicle of meaning but a genuine part of the artistic structure, nor did they realize the interrelationship between the rhythm of the sentence and the rhythm of the narrative situation which it describes. The mellifluous style and the grandiloquent prose of 'Abdullah Fikri, Ḥifni Nāṣif (1865-1918) and Muṣṭafā Luṭfi al-Manfalūṭi occupied the highest status in the scale of linguistic and aesthetic values at that time. The Egyptian short-story writers discovered, from the beginning, that such language was antagonistic to the very nature of narrative discourse and concentrated their efforts in a great campaign against pun, metonymy, verbal decoration and mixed metaphors, in order to gain the readers' acceptance of simple language. By abandoning the vernacular, Taymūr was aiming at a compromise to gain himself a respectable place among the intellectuals of the literary establishment and the traditional reading public.

Taymūr's simplification of the problem of language and his understanding of it as a mere vessel to contain the meaning, and not as an integral part of the meaning itself, were in harmony with his understanding of the nature and function of narrative. The narrative in Taymūr's work depended on "telling" readers all that he wished them to know about the characters and actions. He failed — with a few exceptions

— to "show" them the characters involved in situations which revealed them fully as three-dimensional people, or to go beneath the surface of the action to obtain a reliable view of a character's mind and heart, so enabling the reader to examine the accuracy of the writer's description.[83] This reduced the stories in some cases to bare outlines[84] or, at best, to simplified summaries of the action or synopses of longer tales.[85] There are defects which could easily have been eliminated if the writer had employed his narrative more effectively to suggest rather than deliver information. Failing to achieve the right blend of "telling" and "showing" affected the originality of Taymūr's stories, and lessened their impact upon the writers and the readers of his time. A feature which appeared to be a compensation for this failure was the heavy sentimentality[86] intended to distract the readers' attention from the stories' lack of verisimilitude.

Taken in its historical context, this sentimentality and other shortcomings related to language and direct authorial comment on the characters served as an acceptable compromise in the eyes of the traditional reader, and were, accordingly, praised by some of the reviewers of the period. In spite of these shortcomings, Taymūr's work played an important role in establishing this new narrative discourse, granting it respectability and relevance and gaining considerable support for it from the pillars of the literary establishment. He played a conciliatory role in the transitional phase from the old to the new mode of discourse: his cultural and class background, the way he reacted to and dealt with literary and other related problems, the particular balance he struck at all levels between conformity to the traditional literary canon and innovation and propagation of new values made him a landmark figure in the lengthy process of the genesis of narrative in Arabic literature.

6
The Maturation of the New Narrative Discourse
Maḥmūd Ṭāhir Lāshīn

The arrival of Lāshīn[1] on the Egyptian literary scene in the 1920s marked a turning-point in the history of modern Arabic narrative discourse in general and the short story in particular. He was an outstandingly vigorous pioneer who developed the genre and brought its formative years to a close. His writings represent the culmination, in both form and content, of the work of previous writers and of his contemporaries. He was also the major figure of a versatile literary group, *Jamā'at al-Madrasah al-Ḥadīthah* (the Modern School), which played a decisive role in developing modern Arabic narrative discourse, extending its reading public, and shaping the characteristics of the new sensibility of that period. This new literary sensibility is strongly related to the ethos of the intellectual *nahḍah* (revival), which had had a vital influence on various literary discourses from the middle of the nineteenth century, particularly on the reformulation of the relationship between literature and reality.[2]

Before the advent of the *nahḍah,* Arabic literature's relationship with social reality was rather tenuous, and literature was highly stylized and deeply concerned with verbal and rhetorical accomplishments. The main achievement of the *nahḍah* was to establish the vital link between literature and reality, and to root literary texts in the life of their readers, in order to legitimize the importance of the writer and intellectual in society. The genesis of narrative discourse was an attempt by authors to establish new literary genres capable of portraying the changing social reality and expressing the anxieties and aspirations of their readers in a coherent and artistic manner. The emphasis shifted from the mimetic and the mechanical transmission of raw reality to move gradually towards artistic representation and dialectic interaction between the literary work and its context, without disputing the vital significance of the realistic. This shift towards a balanced and consciously artistic literature reached its acme in the work of *Jamā'at al-Madrasah al-Ḥadīthah* (the New School).

Jamā'at al-Madrasah al-Ḥadīthah

This group did not start as a proper literary school, as the name implies, but rather as a gathering of enthusiastic young writers whose common dream of issuing a paper of their own, to express their views and publish their unconventional works, took almost a decade to be realized. The nucleus of this group was formed, as early as 1917, as a small and zealous study group. It consisted of only four members: Lāshīn, who was a student at the High School of Engineering; Aḥmad Khayri Sa'īd and Ḥusain Fawzi, who were students at the School of Medicine; and Ḥasan Maḥmūd, who was a student at the Faculty of Arts. They attracted new members and developed and shaped their ideas over the next eight years.[3] By the end of 1924 they had managed to reach a degree of uniformity of ideas, justifying their claim to be a literary school. A most important stage in the life of this school was reached when the first issue of its weekly, *al-Fajr: Ṣaḥīfat al-Hadm wa-l-Binā'*[4] (The Dawn: A Paper for Destruction and Construction), appeared in January 1925. The title and subtitle of this journal emphasize the intention to break with previous practices and herald a new dawn, to dismantle the edifice of the old canon in order to build its new literary thought.

The need for this paper was urgent, not only because it provided a means of communication between the group and the reading public, but also because it established important bonds between this new school and young writers with similar views and aspirations in the country at large, and even in the rest of the Arab world.[5] It was also important because it brought the works of the group to the attention of the literary world, and demonstrated that it was radically different from the two major established literary groups at that time.[6] Although many intellectuals shared the ideas of the new school about the stagnation of the old and the falseness of the new attempts which had been undertaken, this versatile literary school was distinguished, in its leader's words, by "its emphasis on modern sciences, fine arts and creative literature",[7] and also by its concern with the social sciences, music, and drama.[8] The totality of their perception and their awareness of the interaction between various literary and artistic endeavours lent their work greater consistency and vigour.

Like many avant-garde literary movements, the *Jamā'at al-Madrasah al-Ḥadīthah* group held their meetings in a pavement café or in the private homes of their members (e.g. Lāshīn and Ibrāhim al-Miṣri). Their cultural views and artistic visions were matured and shaped through fervent discussion. They were influenced mainly by European culture and literature. Ḥaqqi, a member of the group, divided their cultural development into two stages. During the first and less significant stage, they read mainly French, British, American and Italian authors. These included French writers such as La Fontaine, Balzac, Hugo, Dumas *père* and *fils,* Baudelaire, Flaubert, Maupassant, and Rimbaud; British writers such as Shakespeare, Scott, Carlyle, Thackeray, Dickens, Stevenson, and Wilde; American writers such as Poe and Mark Twain; and Italians such as Dante, Boccaccio, and Pirandello.[9] The influence of these authors was largely a theoretical one which increased their knowledge of artistic devices but failed to inspire them.

During the second and crucial stage, which Ḥaqqi calls *marḥalat al-ghidhā' al-rūḥi,* the stage of spiritual nourishment, they fell entirely under the influence of Russian literature until it became the *primum mobile* behind their movement and the main source of their inspiration. They identified easily with the world of pre-revolutionary Russian literature and read Pushkin, Gogol, Lermontov, Turgenev, Dostoevsky, Tolstoy, Chekhov, Gorky, and Artzybashev. The impact of these authors' works upon them was enormous.[10] Some of the leading members of the group went as far as to deny any influence but that of Russian literature;[11] one asserted that Russian literature and music were the closest to "our spirit and our problems",[12] and others devoted a great deal of time and effort to introducing and translating Russian literature.[13] Indeed, there was hardly an issue of *al-Fajr* without one or more Russian writers studied or translated in it.[14] There is also some evidence to suggest the group's acquaintance with the work of Baydas and his translations in his *al-Nafā'is al-'Aṣriyyah.* Indeed, Baydas' collection was published in Cairo a few months before the launching of *al-Fajr.* Even a writer as able as Lāshīn took the liberty of Egyptianizing some of Chekhov's works (without mentioning the origin), only to be attacked by the critics, whose somewhat sardonic reaction demonstrated the fact that adaptation could no longer be tolerated among a certain circle of intellectuals.[15]

In addition to being socially and politically oriented and eager to root the new literary discourse in the life and daily concerns of their readers, this group of young writers was also aware of what Max Weber calls "ideal types", which he defined as "groups of characteristics which may never be found together in any one individual case, but which yet constitute a true type, a meaningful unified analytical entity".[16] The attempt to mirror these "ideal types" of real Egyptians in their works was the basis of their call to create *adab qaṣaṣi qawmi* (national narrative literature).[17] Although they recognized the valuable contributions of earlier writers of narrative discourse, they realized that the short story was still in its infancy and attempts to bring it to maturity were still needed. They worked to develop mature forms of the short story which would be able to go beyond the requirements of local colour and approach the status of world literature with specific national associations — *adab qaṣaṣi qawmi*. The leader of the group, Aḥmad Khayri Sa'īd, proclaimed that the group had grafted the art of modern fiction on to Arabic literature.[18]

Although there is a slight exaggeration in Sa'īd's statement, one cannot deny that it contains an element of truth. The group created in Egypt's cultural life, and in that of the Arabs in general, a current of new ideas and concepts about creative literature and its role and place in the life of society. This current of fresh ideas gained wider public acceptance for the short story as a noteworthy literary genre, and for creative literature in general. It also brought about a more serious approach to creative writing, familiarized the reading public with certain artistic conventions of narrative, and helped the writers develop their technical expertise and widen the scope of their medium.

Their weekly, *al-Fajr,* disseminated these new ideas on a wide scale,[19] and prepared the ground for well-established and respectable magazines to publish short stories and to encourage authors to write them.[20] It also established new criteria in dealing with literature not as something incidental to political and ideological writing, but as a significant, independent activity. This enriched both creative literature and criticism. These new criteria also underlined the relationship between literary work and the other media of artistic expression. The emphasis shifted from the political relevance of the work to its artistic form, without sacrificing its social or edifying role, and a new concept of regional literature was created which was not confined by the limitations of "local colour", but was capable of portraying the human aspects of mature Egyptian characters and scenes.[21] The new criteria also affirmed the role of selectivity in representation, stressed the power of imagination, and emphasized the subtlety of the sophisticated relationship between art and reality.[22]

Because of the favourable atmosphere generated by the spread of these critical concepts and ideas, it was easier for Lāshīn to omit the lengthy introductions which his predecessors had felt compelled to write. In contrast to his predecessors, Lāshīn (surrounded as he was by the other members of the group who were naturally critical as well as supportive) realized the necessity of rewriting and revising his work in order to refine, compress, and improve its structure and style.[23]

Lāshīn commenced writing short stories as early as 1921 or 1922,[24] but he refrained from publishing any of his early attempts and continued to improve on them until late 1924.[25] From then on, he wrote and published frequently in *al-Fajr* and in several other magazines after its closure.[26] He was, in fact, the first member of the group to write short stories to any significant extent, and was the most profound of them. He was also the only one among them who found the courage to collect his works in book form,[27] for, despite the fact that many of his colleagues (e.g. Aḥmad Khayri Sa'īd,[28] Ḥusain Fawzi,[29] and Yaḥyā Ḥaqqi[30]) wrote and published a number of relatively mature and coherent stories, they did not endeavour to collect them in book form. His first collection, *Sukhriyat al-Nāy* (The Flute's Irony), appeared in 1926, and his second, *Yuḥkā Anna* (Once Upon a Time), in 1929/1930,[31] bringing most of his work within the context of *Jamā'at al-Madrasah al-Ḥadīthah*, which went into decline before the end of the 1920s.

Although he tried to write after the breakup of the group, it would appear that working within the group was an important stimulus, for thereafter he found it extremely difficult to continue.[32] However, in his few works he was able to create a coherent artistic vision and to put the new ideas of his group into practice. As well as the works of his elder brother, Muḥammad 'Abd al-Raḥim,[33] who ignited his enthusiasm for literature, Lāshīn read the short stories of his predecessors and assimilated their more significant achievements.[34] He especially tried to avoid treating their themes or dealing with their character types. Nevertheless, he did adopt in his own way some of the 'Ubaids' and Muḥammad Taymūr's themes, but did not overwork them, as they had done. He clearly intended to achieve a wide modulation in theme, character, and structure.

Narrative Survey of the Society

The rooting of the new narrative discourse in social reality, its integration into the life of the new reading public, and its use as a means of altering their perception of themselves and their society had never been as comprehensive or exhaustive as in the work of Lāshīn. The central aim of his work appears to be a literary survey of social life in Egypt in order to integrate the short story into the country's social and cultural consciousness and indirectly expose its social problems and defects. Lāshīn's detailed presentations of characters in their environment implies an attempt to redefine the sensory world, not in its neutral existence, but in relation to the needs and aspirations of individuals. It is part of the larger aim of what Watt calls "the production of what purports to be an authentic account of the actual experiences of individuals".[35]

In this type of social survey through narrative discourse, the author endeavours to make ever larger areas of social reality accessible and comprehensible to the individual. Mediating social experience through narrative discourse provides the reader with a type of knowledge that, although no longer derived from direct experience, is still subject to what Benjamin calls "prompt verifiability". Lāshīn, himself a son of the middle class, naturally focused his work on its characters and values — an attitude he had inherited from previous writers. Yet he does not side with this class at the expense of art or reality, nor does he offer the reader his own views about it. Lāshīn was the first Arab writer to realize, as a critic of the European short story has written, that "the particular domain of the short story is unique. It is a flash of insight that leads to a story; it is not a vision simply of ecstatic moments or aesthetic impressions. It is not the vision of the nature poets. It is a vision of people".[36]

The people who matter in Lāshīn's world represent the whole spectrum of middle-class life: for example, a lawyer who comes home, after studying in France, with ambitious dreams in his mind and tuberculosis in his body which annihilates both his life and dreams, in *"Sukhriyat al-Nāy"*.[37] Another lawyer brings home from France, along with his excellent qualifications, a foreign wife who erodes his happiness, wealth, fame, stability, and honour. The wife fails to adjust her life or habits to those of Egypt, and when she dies she leaves behind a miserable daughter who is unable to feel at home with either the Egyptian community or the ghetto of alien Europeans (*"al-Wiṭwāṭ"*[38] [The Bat]). A third lawyer falls for the widow of his dearest friend and soon turns a discussion of the complicated problem of her inheritance to maudlin talk and kisses (*"wa-Lakinnahā al-Ḥayāh"*[39] [But Life is Like This]). A teacher of geography and calligraphy who is dismissed from his job descends to alcoholism and forces his wife into prostitution, in *"fī Qarār al-Hāwiyah"*[40] (In the Bottom of the Abyss).

A civil servant who has risen from the working class gets married to the domineering daughter of his previous master, who is now bankrupt, in *"Manzil li-l-Ījār"*[41] (A House to Let). Another civil servant pours scorn on the guttersnipes of the overcrowded slums of the city, in *"Jawlah Khasirah"*[42] (A Lost Round). A third civil servant attempts to marry in the old-fashioned manner through a matchmaker (*"Yuḥkā Anna"*);[43] the marriage is unhappy and insecure and drives the husband to excessive drinking (*"Alwū"*[44] [Hello!]). Yet another civil servant seizes the first opportunity to have an affair with the beautiful young wife of the ageing office attendant, who mistreats her, in *"Lawn al-Khajal"*[45] (The Colour of Humility). Most of these civil servants spend a great deal of their time in pavement cafés, chatting over a cup of tea and a hubble-bubble pipe about their fears, interests, and superstitions, as in *"Qiṣṣat 'Ifrīt"*[46] (A Story of a Ghost), or venting their feelings about their sexual frustrations, in *"al-Fakhkh"*[47] (The Trap).

Apart from these civil servants and professionals, there are some other characters from different sections of the middle class: a polygamous, self-made cloth merchant who treats his children badly, in *"al-Infijār"*[48] (The Explosion); a foreign salesman who is rejected by the professionals of his class, in *"al-Wiṭwāṭ"*; and a wicked, educated dropout from the upper class who secures his future by marrying rich old women and fleecing them of their money (*"Bayt al-Ṭā'ah"*[49] [A House with Minimum Legal Requirements]).[50] There are also many others, such as the rich widow who ensnares young men through her wealth and her sensually plump figure, in *"al-Kahlah al-Mazhuwwah"*[51] (The Coquettish Old Woman); the widow who fights at all costs for the future of her children, in *"al-Qadar"*[52] (Destiny); and the rejected wife who follows the news of her previous husband with his new wife in jealousy and despair, in *"Mādhā*

Yaqūl al-Wada'"[53] (What Does Fortune Say?). A student comes from the countryside to complete his higher education in the capital and seduces the wronged wife of his next-door neighbour, in "*Bayt al-Ṭā'ah*", or by his childish curiosity ruins the life of his neighbour, in "*al-Shabaḥ al-Māthil fi al-Mir'āh*"[54] (A Ghost in the Mirror). Corrupt clerics are represented — two Muslims[55] and one Christian[56] — taking advantage of the veneration in which their robes are held.[57]

In addition to all these, there are two other characters who are particularly significant, not only because they offer the reader the first coherent presentation of the frustrated and thwarted character in modern Egyptian literature, but also because they have momentous political implications. The first is the protagonist of "*al-Zā'ir al-Ṣāmit*"[58] (The Silent Visitor), a brave soldier in 'Urābi's army who is dragged down by the disastrous rout of the revolutionary forces; his children are brought up by a defeated and socially frustrated father and subsequently meet with extreme misfortune. The second is one of the activists of the 1919 revolution; his fate, described in "*Taḥt 'Ajalat al-Ḥayāh*"[59] (At Life's Mercy), is no less tragic than that of his predecessor. He also falls dramatically from being a brilliant student at Cairo University, a revolutionary activist, and a far-sighted intellectual to being a frustrated man filled with despair and vague fears.

Without a reasonable understanding of what the failure of 'Urābi's uprising meant to the Egyptians, or what the ramifications were of the brutal destruction of Egypt's aspirations during the 1919 revolution, it is difficult to comprehend fully these two short stories or to appreciate some of their various levels of meaning. It is not mere coincidence that Lāshīn chose a soldier to portray the deep suffering and humiliation of Egypt's defeat by the occupying British forces and a clever student to portray the far-reaching effect of the crushing of the country's hopes for independence, nor that his treatment of the second story is more convincing and artistically more coherent than the first one. Lāshīn himself was one of the intellectuals who were involved in the 1919 revolution and suffered from the dissipation of its hopes.

Apart from all these gradations of the middle-class spectrum which Lāshīn places in the centre of his fictional realm, there is a group of inhabitants of the lower classes who crowd round the fringe of his society but are never allowed to occupy the centre of the stage.[60] Yet lower-class characters are carefully illustrated in Lāshīn's world, despite the obvious overtone of sarcasm and disdain in his representation of them. In fact, he exceeds all artistic licence, turns subtle derision into loud contempt, and uses insulting words and highly charged expressions such as *safalah, ḥuthālah, ri'ā'*, and *dahmā'*[61] (vulgar, scum, riff-raff and rabble), which, apart from being artistically ill-chosen, reveal his hostility towards the poor. As Malcolm Bradbury remarks in his discussion of narrative presentation, the writer "has to persuade us into accepting the laws of, the terms of, the expectations proper to, those principles of development and exploration by which the whole work becomes a structure".[62] Lāshīn's contemptuous treatment of the poor is overt and unpalatable; it fails, in the words of Bradbury again, to "devise a tone — a relationship with the reader which enables him to perceive and share that universe, to respond to it with certain attitudes, certain sympathies and reputations".[63]

Characterization, Themes and Settings

All but one of Lāshīn's stories take place in the city,[64] where he concentrated on two main scenes: the first domestic, inside the houses of the urban middle class, and the second public, in cafés, government offices, and the streets and alleys of the poor quarters of Cairo. This does not mean that Lāshīn offers his reader limited scope of movement in the location of his action. Within the city he introduces a wide range of common and interesting places, achieving a spatial survey. There are variations on the internal scene in the middle-class house with its multifarious degrees of poverty and wealth, tidiness and disorder, cleanliness and filth. When he takes his characters out, he accompanies them to sundry places: pleasant pavement cafés, gloomy bars, the hall of a canonical court, a boat on the Nile, the cemetery, or the tram stop. He also mentions Alexandria, the seaside, and Upper Egypt, without departing from Cairo, which remains the centre of his world. Anywhere else exists only verbally and not factually.

In his *mise en scène* Lāshīn uses three methods. The first is romantic representation, which deals with the location of the action through the emotional and sometimes sentimental moods of the characters involved and denies it any objective, independent existence.[65] The second is photographic representation, which tries to achieve verisimilitude and describes the setting in the most minute detail, regardless of its function in the work.[66] The third is realistic representation, in which the scene, described in a condensed and functional manner, becomes integral to the action without denying the location its independence from both action and character; its main concern is to attain integration and harmony between the various aspects of the work.[67] These three methods do not correspond to three stages in Lāshīn's literary career, but coexist,[68] mainly because of the brevity of the period in which he wrote the bulk of his work. With this wide range of urban characters and locations, Lāshīn provides a comprehensive social survey of Egyptian life in the 1920s. He deals with a range of themes and issues in an attempt to root the short story in the life of the middle class that formed the major part of the new reading public.

Among Lāshīn's themes, three were inherited from previous writers and the rest were new. He uses Nadīm's theme of alcoholism in three stories without freeing himself entirely of the didactic overtones of Nadīm's pithy sermons. In the first, "*Alwū*", he delineates some of the reasons why men drink (mainly as a means of release from their troubled lives) and then fall into the vicious circle whereby drinking causes more trouble and so leads to more drinking. In the second, *"fi Qarār al-Hāwiyah"*, he treats the consequences of alcoholism and how it leads to the tragic disintegration of the family. In the third, *"al-Shabaḥ al-Māthil fi al-Mir'āh"*, he describes how drinking can be a symptom of a state of grave anxiety and remorse and often a prelude to insanity. Beside this Nadīmian theme, there is another which Lāshīn touches upon in *"Manzil li-l-Ījār"*: the drastic effect of gambling upon family ties and a man's status in his immediate surroundings.

Lāshīn also introduces some illuminating variations on the two 'Ubaids' favourite theme of incompatible spouses, without repeating their views, despite the fact that he also emphasizes the problem of cultural disparity between the spouses. Although he appreciates marriage as an institution which has enabled civilized man to channel and control his natural craving for sex and companionship, he attacks marriages which are established on feeble bases and raises various issues concerning the causes and consequences of such marriages. He attacks the laws and conventions which grant the husband rights which he certainly does not deserve and impose heavy burdens on the wife, as in *"Bayt al-Ṭā'ah"*. He indicates the possible grave consequences of resorting to the matchmaker, whose very existence typifies the regressive habits and customs by which marriage takes place. He also deals with the effect of a wide age gap between the partners of a marriage on their social and psychological well-being, in *"Yuḥkā Anna"* and *"Qisṣṣat Zawājih bi-Su'ād"*[69] (The Story of his Marriage to Su'ād).

In *"Ṣaḥḥ"*[70] (Correct), his first published short story, he demonstrates the dominance of the generation gap over any loyalty or traditional respect. In other stories, such as *"al-Zā'ir al-Ṣāmit"*, *"Lawn al-Khajal"*, and *"al-Kahlah al-Mazhuwwah"*, he stresses the cultural gaps which destroy the marriage and lead to adultery or to the death of the tormented wife. In *"Alwū"* and *"Manzil li-l-Ījār"* he shows how the aggravation of the cultural gap by the class gap can cause the destruction of the marriage, and how the couple involved are reduced to a state of wretchedness. The most extreme example of the dramatic effect of this gap upon the married couple and their offspring can be found in *"al-Wiṭwāṭ"*, in which the daughter has to pay heavily when she realizes that her gallicized behaviour has alienated her from her milieu. In *"al-Ḥubb Yalhū"*[71] (Love's Frivolities) the author creates, with some consistency and sophistication, a suggestive picture of a closed social environment, and sheds doubts on the successful future of a marriage arranged in such a milieu. In his evocation of this stagnant atmosphere, he interweaves descriptive details with elements of fate in a way which resembles Greek tragedy.

The third theme Lāshīn derives from the work of his predecessors is that of the corruption and hypocrisy of religious leaders. He criticizes what he sees as their unjustified status in two stories and a sketch, and it appears as a sub-theme in two more stories. The first, *"Mifistūfūlīs"*

(Mephistopheles),[72] illustrates how its protagonist's religious pretensions are wholly insincere and self-interested and how he uses religion to facilitate his sinful behaviour. The second, *"Minṭaqat al-Ṣamt"*[73] (The Domain of Silence), depicts a hypocritical priest who exploits the secrets of the confessional by blackmailing a girl for his own sexual satisfaction. The witty but artistically feeble sketch, *"al-Shaikh Muḥammad al-Yamāni"*, makes little contribution to this theme. The two religious characters of *"al-Kahlah al-Maẓhuwwah"* and *"Ḥadīth al-Qaryah"*, however, add depth to the picture of the evil nature of such people, adding ignorance, deception, pimping, and greed to their vices.

In addition to these three themes which Lāshīn inherited but which he was able to revitalize and give depth to, there are a number of new ones: polygamy and how it militates against the polygamist's children, in *"al-Infijār"*, and inflicts evils on the whole family, in *"Manzil li-l-Ījār"* and *"Jawlah Khāsirah";* the corrupt institutions in social life, particularly that of *bayt al-ṭā'ah,* which is supposed to cement family ties, while in fact it erodes their very existence, in *"Bayt al-Ṭā'ah"*; the lack of healthy accommodation, especially for those on limited incomes, in *"Manzil li-l-Ījār"*; and the need to adapt to new cultural influences properly and carefully, especially those from occidental civilization, and to be constantly aware of their possible consequences, in *"al-Wiṭwāṭ"* and *"Ḥadīth al-Qaryah"*.

He also exposes quack doctors, in *"Jawlah Khāsirah"*, and faith healing, in *"al-Zā'ir al-Ṣāmit"*; the closed horizons of civil servants who have many aspirations they are unable to fulfil, in *"al-Fakhkh"*; and the corrupt policemen who make their judgements according to the size of the bribe offered, in *"al-Shāwīsh Baghdādi"* (Sergeant Baghdadi). He also treats the dramatic effect of superstition on family life, in *"Qiṣṣat 'Ifrīt"* and *"al-Zā'ir al-Ṣāmit"*, and illustrates the suffering of helpless widows in a world without adequate security in *"al-Qadar"* and *"Mādhā Yaqūl al-Wada'"*. He criticizes the hateful traditional interference of mothers-in-law in the life of the newly-weds in *"al-Zā'ir al-Ṣāmit"*, and scorns the greed of those who use marriage as a bridge to wealth in *"Alwū"* and *"Bayt al-Ṭā'ah"*.

Many of these themes are obviously of a social nature and were related to questions that were the objects of lengthy discussion in Egyptian public life throughout the 1920s. As an active participant in an intellectual movement, it was virtually impossible for Lāshīn to escape the influence of the ideas of social reform held by the eminent thinkers of this period. Nevertheless, he has his own personal, critical approach to the ethos of his society, and is not a preacher or social reformer but a short-story writer who deals with the views and values inherent in his fiction. One important personal feature is that his particular artistic view of the world leads him, in his treatment of some of these themes, to introduce fatalism into the action, so that things appear to be predestined and the characters to lack freedom of choice. This is not an accidental element, but rather a deliberate attempt to underline the irony of life and widen the scope of the action.

In the title story of *"Sukhriyat al-Nāy"*, death steals away the young man full of promise and aspirations but spares the old man who lives from day to day without hopes or plans. The heroine of *"al-Qadar"* receives a fatal shock just when she thinks that her torment has come to an end. In *"Alwū"* the hero endures the agony of an incompatible spouse for five years in the hope that his ageing father-in-law may die and leave him a fortune. When he can no longer bear his slavery and divorces his wife, he receives the news of the old man's death on the completion of the divorce procedure. *"Mādhā Yaqūl al-Wada'"* shows how, in six long years, the cycle of destiny turns full circle for the heroine and avenges her grievances. In these stories, Lāshīn uses accidental events in a way which surpasses the naïve, haphazard coincidences of previous writers, and so enriches his action and widens its implications. This also suggests a conscious endeavour on his part to control the structure of his work and to pay attention to various functional dimensions of the action, and not only to its social or moral implications.

A Critical Vision of People and Society

Lāshīn's intention to control the form and content of his work demonstrates itself in his stand *vis-à-vis* human character and women in particular. Apart from being heavily influenced by the Turkish criteria of female beauty, it seems at first glance that Lāshīn supports women's emancipation, but deeper exploration shows this not to be the case. There is evidence to suggest that he considers women to be the origin of malice, vice, evil and anxiety. Even in those stories which seem to defend the wronged woman, e.g. *"Bayt al-Ṭā'ah"* and *"fi Qarār al-Hāwiyah"*, he does not vindicate her on the grounds of her own merits (for instance, for being a sensitive, cultured, attractive person like the 'Ubaids' women), but because she is victim of man's tyranny.

In these same stories, alongside the victims, there are women who play the villain or abet the committing of adultery.[74] In many of his stories, the heroine plans her adultery carefully and skilfully, and promptly takes revenge when ill-treated.[75] With her, fidelity is in short supply; revenge is more important than loyalty; and a justification for her acts is readily found.[76] She can, and does, easily turn her husband's life into a hell, impoverish him without the slightest compunction, betray his memory with his closest friend, or use her influential lover to impose her will upon him.[77] As a mother-in-law, she is wicked and unbearable; as a mother, she can offer nothing but hollow sympathy, and may indeed harm her daughter by her naïve good intentions.[78] The woman is also the cause of many crimes committed by men, and she plays an active role in prostituting her fellow women.[79]

But there is as much justification for calling Lāshīn a misanthropist as a misogynist, for his male characters are often no less degenerate. In his works the man is a ruthless drunkard who compels his young daughter to go out in the severe cold of midnight to buy him drink,[80] or treats his wives malevolently and relieves them of their money.[81] When he makes some money the first idea that crosses his mind is to marry an additional wife and to be parsimonious with his children.[82] If he occupies a religious position he exploits people's confidence in order to satisfy his lust and greed;[83] if he attains a public position, he accepts bribes.[84] He does not hesitate to betray his friends with their wives,[85] or to marry women out of avarice.[86]

But, however dark his portraits of men and women, Lāshīn is by no means a moral preacher, and, among the Arab short-story writers up to the 1930s, he is the least didactic. He tries to bring about reform not through exhortation, but through the provocative effect of his art. His stand against the characters who deserve to be criticized is indicative of a sarcastic and satirical attitude towards certain social phenomena in his society. Some of his contemporaries realized the provocative nature of his satires but failed to see his point.[87] Although they appreciated the highly artistic quality of his work, the dilettanti among them saw nothing in it but local scenes and distorted satirical descriptions of what they called "some artificial aspects of our popular life".[88]

Though Lāshīn presents a gloomy picture of Egypt's social life, it is difficult to say that his way of expressing his disaffection with the dominant social values is based on distortion. His ruthless candour in stripping both character and situation to the bone is supported by sensitive artistry, a wholesome sense of humour, and a deep understanding of the undercurrents of Egyptian life. His fine sense of humour and his alert awareness of the arrangement of his stories saves many of his gloomy pictures from falling into the abyss of melodrama or exaggeration. He has, indeed, the strongest sense of structure among his contemporaries. The analysis of his magnificent story, "*Ḥadīth al-Qaryah*" (Village Small Talk), in the next chapter demonstrates Lāshīn's masterly sense of structure.

Lāshīn's career was both short and chequered, and he was unable to maintain in the rest of his work the standard attained in "*Ḥadīth al-Qaryah*". His work is clearly influenced (like that of his colleagues in *al-Madrasah al-Ḥadīthah*) by Russian literature in general,[89] and by Chekhov's short stories in particular. Any comparison between the stories of Maḥmūd Taymūr and those of Lāshīn reveals a clear difference in artistic approach; namely, that Taymūr's works are endowed with Maupassant-like qualities, while Lāshīn's are characterized by a Chekhovian flavour. "In general Maupassant sought to make his stories dramatic and in order to do that, he was prepared if necessary to sacrifice probability ... Chekhov deliberately eschewed the dramatic. He dealt with ordinary people leading ordinary lives".[90] This is what Lāshīn does; he avoids the dramatic and sudden denouement whenever possible and resorts to simplicity and more contemplative elements.

Indeed, Lāshīn's adaptation of Chekhovian qualities and artistic approaches goes far beyond his attempt to rework the two stories that brought upon him the rage of the sophisticated critics of the 1920s. Although he could not completely eschew the dramatic, he succeeded in playing it down in most of his works. He introduces ordinary men leading normal lives and reveals through his Chekhovian action and characterization the richness and ritualistic qualities of life in a manner that makes small events radiate with poetic significance. The texture of his simple characters' lives, their daily acts, and their sensitive interaction with others are rich in humanity and pride; but it is a unique kind of pride that manifests itself in subtlety and humility. The narrator's pride in *"Ḥadīth al-Qaryah"* prevents him from stooping to the sheikhs' level, and as a result he loses out. Yet, as in *Uncle Vanya* or *The Three Sisters,* he prefers the bitterness of this ostensible defeat to the vanity of a triumph that requires descent into vulgarity.

Vulgarity is a mortal sin in Chekhov's work, and Lāshīn, likewise, portrays it in many of his works[91] as the malady which erodes the soul of the individual. In his many stories of civil servants one finds a mixture of the tragicomic atmosphere of Gogol's "The Overcoat" and Chekhov's "Death of a Civil Servant", with the sensitive characterization of an oppressed marginal group whose tormented souls are subjugated by the vulgarity of their surroundings. Like Chekhov, Lāshīn was appalled by the growing vulgarity round him and accentuated in his work the noble and naïve qualities of his lone, proud characters by setting them in coarse and repugnant surroundings. Like Chekhov also, he is fond of contrasting the savage, crude blindness of vulgarity with the delicate, vulnerable, perceptive grace of refinement. He uses both comic and poetic irony to portray such contrasts in a subtle and effective artistic manner.

Lāshīn's Lasting Significance

Apart from his attempt to avoid his predecessors' technical errors, Lāshīn was fully aware of his readers and was eager to win their support. This awareness accounts for the simplicity of his language, and the frequent occurrence of preambles, in some of which he attempts to address his reader directly.[92] Unfortunately, the poor response he received from both readers and critics, along with his impatience at the task of bearing the cross of the neglected pioneer, discouraged him and was the major factor behind his early abandonment of literature.[93] It is now a platitude that the short-story writer needs to cut out "explanations, preambles, elaborate introductions, apologies, or other notations as to place, time, or occasion",[94] but it was difficult for Lāshīn and his contemporaries to adopt this convention while aiming at a reader whose knowledge of the traditions of modern narrative discourse was almost nil, and who was apt to turn his back on their work if it was beyond his taste or comprehension.

Lāshīn abandoned writing lengthy introductions to his collections of short stories which justified the work and explained its importance and function, believing that this was the task of the literary critic and not the creative writer. Yet, he could not dispense with the preambles within each story, for he and his contemporaries felt the need to acquaint their readers with modern narrative discourse by establishing a bridge, consisting of these undesirable explanations, between them and a more mature fictional form. One needs to bear in mind that, at this period, the dominant literary values were inimical to any realistic representation. They put vivid imagination, lyricism, inspiration, verbal skills, and strong emotional impact at the top of the scale of aesthetic values.

This situation led the writers of fiction to emphasize in their preambles the value and importance of their new opposing aesthetics, which called for a closer relationship between art and reality and preferred the cognitive to the expressive, the dramatic to the lyrical, the human to the sublime, and the realistic to the imaginary. In their reaction to the dominant literary values they went a little too far in order to win their readers' interest, and tried to convince them that they were conveying bold reality and not writing fiction. Lāshīn was aware, perhaps more than most of his contemporaries, of the difficulty of abandoning these rudimentary explanations without widening the gap between his work and the reading public, but at the same time he recognized the necessity of at least diminishing them in the interests of artistic criteria. Their retention, however, is indicative of the importance Lāshīn attached to the reader's perception of his work as one marked by its tenacious affinities with reality without implying an imitation of its logic, for he also was keen to separate the logic and dynamics of art from those of reality.

On the horns of this dilemma, Lāshīn tried to make preambles as short as possible and to integrate them into the work. Some of the shortcomings related to the use of this explanatory technique are as follows: a tone of apologetic self-justification or vindication, and of didacticism; the emphasis on action at the expense of character, with a failure to motivate some of the character's actions internally and thus maintain plausibility by means of external references; the occurrence of snippets of action which have no organic relation to the main one; the portrayal of certain portions of individual lives and various details of action for the sake of exhibiting wide varieties of characterization and situations, without relating them to the general theme of the story or transcending the level of mere examples; the passing of moral judgements on a character or certain aspects of the action by means of direct statements from the author; and the failure to understand that "description is always a form of characterization".[95] These faults manifest both the writer's dilemma, as he is torn between his commitment to his art and the need to respond to his reader's demands and mentality, and his craving to convey a strong sense of verisimilitude in order to accomplish his social survey of his country's life through fiction.

This dilemma is evident in Lāshīn's fluctuations between contradictory elements: purely descriptive writing concerned with an often romanticized, simplistic or naturalistic depiction of regional features and types coexists with writing that transcends this parochialism and at the same time gives a more realistic and dramatic representation of particular and specific characteristics.[96] The critics' response intensified his dilemma — some praised the local colour,[97] whereas others deprecated it[98] — and they did not help him to distinguish a work of art from a slice of life, or to avoid "the danger of details becoming important in themselves".[99] They could not help him to realize that "with the loss of the art of narration, details cease to be transmitters of concrete aspects of the action and attain significance independent of the action and of the lives of the characters".[100]

Therefore he continued to fluctuate between unfruitful alternatives and was not able to lift his writing out of the old pattern and lead it towards a more mature artistic phase; he attempted to delineate realistic elements but could not free his work from sentimental expressions of sadness and grief;[101] he tried to rescue his work from the generalizations, simplifications, and sentimental exaggerations of his predecessors, and to lend precision and accuracy to his presentation, but, despite this, the issues in his stories remain blurred and his characters often lack discernible motivation for their actions. None the less, on many occasions he does succeed in maintaining a delicate balance between characterization and the presentation of action. His awareness of the importance of characterization as a major principle of any mature short story was far in advance of that of his predecessors because he realized that the essential difference between the short story and previous traditional tales and *maqāmāt* lay in the concept of characterization. His characterizations, especially in his best works, constitute a distinct landmark between two phases in the development of Arabic narrative discourse. Traditional fictional writing does "not attempt to create *real people* so much as stylized figures which expand into psychological archetypes".[102] Lāshīn sought to create real people in plausible situations who could also expand into psychological archetypes.

Narrative Discourse and the Reader's Consciousness

Because of Lāshīn's desire to accomplish his social survey and root narrative discourse in the reader's consciousness, most of his stories emphasize the elements engaged in the presentation of this survey, that is, the setting, events, description, dialogue, interaction between characters and between them and the situation, and the actual progression of the action. He realized that character is the cornerstone of any narrative discourse and paid considerable attention to its construction, to the extent of dedicating some of his works to the illustration of certain character types.[103] He also employed his skill at writing repartee and his powerful sense of humour to provide his characters with many witty and humorous remarks which, despite a few lapses into superficial entertainment, enhance their presentation, lend his work vividness, produce a shock of comic surprise, and undermine the melodramatic elements which occasionally occur.[104]

His remarkable sense of comedy sharpens the effectiveness of his racy description and provides his language with suggestive power.[105] This would seem to be because his humour springs from his real experience of human character and not from mere observation of external conduct. Lukács observes: "The opposition between experiencing and observing is not accidental. It arises out of divergent basic positions about life and about the major problems of society and not just out of divergent artistic methods of handling content or one specific aspect of content."[106] Some of Lāshīn's witty remarks may be categorized as wry humour, especially when he has no sympathy for the character,[107] or when he intends to ridicule a certain character or censure some specific behaviour.

In the sphere of language, Lāshīn's style "succeeds in shedding the trappings of archaic traditional prose, inherited from the epoch of Ibn al-Muqaffa' and al-Jāḥiẓ to the era of Tawfīq al-Bakri, yet it fails to escape from the influence of al-Manfalūṭi and al-Muwayliḥi".[108] He uses many Qur'ānic expressions[109] and traditional or highly classical verbal structures, but for different purposes.[110] By grafting these expressions onto his language, Lāshīn kills two birds with one stone: he assures his reader that he can write in the traditional manner if he likes (in fact some of his critics swallowed the bait and praised his elegant classical style),[111] and at the same time, he demonstrates the absurdity of writing in such an undescriptive language. Lāshīn turns what has been for too long a highly respectable style into the subject of mockery, "as if the use of the classical style reaches a point where its new function is to create a comic effect".[112] Ironically, he juxtaposes highly classical expressions, with their inherent wordplay and metonymy, alongside vernacular or transcribed foreign words,[113] a feature which reveals another facet of his dilemma.

His use of language is more sensitive, skilful and aware of the nature of narrative linguistic demands than that of any other short-story writer in the Arab world before 1930. He understood the specific nature and the multitude of functions of the language of fiction: the necessity of informing by means of implication, the fine difference between "emotive" and "referential" language,[114] the significance of comic irony and suggestive remarks, and the need to avoid exaggeration, authorial comment, or any kind of direct authorial interference in the narrative. However, it should not be concluded from these remarks that Lāshīn is a pure stylist; on the contrary, one could maintain that he is "interested in style only insofar as it will make what he has to say more lively and memorable, and he knows that events, however improbable or even impossible, can only be made lively and memorable in narration if the language in which they are expressed, in addition to carrying the main line of the meaning, can simultaneously make vivid contact with experience as known to the most unadventurous".[115] He realizes that his language is his medium and that his business, as Chekhov says, "is to be talented, that is, to be able to distinguish important testimony from trivia, to illuminate the figures and speak their language".[116]

Lāshīn's comparatively advanced understanding of the nature of the language of narrative contributes enormously to the artistic coherence of his work and widens the scope of his vision. An anonymous reviewer wrote of him, "He has a remarkable talent for form, and a gift to harmonize different elements of structure. The mentality of an engineer may have provided him with this strong sense of structure and harmony".[117] He tried to modulate the form from one story to another, and used varied techniques: the connected narrative with its syllogistic progression which purports to reveal various dimensions of the character and action; the fixed image of a character or incident which, often, seems flat or motionless; the first person who seems as if he is actually telling the story or writing it;[118] the story in the form of a letter; the diary form in which the story pretends to be a factual document; the fictional sketch (which, mostly, fails to produce a good story); and the story constructed from a group of episodes or flashbacks. In these various types of narrative, some of which appear in the Arabic short story for the first time in his work, Lāshīn achieved an interaction between form and language in a way that both enriched and created plausible characterization. Lāshīn is indeed the first Arab advocate of the importance of revision and rewriting in the field of narrative fiction, for he realized that "revision is a means not only of polishing, but also of compressing. For perfect brevity can seldom be had without long filing and cutting".[119]

Lāshīn, it may be recalled, was a member of a wider group of writers — *Jamā'at al-Madrasah al-Ḥadīthah* — who struggled, in one of its founders' words, "to create authentic, indigenous, Egyptian literature, to bring about a new style free from decoration and obfuscation, to establish the short story in Egypt, and to propagate the trend towards realism";[120] in short, to shape and express a new artistic sensibility. The strength and sophistication of their work, which can be seen in the detailed examination of one of Lāshīn's stories in the next chapter, completed the process of change towards the realistic sensibility and anchored literature firmly in its social context. The domain of their narrative exploration remained for many subsequent years the recognized realm of narrative investigation and provided Arabic narrative discourse with the relevance and legitimacy it required. The realistic sensibility which they established provided both modern Arabic literature and its readers with a strong sense of identity and enhanced their ability to understand themselves.

This pioneering literary group developed the new narrative discourse, participated in delineating its genres, and brought it to maturity, a process which had started sixty years earlier with the first works of Salīm al-Bustāni and 'Abdullah Nadīm. Although the discussion has concentrated on Lāshīn's short stories, his novel, *Ḥawwā' bilā Ādam* (Eve without Adam, 1933), and that of Aḥmad Khayri Sa'īd, *al-Dasā'is wa-l-Dimā'* (Blood and Conspiracies, 1935), played as important a role in the maturation of the novel genre. The strength, both in quality and quantity, of their writing established and broadened the base of this new literary discourse and gained for it the respectability it needed in order to flourish. The impact of their work upon the intelligentsia and the reading public could be seen throughout the next three decades and in the works of other writers from the same generation,[121] and those of the succeeding generation,[122] one of whom (Najīb Maḥfūẓ) was the first Arab writer to win the Nobel Prize for literature, primarily for his realistic narrative work.

7
The Culmination of a Sophisticated Discourse
"Ḥadīth al-Qaryah"

The genesis of modern Arabic narrative discourse brought together various cultural, literary, textual and social strands and wove them into a cohesive whole. The previous chapters of this book elaborated these strands separately and discussed the lengthy process of weaving them together into a distinct narrative discourse and autonomous literary genres. The aim of this concluding chapter is to reverse the critical process of constructing a broad literary history and to analyse a single story to show the intricacy of the weaving procedure and identify as many of the elements which went into its composition as possible, and, more importantly, their interaction within the literary discourse. It will explore how elements of continuity merge with those of discontinuity, how different discourses coexist and clash within the same literary text, and, more significantly, how this interaction between different elements and discourses is vital in the emergence of a mature narrative. The necessary tension within the new narrative discourse stems from the rupture with the dominant traditional modes of expression and their system of manipulating and controlling reality.

Another aim of the detailed analysis of this single narrative text is to establish how it succeeded in creating a structure analogous to reality and the collective consciousness it aspired to express, and how the world-view and the collective consciousness are elaborated implicitly in the overall behaviour of individuals. This is achieved not through ideological speculations but through the examination of textual rubrics and intertextual networks. In this way it becomes clear that the narrative text, whose realization relies on an intricate process of interplay between language, social institutions, subjectivity and power, reflects the various characteristics of "discursive fields" in Foucault's sense of the term.

The text chosen for analysis in this chapter is naturally one of Lāshīn's short stories; a story from his second collection, *Yuḥkā Anna,* entitled "*Ḥadīth al-Qaryah*"[1] (Village Small Talk). This story (its English translation is given in the Appendix) has been selected because it demonstrates the degree of maturity and sophistication which Arabic narrative discourse had attained by 1929, and also because its theme is nothing other than the very process that brought the new narrative discourse into existence: the search for modes of development and progress. The means of realizing this momentous theme within the text is also relevant to the genesis of narrative discourse because it is elaborated through nothing other than the very act of storytelling, of the manipulation of narrative, the use of the story within the story. It is, therefore, thematically and structurally relevant to the very subject of this book, the genesis of narrative discourse.

But Lāshīn's magnificent story is not only relevant to a literary exercise, but is also a rich and important story in its own right, and the analysis undertaken here aims to demonstrate Lāshīn's masterly sense of structure. It also intends to show how the new narrative discourse, culminating in the Arabic short story at the time, attains authenticity and maturity, and how this in turn brings the period of its genesis to a close. It is a momentous story, not only because it constitutes the real birth of the coherent, indigenous, realistic Arabic short story, but also because it focuses its attention on the crossroads at which modern Egypt stood, where the conflict between rural and urban values, between modernism and traditional religious thought, between occidental and oriental cultures was at its height.[2] Yet it treats these complicated issues without falling into the trap of presenting foregone conclusions; though it uses stereotypes, it shuns exaggeration and resorts only to sophisticated literary presentation.

The fact that Lāshīn wrote this text demonstrates Goldmann's precept concerning the ability of an author to create a narrative work which corresponds to the mental structure and the world-view of a particular social group with whom he or she has very little relation.[3] With the publication of "*Ḥadīth al-Qaryah*" in 1929, the process of the genesis of narrative discourse came to its happy end, for it is the most mature literary text that emerged, and contains within its textual structure most of the elements that brought this process to fruition. The aim of this chapter is both to analyse the story as a literary text in order to show these elements at work, and to illuminate the forces at play in the process of the realization of modern Arabic narrative. The elaboration of the elements of composition in this text is also intended to balance the prevalence of thematic analysis in the previous chapters, which was dictated by the simplistic nature of the earlier texts and by the need to identify the elements participating in the genesis of narrative discourse.

Naming as a Prefatory Narrative Device

The first element the reader encounters with the story is its title. The title is the prefatory element of a more comprehensive textual strategy of naming which includes the naming of characters and places within the story. Lāshīn calls his story *"Ḥadīth al-Qaryah"* to draw attention to the nightly gathering which forms the core of the story, and to emphasize that the story is not that of 'Abd al-Samī''s tragedy of adultery and revenge, which occupies no more than one-third of the whole work, but that of the more general talk which preceded, accompanied, and followed it, including the telling of 'Abd al-Samī''s story. The revealing nightly chat starts even before the beginning of 'Abd al-Samī''s story, continues in the peasants' comments on its various details and the suggestive description which accompanies its telling, and goes on after its end.

The linguistic bond, *iḍāfah,* between the two words of the title creates a dialectical relationship between them in which each is emphasized in a different way, the talk by the virtue of its primacy in the word order of *iḍāfah,* and the village by being the syntactic cornerstone of the linguistic construction. The descriptive title focuses our attention equally on both the village and its talk, and establishes from the start the mimetic nature of the story. The title is descriptive rather than metaphorical or interpretive; it points to something that takes shape within the story and not to a value or a message that can be inferred from it. The village is not merely the locus of the talk; it is also the focus of its attention and the real issue in the debate. The talk penetrates the action and frames the various contradictory views expounded in the story of 'Abd al-Samī'. The talk has two functions: the elaboration of the enframed story and the structuring of the whole story in imbricating layers organized in a carefully controlled manner, for what each layer hides is as important as what it reveals. The talk which forms the substance of the story has some of the qualities of the process of imbrication, for it oscillates between revealing and concealing, and in the process employs different modes of mimesis and diegesis. It is also conducted by characters most of whose names are withheld or even suppressed.

There are only two named characters in the story: Sheikh Muḥsin and 'Abd al-Samī'; the rest, including the narrator himself, are nameless. Providing some characters with names while denying names to others was done haphazardly in most of the work of Lāshīn's predecessors. But in this story, Lāshīn understands the significance of the naming device and uses it to the full. Although the story is that of the narrator's weekend visit to the village of his friend, neither the name of the narrator nor that of his friend are provided. The name of the village is also suppressed, for it is not the story of a specific village, but of the archetypal village and of the whole country. The first name which the reader encounters is that of the village *imām*, Sheikh Muḥsin, whose name means the benevolent, the charitable. Sheikh Muḥsin is named ironically, for he is clearly lacking in benevolence and compassion; indeed, he is a highly pragmatic and self-interested person who guards his stakes ruthlessly.

As soon as Sheikh Muḥsin appears, his first utterance brings in the second named character, the protagonist of the story within the story, 'Abd al-Samī'. This establishes a further connection between the two named characters; they are not only named, but they are also connected. The link between the two named characters is in marked contrast to the lack of nexus between the unnamed ones. 'Abd al-Samī' is brought into the narrative by Sheikh Muḥsin solely for his own benefit, to be used as a concrete example; hence the importance of identifying him by name. His is a name that is well known to the peasants, but not to the urban visitors, and this grants Sheikh Muḥsin complete control over the presentation of his story. The name 'Abd al-Samī' means the slave or follower of the one who hears or listens. If the story, on one level, is about the lure of the call for change and the victims of its false assumptions, Lāshīn could not have selected a better name for his character. Within the narrative domain, 'Abd al-Samī' is also the slave of Sheikh Muḥsin and the subject of his total manipulation; his story, and subsequently his narrative existence, depends entirely on the sheikh. An additional significance of the name is related to the verbal fencing-match round which the story is constructed. Although 'Abd al-Samī' is absent from the debate, he is the proof of all that is heard in it, as if he hears and responds to different aspects of the argument; at least, he is used as such.

The Beginning and Its Assumptions

Another prefatory device is the beginning of the story and how it adumbrates certain aspects of its action and theme. In his analysis of the technique of the short story, Bonheim confirms that

> The opening of the short story is more important than that of the novel. Insofar as we can measure in sentences and paragraphs at all, the opening may be shorter in the short story; but of course it occupies a greater percentage of the text. Then too, the short story tends to require a more tightly knit structure, so that the initial sounding of theme and tone is likely to reverberate through the middle and end in a way which is neither called for nor possible in a novel.[4]

In Arabic narrative discourse, the lack of established literary conventions burdened most preceding attempts in this genre with unfunctional preambles. Previous works used textual devices which sought to neutralize the subsequent narrative by feigning to make it the outcome of some natural circumstance and thus, as it were, "disinaugurating" it, to use Barthes' term.[5] The use of certain initiatory devices (e.g. discovered manuscripts, diaries or a bundle of letters, a narrator who confides in the author, or private confessions that are overheard) constituted a denial of narrativity and an attempt to pass the text as reality. It also served as a means to root narrative in reality and to accustom the reader to its conventions.

In his work Lāshīn was aware of the importance of eliminating these unnecessary introductions, and he attempts to reach a satisfactory conclusion in this story. The significance of Lāshīn's achievement in this respect cannot be exaggerated. He starts by eliminating all preambles and goes straight into the story, using report, a mode of narration common to a large number of mature short stories. "Detailed analysis of the modern short story has shown that report and speech have become the dominant mode of the short story in this century ... But only report vies with description in the opening sentences in modern short stories, occurring four times as much as does speech".[6] Bonheim notes that the turn towards the emphasis on report came with James Joyce's *Dubliners,* which was written at roughly the same time as Lāshīn was writing his work.

Lāshīn's beginning uses a report which, by a stroke of genius, incorporates scenic description, anterior necessary information and motivation of the action. The first paragraph provides us with the temporal and the spatial elements of the story. The time of the story is a Friday, the Muslim weekend, a day of rest and of enhanced religious awareness because it is the day of the weekly congregation, the day of the sheikh *par excellence*. The space is the village as observed by the narrator, who is enchanted by its scenic landscape, but affected by the human misery he sees. The introduction of the village through the eyes of the city-dweller sets the scene for the clash between the two which occupies centre stage in the story. The opening also provides us with the necessary information about the background of the two visitors, not directly or abstractly, but through their response to the scene. The scene aptly introduces the reader to both the landscape and the people inhabiting it: the men working in the field under the blazing heat, the women sitting in front of their adobe houses hiding themselves from onlookers with their tattered rags, the children playing with the animals, and the chickens scratching in the crooked narrow alleys of the village.

This is introduced by the narrator in a report in which the character reporting is also the subject and focus of the act of reporting, a narrator reporting events in which he is involved. Self-reporting is normally characterized by a constant tension between revealing and concealing, selection and omission, a dynamic operation that need not necessarily be conducted consciously, for it also involves subtle elements of self-deception. Such characteristics are in harmony with the technique of imbrication. Imbrication of narrative elements performs a number of functions, one of which is the interaction between these elements, and another is the use of overlapping as a device ordering these elements in a hierarchical manner. Yet another is the deviation from traditional discourse and the achievement of what Said calls "convergence of difference and repetition".[7] This also implies that inherent in self-reporting is an elusive manipulation of discourse, and this is revealed from the first sentence of the story. It starts with *"da'āni ṣadīqi"* (my friend invited me), identifying the narrator from the very first word, not as the subject of the verb, and later the action, but as its object, as the recipient of the action, adumbrating his later passivity. He is reporting the action in first-person narrative, but, at the same time, subtly absolving himself from any responsibility for it.

This detachment from the action is soon confirmed when, in the second sentence, the narrator describes himself in third-person narrative as *ibn al-madīnah* (a city-dweller), and when he oscillates between two modes of narrative, personal and apersonal,[8] before the end of the first paragraph. Even before this one can still detect such detachment in the first sentence where he sets himself apart from his friend, for he uses the verb "to spend" twice, initially with a first-person-plural subject, then in the third-person-singular referring to his friend. This indicates that they have common reasons for spending this weekend in the country, but also different ones too; the friend is visiting the village to attend to his business there, while the narrator has no business in the village, a very perceptive opening remark. By the second paragraph, the text makes us aware that the two characters, despite their stated friendship, are different in inclinations, temperament and motivation, and this is highly significant for the understanding of the various layers of meaning within the story.

The economic introduction of elements of anteriority, which is associated with the use of the perfect (past) tense, is coupled with an elaborate exposition of the story's argument which is animated by the shift to the imperfect tense, even in the opening sentence. This slide between the tenses enables the opening to move between various types of narrative and to increase the expositional quality both by descriptive passages and by the amount of comment embedded in the narrated monologue. This in turn provides the reader with the initial theme and tone which reverberate throughout the story. Before the end of the second paragraph, it becomes clear that the views and sentiments of the narrator are in marked contrast to those of his friend, and the two immobile stances are actually searching for a catalyst to animate and verify them. The exposition of the conflicting views of the two urban visitors, inconspicuous and brief as they are, continues to resonate throughout the story. This establishes the frame story as the main driving force in the narrative and contains the enframed story, the story within the story, in its perspective. The author selects first-person narrative for this exposition in order to underline its subjectivity and provide it with elements of equivocation, setting the tone for the clash between country and city.

Dialectics of *Fabula* and *Sjuzhet*

The Russian formalists elaborated three critical terms in their analysis of narrative discourse, almost at the same time as Lāshīn wrote his story. They are *fabula, sjuzhet* and *skaz*.[9] These terms had been enriched and refined through the work of their contemporary, Mikhail Bakhtin,[10] and were later picked up and elaborated by the structuralists, particularly through the work of Barthes[11] and Genette.[12] Using the formalists' basic terms for the analysis of narrative is appropriate for the work of a writer who was heavily influenced by Russian literature, but this does not mean embracing the whole method of formalistic analysis, and it will be clear from our analysis and from the rest of this book that their dehumanization of art and their attempt to divorce it from history, social context and value judgement have been discarded.

The term *fabula* refers to the basic story or the total sum of events and material for narrative construction as they occurred in their chronological order. The term *sjuzhet* refers to the story as it unfolds in the narrative text and the way in which it is told, or its events are reordered or linked together. The *sjuzhet* is naturally the main concern of narrative criticism, for the *fabula,* which can only be perceived through the *sjuzhet,* only serves to articulate the significance of the *sjuzhet* and its reordering of events and manipulation of time and characters. The *fabula* alone, without its artistic embodiment, can never account for the efficacy of narrative discourse; its significance lies in its dialectical interaction with the *sjuzhet.* Art in general, and the art of narrative in particular, depends on the intricacy of the organizational principle. Thus, the task of criticism, as Tolstoy suggested, is "to inquire into the laws governing that labyrinth of linkages, *labirint scepleij,* which is literary art".[13]

The *skaz,* as an important critical term, was elaborated by Bakhtin to denote a technique or mode of narration that imitates or rather internalizes the discourse of an individual. It is a term that merges the concepts of point of view, voice, and tone of narration together into one dynamic unity in order to identify the role of the teller and infer his implied motivation from his production of such discourse. Genette uses the term focalization[14] as an approximate equivalent, after emphasizing the need to perceive focalization not in its purely visual sense, but in a broader perspective which includes cognitive, emotive, and ideological orientation. A narrative text can contain one or more *skaz,* each with its own characteristics and point of view, and the understanding of their different modes is vital for the comprehension of the various facets of the interaction between the *fabula* and the *sjuzhet.*

The *fabula* of "*Ḥadīth al-Qaryah*" can be paraphrased in a few sentences despite the fact that it lasts for a long time, from the arrival of *mu'āwin* (a government official) to the end of the nightly chat. It is the story of a *mu'āwin* who comes from the city to the village, where he sees the beautiful wife of 'Abd al-Samī', who is probably singing that night. He offers her husband a job in the city and asks him to bring his wife to help with the domestic chores in the house of the *mu'āwin.* 'Abd al-Samī' discovers that they are having an affair, surprises them in bed and kills them together; then he goes to the police station and confesses. This story is told by Sheikh Muḥsin to the two urban visitors in a nightly chat. The *fabula* has all the elements of a classic *ménage à trois* which ends in the traditional *crime passionnel*, a popular narrative genre, on which many variations have been written by Lāshīn's predecessors.

Organizing this *fabula* in a *sjuzhet* opens endless possibilities, the most obvious of which would be to fall for the trappings of intrigue and seduction in the *ménage à trois* or the psychological examination of either the wronged husband or the smooth and experienced urban *dragueur*. A third possibility, which Lāshīn uses as an ironic device in his story within the story, is to emphasize the elements of sex and violence to the maximum in order to produce a sensational text. Lāshīn ignores all these and other similar possibilities and opts for a different organizational principle. The examination of his *sjuzhet* reveals that he is aware of the popularity and power of the narrative of adultery and revenge, chooses to subject it to a more complex design, and uses it to serve different ends. The order of the *sjuzhet* is markedly different from that of the *fabula*, for the very order of the *fabula* emphasizes the classic elements of seduction, intrigue and revenge. The *sjuzhet* deliberately inverts this order and starts the story from the end, or near the end, with the arrival of the two urban visitors.

The selection of their arrival as the beginning of the *sjuzhet* structures their visit not as an incidental event, but as a cyclical event in an extended experience, the village's experience of the city-dwellers meddling in its affairs, or, at another level, the subjection of the country to the rubrics of modernization. The beginning with the two urban visitors sets the context in which 'Abd al-Samī''s story is narrated, used, discussed and finally perceived by the reader. This careful setting renders the story of 'Abd al-Samī' cotextual (that is, containing references interior to the narrative rather than verifiable in the outer, non-fictional world) rather than contextual. As such, it becomes a textual strategy, a story within the story. But one of its problematics is that it is easily conceived as contextual, and this in itself enhances its ability to trap both the characters and the readers in its snares, hence ceasing to be contextual and becoming cotextual again. The double function in the enframed story is one of the manifestations of a wider system of binary structures (that will be discussed below) in which many elements of the narrative are organized dyadically, i.e. in pairs of opposing, yet integrated qualities.

The complexity of the structure in which the story-within-a-story technique is used is in itself a rejection of the simplifications of the traditional story of *crime passionnel*. This simple plot with its connected causal narrative is confined to the enframed story in which the characters have become objects of both the author's design and the talk of the frame story. The frame story is dialogically constructed and structurally open-ended, while the enframed is monologically perceived and understood as complete and finite. The marked difference between the compositional principles of the frame and the enframed stories functions as a further factor in the process of manipulating the traditional narrative genre in the service of the new one. It also turns the frame into the arena in which the various interpretations of the enframed story are debated.

This is a by-product of the *sjuzhet*'s inversion of the chronological order of the *fabula*. On a structural plane the elaboration of the complex plot can be seen as a formal device to eschew the tendency to regard fictional incidents as a direct reflection of social mores. This is reinforced by taking social mores themselves as a subject for the text's debate, and by presenting constantly conflicting points of view. From the very beginning of the story, the narrator's romantic or, rather, romanticized view of the beautiful countryside with its distant horizon and wretched peasants is balanced by the friend's cynicism as he mocks his romanticism, seeing only the vices of the peasants, and believing that their deplorable state suits them well. A further set of conflicting views is elaborated when in the evening the city-dwellers, with their different but equally misplaced views, encounter Sheikh Muḥsin and debate the position of the peasants with him.

One of the major ironies created by the very structure of the *sjuzhet* is its positioning of the peasants, the subject of the debate, as the centre of interest but completely alienated from it. Whether in the first conflict between the narrator and his friend, or in the second between him and Sheikh Muḥsin, the situation of the peasants and their future is the subject of the debate. It is debated in the presence of the peasants but without their participation. They are either absent or reduced to a mere chorus, and the debate is either unintelligible to them because of the use of English, as in the first conflict between the narrator and his friend, or misunderstood, as in the second with Sheikh Muḥsin. But there is some evidence to suggest that they wanted to communicate with the city dwellers, for they sent for Sheikh Muḥsin to represent them and speak on their behalf. Another irony is that their appointed representative is the one with a vested interest in alienating them from the calls of progress coming from the city.

The *sjuzhet* also shows that the various elements making the new discursive field have reached in this text a stage of fusion, including the audience without whose participation and response the story would not have taken place. The peasants are used within the story as the audience for the debate, and their response, though subtle and reduced to the minimum, is vital for the determination of the outcome, and even for the progress of the debate, and the grading of its warring discourses. The hierarchy of discourses is established within the domain of the talk through the audience response and the nature of their conduct. Apart from the direct response of the peasants, there are two reported descriptions of their behaviour, the first given by the narrator in first-person narrative when he sees in the middle of his emotional outburst two of the peasants whispering to each other and paying no attention to him. This is the point at which he becomes divided within himself and starts to doubt the value and relevance of his intervention and probably of the whole debate.

The second description is reported in neutral third-person narrative, which seems, despite its neutrality, to be observed by the narrator. It tells of the attempt of one of the peasants to adjust the lantern and how he was promptly disparaged, not by one person but by the whole collective audience acting as one. The two converse actions speak clearly for themselves, but the different modes of discourse communicate through their different organizational principles two distinct messages. The narrator is the only one who sees his own defeat, for it is reported through his interior monologue, while the appreciation of his opponent is objectively reported in third-person narrative for everyone to see. The modes of discourse indicate that a subtle process of self-deception is developing beneath the ostensible battle between the two protagonists of the piece: the narrator and Sheikh Muḥsin.

Vladimir Propp has shown that the functions of narrative in the tale are the crucial elements in the unfolding of its discourse, and this helps us to see the story as a series of functional transformations.[15] The *sjuzhet* reorders the narrative functions in a new hierarchical organization by rearranging them in a different series of functional transformations. By reversing the order, the *sjuzhet* encrusts the chronological beginning of the *fabula* in a completely different discourse, the most sacred of all Arabic discourses: the Qur'ānic discourse. This bestows parabolic qualities on the enframed story and renders the exaggeration of its elements of sex and violence a rhetorical device, showing the manipulative nature of Sheikh Muḥsin to be more than a mere exposition of its events. This is so because the frame story is both the generative force behind the production of the enframed story and the filter through which its elements are mediated and sifted.

Skaz and Characterization

The very orientation of the narrative plays an important role in the text, and this is equally true of a narration by the author, by a narrator, or by one of the characters. These three types of narration are employed in the text for different purposes and from varying points of view. The position from which a story is told, a portrayal is built or information is provided is constantly modified according to the nature and aim of the discourse, whether representational, informational or judgemental. In Lāshīn's story, the narrator (whether actual or implied) is neither an expression of an "I" external to the text and residing outside it, nor an omniscient, impersonal consciousness who tells the story from a superior point of view, but a narrator who mostly limits his narrative to what the characters can observe or know. This allows the narrative to proceed as if each of the characters in turn were the generator of the discourse.

Although the story is narrated by, or at least mediated through the consciousness of, the narrator, it contains more than one *skaz*. This is so because of the technique of imbrication mentioned above, and because it adopts a detached first-person narrative that conveniently slips into the third person. It starts as first-person singular, then slips to first-person plural then to a reported third-person narrative, changing the *skaz* without radically altering the terms of focalization, except when the shift into the third person is complete and the narrative assumes the mode of the omniscient author, as is the case when it comments on the utterance of one of the peasants and volunteers to speculate on what was going in his mind at the moment of the utterance. Lāshīn is obviously aware that it is difficult to speak without betraying a point of view, and he shifts the *skaz* primarily between the two main characters, in order to grant the city and the country views equal weight. This is a tremendous development from the simplistic and one-dimensional polarization of, say, Jibrān's romantic conflict between the country and the city where the narrative was solely projected through the eyes of the omniscient author.

Another technical development is the presentation of each of the opposing characters in the eyes of the other. In the eye of the beholder, each behaves despicably but justifiably so. Sheikh Muḥsin misconstrues the words of the narrator, not behind his back, but in his presence. The technique of negative mirroring, in which the story allows each of the protagonists to see himself only in the eyes of his enemies, polarizes the argument and accentuates the relativity of truth. This technique participates in shaping the various characteristics of binary opposition as a structural feature in the text and makes ambivalence one of its major traits.

"Ḥadīth al-Qaryah" has two different types of characters: the narrator, who interests Lāshīn as a particular perspective on the world and on the self, as a position which enables the writer, and probably the whole Arab intellectual class, to interpret, evaluate and comprehend their surrounding reality; and Sheikh Muḥsin, as some manifestation of reality that possesses fixed and specific social traits. He interests Lāshīn as a specific profile assembled out of unambiguous and objective features which taken together reflect certain aspects of reality. As a representative of the new educated class and its rational attempt to comprehend reality and search for meaning, the narrator is primarily interested in how the world appears to him; while the sheikh, who represents the graduates of the theocentric education with its static world-view, is concerned about how he appears to the world. This in turn requires two different types of *skaz*, different in language, tone, point of view and motives.

The perception through which the story is rendered is that of the narrating self and not of the experiencing self. The first-person narrative here is not the narrative of the retrospective narrator retrieving past events, delving into his inner self, following his thoughts with their free associations or reflecting on his involvements in problematic issues; it is, rather, a reporting narrative similar to that of the third person. But the reporting here is different from that of the absent but omnipresent observer, for it is done by a character within the represented world, yet temporarily capable of standing outside it. Hence the *skaz* of the narrator has a certain tone of objectivity, even neutrality, about it, and this is in marked contrast with that of Sheikh Muḥsin whose involvement in the situation is much greater than that of the merely visiting narrator, and whose discourse therefore has the characteristic of a highly impassioned plea. Sheikh Muḥsin is not a rogue, and it is clear that he is acting with good intentions to protect the villagers. He represents himself from the beginning, not as a graduate of al-Azhar, but as a failed Azharite student, and his interpretation of the Qur'ān demonstrates the limited knowledge and narrow-mindedness of a semi-educated Azharite.

Another marked difference between the two discourses is that the narrator's *skaz* has the task of articulating not only the narrator's views but the contrasting urban views about the village and the peasants, while Sheikh Muḥsin's has only one unified view. The views of the peasants, who comment on and respond to both the *imām*'s account of the story and the visitor's critical remarks, are complementary to those of Sheikh Muḥsin and provide variations on his themes. The views of the two urban visitors have utopian characteristics;[16] namely that the narrator is intellectually so interested in the realization of his dream of a beautiful village, and in the substantiation of his own ideas about the village, that he unwittingly sees only the elements in the situation which tend to realize his own ideal. His inability to recognize the forces that work against the realization of his collective paradise in which all the peasants are in the same harmony as nature round them is a factor in his downfall. He is incapable of diagnosing the existing conditions correctly, and fails to communicate with those whose condition he seeks to transform.

The views of Sheikh Muḥsin typify the "ideology" of this reality. He starts his talk by affirming his association with the ruling clique: the *'umdah* (mayor), and *mandūb al-ḥukūmah* (the government representative). It is rather significant that Sheikh Muḥsin is vague and does not specify the nature of the government representative or his specific position. The function of the remark is to grant him the maximum power by association and to establish his connection with authority. It is therefore appropriate that the representative of the government is not specified, for the more ambiguous he is, the more representative he becomes. It is also likely that the representative of the government who is normally sent to villages is a *mu'āwin idārah*, and specifying his rank and position would diminish the effect and confuse him with the deceased who was also a *mu'āwin idārah*.

This association with authority is introduced as a function of Sheikh Muḥsin's importance, for he was assisting in *"yunīr lahum ṭarīq al-taḥqīq fi qaḍiyyat 'Abd al-Samī'"* (shedding light and opening a venue for the investigation of 'Abd al-Samī''s case). A side benefit of this association is the privileged access to secret information concerning the details of 'Abd al-Samī''s crime. Before divulging this secret information revealed to him by the interrogators he reiterates that he has been granted such vital information because of his status and their confidence in him. It is clear from the outset that Sheikh Muḥsin is interested in using this association to enhance his power, for he starts his talk by setting the bait and dictating the terms of the debate. As soon as he arrives, he drops a hint concerning 'Abd al-Samī''s case, and, like a bait, it has to be left for a while before one of the peasants finally rises to it and asks him about the recent developments in the case.

The story does not end before demonstrating to us this enhanced power at work. When he finishes his talk, he winds up the meeting, indicating that he has to go back to the mayor and the other notables, the ruling group. But he does not leave alone; the peasants, after performing the ritual of collective submission characterized by kissing his hand, follow him back to his own domain. It has become evident that the only one who went astray, 'Abd al-Samī', destroyed himself. The demise of 'Abd al-Samī' was preceded by his adopting the urban attire of a jacket and a fez and abandoning peasant dress. The change in appearance is a marker for a more substantial change in social position, an attempt to attain social mobility and to rise above the station ordained for him in a rigidly controlled social system. Sheikh Muḥsin uses the opportunity of the destruction of the one who defied the rules to assert himself as peasants' spokesman and negotiator with the outside world and reaps the fruits of this assertion in the hand-kissing ritual.

The association with the community's civil leaders, with whom the sheikh has discussed 'Abd al-Samī''s case, gives both the listeners and the readers an intimation of their views concerning this case. Like the narrator with his utopian dreams, the sheikh, in his ideological thinking, offers an example of how "the ruling groups can in their thinking become so intensively interest-bound to a situation that they are simply no longer able to see certain facts which would undermine their sense of domination. There is implicit in the word 'ideology' the insight that in certain situations the collective unconscious of certain groups obscures the real conditions of society both to itself and to others and thereby stabilizes it".[17] This collective element explains why many of the peasants echo the sheikh's views and complement them, and fail to sympathize with the urban visitor, who tries to suggest how they might change their appalling conditions.

But despite their marked difference the two discourses have something in common, for

> all ideology in the strongest sense, including the most exclusive forms of ruling-class consciousness just as much as that of the oppositional or oppressed classes, is Utopian ... insofar as it expresses the unity of a collectivity. Yet it must be added that this proposition is an allegorical one. The achieved collectivity or organic group of whatever kind — oppressors fully as much as oppressed — is Utopian not in itself, but only insofar as all such collectivities are themselves *figures* for the

> ultimate concrete collective life of an achieved Utopian or classless society.[18]

The collectivity of both conflicting views in the story, whose common ground is outlined here, is discussed below. But the convergence of difference and similarity in the two views is as important a structural feature as other forms of pairing and duplicity.

There are two main groups of characters in this story: the villagers, their sheikh and the tragic hero 'Abd al-Samī', on one side, and, on the other, the city people — the two visitors and the assistant prosecutor — who, for various reasons, try to meddle in the village's affairs. The two groups are antithetical, but are not without some points in common. The construction of the two groups is highly significant and is based on the principle of pairing and binary opposition: Sheikh Muḥsin and the narrator, the assistant prosecutor and 'Abd al-Samī' and the villagers and the friend of the narrator. The composition of each of the two groups mirrors that of the other: two speakers who behave as if they were self-appointed representatives of their respective groups (Sheikh Muḥsin and the narrator); two actants who are both victims and perpetrators of harm (the assistant prosecutor and 'Abd al-Samī'); and two audiences (a rural one represented by the villagers, and an urban one whose sole representative is the friend of the narrator — the only city-dweller who escapes severe punishment to a certain extent).

The two groups have common characteristics and contrasting ones; for instance, the intervention of the city-dwellers in the life of the village is based on both sympathy and aggression, and the reaction by the peasants to each one corresponds to the nature of his motives and the degree of his involvement in the peasants' affairs. Both the narrator and the assistant prosecutor meddle in the village's affairs and both are punished. The nature of the punishment corresponds to the magnitude of the interference, and since the crime of the assistant prosecutor is so grave, its punishment seems to extend to his fellow city-dweller — the narrator — despite the latter's good intention. Even the assistant prosecutor who ruined 'Abd al-Samī''s life behaves with an amalgam of carnal desire (almost affection) and aggression and tries to improve 'Abd al-Samī''s standard of living. He is neither an absolute rogue nor innocent of blame, and this is also the case with the narrator, who misrepresents his own good intentions and proves how misguided his calls for reform are. His response to Sheikh Muḥsin's performance is not entirely free from certain elements of aggression or at least self-retribution. On the other hand, Sheikh Muḥsin is no less a perpetrator of harm, for his good intentions have misled the villagers and exploited their trust. By underlining the elements of contrast and similarity in his characters, Lāshīn avoids the polarization of certain peculiarities, grants the characterization plausibility and shuns naïve simplification.

Molestation, Duplicity and Authority

Here one is aware of Benjamin's observation of the decline of the authority of the storyteller, but this should also be seen as leading to the need for the story to take on more authority itself. The question of authority is one of the major themes of this story through which the nightly chat becomes a microcosm of the struggle for leadership and control between the new and traditional groups of intellectuals. The struggle for authority on the thematic plane corresponds to another textual struggle for authority on the structural and narrative ones. In this respect it is clear that the three special conditions which Said suggests as vital for the generation of fictional narrative are at work here. The story is a perfect example of his proposition of molestation and authority as a defining characteristic of narrative.

"The first special condition is that there must be some strong sense of doubt that the authority of any single voice, or group of voices, is sufficient unto itself".[19] This is clearly demonstrated not only in the constant tension between the various voices in the text, but also through the attempt of each to undermine the authority and the validity of the other. At a certain level of interpretation, the story is that of the dynamics of undermining authority and the attempt by those in control to consolidate their power. The conflict between the narrator and Sheikh Muḥsin is not a polemical debate concerning the interpretation of a verse in the Qur'ān, but the struggle for the formulation of the blueprint for the future, the national project. What unfolds in the text is not a multitude of characters living in a single objective world, but rather a duality of consciousness, with equal rights, each with its own world.

The two main characters in the story are treated as ideologically authoritative and independent; each is perceived as the author of a fully motivated ideological conception of his own, and not as the object of the author's vision. Each project strives to prove that it is both rooted in reality and offers the best solution for its problems, but the very interpretation of reality, and consequently what is problematic in it, differs radically, and this in turn undermines the authority and even sincerity of each voice. At the root of the very authority of one project is the denial of the other, and in this way the two projects cancel each other out, or at least weaken each other's monopoly on the truth.

The "second special condition is that the truth — whatever that may be — can only be approached indirectly, by means of a mediation that because of its falseness paradoxically makes the truth truer. In this context a truer truth is one arrived at by a process of elimination: alternatives similar to the truth are shed one by one. The elevation of truth-resembling fictions to preeminence becomes a habitual practice, because fiction is thought to be the trial of truth by error".[20] The elaboration of this second condition in the narrative requires an awareness that the implied author seems not to subscribe to either view; he identifies neither with the views of the narrator, nor with those of Sheikh Muḥsin. "Unlike the narrator the implied author can tell us nothing. He, or better it, has no voice, no direct means of communicating. It instructs us silently, through the design of the whole, with all the voices, by all the means it has chosen to let us learn".[21]

Like the body of Osiris scattered over the valley, the truth is dispersed in the text and is portioned out between its various elements. The more the character claims that he has a monopoly on truth, the further from the truth he moves. This does not mean that the more doubt he expresses the closer he moves to the truth, since excessive doubts could be a mere narrative device. Like the implied author, the truth is also elusive and implied. The voice of the storyteller can be heard through the effect achieved by sound patterns, puns, comic effects, illogical anti-climaxes, and other narrative devices as the carefully selected profession for 'Abd al-Samī', the use of traditional and rhymed discourse by the sheikh, and the use and manipulation of the Qur'ānic verses.

"A third special condition for the generation of fictional narrative is an extraordinary fear of the void that antedates private authority".[22] This is also present in the text, for, as Said observed, the narrative character gains his fictional authority in the desire to escape death, and this is the case with Sheikh Muḥsin. Like the one-eyed among the blind, his position in the village is both authoritative and precarious; it is based on partial knowledge, as indicated by his reference to his incomplete study at al-Azhar. But in the land of the illiterate this provides him with a strong advantage, which the advent of the narrator with his enlightening remarks threatens. One of the ruses for hiding his disability is the constant use of the sacred text, the Qur'ān, and his appropriation of its power to consolidate his own. Another ruse is his repeated reference to his association with authority and his usefulness to the ruling establishment, whose ambiguity has been explained above.

He sees the narrator's intervention as an attempt to undermine his authority, and his life and position in the village is conditional on his success in saving his flock from being ensnared by the narrator's argument and subjected to his authority. He is aware that as soon as they open their eyes they will discover his inadequacy, and this marks his discourse with defensiveness. The defensive nature of the discourse appears in two opposing but complementary forms: bellicosity and remorse. The two forms materialize in succession and often in an imbricated form, for each contains an element of the other. The use of Qur'ānic terminology, proverbs, customary parlance and certain turns of phrase helps Sheikh Muḥsin slip easily from one form into the other. The narrator's discourse is no less complex in this respect, and his lack of self-confidence percolates through every turn of phrase and infiltrates every move. Implicit in the Utopian nature of his discourse is a sense of fear of the perpetuation of the present, or, even worse, a return to the past. Each of the two main characters is acting to ward off an impeding sense of his own duplicity and an inexplicable premonition of his own doom. The demystification of illusion, which is the central theme of the story, enacts these fears and intensifies their hold on the narrator, for the more he knows about the village the more real the fear of perpetuating its present becomes. There even a hint that the narrator's failed attempt to exorcise these fears leaves him in a state of paralysis at the end of the story, while the only movement, that of the peasants following their sheikh in the dark, is towards the thickness of darkness.

The Polyphony of Discourses and Intertextuality

Intertextuality is realized in this text on two different planes: the linguistic and the structural; the former results in the polyphony of discourses and the latter in the dialogue with preceding narrative genres. The previous sections of this analysis have already alluded to the juxtaposition of a number of discourses in the text. One of the major achievements of Lāshīn's story is its ability to harmonize elements of traditional modes of expressions with those of the new narrative discourse, and even internalize many of the former into the structure of the latter and completely digest them. The new narrative discourse is marked by its heterogeneity and its personal narrative system, while traditional modes of narrative tend to be more apersonal in orientation.[23] The story uses both systems effectively to illuminate various aspects of the narrative and to categorize various discourses in a subtly hierarchical order.

The polyphony of discourses and the multiplicity of its manifestations can be categorized into three distinct groups corresponding to the three types of characters: the modern, which corresponds to the city-dwellers; the traditional of Sheikh Muḥsin, with his explicit use of the Qur'ān and other classical references; and the popular, which is prevalent in the interventions of the peasants with their proverbs and trite remarks. Naturally, the last two groups are closer to each other than to the first, although all three have certain common characteristics, and this enables the reader to perceive a certain polarity of discourses. Lāshīn's main characters are, by the nature of his creative design, not only objects of authorial discourse but also subjects of their own directly signifying discourse. Yet the multiplicity of discourses is organized along a binary divide in which discourses act as both reaction and complement to each other. The binary division is both structural and discursive and corresponds to the two protagonists of the piece.

The division on the structural plane between the frame story and the enframed one and on the plane of characterization between the narrator and Sheikh Muḥsin, the named and the unnamed, is represented in the discursive field in the opposition between two opposing and complementary discourses. The modern discourse is associated with the city, the secular, urban attributes, abstraction, light, resort to truth, dream, romantic qualities, Utopia, authenticity, reason, education, sensitivity, etc. The traditional discourse is symmetrically opposite, for its affinities are with the country, religion, rural characteristics, the concrete, darkness, resort to authority, manipulation, pragmatism, ideology, distortion, fatalism, illiteracy or semi-illiteracy, coarseness, etc. The two sets of qualities can be arranged in a table of coupling by contrast that offers opposing and complementary polarity. These two major discourses can in turn subdivide along their internal binary scheme. The former can be divided along the opposing views of the narrator and his friend, and the latter along the subtle differences between Sheikh Muḥsin and the peasants. This binary opposition shows both the polyphony of discourse and the dramatic tension that runs through it and fuses it into a complex whole denoting the degree of complexity in the world-view that generates it. Beneath the juxtaposition of discourses one detects a juxtaposition and even an interaction of genres: the comic, the romantic, the tragic and even the mythological.

The multiplicity of discourses is not only linguistic but also structural, for there is an implicit intertextual dialogue with the structure of the two major classical Arabic narrative genres: the *maqāmah* and *Alf Laylah wa Laylah* (*The Arabian Nights*).[24] The story incorporates a superficial resemblance to the *maqāmah* and involves a profound intertextuality with *The Arabian Nights,* and this is one of its substantial achievements in subverting the link with the *maqāmah* from within and at the same time strengthening the bonds with the more impressive narrative of *The Arabian Nights.* The basic structure of the *maqāmah* rests on the duality of its characterization: a hero who experiences the world and endures its tribulations, and a narrator who filters the experience of this hero through his own consciousness. The story includes the two, but instead of their static relationship in the *maqāmah,* they engage here in a highly dynamic relationship. The narrator who tells about a hero is neither a friend nor a confidant of the hero, nor is he the filter of the discourse, for now the power of narrative discourse defies any unilateral control. In addition, the pair are both a reproduction of the relationship, in the form of the narrator and his friend, though in an inverted form, and a subversion of it, in the case of the narrator and Sheikh Muḥsin.

Interesting as it may be, the intertextuality with the *maqāmah* is less important than that with *The Arabian Nights.* Since *The Arabian Nights* is the archetypal narrative *par excellence,* for one of its main concerns is to cover the entire spectrum of narrative including religious *exempla*, animal fables, magic tales, historical romances, travel, adventure tales, etc., it is not difficult to find elements of partial similarity between it and any narrative text. But the test of any real interaction between a given text and *The Arabian Nights* remains in the structural similarity rather than in the affinity with the heterogeneity of discourses in the archetypal text. As in *The Arabian Nights,* we have a frame story and an enframed. The frame story is ostensibly suspended, creating a lull in the narrative for the enframed story to unfold, and as soon as it ends, the frame story continues.

Again like *The Arabian Nights,* the structure of the frame story is constantly interacting with that of the enframed, and their dialectics generates the main theme. The two visitors of the frame correspond to the two kings of the frame story in *The Arabian Nights*, Shahryār and Shāhzamān, achieving on the structural level both pairing and duplicity. Pairing along binary opposing and contrasting principles and duplicity suggest similarity. Like the two kings, they are bent on the discovery of the truth and their search leads to the generation of the enframed story. The story of 'Abd al-Samī' is in many ways similar to that of the two kings: his wife betrayed him and he killed her and her lover. It is almost a reproduction of the primeval story of Shāhzamān in *The Arabian Nights,* who returned home unexpectedly, surprised his wife in his bed with her lover and killed them both.

But in addition to these similarities in the surface structure, there are more similarities at the deeper level. In *The Arabian Nights,*

> the narrative line can be retold in more abstract terms as that of the rupture leading to a curse and its ultimate undoing. This invariably carries with it overtones of Semitic myths of Creation where an initial order and equilibrium are lost. *The Arabian Nights* is essentially a demotic version of paradise lost and recovered. The bliss of the original couple was ruptured by their eating the fruits of the forbidden tree, that is, by their tasting the fruits of knowledge. Similarly, taboo and knowledge are keys to the unfolding of *The Arabian Nights.* Sin and death go hand in hand in both.[25]

Like *The Arabian Nights,* the success of Sheikh Muḥsin depends on his ability to evoke dormant mythological discourse, and the accomplishment of "*Ḥadīth al-Qaryah*" itself relies on its ability to present the city's meddling in the country's affair as a drastic disturbance of its harmony and equilibrium.

The original bliss not only of 'Abd al-Samī''s domestic life, but of the whole village, was disrupted by the arrival of the *mu'āwin.* This disruption brought sin and death, and order was not restored until a second cycle of events occurred and Sheikh Muḥsin killed the urban dragon, or at least tamed him by the magic of his knowledge and the light of his lantern. Hence the significance of the symbolic act of leaving the lantern behind, as if it were a spell that holds the two visitors at bay. Here another parallel with *The Arabian Nights* emerges. Shahrazād tames the despotic king by replacing his steady diet of women by tales of women, and Sheikh Muḥsin uses the same technique by replacing the narrator's desire to interfere in village life by a tale about interference. But here the similarity ends and the difference starts.

"Shahrazād's genius lies in turning women from objects of sex to objects of sexual fantasy. This entry into the symbolic is the most critical step undertaken by Shahrazād. This is a crucial transformation that parallels the substitution of ritual prayer for the concrete sacrifice in religion. Once the signifier replaces the signified, language becomes possible and once language is installed, an unlimited number of discourses becomes possible".[26] But Sheikh Muḥsin, for obvious reasons, is incapable of maintaining the argument at the level of discourse, and his offering of the story of 'Abd al-Samī' can be seen as reverting to the stage of concrete sacrifice. His intentional exaggeration of the elements of sex and violence in the story makes the sacrifice raw and dripping with blood to enhance the value of his offering. By the twist of the tale Sheikh Muḥsin turns the story of 'Abd al-Samī' from the arena of the struggle to a tool in his incantatory ritual of appeasing the monster. But the sheikh is also playing up the sex and violence in 'Abd al-Samī''s story in keeping with the traditional folk tales of honour and revenge, the discourse that is guaranteed to appeal to the peasants.

This is enhanced by the fact that Sheikh Muḥsin's relating of the enframed story is ostensibly delivered for the sake of the narrator and his friend, for all the peasants know the story well, but it is also narrated for the peasants. As far as he is concerned, they are the only audience that matters, because the urban visitors are not only transient and temporal, but are used to enhance his control over his audience. And this aspect of his performance brings in the other mythological element that separates him even further from Shahrazād, that is, the binary opposition of Eros and Thanatos. The enframed story is a story of love and death, and the frame story echoes this theme through the narrator's love of the countryside and compassion for the poor peasants, and through Sheikh Muḥsin's symbolic sacrifice of 'Abd al-Samī'. Like Thanatos, the son of Nyx (night) and the brother of Hypnos (sleep), Sheikh Muḥsin is associated with darkness and uses the power of oratory to hypnotize the peasants. He also uses the gift of words, the city's tool of seduction, to placate the city-dwellers, and, more importantly, to cancel the discourse altogether and replace it by concrete sacrifice. The ending of the story accentuates again his association with the two qualities of darkness and hypnosis.

The narrator does not purely represent the mythological Eros, though he has some shades of the pluralistic Erotes with their sometimes gold-tipped, sometimes lead-tipped arrows. He is more like Sisyphus who tricked Thanatos but suffered everlasting torment as punishment. The narrator is left alone at the end of the story with his symbolic stone of Sisyphus in the shape of the lantern, the light of knowledge and realization. As Thanatos knew that Sisyphus had had a past association with Autolycus, the master thief, whose daughter Anticlea he seduces, Sheikh Muḥsin associates the narrator with the master thief of the enframed story, the *mu'āwin.* These various layers of intertextuality widen the scope of meaning in the story and demonstrate the complexity and heterogeneity of the elements that participated in the genesis of the new narrative discourse.

Thematic Interpretation and the Use of Description

If narrative presentation is seen in a purely formalist tradition not as a reflection of actual reality, but as a conventional deformation of it in which the plot is perceived not as a mere sum total, but as an artistically ordered presentation of motifs, the text yields several interpretations. "The term deformation has no derogatory implication; it means simply the changes imposed on the material, the effect achieved, for instance by poetic language in contrast to the language of prose, the patterning by sound repetitions and figures, the nods and turns of novelistic plot — in short all the devices, procedures, or instruments of art".[27] The story uses such devices not only to deal with the ever recurring themes of city versus country, new versus old, secular versus religious (an issue of continuing and renewed importance in the Arab world), but also to elaborate the more fundamental question of "the development of self-consciousness and the exercise of free will in opposition to a traditional passivity and an acceptance of God's will".[28]

The concept of preordained fate was the cornerstone of the world-view whose demise and replacement by a radically different outlook gave rise to the genesis of the new narrative discourse. The story endeavours through its theme as well as its narrative structure to investigate the remains of the old world-view and the nature of its relationship with the new one. In order to probe this question thoroughly, the story selects the hero of its enframed story ('Abd al-Samī') very carefully to shape by this choice the nature of various types of identification with the argument. Through a stroke of genius, Lāshīn makes 'Abd al-Samī' a character whom the peasants can identify with easily and yet be detached from, look down upon as a cobbler and not a proper *fellah* (Egyptian peasant), and mock for his ridiculous attempt to climb the social scale. The narrator seems passionate and sincere in his calls for reform, but what is the point of mere talk, however virtuous, when seen in the light of the deeds of the other city-dweller, the *mu'āwin,* who fooled their fellow villager and destroyed his life? There is also the way in which the narrator expresses his views: he is described by his friend as too rational, dry, and difficult to understand,[29] and this hinders his communication with his audience. Therefore it is quite understandable that they comment collectively, "God damn urban life, God forbid modernization and the day we ever heard of it",[30] identifying modernization with evil and being suspicious of any message from the town.

But that does not mean that the story itself condemns the call for modernization; rather it criticizes the insularity of those who call for it without understanding the existing reality or the important elements of modernity. The narrator's comments on 'Abd al-Samī''s story are few, but his almost spontaneous slip of the tongue, "I wish I had been with them", is both astonishing and revealing. It discloses his desire to understand 'Abd al-Samī''s, and consequently the villagers', logic and viewpoint. At another level of interpretation, it also proves, though ironically, his argument about the importance of the human will, without which 'Abd al-Samī' would not have been able to retaliate.[31] At a third level, it indicates that he is fascinated by the spontaneous and conventional response of 'Abd al-Samī', despite his preaching about reason and human will. The assimilation of the narrator into the action has a vital corollary: the move from description to narration in Lukács' sense of the terms. Lukács explains in his article "To Narrate or To Describe" how the two strategies differ in quality and in point of view.[32]

The story is rich in meaning, economic in style, and pertinent in its profound analysis of the clash between the various contradictory views. It maintains a delicate artistic balance between the narrative elements, and uses words to their full poetic value. It employs some suggestive symbols which draw upon the different shades of light for illuminating both the scene and the characters. For example, the crescent moon casts only a feeble light at the beginning of the evening gathering; the half moon leads 'Abd al-Samī' to the recognition, in the Aristotelian sense, of his problem and guides him to the iron rod and to the course of action he should take; the light of the lantern surrounds the arrival of the sheikh, and stays with the lonely visitors after they have had the veil of their illusions torn from their eyes; and when the sheikh leaves, followed by the peasants, he is enveloped by utter darkness.

The use of light imagery in the text is not a gratuitous description of nature, for it constitutes what Ghazoul calls a code, "a combination of thematic elements that constitute a sub-language. The codes are extended translations of the matrix, and when isolated they can serve to verify the matrical statement. Flaubert, for example, uses weather code words such as sunny, rainy, stormy, etc., to constitute the internal states of the hero in *La Légende de Saint Julien l'Hospitalier*".[33] The use of light code words in the story permeates the text and operates in both the frame and the enframed stories.

The light code consolidates the impact and suggests that, although the encounter between the two protagonists ends with the defeat of the narrator, his opponent, like the master of darkness, reigns over his subjects only under its protective carapace. The association with darkness is intended, not only as a contrast to the narrator's fondness and preoccupation with light, but also as a significant commentary on Sheikh Muḥsin's use of the only glimmer of light that he has appropriated from the city, the gift of oratory gained during his fruitless years at al-Azhar. On one level, the light of knowledge which Sheikh Muḥsin had acquired in the city enabled him to rule over his subjects in the village, but when the moment comes for using it, like a magic spell, against the city-dwellers and their attempt to violate the village, he prefers to abandon it completely in order to preserve the chastity of his village, and leaves it behind. Through the light code the story of profanity and adultery is reproduced, with the sheikh attempting to use the little light he has to tame or rather kill his own *mu'āwin,* the narrator.

Apart from all these symbolic shades of light and darkness, the rod which 'Abd al-Samī' finds by the tracks is treated similarly. Like the blazing sun in Camus' *L'Étranger*, the weight of the rod and the shining moon lead him to return to his house and compel him to kill. Throughout the story, Lāshīn uses the description of the setting to enrich his action and characterization with suggestion and implication and to accomplish the integration of fictional elements. The constant presence of both the landscape and the temporal changes contextualize the action and frame both stories in their undisturbed, almost apathetic, continuity. His descriptions of nature also accompany the action in such a way as to illuminate the setting and enrich the situation. Lāshīn also uses the device of recording the reactions of various characters to a single event so as to dramatize the different aspects of the fictional situation and at the same time to reveal the inner depths of each character. He uses in this story, and in many others, elements of structural irony and parallelism, especially in the contradictory characters and their coherent interrelationship.

The story pays attention to the "beginning, the balance of factors, or tension; writing in scenes as far as it is mortally possible, the motivation for action; and the making of skilful, unnoticeable transitions".[34] This story is the culmination of Lāshīn's attempt to create a suitable language for the short story which has its own stylistic and aesthetic values and is free from decorative and mellifluous elements. Without recapitulating Ḥaqqi's elaborate testimonial in this respect,[35] one may say that the language of his story is economical, smooth, and highly suggestive. It appreciates that "style is not a decorative embellishment upon subject matter, but the very medium in which the subject is turned into art".[36] The shift from action or dialogue to reporting is controlled by careful consideration for economy and brevity. "Language itself is in an ontological relation with reality, as all older philosophers of language and even Heidegger assert".[37]

The Open Ending and Its Significance

"Endings are interesting. Writers obviously devote special care to their composition and readers, not only professional critics, probably give them particular attention. We expect endings, much more than beginnings, to show what the story was about, what special effect was to be achieved".[38] Endings are commonly divided into closed and open endings. In a closed ending a variety of signals announce that the story is drawing to a close either by a repetition of some earlier elements in a different form, or by one of the closing devices such as the departure of the character from the scene of the story, or the closing of doors, windows or even of lives, by death. "In an open ending, on the other hand, action and dialogue continue to the very end; conflicts, if any, are left unresolved or insoluble, or 'a slice of life' is left uncovered and without any particular container: hanging, as it were, in mid-air. The action is suspended rather than concluded".[39]

A natural closed ending to *"Ḥadīth al-Qaryah"* would have been the end of the visit and the return to the city, or a final comment concerning the irreconcilability of town and country. But the author deliberately eschews such closed endings and leaves his visitors in the village at the end of the story and hence opens his ending. A closed ending of this story would have involved a crude manipulation of the story's content, and, in so doing, have constituted an anomalous imposition on its fine structure. It would have introduced authorial intrusion, the quality which Lāshīn purges successfully from his text. It would have adopted "telling" as opposed to "showing" and resorted to comment rather than reporting. Opting for a different ending with the necessary set of textual strategies enhances the structural quality of the story and enriches its content.

It seems that at least by intuition, if not by design, Lāshīn was aware that "in the twentieth century the open ending has become more or less the standard strategy, whereas the stories of Poe, Hawthorne and Melville usually have closed endings".[40] But those of Mansfield, Joyce, Lawrence, Scott Fitzgerald, Faulkner and others have open ones.[41] The story ends with the application of the imbrication technique to its ending, by arranging the ends of the enframed and the frame stories in an overlapping manner. The distance between the two beginnings is contrasted by the closeness of the two endings. But there is a correspondence between beginning and ending to counterbalance this contrast. If the beginning contains the minimum anteriority and provides the reader only with the necessary background information about the city-dweller and his first visit to the country, the end also provides us with minimum posteriority, and does not concern itself with any predictions about the future.

Although the enframed story does not start until nearly the middle of the text, the ending of the enframed story signals that of the frame, yet there is a marked difference between the two. The enframed story employs a closed ending, or rather a semi-closed one, while the frame culminates in an open ending. The dialectics of the two endings suggests a re-examination of that of the enframed, for the ending of the enframed story appears as a closed ending regarding the retribution and the arrival of Thanatos after the exploits of Eros, but it is a tentatively open one with respect to the fate of 'Abd al-Samī' himself, which is left undecided. The lack of information about the fate of 'Abd al-Samī', despite the fact that his whole story was initiated by a question of one of the peasants about his fate, is highly significant, and confirms his symbolic murder by Sheikh Muḥsin. The deliberate ambiguity is amplified by the reader's anterior knowledge that Egyptian law is extremely lenient regarding husbands who commit a *crime passionnel.* But the final ending of the frame story with its intentional linking of Sheikh Muḥsin and darkness contains an implicit reference to the Thanatos side of his character.

More questions arise about Sheikh Muḥsin's intention in relating the enframed story when he repeats at the end the same remarks about his association with the mayor and the other notables, and indulges his authority by offering the peasants his hand to kiss. The peasants were actually prompted to do so by Sheikh Muḥsin's final utterance, its religious overtone indicating a shift from the narrative discourse, with its democratic interaction, to the religious one, with its rigidly hierarchical and authoritarian nature. The ending refers back to the Qur'ānic discourse in which the beginning was embedded. This has the effect of rendering the enframed story in retrospect as part of Sheikh Muḥsin's parabolic discourse, and probably explains Sheikh Muḥsin's lack of interest in the fate of 'Abd al-Samī' or at least in providing any information about it.

By its very nature, the ending echos elements tucked away in the interior of the story and sheds new lights on others. "By the time the reader arrives at the end of a story he has probably amassed a fund of information about character, event and theme".[42] The ending recalls this information and draws attention to certain aspects more than others, affecting its hierarchical rearrangement. The departure of the peasants with Sheikh Muḥsin echos their sending for him at the beginning of the evening. The leaving of the lantern, a symbolic act which seals the reader's acceptance of the story's code, draws the reader's attention to the significance of the light code and its corollary acoustic code.

The melancholy and wistful tunes of the distant flute resonate throughout the story in their rapport with the imagery of the light code. It punctuates certain aspects of the story before yielding its place to the orchestral croaking of frogs, and then to the slurp of Sheikh Muḥsin's drinking from the pitcher. The gradual acoustic change from the melodious sound of the flute to the vulgar sound of the slurping through the croaking of the frogs, corresponds to the change in the visual imagery from the crescent moon to the utter darkness through the light of the lantern. These two codes correspond in turn to the psychological change experienced by the narrator, from the hopeful romantic dreamer to the bewildered and alienated subject.

The ending of the enframed story heralds that of the frame which follows promptly and consists of only one reporting sentence with no description or speech. The final reporting sentence starts with *and*, a device often used in the short-story ending to suggest a strong nexus with what has come before.[43] The *and* of the reporting final sentence follows the hand-kissing ritual and links the end of the enframed story with that of the frame. The reporting final sentence tells us how Sheikh Muḥsin left, followed by the peasants, leaving the lantern for the two urban visitors, who wanted to stay behind. By injecting the single word, *qani'ū* (they were content), in the non-scenic report at the end of the story, the author fused an element of comment into the report. This may stem not so much from the author's wish to put the story into a clearer focus by means of an abstraction, as from the need to elevate the diction at the end, thus giving a signal, as it were, that the work is over. It also calls into question the very issue with which Sheikh Muḥsin ends his talk, the advocacy of the acceptance of the preordained, for the contentment here is a consent to darkness.

The injection of *qani'ū* into the reporting sentence gives it a special twist, for the word's connotation with satisfaction and contentment has the effect of both gratification and appeasement. But the application of this word to the act of the peasants following not their *sheikh* or *ma'dhūn* or *imām*, the words used to describe Sheikh Muḥsin in the text before this final sentence, but *faqīh* (jurisprudent expert), gives the final sentence an ironic ring. The reader by then is quite aware of the nature of Sheikh Muḥsin's expertise and would not miss the sarcasm implicit in calling him, for the first time in the story, *faqīh,* and even adding to this new word the suffix *hum* (third person plural pronoun suffix) confirming the strong affinity between the peasants and *faqīhahum* (their *faqīh*) and, at the same time, detaching all of them from the narrator, thus accentuating his isolation. But the major part of the closing sentence concerns the two visitors' decision to stay behind and the action of leaving the lantern behind, a symbolic or iconic action which typifies the central value of the story. This is reported in first-person-plural narrative, a shift from the personal to the collective.

The collective voice in the first part of the closing sentence, and the sarcastic tone in its second part, ameliorate the absence of any suggestion of posteriority in focusing the reader's attention on the momentous issues it raises. The open ending here has some of the qualities of the Brechtian dramatic technique of persuading the audience to contemplate the issues it provokes rather than purging their emotions by catharsis. The contemplative nature of the ending with its frozen final scene dimly lit and left to hang *in medias res* has the effect of the frozen picture in film techniques, for it poses more questions than it offers answers. It recalls the significance of the reported incident of the two talking peasants when the narrator was elaborating his views, grades the discourse retrospectively in a hierarchical fashion, and suggests that the audience shows its lack of interest in the new intellectuals as soon as they start to doubt themselves.

The end, particularly the open ending, implies a return to the beginning. Leaving the two urban visitors alone and together, crucified in their paralysis and self-doubt, shows that their two ostensibly irreconcilable urban views face the same fate, for they are in reality two sides of the same coin. But the story's main character was its narrator, and his pride has prevented him from stooping to the sheikh's level; as a result, he has lost out. Yet, as in *Uncle Vanya* or *The Three Sisters,* he prefers the bitterness of this ostensible defeat to the vanity of a triumph that requires descent into vulgarity. Both the visual and the acoustic codes demonstrate that the story in one sense is a cry against the regression into vulgarity. In this sense and in many others, the conflict between the story's two characters and opposing discourses is still being waged, sixty years after its publication, between the Islamic descendants of Sheikh Muḥsin and the secular progeny of the narrator. It remains unsolved today and it will probably continue for many years to come to be the major debate in the Arab world.

The intertextual interaction with the *maqāmah* through the use of the dual hero or the split authorial voice acting both as a narrator and as a commentator on the action, and at other times as the one who experiences it, roots the narrative in the major traditions of Arabic discourse. The oscillation between acting and narrating in the *maqāmah* genre has reached its maturity, ten centuries after its inception, and the narrator has become completely integrated into the action. The impact of the structure of *The Arabian Nights* and other elements from popular narrative can also be detected in the story, bringing another element of classical Arabic narrative to bear on the genesis of narrative discourse. The complexity of the structure, the multiplicity of its elements and the polyphony of discourses are the manifestation of a new world-view and the expression of a different artistic sensibility and a changing literary canon, a manifestation that takes a new shape and creates a new literary discourse, a mature and sophisticated narrative discourse.

The conclusion of a study of this nature cannot be complete without launching the reader into the new codes and conventions of the emerging discourse, and the close reading of Lāshīn's story was devoted to this. The analysis of "Village Small Talk" concludes this study by demonstrating how the lengthy process of the genesis of Arabic narrative discourse culminated in a mature and sophisticated narrative. The close reading of the story showed how the various elements of the literary historical process, including the emergence of new reading public and the conflict of the new discourse with the old, filtered through the text and participated in the shaping of its complex structure and fine literary composition. It also showed how intertextual elements are fused into the fabric of the story in a manner that enhances its ability to absorb and articulate the diverse sociocultural processes which gave rise to the new narrative discourse. The story demonstrates how the new discourse, with its secular and rational understanding of reality and dynamic vision of man and society, is emerging out of the struggle with the old one-dimensional approach to reality and the static vision of truth. This struggle has been at the heart of the genesis of the new narrative discourse in Arab culture and has led to the strong tendency, from the early days of its formation, to integrate the elements of realistic presentation with elements of assessment.

The direct commentary which characterized the early vignettes of Nadīm took fifty years to transform itself into an organizational principle integrating its evaluative stance into carefully arranged narrative sequences whose scenes reflect ironically upon each other without giving the reader a sense of obtrusive manipulation. The journey has been long and arduous and involved complex processes and transformations, for the genesis of this discourse was both a literary project and an elaborate sociocultural process. As a new and cohesive discursive field, its genesis was a gradual process of altering and transforming both the perception of space and the nature of the social experience and with it rearticulating certain aspects of the discourse which reflects and expresses them. This process involved selection and exclusion on the part of the writers whose quest for an effective role in their societies was inseparable from their search for and shaping of the new discourse.

The genesis of Arabic narrative discourse was a complex sociocultural process; thus it was necessary in this study to draw upon several fields of scholarship. The homology between social, political and cultural experience and their subtle manifestation in a discursive field established the comprehensive nature of the process. The study of the changing sociocultural experience and its interaction with the quest for individual and national identity paved the way to understanding the new world-view which altered individuals' perception of themselves and their society. This emerged as a collective endeavour in which both the individual "I" and the collective "we" underwent radical transformation which affected the perception of both time and space in a manner that gave impetus to the generation of the new discourse. The survey of the composition of the new reading public and the probing of its expectations showed how the new educational system had developed a reader whose critical faculties made him increasingly dissatisfied with classical Arabic narrative with its prevalent direct commentary; he demanded a discourse that allowed more verifiability and freedom to exercise independent judgement.

The search for effective means of enhancing the verifiability of narrative discourse led to the study of sources and the transition of literary influences and other elements of comparative literature methodology. This started by establishing the channels through which both Russian and French literary influences filtered through to the Arab intellectual scene. Once these have been established, the intricacy of selection, exclusion and integration of heterogeneous elements of discourses into a new one started, and with it the alteration and transformation of horizons of expectations. The influence of the discourses emerging through these channels continued to clash and interact with the prevalent forms of discourses in the culture. The fusion of these heterogeneous forms into a new discourse was a collective endeavour in which many writers, within the unifying domain of Arabic culture and from different literary, social and national backgrounds within the Arab world worked together and echoed each other's attempts sometimes without any direct contact between them.

In an attempt to demonstrate both the collective and individual aspects of this process, the study used both genealogical aspects and critical ones, and in addition went even beyond their confines; for "the genealogical aspects concern the effective formation of discourse, whether within the limits of control, or outside of them, or as is most frequent, on both sides of the delimitation. Criticism analyzes the process of rarefaction, consolidation and unification in discourse; genealogy studies their formation, at once scattered, discontinuous and regular. To tell the truth, these two tasks are not always exactly complementary. We do not find, on the one hand, forms of rejection. exclusion, consolidation or attribution, and, on a more profound level, the spontaneous pouring forth of discourse, which immediately before or after its manifestation, finds itself submitted to selection or control".[44] The lengthy process of the genesis of Arabic narrative discourse showed how, both on the structural and thematic planes, the forms of rejection, consolidation or attribution continued to interact with the spontaneous pouring forth of discourse and shape its new conventions.

The function of the new narrative discourse was to mediate between the dreams of the new educated public and the sorrow of their nations' condition. The only triumph of the narrator in the story, if one needs to look for any such concept, is that he was capable of self-doubt and willing to rethink his ideas and his strategies. The will to learn, fathom the complexity of reality, probe its mysteries and shape the discourse capable of comprehending it was at the heart of the process which engendered this new narrative discourse. Without this will it would not have been able to raise a simple individual experience to the level of a national and human dilemma. The end of "Village Small Talk", which left the elucidators of the new discourse in the flicker of the lantern light and enveloped the exponents of the old in darkness, heralded the great future of this new way of mediating experience and rationalizing it. The development of the new form of Arabic narrative discourse in its various genres (the novel, the short story and drama) since 1930 has demonstrated its validity and its relevance, and even its necessity, to a new mode of existence and a different social and political reality. The ever-increasing number of Arab writers and the rich variety of their output after 1930 continued to enhance the role of the new discourse in mediating, comprehending, elaborating, and even transforming reality.

Appendix
Village Small Talk
an English translation of *"Ḥadīth al-Qaryah"*

My friend asked me to visit his village with him so that we could spend Friday in the heart of the country, and he could see to some of his estate business. So we went and found beauty and joy there. But that lush radiance which charms the city-dweller in the never-ending expanses of the countryside, and that pleasure which suffuses his whole being when he sees nature glowing joyfully at him wherever he turns his face, was tainted for me by the pity I felt for the peasants. The men were half-naked and worked the earth with hoes and scythes, bent double, clearly exhausted, pouring with sweat in the blazing heat. The women squatted submissively in front of their reed and mud huts and as we walked along the narrow, twisting lanes looking down at them, they seemed to melt into one another, veiling themselves from us with their tattered rags, which were as thick with dust as the ground at their feet.The small children, half-naked like their fathers, grubby like their mothers, grazed with the goats and chickens in the winding alleys, or on dusthills and around the stagnant pond nearby.

I started telling my friend how uncomfortable I felt, but he obviously did not share my sentiments. On the contrary, he began trying to convince me that this was the most suitable way of life for these people, that they themselves saw nothing wrong with it, and he quoted from his own experiences to demonstrate that beneath their primitive exteriors lurked the treachery of wolves and the cunning of foxes. Then he proceeded to make fun of my poetic sensibilities and my naivety.

When evening approached and the fields were bathed in the calm, sad splendour of dusk my poetic sensibilities — as my friend called them — got the better of me, and I felt profoundly depressed. We were walking down a dusty path between rows of maize plants. The shadows were lengthening and silence engulfed us, broken from time to time by the soft tread of oxen wandering indolently homewards, or peasants greeting us lackadaisically as they made their weary way in from the fields. We remained silent, and I thought about these people passing by.

What sort of conversation would they have with their wives when they reached home? Did they really not notice the hardship and poverty in their lives? Where did they find happiness and consolation?

I was unable to work out any satisfactory answers and unwilling to ask my friend. We were on our way to the little open-air mosque and by the time we reached it, the twilight had faded and the world was in darkness. The mosque was a piece of ground on the canal bank, carpeted with reed matting and enclosed by a low brick wall, mid-back height on those sitting propped against it. Here the men from the village gathered in the evenings to pray and chat. They rose to greet us and only sat down again when we indicated that they should do so. After my friend had given directions to someone who was concerned about his duties on the estate, a strained silence fell, broken only by their continuing expressions of welcome to us. I murmured to my friend that we had perhaps interrupted their conversation.

"What could they have been saying of any conceivable importance?" he retorted in English.

Then one of them suggested that Sheikh Muḥsin should be sent for and an emissary hurried off to find him. We were informed that the man in question was the *ma'zun,* chief legal official of the village, and the most suitable interlocutor for people like us. Then all were silent, until the awaited guest arrived, preceded by the messenger holding up a paraffin lamp in whose glow you could see that the sheikh had cut his moustache but let his beard grow freely, that he wore a red turban and, believe it or not, a red robe to match.

The sheikh certainly knew why he had been summoned. As soon as he had settled down and the introductions were completed, he broke into a long, expansive discourse. The first part of this consisted of him telling us how he had just been with the local mayor and the government deputy, enlightening them as to how they should proceed in trying the case of one 'Abd al-Sami'. In the middle section he informed us that he had been a student at al-Azhar for a number of years, and in the conclusion gave us a disquisition on a calico factory set up by Muḥammad 'Ali Pasha. Then he swayed gently in his place, preening himself, while his audience shot glances in our direction which plainly said, "Could you give a speech like that?"

The crescent moon had climbed up the sky and the still water received its pale light like a tender mother taking a sick child in her arms. By a distant fire a reed pipe started up a plaintive lament. I was captivated by the magic of the surroundings and temporarily ignored those around me. My friend roused me, and there was the sheikh immersed in an explication of some verses of the Qur'ān, wringing the meaning out of them, so that their spirituality was utterly lost, and using his interpretation as a balm which dropped on his listeners' hearts and left them unscathed.

This was hard for me to bear and my friend, noticing my obvious disquiet, whispered that it would do no good to intervene. I ignored his advice and, as gently as I could, set about opposing the hero of the gathering. He resisted my arguments stubbornly, resorting to myths and fabrications which afforded my friend much surreptitious mirth, although he refused to be drawn into the discussion. At this I no longer held back. Determined to disprove the sheikh's lies and destroy his empty debating points, I waited until I noticed him wavering in his argument and jumped in, seizing the opportunity to discuss the peasants' living conditions. I spoke openly to them about their miserable situation and their harsh way of life, mentioned their children, their wives, their primitive housing, and outlined the way they could change their lives for the better if they wanted to. Then I elaborated on the subject of free will combined with action, explaining that they could accomplish miracles if they became conscious of their existence and resolved to justify it.

I talked passionately, my voice trembling with emotion, calculating that by addressing such a sensitive area, I would find a way to their hearts without any trouble. However, each time I paused to see what effect I was having, I found them open-mouthed in dumb amazement, looking from me to their mentor, as if they would have liked to ask for an explanation of my behaviour. As I thundered along, carried away in a frenzy of enthusiasm, I caught sight of two members of my audience, their heads close together, whispering to one another and not paying me the slightest attention. I was torn by conflicting emotions.

"How stupid you are!" a voice inside me cried. "You're tiring your lungs for nothing. They'll never understand you because you're an outsider, an interloper."

I gave in, and brought my speech to a premature close. The moment I finished, one of the two who had been whispering spoke out.

"Tell us then, Master — did the mayor testify for 'Abd al-Samī' or against him?"

Then the whole gathering erupted into a babble of noisy remarks on the same subject and I ceased to exist along with my words. My friend was visibly embarrassed by me and we avoided each other's eyes for some time. The sheikh remained silent until calm had returned.

"God forgive me," he murmured, then turned to address his audience in grand style.

"Disasters befall us, yet we do not weep. This failure to weep is the result of eyes that are like stones. Such eyes come from a hard heart, which is caused by an abundance of sins. An abundance of sins is the result of an excess of hope, which in turn is the product of a love of the material world. The source of such a love is the will. That is, the idea that the will of man, the created one, is everything and the will of the Creator, Almighty God, is nothing."

He swivelled his eyes around his listeners and they bowed their heads and sucked in the corners of their mouths to show their distress and anguish. My friend looked at me.

"This is their man," he said in a low voice. "You invaded their minds and they didn't understand you. But he spoke to their hearts. And that's the kind of people they are, as you see."

The crescent moon had sunk close to the blazing fire and turned red in its glow, as if it was burning fiercely. It was an extraordinary spectacle and my eyes were instinctively drawn to it, but my ears were focused on the speaker, who had begun to take my speech to pieces.

"This gentleman, people, has led us to consider a fine concept, that is, the will, in the sense that if one wants something, all one has to do is to say 'Be' and it will be."

I shuddered at this unpalatable sarcasm and the ridiculous misconstruction of my arguments, and bit my lip in an attempt to master my feelings and suppress the obscenities I was on the point of hurling at this bearded miscreant. My friend pressed me on the leg and whispered, "You may not have the chance of seeing anything like this again in your life, so why don't you keep quiet and listen."

I did as I was told. The sheikh was haranguing those around him.

"Which of you would not like to be a village mayor?" he shouted.

A skinny peasant with narrow slits of eyes interrupted.

"Or even a pasha!" he said, chasing away a mosquito from his face.

All those who understood that this interjection made no sense laughed heartily. Sheikh Muḥsin, stony-faced, retrieved the situation and went on.

"No, no. We're mistaken. The gentleman here stipulates action together with the exercise of the individual will. Let us say straight away that 'Abd al-Samī' pursued this course. And how unfortunate that turned out to be!"

A chorus of voices: "God be merciful to him! God help him!"

The man with small eyes straightened up, raised his hands heavenwards and prayed fervently.

"O God, preserve us from the evil in ourselves, and from the Devil's wicked work. O, Lord!"

What he was really doing with this earnest prayer was banishing from his mind the spectre of the spiteful trick he had played against the owner of the field next to his.

The sheikh began to relate the story of 'Abd al-Samī' especially for our benefit, and at the same time the frogs started up somewhere in the distance, providing a kind of orchestral accompaniment to his tale.

"This 'Abd al-Samī' was — if I might mention it — a cobbler, living always on the backs of those whose shoes he patched. [He laughed at his own joke and there were gales of laughter on all sides.] But he was not satisfied with his lot. He decided of his own free will [here he brought his hands together with a vigorous smack to emphasize the word] to raise himself to a station not ordained for him in eternity."

A voice: "The ancients said, 'Greed debases the greedy'."

"God led him on — for God is the most skilful deviser of stratagems to defeat his enemies. God sent 'Abd al-Samī' the assistant prosecutor — one of those young men who have traded the next world for this. He appointed 'Abd al-Samī' as his personal doorkeeper at work, welcomed him into his home, heaped material comforts upon him. 'Abd al-Samī' became a city-dweller, wore a jacket and tarboosh and walked around exulting at his good fortune, even though the Almighty has said, 'Walk not triumphantly in the land, for you will never cleave the earth, nor equal the mountains in stature'."

Voices wove together saying, "Glory be to Him who spoke these words."

These were followed by sighs of appreciation, and some of them turned to look at us, eyes shining in admiration at the eloquence of the speaker, while others bowed their heads until their faces almost touched the ground and the rest exchanged glances, waving the mosquitoes away from their noses.

The sheikh gathered the skirts of his robe around him, adjusted his turban and inserted his fingers into his beard in a manner which suggested that he was ready to move on to a significant point in his story. A brief silence descended. The melodies of the distant flute stirred vaguely like a gentle breeze, endless, sad.

"The new job and the life of ease were not aimed at 'Abd al-Samī', but in fact — and God forgive me for what I'm about to say — at his wife. Despite being poor, she is extremely beautiful, as you know, and the assistant prosecutor had often noticed her at her husband's side when he was patching sandals for him. He convinced the husband that it would be a good idea to bring her with him when he came to work for him permanently. Then he could keep an eye on her and she could do the housework, seeing that he himself was a bachelor. The master had his way, but did 'Abd al-Samī''s efforts really do him any good? Absolutely not. After a while, God began to fill his head with overwhelming doubts..."

"God preserve us!"

"...and worry got the better of him."

"God protect us!"

"He became unable to enjoy life, and his peace of mind was destroyed."

The sheikh paused to let his listeners express their reactions as they fancied. He reached for a round earthenware pitcher of water and began to drink from it, making the loudest, most irritating noise possible. The moment he finished, the man sitting next to him hurried to take the pitcher from him and return it to its place, while Sheikh Muḥsin drew a large handkerchief from his pocket, a quarter of which would have made a fair-sized one, belched, asked God's forgiveness, then wiped his mouth, murmuring, "Thanks be to God."

When he had replaced his handkerchief and played with his beard to his heart's content, he continued talking.

"How could he have any peace of mind, when one thing naturally led to another? I fear I've gone on for too long, gentlemen. [This remark was directed at us and we answered it as best we could.] The wretched cobbler's wife who used to sing at saint's day celebrations and receive alms — goodness me, goodness me — became a lady, saying what should and shouldn't be done. And the only person she could find to lord it over was her husband. [Sounds of distress, amazement, anger.] If ever he rebuked her, she would rush to her master, weeping and wailing, and he in turn would rebuke the husband and accuse him of being a peasant with no notion of a woman's worth."

"There is no power or strength save with God!" murmured the voices disapprovingly.

"The poor man often complained to me about his situation, and I advised him to leave what was not his and return to the life he was fitted for.

"But he was like a drowning man and continued down the same path until there was no room for doubt. Then he began to be tormented by raging fires of jealousy. He was distraught, continuously unhappy, took no pleasure in life and found no escape from his trials in sleep. All the same, he was incapable of extracting himself from this purgatory.

"One: it was hard for him to give up the easy life laid on for him.

"Two: Satan was playing with his mind, so every time he resolved to change things, he developed a fixation that he really was just a peasant, and that urban life was like this. Then he calmed down and gave up the struggle."

Voices: "God damn urban life, and the day we ever heard of it."

"Things went on as they were until that dreadful night when the assistant prosecutor asked 'Abd al-Samī' to take a message to the mayor — here — and to bring him the reply, not straight away, but the next morning."

At this point one of the audience remarked suddenly, "Very odd," in a long drawn-out, humorous tone, clowning around, and the rest laughed briefly.

Then the sheikh lowered his voice to a deep, thrilling pitch and told his audience that what they were about to hear was secret information which the examining magistrates had given him access to because of his high standing in their eyes, and because of the confidence they had in him. He requested them to keep it to themselves, and they nodded eagerly. At that moment one of them decided to adjust the lamp — it had been placed in the centre of the circle and squadrons of mosquitoes hovered over it and swooped down around it in frenzied attacks — and the rest chided him for his lack of manners when the teacher was talking.

"'Abd al-Samī' made his way along the railway embankment, thinking about the state of his life, his heart full of doubt. The moon lit his path and as he went along he noticed, lying between the rails, a piece of iron as a long as a man's arm — I've seen it with my own eyes. He picked it up and the moment he discovered how heavy it was, he was seized by a desire to return. The poor wretch claims he tried to conquer this desire without success: it was as if the invisible hand of the Almighty was pulling him backwards. He finally gave in, returned and found the house in darkness. He opened the doors warily, one by one, until he came to his master's room, and there he saw — God forbid — he saw his master in ... the husband's place ... with his own wife."

The gathering erupted once more, this time with noises of disapproval and disgust and countless appeals to God. Sheikh Muḥsin took the opportunity provided by this uproar to repeat his welcome to us. He would have liked to add, "Am I not an eloquent speaker?"

Once calm was restored, he continued.

"The two of them were asleep when he went in, and he could not restrain himself from bringing the iron bar crashing down on their skulls. They died at once."

Approving noises.

"However, he did not stop there. The desire for revenge was still burning fiercely in him, and he beat their heads to a pulp. The examining magistrates actually found pieces of brain ... of brain, Heaven forbid, sticking to the wall."

Noises of approval and disgust at the same time.

The gathering went quiet for a spell. The croaking of the frogs was the only sound in the still air, since the reed flute's lament had long since died away.

"The strangest thing was that, once his thirst for revenge was satisfied, he fetched the utensils he needed to make tea and sat up with the corpses for the remainder of the night, drinking tea and smoking."

"What kind of monstrosity are we talking about?" demanded my friend, aghast.

To my astonishment, I heard myself saying, "I wish I could have been with them that night."

The gathering echoed to expressions of horror.

"At dawn," continued the sheikh, "'Abd al-Samī' took the piece of iron, went to the police and made a clean breast of all that had happened."

Once again the sheikh reached for the water jar and drank from it in the same manner as before.

Then he said, "And so, my sons, life on earth is about worship, not free will, and the best way is always God's way."

He prepared to leave, claiming that the mayor and many of the notables were expecting him. The peasants went up to him one by one to kiss his hand, contented and at ease, thanking God that through His grace they were protected from scandal.

We preferred to stay behind, my friend and I, and so they left the lantern, happy to follow their teacher into the darkness.

Maḥmūd Ṭāhir Lāshīn, 1929

Notes

Foreword

1. Norman Friedman, *Form and Meaning in Fiction* (Athens, Georgia, University of Georgia Press, 1975), p. 169.

2. Hans Robert Jauss, *Towards an Aesthetic of Reception,* trans. Timothy Bahti (Minneapolis, University of Minnesota Press, 1982), p. 80.

3. Such as Maḥmūd Ṭāhir Lāshīn, Yaḥyā Ḥaqqi, Maḥmūd al-Badawi, Yūsuf al-Shārūni in Egypt; 'Abd al-Salām al-'Ujayli, Sa'id Ḥūrāniyyah and Zakariyyā Tāmir in Syria; Samīrah 'Azzām and Ghassān Kanafāni in Palestine; and Dhū-l-Nūn Ayyūb and 'Abd al-Malik Nūri in Iraq.

4. Arab culture has its fair share of these genres and other narrative forms from the epics of *'Antrah, al-Zīr Sālim, Sayf ibn Dhi Yazan, al-Hilāliyyah, Sirat Dhāt al-Himmah,* and *'Ali al-Zaibaq* to the elaborate and fascinating narrative of *Alf Laylah wa-Laylah,* the stories of the Qur'ān and those of *al-Bukhalā'* and others.

5. James T. Farrel, "International Symposium on the Short Story", *Kenyon Review,* XXXII, 1, 1970, p. 88.

6. James Cooper Lawrence, "A Theory of the Short Story", in *Short Story Theories,* (ed.) Charles E. May (Columbus, Ohio, Ohio University Press, 1976), p. 61.

7. Elizabeth Taylor, "International Symposium on the Short Story", *Kenyon Review,* XXXI, 4, 1969, p. 370.

8. Published in *Kenyon Review,* XXX, 1, 1968; XXXI, 1 and 4, 1969; and XXXII, 1, 1970.

9. The explanation provided by the German writer Hans Bender for the revival of the short story in post-World War II Germany sheds some light on this phenomenon, for it makes it a part of a newly emerging culture, similar to those of the developing countries. Like that of developing countries, the literature of post-World War II Germany strove for a new beginning, and "the short story began a new life, so sudden, vigorous and fresh was its appearance that it became the most characteristic genre of the new beginning ... It was well liked also because it stood in contrast to the kind of literature which had mainly been produced, read and promoted during the preceding twelve years". See Hans Bender, *Kenyon Review,* XXXI, 1, 1969, p. 86.

Introduction

1. Ian Watt, *The Rise of the Novel* (Berkeley, University of California Press, 1957), and Q.D. Leavis, *Fiction and the Reading Public* (London, Penguin Books, 1965).

2. Georg Lukács, *The Theory of the Novel,* trans. Anna Bostock (London, Merlin Press, 1971), and M. M. Bakhtin, *The Dialogic Imagination,* trans. Caryl Emerson and Michael Holquist (Austin, University of Texas Press, 1981).

3. René Girard, *Mensonge romantique et vérité romanesque* (Éditions Bernard Grasset, 1961), translated into English as *Deceit, Desire, and the Novel* by Yvonne Freccero (Baltimore, Johns Hopkins University Press, 1965).

4. See, for example, Muḥammad Muḥammad Ḥusain, *al-Ittijāhāt al-Waṭaniyyah fi-l-Adab al-Mu'āṣir,* 2 vols (Cairo, al-Maṭba'ah al-Namūdhajiyyah, 1956); Fārūq Khūrshīd, *fī al-Riwāyah al-'Arabiyyah fī 'Aṣr al-Tajmī'* (Cairo, Dār al-Qalam, 1960); Jamīl Sulṭān, *Fann al-Qiṣṣah wa-l-Maqāmah* (Beirut, Dār al-'Anwār, 1967); Aḥmad Haykal, *al-Adab al-Qaṣaṣi wal-Masraḥi fī Miṣr* (Cairo, Dār al-Ma'ārif, 1970); Muḥammad Rushdi Ḥasan, *Athar al-Maqāmah fī Nash'at al-Qiṣṣah al-Miṣriyyah al-Ḥadīthah* (Cairo, al-Hay'ah al-Miṣriyyah al-'Āmmah li-l-Kitāb, 1974); and in English Roger Allen, *Muḥammad Ibrāhīm al-Muwayliḥi: A Study of Ḥadīth 'Īsā Ibn Hishām,* on microfiche (Albany, State University of New York, 1974), and Ali al-Rā'i, "Some Aspects of Modern Arabic Drama", in *Studies in Modern Arabic Literature,* ed. R.C. Ostle (Warminster, Aris & Philips, 1976), pp. 167-78.

5. M.M. Badawi, *Modern Arabic Literature and the West* (London, Ithaca Press, 1985), p. 128.

6. See Maḥmūd Taymūr, *Nushū' al-Qiṣṣah wa Taṭawwuruha* (Cairo, al-Maṭba'ah al-Salafiyyah, 1936); Suhayl Idrīs, *Muḥāḍarāt 'an al-Qiṣṣah fī Lubnān* (Cairo, Dār al-Ma'rifah, 1957); 'Abd al-Muḥsin Ṭaha Badr, *Taṭawwur al-Riwāyah al-'Arabiyyah al-Ḥadīthah fī Miṣr* (Cairo, Dār al-Ma'ārif, 1963); Muḥammad Yūsuf Najm, *al-Qiṣṣah fī al-Adab al-'Arabi al-Ḥadīth* (Beirut, al-Maktabah al-Ahliyyah, 1966); 'Abbās Khaḍr, *al-Qiṣṣah al-Qaṣīrah fī Miṣr: Mundh Nash'atihā Ḥattā Sanat 1930* (Cairo, al-Dār al-Qawmiyyah, 1966); and 'Abd al-Ḥamīd Ibrāhīm, *al-Qiṣṣah al-Miṣriyyah wa-Ṣūrat al-Mujtama' al-Ḥadīth* (Cairo, Dār al-Ma'ārif, 1973).

7. See Lucien Goldmann, *Le Dieu câché* (Paris, Éditions Gallimard, 1956) translated into English as *The Hidden God* by Philip Thody (London, Routledge & Kegan Paul, 1964), p. 35.

8. For a detailed discussion of this concept as well as those of "authority" and "molestation", see Edward Said, *Beginnings: Intention and Method* (New York, Columbia University Press, 1985), especially chapter 3 "The Novel as Beginning Intention", pp. 81-275.

9. Georg Lukács, op. cit., p. 88.

10. Edward Said, "Introduction" to *Days of Dust* by Halim Barakat, trans. Trevor Le Gassick (Wilmette, Illinois, Medina University Press, 1974), p. xii.

11. Goldmann, *The Hidden God,* p. 15.

12. Lucien Goldmann, *Method in the Sociology of Literature,* trans. William Q. Boelhower (Oxford, Basil Blackwell, 1980), p. 111.

13. Edward Said, *Beginnings,* p. 81, and also in "Molestation and Authority in Narrative Fiction" in J. Hillis Miller (ed.), *Aspects of Narrative* (New York, Colombia University Press, 1971), p. 47.

14. Edward Said, *The World, the Text, and the Critic* (Cambridge, Mass., Harvard University Press, 1983), p. 39.

15. Said, *Beginnings,* p. 81.

16. Said, "Molestation and Authority in Narrative Fiction", p. 48.

17. Said, "Introduction" to *Days of Dust,* p. xiv.

18. Ibid., p. xv.

19. Wallace Martin, *Recent Theories of Narrative* (Ithaca, New York, Cornell University Press, 1986), p. 7.

20. Jacques Berque, *Cultural Expression in Arab Society Today* (Austin, University of Texas Press, 1978), pp. 259-60, also quoted in Roger Allen, *The Arabic Novel: An Historical and Critical Introduction* (Manchester, University of Manchester Press, 1982), pp. 17-18.

21. M.M. Bakhtin and P.M. Medvedev, *The Formal Method in Literary Scholarship: A Critical Introduction to Sociological Poetics* (Cambridge, Mass., Harvard University Press, 1985), p. 129.

22. M.M. Bakhtin and V. N. Volosinov, *Marxism and the Philosophy of Language,* trans. L. Matejka and I. R. Titunik (New York, Simenar Press, 1973), p. 79.

23. Alan Swingewood, *Sociological Poetics and Aesthetic Theory* (London, Macmillan, 1986), p. 19.
24. Bakhtin, *The Dialogic Imagination*, pp. 262-3.
25. Ibid., p. 261. Something similar to the linguistic stratification outlined here started to emerge in the Arabic language as a result of the development of different educational systems and varying modes of social experience. The dichotomy between the written and the spoken was no longer the only linguistic distinction, several linguistic strata started to appear and pave the way for multifarious discourses.
26. Ibid., p. 411.
27. Lucien Goldmann, *Pour une sociologie du roman* (Paris, Éditions Gallimard, 1964), translated into English as *Towards a Sociology of the Novel* by Alan Sheridan (London, Tavistock Publications, 1975), p. 9.
28. Ibid.
29. Ibid.
30. Ibid.
31. Ibid., p. 14.
32. Owen Miller, "Intertextual Identity", in Mario Valdés & Owen Miller (eds.), *Identity of the Literary Text* (Toronto, University of Toronto Press, 1985), p. 20.
33. See Julia Kristeva, *Semeiotikè: Recherches pour une sémanalyse* (Paris, Éditions du Seuil, 1969), p. 255.
34. A. J. Greimas and J. Courtés, *Semiotics and Language: An Analytical Dictionary*, trans. L. Crist et al (Bloomington, Indiana University Press, 1982), p. 161.
35. Jonathan Culler, *The Pursuit of Signs: Semiotics, Literature, Deconstruction* (London, Routledge & Kegan Paul, 1981), p. 103.
36. Ibid.
37. Janet Wolff, *The Social Production of Art* (London, Macmillan, 1982), p. 67.
38. Jauss, op. cit., p. 88.
39. Diana Spearman, *The Novel and Society* (London, Routledge & Kegan Paul, 1966), p. 227.
40. Chris Weedon, *Feminist Practice and Poststructuralist Theory* (Oxford, Basil Blackwell, 1987), p. 21.
41. Diana Spearman, op. cit., p. 236.
42. Anthony Giddens, *New Rules of Sociological Method* (London, Hutchinson, 1976), p. 161.
43. John Frow, *Marxism and Literary History* (Oxford, Blackwell, 1986), p. 125.
44. Bakhtin and Medvedev, op. cit., p. 120.
45. Weedon, op. cit., p. 22.
46. For a detailed discussion of the concepts of discursive formation and discursive field, see Michel Foucault, *The Archaeology of Knowledge and the Discourse on Language*, trans. A.M. Sheridan Smith (New York, Pantheon Books, 1972), pp. 21-78.
47. Ibid., p. 229.
48. Ibid.
49. Ibid.
50. Spearman, op. cit., p. 236.
51. Janet Wolff, *Aesthetics and the Sociology of Art* (London, George Allen & Unwin, 1983), p. 105.
52. Jauss, op. cit., p. 22.
53. Frow, op. cit., p. 128.
54. E. D. Hirsch, *Validity in Interpretation* (New Haven, Yale University Press, 1967), p. 71.
55. Hans Robert Jauss, *Towards an Aesthetic of Reception*, trans. Timothy Bahti (Minneapolis, University of Minnesota Press, 1982), pp. 76-109; a French version of this appeared in *Théorie des genres* (Paris, Éditions du Seuil, 1986), pp. 37-76.
56. Ibid., p.79.
57. Bakhtin and Medvedev, op. cit., p. 129.
58. Benedetto Croce, *Estetica*, 2nd ed. (Bari, 1906), p. 40, quoted in Jauss, op. cit., p. 78.
59. Jauss, op. cit., p. 88.

60. Ibid.
61. Ibid., pp. 81-2.
62. Hirsch, op. cit., p. 78.

Chapter 1

1. Ian Watt, *The Rise of the Novel* (Berkeley, University of California Press, 1957), p. 7.
2. Hans Robert Jauss, *Towards an Aesthetic of Reception*, trans. Timothy Bahti (Minneapolis, University of Minnesota Press, 1982), pp. 26-7.
3. Ibid., p. 27.
4. Edward Said, "Introduction" to *Days of Dust* by Halim Barakat, trans. Trevor Le Gassick (Wilmette, Illinois, Medina University Press, 1974), p. xiii. Said is clearly elaborating here certain aspects of Michel Foucault's ideas of identities and differences, and signs and similitudes in chapter 3 of *Les mots et les choses*, translated into English as *The Order of Things: An Archaeology of the Human Sciences* (New York, Vintage Books, 1970), pp. 46-76.
5. Soon after its foundation this school was put under Jesuit administration. Although it was a Christian theocentric school dominated by the Vatican ethos, it presented an advanced step, by the standard of the time, towards a more balanced and European-oriented education.
6. Philip Hitti, *The Middle East in History* (Princeton, New Jersey, D. Van Nostrad, 1961), p. 443.
7. See his elaborate introduction to the new edition of his book *al-Mutanabbi* (Cairo, Maktabat al-Khānji, 1964). More than twenty years later, this introduction appeared as an independent book entitled *Risāla fi-l-Ṭarīq ila Thaqāfatina* (Cairo, Dār al-Hilāl, 1987).
8. Al-Jabarti, the father of the famous historian 'Abd al-Raḥmān, was one of the great scholars, scientists and engineers of his time; his home housed one of the largest libraries of the period. Shākir provides evidence that a number of orientalists came to study under him, some of whom returned afterwards with the French expedition. See *Risāla fi-l-Ṭarīq ila Thaqafatina*, pp. 125-206.
9. Peter Gran, *Islamic Roots of Capitalism: Egypt 1760-1840* (Austin, University of Texas, 1979).
10. Aḥmad Ṣādiq Sa'd published many articles and books on the subject; prominent among them are his three books; *Nash'at al-Takwīn al-Miṣri li-l-Ra'smāliyyah wa-Taṭawwuruh: fī Ḍaw' al-Namṭ al-Āsyawi li-l-Intāj* (Beirut, Dār al-Ḥadāthah, n.d.); *Tārīkh Miṣr al-Ijtimā'i al-Iqtiṣādi* (Beirut, Dār Ibn Khalhūn, 1979); and *Taḥawwul al-Takwīn al-Miṣri min al-Namaṭ al-Āsyawi ilā al-Namaṭ al-Ra'smāli* (Beirut, Dār al-Ḥadāthah, 1981).
11. Aḥmad Ṣādiq Sa'd, *Taḥawwul al-Takwīn al-Miṣri min al-Namaṭ al-Āsyawi ilā al-Namaṭ al-Ra'smāli*, pp. 75-104.
12. Ibid., pp. 152-61.
13. 'Abd al-Raḥīm 'Abd al-Raḥmān 'Abd al-Raḥīm, "*al-Qaḍā' fī Miṣr al-'Uthmāniyyah*", in *Buḥūth fī Tārīkh Miṣr al-Ḥadīth* (Cairo, 'Ayn Shams University, 1976), pp. 129-30.
14. Gran, op. cit., pp. 35-6.
15. Tawfīq al-Ṭawīl, *al-Sha'rāni: Imām al-Taṣawwuf fī 'Aṣrih* (Cairo, 'Īsā al-Bābi al-Ḥalabi, 1945), p. 87.
16. Aḥmad Ṣādiq Sa'd, *Taḥawwul al-Takwīn al-Miṣri*, p. 164.
17. This explains the ease with which Muḥammad 'Ali was able to dispense with the *'ulamā'* soon after his rise to power, for they continued to lose the support of the people steadily, then their national status suffered a serious blow during the French occupation.
18. Tawfīq al-Ṭawīl, op. cit., p. 109. Quoted in Aḥmad Ṣādiq Sa'd, *Taḥawwul al-Takwīn al-Miṣri*, p. 165.
19. Ibid., p. 56.
20. Zaki Mubārak, *al-Taṣawwuf al-Islāmi fī al-Adab wa-l-Akhlāq*, 2 vols (Cairo, Maṭba'at al-Risālah, 1946), Tawfīq al-Ṭawīl, op. cit., and Ṭaha 'Abd al-Bāqi Surūr, *al-Taṣawwuf al-Islāmi wa-l-Imām al-Sha'rāni* (Cairo, Maktabat al-Nahḍah, 1955).

21. Tawfiq al-Ṭawīl, op. cit., p. 57.
22. The *Wafā'iyyah* was one of the major *Ṣūfi ṭarīqah* at the time.
23. Ibid., p. 59.
24. Ibid., p. 68.
25. Most of the historical accounts of the development of modern Arabic literature or thought postulate that the condition before the contact with European culture was one of complete decline, cultural degradation and even decay.
26. He was the most outstanding of the four scholars of the family: Isṭifān 'Awād al-Sam'āni (1709-82), Yūsuf Liwīs al-Sam'āni (1710-82), and Sham'ūn al-Sam'āni (1752-1821), who all studied in the Maronite Institute in Rome and produced copious literary and linguistic works.
27. This Syrian was Sa'īd ibn Muḥammad al-Ḥalabi; for more details see 'Umar al-Daqqāq, *Funūn al-Adab al-Mu'āṣir fi Sūriyyah* (Beirut, Dār Sharq, 1971), pp. 15-27.
28. This was the Greek Orthodox press of St Georgios.
29. Some of the ideas expressed in the work of this chronicler are to be found in the work of later generations outside Egypt such as Ibn Abi Ḍiyāf in Tunis, al-Biṭār in Damascus, and Sulaymān Fa'iq in Baghdad.
30. See A. al-Jabarti, *'Aja'ib al-Āthār fi al-Tarājim wa-l-Akhbār,* vols 4 and 5 (Cairo, Dār Iḥyā' al-Kutub al-'Arabiyyah, n.d.).
31. An Azharite student from Aleppo who assassinated Bonaparte's successor in Cairo, General Klieper.
32. See the full text of this proclamation in 'Abd al-Raḥman al-Rafi'i, *Tārīkh al-Ḥarakah al-Qawmiyyah wa-Taṭawwur Niẓām al-Ḥukm fi Miṣr* (Cairo, Maṭba'at al-Nahḍah, 1929), vol. I, pp. 85-9.
33. For a significant analysis of this proclamation and its main ideas, see Liwīs 'Awaḍ, *al-Mu'aththirāt al-Ajnabiyyah fi al-Adab al-'Arabi al-Ḥadīth* (Cairo, Dār al-Ma'rifah, 1963), vol. 1, pp. 8-12.
34. See al-Rafi'i, op. cit., chapters 3 and 4, for an account of these institutions.
35. The tragic nature of the relationship between the intellectuals and the state continued throughout the modern history of the Arab world, and was aggravated by the lack of democracy, for both were seen, and even conceived of themselves, as vying for influence and power, and each claimed to represent the interests of the silent majority and to possess its unequivocal mandate.
36. This was the case with most of the *'ulamā'* (intellectuals) of al-Azhar, who were attracted by authority or given substantial gifts of money or land.
37. This was the case with 'Umar Makram, the head of the *Ashrāf* (descendants of the Prophet), who refused to be silenced and remained committed to the spirit of opposition. He was exiled by Muḥammad 'Ali, with the valuable help of those whom he had bought off.
38. This was the fate of popular militants such as Ḥajjāj al-Khuḍari and others.
39. C. Wright Mills, *Power, Politics, and People: The Collected Essays,* ed. Irving Louis Horowitz (Oxford, Oxford University Press, 1963), p. 413.
40. 'Abbās al-'Aqqād, *Muḥammad 'Abduh* (Cairo, Maṭa'bat Miṣr, 1962), p. 16.
41. P.J. Vatikiotis, *The Modern History of Egypt* (London, Weidenfeld & Nicolson, 1969), p. 99.
42. Ḥasan al-'Aṭṭār was one of the leading intellectuals of his time and became the Rector of the University of al-Azhar. Like many of the intellectuals of his time, he travelled extensively in the Arab world, from Morocco to Damascus and Mecca, and his approach to learning was encyclopaedic in its scope, with a strong emphasis on scientific subjects, in which he is reputed to have excelled.
43. Ṣalāḥ 'Īsā, *al-Thawrah al-'Urābiyyah* (Beirut, al-Mu'assasah al-'Arabiyyah li-l-Dirāsāt wa-l-Nashr, 1972), p. 187.
44. Henceforth referred to as *Takhlīṣ*.
45. In translating the rhyming titles of books, a common feature of nineteenth-century writing, certain liberties have been taken in order to reflect the main thesis of the book concerned. Literal translation of such titles into English is pointless, and is only adopted when it emphasizes certain points under discussion.
46. Henceforth referred to as *Manāhij.*

47. Jacques Berque, *Egypt: Imperialism and Revolution,* trans. Jean Stewart (London, Faber & Faber, 1972), p. 16.
48. The Marrāshs were a well-established, learned Christian family from Aleppo. They produced Buṭrus Marrāsh (d. 1818), who was killed by Orthodox fundamentalists for his religious views; Fatḥ-Allah, Francis' father, who wrote a blasphemous book and created another scandal. Fatḥ-Allah had also another son, 'Abdullah (1839-1900), who was a well-known intellectual; and a daughter, Marian, was a noted poet.
49. For a detailed account of his life and work, see Ḥaydar Ḥāj Ismā'īl, *Francis Marrāsh* (London, Riad El-Rayyes Books, 1989).
50. Fritz Steppat, "National Education Projects in Egypt before the British Occupation", in William R. Polk and Richard L. Chambers (eds.), *Beginning of Modernization in the Middle East: The Nineteenth Century* (Chicago, University of Chicago Press, 1968), p. 283.
51. This third mission is known as *Ba'that al-Anjāl* (the mission of the children), because it contained a large number of Muḥammad 'Ali's family.
52. Vatikiotis, op. cit., p. 94.
53. For a detailed account of Ismā'īl's educational, literary, and scientific renaissance, see 'Abd al-Raḥman al-Rāfi'i, *'Asr Ismā'īl* (Cairo, Maṭba'at al-Nahḍah, 1932), vol. I, pp. 208-17.
54. For detailed information, see Ibrāhīm 'Abduh, *Taṭawwur al-Ṣiḥāfah al-Miṣriyyah: 1797-1951* (Cairo, Maktabat al-Ādāb, 1951), particularly the section entitled *"Jadwal al-Ṣuḥuf al-'Arabiyyah"*, pp. 259 ff.
55. Vatikiotis, op. cit., p. 74.
56. It is highly significant that this national manifesto was signed not only by 60 members of the Consultative Council, but also by 60 *'ālim* and religious leaders, including the sheikh of al-Azhar, the Coptic patriarch, the Jewish rabbi, 42 leading merchants, 72 senior civil servants and 93 officers. It sowed the seeds of the alliance between the notables, merchants, middle class and intellectuals. See 'Abd al-Raḥman al-Rāfi'i, *'Aṣr Ismā'īl,* vol. II, pp. 182-4.
57. Ṣalāḥ 'Īsā, op. cit., p. 154.
58. Patrick O'Brien, "The Long-term Growth of Agricultural Production in Egypt: 1821-1962", in P.M. Holt (ed.), *Political and Social Change in Modern Egypt* (Oxford, Oxford University Press, 1968), p. 163.
59. Steppat, op. cit., pp. 283-4. Steppat states that "from 1857 to 1861, an average of 30,000 foreigners came into the country each year; in 1862 they numbered 33,000; in 1863, 43,000; in 1864, 56,600; in 1865, 80,000". See also David S. Landes, *Bankers and Pashas: International Finance and Economic Imperialism in Egypt* (London, 1958), pp. 87-8; and Rif'at al-Sa'īd, *al-Asās al-Ijtimā'i lil-Thawrah al-'Urābiyyah* (Cairo, Dār al-Thaqāfah al-Jadīdah, 1967), p. 137.
60. Anwar 'Abd al-Malik, *Nahḍat Miṣr* (Cairo, al-Hay'ah al-Miṣriyyah al-'Āmmah li-l-Kitāb, 1983), p. 87.
61. Ira M. Lapidus, *A History of Islamic Societies* (Cambridge, Cambridge University Press, 1988), p. 640.
62. Albert Hourani, "Ottoman Reform and the Politics of Notables", in Polk and Chambers, op. cit., p. 65.
63. Peter Mansfield, *The British in Egypt* (London, Weidenfeld & Nicolson, 1971), p. 7.
64. Vatikiotis, op. cit., p. 90.
65. For a detailed study of the genesis of the colonial economy, see Berque, "The Establishment of the Colonial Economy" in Polk and Chambers, op. cit., pp. 223-43.
66. George Antonius, *The Arab Awakening: The Story of the Arab National Movement* (London, Hamish Hamilton, 1938), p. 39.
67. Hitti, op. cit., p. 479.
68. For a detailed study of the impact of these schools on the Palestinian cultural scene at the turn of the century, see 'Abd al-Raḥmān Yāghi, *Ḥayāt al-Adab al-Filasṭīni al-Ḥadīth: min Awwal al-Nahḍah ḥattā al-Nakbah* (Beirut, al-Maktab al-Tijāri, 1968), pp. 62-82.
69. 'Abd al-Raḥmān Yāghi, op. cit., pp. 64-8.

70. Hitti, op. cit., p. 449.

71. There is some debate concerning the first newspaper in Iraq. Rūfā'īl Buṭṭi argues that the first Iraqi newspaper, *Journal al-'Irāq*, appeared in 1816 during the rule of Dāwūd Pasha. See his *Tārīkh al-Ṣiḥāfah fī al-'Irāq* (Cairo, Dār al-Ma'rifah, 1955). But most historians support the view that *al-Zawrā'*, whose first issue appeared on 5 Rabī' Awwal 1286AH, is the first Iraqi newspaper to have appeared. Some reference to the alleged earlier one was found, but none of its issues have survived. If proof of the existence of the *Journal al-'Irāq* were to be found, then it would be the first Arabic newspaper.

72. For more details, see 'Abd al-Razzāq al-Hilāli, *Tārīkh al-Ta'līm fī al-'Irāq fī al-'Ahd al-'Uthmānī: 1638-1917* (Baghdad, Sharikat al-Nashr al-Ahliyyah, 1959).

73. The work of the two Taymūrs is discussed in chapters 4 and 5 below.

74. See *Fihris Maktabat 'Umar Makram* (Cairo, Maṭba'at Dār al-Kutub al-Miṣriyyah, 1933).

75. For a detailed discussion of the early output of Būlāq press, see Reinhard Schulze, "Mass Culture and Islamic Cultural Production in the 19th Century Middle East", in George Stauth, Sami Zubaida (eds), *Mass Culture, Popular Culture and Social Life in the Middle East* (Frankfurt am Main, Campus Verlag, 1987), pp. 189-222. Schulze also gives figures and subject distributions of the Arabic books published in Istanbul in the same period, indicating that, unlike those of Cairo, literature, language and Islamic studies accounted for nearly 70% of Istanbul's publications.

76. Ibid., p. 197.

77. See Yusūf Ilyās Sarkīs, *Mu'jam al-Maṭbū'āt al-'Arabiyyah wa-l-Mu'arrabah* (Cairo, Maṭba'at Sarkīs, 1928).

78. Edward William Lane, *Manners and Customs of Modern Egyptians* (London, 1836), 1894 edn, pp. 222, 283.

79. See *Fihris al-Khizānah al-Taymūriyyah* (Cairo, Maṭba'at Dār al-Kutub al-Miṣriyyah, 1948).

80. 'Abd al-Raḥmān Yāghi, op. cit., p. 34.

81. P.L. Cheikho, *al-Ādāb al-'Arabiyyah fī al-Qarn al-Tāsi' 'Ashar* (Beirut, al-Maṭba'ah al- Yasū'iyyah, 1910), vol. 2, p. 64.

82. For a detailed account of the development of journalism, particularly literary and cultural periodicals, see Filīb Ṭarrāzi, *Tārīkh al-Ṣiḥāfah al-'Arabiyyah* (Beirut, al-Maṭba'ah al-Adabiyyah, 1913).

83. These were the Opera House and Azbakiyya playhouse in Cairo in the 1860s, and the Zīzīnyā and Alfiriyā playhouses in Alexandria in the 1870s.

84. This was the beginning of a radical change in the artist-public relationship, for tickets appeared extensively for the first time; thus the artists were selling their product to an anonymous public.

85. For more details on the period, see M.M. Badawi, *Early Arabic Drama* (Cambridge, Cambridge University Press, 1988), pp. 31-42.

86. Charles Issawi, "Economic Change and Urbanization in the Middle East", in Ira M. Lapidus (ed.), *Middle Eastern Cities: A Symposium on Ancient, Islamic and Contemporary Middle Eastern Urbanism* (Berkeley, University of California Press, 1969), pp. 102-3. In order to point out the high degree of urbanization in these Arab countries, Issawi gives similar figures for some European countries at the time. In 1800 the percentage of the total population living in towns of 100,000 or over has been put at 7 per cent for England and Wales, 7 per cent in the Netherlands, 2.7 per cent in France, 1.6 per cent in Russia and 1 per cent in Germany. The 1790 census showed that only 3.3 per cent of the population of the United States lived in towns of 8000 or more.

87. Gabriel Baer, "Social Change in Egypt: 1800-1914" in Holt (ed.), op. cit., p. 155, and see also Baer's "Urbanization in Egypt, 1820-1907", in Polk and Chambers, op. cit., pp. 155-69.

88. Issawi, op. cit., p. 108.

89. Hans Kohn, *Western Civilization in the Near East* (London, George Routledge & Sons, 1936), p. 155.

90. Hitti, op. cit., pp. 490-1.

91. This may be attributed to the fact that Arab societies were segmented rather than stratified at the time.

92. Anwar 'Abd al-Malik, op. cit., pp. 104-19.

93. The first national library, Dar al-Kutub al-Khidiwiyyah (the Khedivial Library), was founded in 1873.

94. The interweaving of cultural and national issues is the main theme in any account of the development of literary genres or cultural institutions. See, for instance, Ibrāhīm 'Abduh, op. cit., or Muḥammad Yūsuf Najm, *al-Masraḥiyya fī al-Adab al-'Arabī al-Ḥadīth* (Beirut, 1956).

95. At this point one should mention that many traditional works of Arabic fiction were printed or reprinted at that time in order to substitute for the lack of new translations. These publications included *Kalīlah wa-Dimnah* (1868), *Maqāmāt al-Ḥarīrī* (1873), *Nawādir Juḥā* (1883), *Maṣāri' al-'Ushshāq* (1883), *Alf Laylah wa-Laylah* (1887), *Maqāmāt al-Hamadhāni* (1889), *al-Faraj ba'd al-Shiddah* (1891), and many other similar books.

96. Polk and Chambers, op. cit., p. 13.

97. 'Ali Mubārak, *'Alam al-Dīn*, vol. I, p. 139.

Chapter 2

1. George Antonius, *The Arab Awakening: The Story of the Arab National Movement* (London, Hamish Hamilton, 1938), p. 86.

2. Leslie Stephen, *English Literature and Society in the Eighteenth Century* (London, 1904), p. 26, quoted in Ian Watt, *The Rise of the Novel*, p. 36.

3. 'Abdullah Nadīm, *al-Ustādh*, 15 November 1892.

4. As opposed to the traditional theocentric education, *al-ta'līm al-dīni*, of al-Azhar in Cairo or of the traditional religious schools in the Levant.

5. For a comparison with the English reading public, see Watt, op. cit., pp. 36-61.

6. 'Abd al-'Azīm Muḥammad Ramaḍān, *Taṭawwur al-Ḥarakah al-Waṭaniyyah fī Miṣr: 1918-1936* (Cairo, Dār al-Kātib al-'Arabī, 1968), p. 27.

7. 'Abdullah Nadīm, *"al-Ma'ārif bi-Miṣr: Ḥālunā Ams wa-l-Yawm"*, *al-Ustādh*, 21 March 1893.

8. Ibid.

9. Anwar 'Abd al-Malik, *Nahḍat Miṣr* (Cairo, al-Hay'ah al-Miṣriyyah al-'Āmmah li-l-Kitāb, 1983), p. 171.

10. For more details and figures, see Ḥasan al-Fiqi, *al-Tārīkh al-Thaqāfi lil-Ta'līm fī Miṣr* (Cairo, Dār al-Ma'ārif, 1971), p. 84.

11. For a detailed discussion of these two, see ch. 4 of Ḥasan al-Fiqi, ibid., pp. 67-98, and see also J. Heyworth-Dunne, *An Introduction to the History of Education in Modern Egypt* (London, Luzac, 1938), pp. 96-285.

12. The population of Egypt at that time was 5,803,381, according to the census of 1882.

13. T.B. Bottomore, *Elites and Society* (London, Penguin Books, 1973), p. 97.

14. Wright Mills, *The Sociological Imagination* (London, Penguin, 1970), p. 199.

15. Sir Evelyn Baring, later Earl of Cromer, generally known as Lord Cromer, was the architect of the the long-term policies of the British occupation in Egypt. He was the British Agent-General in Egypt from September 1883 to May 1907. But he aggressively transformed his job from an Agent-General appointed rather vaguely to advise and assist the Egyptians in reforming their government to the virtual ruler of the country.

16. Jacques Berque, *Egypt: Imperialism and Revolution*, trans. Jean Stewart (London, Faber & Faber, 1972), p. 182; see also Peter Mansfield, *The British in Egypt* (London, Weidenfeld & Nicolson, 1971), p. 139.

17. Muḥammad Anīs, *Thawrat 23 Yūliū 1952 wa-'Uṣūluhā al-Tārīkhiyyah* (Cairo, Dār al-Nahḍah al-'Arabiyyah, 1964), p. 128.

18. Mansfield, op. cit., p. 141.

19. Afaf Lutfi al-Sayyid, *Egypt and Cromer: A Study in Anglo-Egyptian Relations* (London, John Murray, 1968), p. 167.

20. Pierre Cachia, *Taha Ḥusayn: His Place in the Egyptian Literary Renaissance* (London, Luzac, 1956), p. 27.
21. Antonius, op. cit., p. 93.
22. Nada Tomiche, "The Situation of Egyptian Women in the First Half of the Nineteenth Century", in William R. Polk and Richard L. Chambers (eds.), *Beginning of Modernization in the Middle East: The Nineteenth Century* (Chicago, University of Chicago Press, 1968), p. 183.
23. For a detailed study of his educational reform, see Aziz S. Atiyah, *A History of Eastern Christianity* (London, Methuen, 1968), pp. 103-7.
24. Anwar 'Abd al-Malik, op. cit., p. 171.
25. The Imperial Orthodox Palestine Society is discussed in some detail later.
26. Derek Hopwood, *The Russian Presence in Syria and Palestine: 1843-1914* (Oxford, Clarendon Press, 1969), pp. 147-8.
27. For the role of al-Ṭahṭāwi's work in this respect, see Liwis 'Awaḍ, *al-Mu'aththirāt al-Ajnabiyyah fī al-Adab al-'Arabi al-Ḥadīth* (Cairo, Dār al-Ma'rifah, 1963), vol. II, and Anwar 'Abd al-Malik, op. cit., pp. 328-36.
28. Salīm al-Bustāni, *"al-Inṣāf"* (Fair Treatment), *al-Jinān,* 1870, pp. 369-71.
29. Salīm al-Bustāni, *"Inn allati Tahuzz al-Sarīr bi-Yusrāhā Tahuzz al-Arḍ bi-Yamīnihā"* (The One who Swings the Cot with her Left Hand Raises the Earth with her Right), *al-Maqtaṭaf,* 1883, vol. 7, pp. 709-12 and vol. 8, pp. 7-11.
30. In the Egyptian newspaper, *al-Mu'ayyad,* 1 July 1910.
31. Philip Hitti, *The Middle East in History* (Princeton, New Jersey, D. Van Nostrand, 1961), p. 492.
32. Hitti, op. cit., p. 492.
33. See al-Ṭahṭāwi, *Manāhij,* and *Nafīr Sūriyyā* (Beirut, 1860-1), 25 October 1860. This appeared on the heels of the massacre of Christians by the Druse in the Shawf mountains. Buṭrus al-Bustāni's *al-Jinān* (1870-86) made its slogan *Ḥubb al-Waṭan* (love for the homeland), and continued to promote this concept in many of its articles; see also A. Hourani, *Arabic Thought in the Liberal Age:1798-1939* (Oxford, Oxford University Press, 1962), p. 101.
34. *The Times,* 11 April 1876, p. 5.
35. Antonius, op. cit., p. 84.
36. For the impact of the Western economic onslaught on Syria, see Dominique Chevallier, "Western Development and Eastern Crisis in the Mid-Nineteenth Century: Syria Confronted with the European Economy", in Polk and Chambers, op. cit., pp. 205-22.
37. Egypt was never officially declared a part of the British Empire or even a colony. Between 1882 and 1907 Britain made 120 declarations of her intention to withdraw from Egypt, according to Afaf Lutfi al-Sayyid, op. cit., p. xi, and 72, according to Mansfield op. cit., p. xi.
38. This, for example, was the main guarantee for the settlement of Egypt's heavy debts: exports grew from £E11.7 million in 1883 to £E28.1 million in 1910.
39. Robert Mabro, *The Egyptian Economy* (Oxford, Clarendon Press, 1974), pp. 11-12.
40. In 1913, Ṭal'at Ḥarb published his book *'Ilāj Miṣr al-Iqtiṣādi wa-Inshā' Bank lil-Miṣriyyīn,* which included most of the important issues discussed in this conference.
41. The report of this committee was considered for a long time to be the sacred constitution of Egyptian national policy in commerce and industry.
42. Albert Hourani, op. cit., p. 206.
43. Early in his life Kāmil met Nadīm several times before the latter was banished from the country by Cromer. Through these meetings Kāmil came to realize the importance of oratory in awakening the dormant patriotic feelings of his fellow Egyptians, especially in a country where illiteracy was extremely high; hence, sentiments were more important than reasoning.
44. A. Hourani, op. cit., p. 208.
45. In 1905, the victory of Japan over Russia in the 1904-5 war provided Kāmil with a strong vindication of his argument that "oriental" people could gain victory over a

dominating occidental power. This event inspired many Egyptian poets to sing the praises of that victory and incite their country to follow in Japan's footsteps.

46. In 1907 four parties were founded: *al-Ḥizb al-Waṭani* (the National Party), *Ḥizb al-'Ummah,* (the Nation's Party), *Ḥizb al-'Iṣlāḥ 'alā al-Mabādi' al-Dustūriyyah* (the Constitutional Reform Party), and *al-Ḥizb al-Waṭani al-Ḥurr* (the Liberal National Party).

47. These were *Ḥizb al-'A'yān* (the Notables' Party) and *Ḥizb al-Miṣriyyin al-Mustaqillīn* (the Party of Independent Egyptians).

48. Gabriel Charmes, *Voyage en Syrie,* pp. 171-2.

49 This is Denis de Rivoyre, *Les vrais Arabes et leur pays,* pp. 294-5.

50. Antonius, op. cit., pp. 89-90.

51. Ira M. Lapidus, *A History of Islamic Societies* (Cambridge, Cambridge University Press, 1988), p. 641.

52. When the distinguished Syrian writer, Zakariyyā Tāmir, the editor-in-chief of the Syrian monthly *al-Ma'rifah,* republished one of al-Kawākibi's articles in his magazine in February-March 1980, the issue was banned, the editor lost his job, and life was made extremely difficult for him until he left the country and settled permanently abroad.

53. For a discussion of these novels, see Muḥammad Yūsuf Najm, *al-Qiṣṣah fī al-Adab al-'Arabi al-Ḥadīth* (Beirut, al-Maktabah al-Ahliyyah, 1958), pp. 173-204.

54. For an account of the nationalistic activity of the period, see Zeine N. Zeine, *Arab-Turkish Relations and the Emergence of Arab Nationalism* (Beirut, 1958).

55. Antonius, op. cit., p. 113

56. Hitti, op. cit., p. 496.

57. Syria, Lebanon, Palestine and Iraq were made class A mandates administered under the League of Nations. The relevant article in the covenant of the League acknowledged such communities as having reached a stage of development such that their existence as "independent nations can be provisionally recognized, subject to the rendering of administrative advice and assistance by a mandatory power until such time as they are able to stand alone".

58. For an account of the events and implications of these three occasions, see 'Abd al-'Azīz Rifa'i, *Thawrat Miṣr Sanat 1919* (Cairo, Dār al-Kātib, 1966), pp. 89-203.

59. For details and names of its members see P.L. Cheikho, *al-Ādāb al-'Arabiyyah fī al-Qarn al-Tāsi' 'Ashar,* (Beirut, al-Maṭba'ah al- Yasū'iyyah, 1910), vol. 1, p. 71.

60. Hitti, op. cit., p. 487.

61. Antonius, op. cit., p. 111.

62. Jurji Zaydān, *Tārīkh Ādāb al-Lughah al-'Arabiyyah* (Cairo, Maṭba'at al-Hilāl, 1914), vol. 4, p. 105.

63. For the role of orientalists in modifying the views of the Arab intellectuals and introducing them to new ideas and new forms of scholarship, see ibid., pp. 157-83.

64. For a detailed account of these societies, see ibid., pp. 78-104.

65. Ibid., pp. 97-104.

66. A detailed account of these theatrical societies is given in Muḥammad Yūsuf Najm, *al-Masraḥiyya fī al-Adab al-'Arabi al-Ḥadīth* (Beirut, 1956), pp. 168-86.

67. See Ibrāhīm 'Abduh, *Taṭawwur al-Ṣiḥāfah al-Miṣriyyah: 1797-1951* (Cairo, Maktabat al-Ādāb, 1951), pp. 443-55.

68. The major newspaper which supported Ismā'īl and led a strong campaign against the Ottoman Turks in support of the Khedive and the Russians was the Egyptian newspaper, *al-Waṭan,* edited by Mīkhā'īl 'Abd al-Sayyid. Many Lebanese periodicals, particularly *al-Jinān* and *al-Akhbār,* received his strong financial backing, thus supporting his cause against the Ottoman.

69. For more details of Levantine journalism, see Kamāl al-Yāziji, *Ruwwād al-Nahḍah al-Ḥadīthah fī Lubnān* (Beirut, Maktabat Ra's Beirut, 1961), pp. 131-8.

70. See Yūsuf As'ad Dāghir, *Qāmūs al-Ṣiḥāfah al-Lubnāniyyah: 1858-1974* (Beirut, Lebanese University Press, 1978).

71. For more details, see Fīlīb Ṭarrāzi, *Tārīkh al-Ṣiḥāfah al-'Arabiyyah* (Beirut, al-Maṭba'ah al-'Adabiyyah, 1913).

72. See the list of some of these in 'Abd al-Ilāh Aḥmad, *Nash'at al-Qissah wa-Taṭawwuha fi-l-'Irāq* (Baghdad, Maṭba'at Shafīq, 1969), pp. 432-6.

73. S. Radwan, *The Development of the Egyptian Economy in Historical Perspective,* in press.
74. Between 1880 and 1900 the average price of a newspaper was 7-15 millims (1-2 pence), the average weekly magazine was sold at 2-3 piastres (2-4 pence) and its average annual subscription was 1 Egyptian pound. The monthly reviews and books of fiction were between 5 and 10 piastres (5-10 pence). In 1882 a subscription to *al-Muqtaṭaf* was 1 Egyptian pound and that of *al-Hilāl* in 1892 was 50 piastres (53 pence). The novels of Jurji Zaydān published before 1900 were sold for 6-10 piastres a copy (6-11 pence).
75. These statistics show that the paper with the highest circulation was *al-Ahrām,* 3000; followed by *al-Ustādh,* 2288; *al-Mu'ayyad,* 1600; *al-Muqaṭṭam* 1445; *al-Muqtaṭaf,* 1300; *al-Ādāb,* 1000; *al-Nīl,* 1000; *al-Waṭan,* 1000; *al-Tallighrāf,* 880; *al-Maḥrūsah,* 800; *al-Hilāl,* 740; *al-Zirā'ah,* 600; *al-Fallāḥ,* 545; *al-Gazzette,* 438; *al-Fa'r,* 432; and *al-Busfūr,* 424. See *"Iḥṣā' al-Jarā'id"*, in *al-Ustadh,* 3 January 1893.
76. Nadīm mentioned in the same reference that there were another twenty-two papers which did not appear in the statistics. But he declined to tell us if this was because of their diminutive circulation or a mere lack of information.
77. See *"Kuttāb al-Jarā'id wa-l-Majallāt", al-Hilāl,* October 1897, p. 131.
78. Q. D. Leavis, *Fiction and the Reading Public,* (London, Chatto & Windus, 1965), p. 125.
79. See *"Ḍarar al-Riwāyāt wa-l-'Ash'ār al-Ḥibbiyyah"*(The Harm Caused by Amorous Novels and Love Poems), *al-Muqtaṭaf,* August 1882.
80. See *"al-Riwāyāt"* (The Novels), *al-Muqtataf,* October 1890.
81. See *"Qirā'at al-Riwāyāt"* (Reading Novels), *al-Muqtaṭaf,* August 1907.
82. See *"Kuttāb al-'Arabiyyah wa-Qurrā'uhā"* (The Writers of Narrative and Their Readers), *al-Hilāl,* March 1897.
83. See *"Kuttāb al-'Arabiyyah wa-Qurrā'uhā"* (Arab Writers and Their Readers), *al-Hilāl,* February 1897.
84. The same type of argument was reproduced in Iraq fifteen years later, in the debate about the morality of narrative fiction started in the weekly *Ṣadā Bābil* (issue 59, 1910) and continued later in *Lughat al-'Arab* (issue 7, 1913). For a detailed discussion of this, see 'Abd al-Ilāh Aḥmad, op. cit., pp. 27-9.
85. Hitti, op. cit., p. 493.
86. Ibid.
87. S. Prawer, *Comparative Literary Studies* (London, Duckworth, 1973), p. 74.
88. Ibid., pp. 80-1.
89. For a detailed account of translated works and writers throughout the nineteenth century, see Jāk Tājir, *Ḥarakat al-Tarjamah fi Miṣr Khilāl al-Qarn al-Tāsi' 'Ashar* (Cairo, Dār al-Ma'ārif, 1945) and Anīs al-Maqdisi, *al-Ittijāhāt al-Adabiyyah fi al-'Ālam al-'Arabi al-Ḥadīth* (Beirut, Dār al-'Ilm li-l-Malāyīn, 1952).
90. For a study of al-Ṭahṭāwi' s translation, see Muḥammad Rushdi Ḥasan, *Athar al-Maqāmah fi Nash'at al-Qiṣṣah al-Miṣriyyah al-Ḥadīthah* (Cairo, al-Hay'ah al-Miṣriyyah al-'Āmmah li-l-Kitāb, 1974), pp. 78-83, 177-180.
91. In the same vein were the works of at least ten other translators, such as Najīb Gharghūr, Khālid Ḥimṣi, Yusūf Sarkīs, Iskandar 'Ammūn, Adīb Isḥāq, and Najīb Mīkhā'īl. For a fuller list, see Jāk Tājir, op. cit.
92. Goethe's quotation is from his eulogy to Wieland, and is quoted in S.S. Prawer, *Comparative Literary Studies* (London, Duckworth, 1973), p. 75.
93. Locke, *Essay Concerning Human Understanding* (1690), bk. III, Ch. 3, sec. vi, quoted in Ian Watt, *The Rise of the Novel,* p. 21.
94. The great success of the first translated novel of Alexandre Dumas *père, Le Comte de Monte-Cristo,* in 1871, attracted ten different translators to work on his novels, and this led to the publication of another fourteen of his novels in Arabic before 1910. Also the success of the translation of Jules Verne's *Cinq Semaines en Ballon* in 1875 led to the translation and publication of another three of his works before 1894.
95. After the success of al-Ṭahṭāwi's translation, *Télémaque* was retranslated three more times before 1912.
96. In Egypt, the proportion of those who had French as their first foreign language and those who chose English was 74 per cent to 26 per cent in 1889, 59 per cent to 41

per cent in 1897, 33 per cent to 67 per cent in 1898, and 22 per cent to 78 per cent in 1899. See Berque, op. cit., p. 206.

97. The most significant and frequently translated of them are François Fénelon, François Chateaubriand, Bernardin de Saint-Pierre, Alexandre Dumas *(père)* and *(fils)*, Victor Hugo, Jules Verne, François Coppée, Henri Bordeaux, Guy de Maupassant, Henri Lammens, Pierre Loti, Jules Mary, Pierre Decourcelle, Xavier de Montépin, Michel Zévaco and Maurice Leblanc. For a full list of the writers and the works translated, see Henry Peres, "Le Roman, le conte et la nouvelle dans la littérature arabe moderne", *Annales de l'Institut d'Études Orientales*, vol. 3, 1937, pp. 266-337.

98. The most significant of them were William Shakespeare, Daniel Defoe, and Walter Scott.

99. Hopwood, op. cit., p. 33. The book provides a detailed history of the motives behind Russian activities in the area and the means of their realization.

100. Ibid., p. 53.

101. These were the years of expanding Russian activities and developing interest in the outside world. In the same year, 1858, the Moscow Slavonic Benevolent Committee was founded to direct the rising Panslav movement. Porfiri Uspensky was a founding member and the first president of its Kiev sister committee. One of the main aims of the committee was to give aid to the Orthodox churches and schools under Ottoman rule.

102. Ibid., p. 108.

103. Ibid., p. 141.

104. One of the pupils of this school was the late Mīkhā'īl Nu'aymah, who left a vivid portrait of Kuzmā, who was known in the Seminary as *"al-Mu'allim Iskandar"*, for his full name was Iskandar Jibrā'īl Kuzmā, in his autobiography, *Sab'ūn* (Beirut, Dār Ṣādir, 1959), vol. I, p. 118.

105. Hopwood, op. cit., pp. 144 and 146.

106. There was a boys' and a girls' school in the village.

107. Hopwood, op. cit., p. 152. The quotation is from George Hannā, *Qabl al-Maghīb: Tajārib wa-Dhikrāyāt min Ḥayāti* (Beirut, Dār al-Thaqāfah, 1960), pp. 86-7.

108. See Nu'aymah, op. cit., p. 75, and Hopwood, op. cit., p. 152.

109. F.J. Cox, "Khedive Ismail and Panslavism", *Slavonic Review*, XXXII December 1953, pp. 151-67 and Derek Hopwood, op. cit., p. 80.

110. Hopwood, op. cit., p. 97.

111. Ibid., p. 159.

112. A. Krachkovski, *Nad arabskimi rukopisyami* (Moscow, 1946), pp. 49-50, quoted in Derek Hopwood, op. cit., pp. 152-3.

113. The list of the translators of Russian literature who wrote, with varying degrees of success, novels, short stories or even plays is very long. It suffices to mention a few here such as Nu'aymah, Ḥaddād, Khalīl Baydas, Najāti Ṣidqi, Kalthūm 'Awdah, Anṭūn Ballān in the Levant, and most of the writers of *al-Madrasah al-Ḥadīthah*, Ibrāhīm al-Māzini and Maḥmūd al-Badawi in Egypt.

114. The contribution of Ḥaddād and Nu'aymah is discussed in chapter 4 below.

115. The word *mahjar* means the land of expatriation, but as a literary term it is used to identify a literary movement which emerged among the Arab immigrants in the Americas in the early part of this century.

116. *al-Nafā'is* appeared in Jaffa as a weekly on 1 November 1908, changed its name in November of the following year to *al-Nafā'is al-'Aṣriyyah* and became fortnightly. In January 1911 it moved to Jerusalem and continued there until the outbreak of World War I. After the war it resumed publication in 1919 but was closed the following year.

117. *al-Nafā'is*, vol. I, issue 1, 1908, p. 1.

118. When its editor, Khalīl Baydas, wanted to publish his first collection of short stories, *Masāriḥ al-'Adhhān*, he found an Egyptian publisher among the admirers of his magazine to do the job, and the collection appeared in Cairo in 1924.

119. Marie Corelli's (1855-1924) novel *Romance of Two Worlds* (1886) was translated into Russian with a modified title, and then translated by Baydas in 1908 from Russian into Arabic, with the title changed to *Shaqā' al-Mulūk* (The Misery of Kings).

120. Bandali Ṣalībā al-Jawzi, Jibrān Maṭar and Ilyās Naṣrallah translated from German; Ibrāhīm Ḥannā, Rūz Ḥassūn, Tawfīq Zaibaq, Aḥmad Shākir al-Karmi, Wadī' al-Bustāni and Būlus Ṣidqi from English; Muḥammad Rawḥi al-Khālidi, 'Ādil Zu'aitar, Jamīl al-Buḥairi, 'Ādil Jabr and Isḥāq al-Ḥusaini from French; and Jūrji al-Khūri from Greek.

121. Nu'aymah, *Sab'ūn*, I, p. 156, and Derek Hopwood, op. cit., p. 158.

122. 'Abd al-Raḥman al-Rāfi'i in *Tārikh al-Ḥarakah al-Qawmiyyah*, vol I, and Liwīs 'Awaḍ, op. cit., vol. II.

123. Muḥammad Ṣabry, *Genèse de l'esprit national* (Paris, 1924), Ṣubḥi Waḥīdah, *fi Uṣūl al-Mas'alah al-Miṣriyyah* (Cairo, Maktabat al-Anglū, 1958), Jamāl Ḥimdān, *Shakhṣiyyat Miṣr* (Cairo, 'Ālam al-Kutub, 1968-80), Hourani, op. cit., and 'Abd al-Malik, op. cit.

124. This was the Egyptian newspaper which appeared in 1877, edited by Mīkhā'il 'Abd al-Sayyid.

125. Coleridge, *Biographia Literaria*, ed. Shawcross (London, 1907), I, p. 87.

126. Ian Watt, op. cit., p. 26. His semantic reference is also valid in Arabic where the words *ḥāḍir, wāqi', ān* or *muḍāri'* (present) and *daqīqah* or *burhah* (minute) have spatial as well as temporal meaning.

127. Liwīs 'Awaḍ, *Dirāsāt fi Adabinā al-Ḥadīth* (Cairo, Dār al-Ma'rifah, 1961), pp. 61-73.

128. See particularly 'Abd al-Malik, op. cit., pp. 215-48, and Ḥusain Fawzi al-Najjār, *Rafā'ah al-Ṭahṭāwi* (Cairo, al-Dār al-Qawmiyyah, 1966).

129. Fritz Steppat, "National Education Projects in Egypt before the British Occupation", in Polk and Chambers, op. cit., pp. 284-5.

130. Hitti, op. cit., p. 491.

131. Reinhard Schulze, "Mass Culture and Islamic Cultural Production in the 19th Century Middle East", in George Stauth, Sami Zubaida (eds), *Mass Culture, Popular Culture and Social Life in the Middle East* (Frankfurt am Main, Campus Verlag, 1987), p. 198.

132. This is probably true up to the most recent ideologues of Muslim fundamentalism in the Arab world.

133. For a detailed study of the impact of the new city on culture and literature, see R.C. Ostle, "The City in Modern Arabic Literature", *Bulletin of the School of Oriental and African Studies*, vol. XLIX, part 1, 1986, pp.193-202.

134. Ian Watt, op. cit., p. 21.

135. For a detailed discussion of their role and impact on the Egyptian cultural and nationalist movement, see 'Abd al-Malik, op. cit., pp. 203-13, and Muḥammad Ṭal'at 'Īsā, *Atbā' Sān Simon: Falsafatuhum al-Ijtimā'iyyah wa-Taṭbīquha fi Miṣr* (Cairo, al-Dār al-Qawmiyyah, 1957).

136. The discussion of some of the purely literary ideas will be taken up in the following chapters.

137. Such as that of 'Ukāẓ and Mirbid, and later in the actual market-place where the bards used to recite poems or narrate folk epics.

138. Hitti, op. cit., p. 489.

Chapter 3

1. For a detailed discussion of the critical discourse of the period, see: 'Abd al-'Azīz al-Disūqi, *Tārīkh al-Ḥarakah al-Naqdiyyah* (Cairo, al-Hay'ah al-Miṣriyyah al-'Āmmah li-l-Kitāb, 1977); Isḥāq Mūsā al-Ḥusaini, *al-Naqd al-Adabi al-Mu'āṣir fi al-Rub' al-Awwal min al-Qarn al-'Ishrīn* (Cairo, Dār al-Ma'rifah, 1967); and Ḥilmi Marzūq, *Taṭawwur al-Naqd wa-l-Tafkīr al-Adabi al-Ḥadīth fi al-Rub' al-Awwal min al-Qarn al-'Ishrīn*, (Cairo, Dār al-Ma'ārif, 1966).

2. The romance of 'Antar was published in Cairo in 1893, and other romances followed, particularly those of Abū-Zaid and Saif Ibn Dhi-Yazan. Other forms of traditional narrative texts from Kalīlah wa-Dimnah to the Fables of Luqmān and from the stories of the Qur'ān to those of al-Tunūkhi's *al-Faraj Ba'd al-Shiddah* were also printed.

3. Edward William Lane, *Manners and Customs of the Modern Egyptians* (London, Everyman's Library, n.d.), ch. VIII, particularly pp. 395-8.
4. See M.M. Badawi, *Early Arabic Drama* (Cambridge, Cambridge University Press, 1988), p. 8.
5. The English translation of the titles of books or stories is normally given except when the title is a proper name of a person, as is the case here.
6. Ṭaha Ḥusain, *al-Ayyām*, vol. 1, (Cairo, Dar al-Ma'ārif, 1929).
7. See his novel, *Zuqāq al-Madaq*, (Cairo, Maktabat Miṣr, 1946) ch. 1; English translation by Trevor Le Gassick entitled *Midaq Alley* (London, Heinemann, 1966).
8. Ibid., p. 5.
9. For a full list of these books see Muḥammad Yūsuf Najm, *al-Qiṣṣah fi al-Adab al-'Arabi al-Ḥadīth* (Beirut, al-Maktabah al-Ahliyyah, 1966), pp. 6-21.
10. Yūsuf As'ad Dāghir, *al-Adīb*, Beirut, Vol.VII, No. 6.
11. Such as *al-Maqtaṭaf*, as mentioned before.
12. This is true for many literatures and has been observed in a number of European and other literatures.
13. See, for example, his translation of Bernardin de Saint-Pierre's *Paul et Virginie* as *al-Amāni wa-l-Minnah fi Ḥadīth Qabūl wa-Ward Jannah*, in which he tried to find the nearest Arabic names to those of the French characters — Paul became Qabāl and Virginie became Ward Jannah — and changed the location of the story accordingly.
14. As in *al-Riwāyāt al-Mufīdah fi 'Ilm al-Trājīdah* (Tragedies with a Message) and *al-Arba' Riwāyāt min Nukhab al-Tiyātrāt* (Four Best Plays).
15. Najm, *al-Qiṣṣah*, pp. 21-6 and *al-Masraḥiyyah*, pp. 195-290.
16. Najm, *al-Qiṣṣah*, pp. 22-4.
17. Peter Gran, *Islamic Roots of Capitalism: Egypt 1760-1840* (Austin, University of Texas, 1979), p. 58.
18. *Maqāmāt al-Ḥarīri* was printed again in 1873.
19. This is the first complete edition of *Alf Laylah wa-Laylah*, but there were many other editions of single stories from the collection and of anthologies of a number of stories. Sarkīs lists seventeen different books of this kind.
20. The full text of al-'Aṭṭār's *maqāmāt* is still a manuscript in the Egyptian National Library, no. 7574. But one of his *maqāmāt, Maqāmat al-Adīb al-Ra'īs al-Shaykh Ḥasan al-'Aṭṭār fi al-Faransīs*, was printed with Maqāmāt al-Suyūṭi in 1858.
21. Gran, op. cit., p. 206.
22. For details, see Clément Huart, *A History of Arabic Literature* (Beirut, Khayats, 1966), p. 425.
23. For an account of these works, see 'Umar al-Ṭālib, *al-Fann al-Qaṣaṣi fi al-Adab al-'Arabi al-Ḥadīth: al-Riwāyah al-'Arabiyyah fi al-'Irāq* (Baghdad, Maktabat al-Andalus, 1971), vol. 1, p. 26.
24. His *Maqāmāt al-Alūsi* was printed for the first time in Karbalā' in 1856.
25. For a more detailed account of their *maqāmāt*, see P.L. Cheikho, *al-Ādāb al-'Arabiyyah fi al-Qarn al-Tāsi' 'Ashar* (Beirut, al-Maṭba'ah al-Yasū'iyyah, 1910), and Yusūf Ilyās Sarkīs, *Mu'jam al-Maṭbū'āt al-'Arabiyyah wa-l-Mu'arrabah* (Cairo, Maṭba'at Sarkīs, 1928).
26. Sarkīs, op. cit.
27. *Al-Ahrām*, 11 May 1881.
28. A novel under the Arabic title *al-Intiqām* (Revenge).
29. A famous example is the conflict between Ya'qūb Ṣannū' and the Khedive Ismā'īl over the play *al-Ḍarratain* (The Two Wives), which led to the closure of his theatre in 1872.
30. Such as Sa'īd al-Bustāni and Alīs Buṭrus al-Bustāni.
31. *Al-Jinān*, I, 1 (1870), pp.19-21.
32. Ibid., pp. 23-48.
33. Such as *Zunūbiā* (*al-Jinān*, II, 1871), *Budūr* (*al-Jinān*, II, 1871) and *al-Hiyām fi Futūḥ al-Shām* (Love and the Conquest of Syria) (*al-Jinān*, IV, 1873).
34. *Al-Jinān*, II (1871), p. 201.
35. Ibid., IV (1873), p. 859.
36. Ibid., II (1871), p. 447.

37. Ibid., IV (1873).
38. Ibid., VI (1875).
39. Ibid., VIII (1877).
40. Ibid., IX and X (1878-9).
41. Ibid., XIII and XIV (1882-4).
42. Ibid., III (1872), p. 732. Quoted in Najm, *al-Qiṣṣah*, p. 42.
43. Shukri Muḥammad 'Ayyād, *al-Qiṣṣah al-Qaṣīrah fī Miṣr: Dirāsah fī Ta'ṣīl finn Adabi* (Cairo, Dār al-Ma'rifah, 1968), pp. 10-11.
44. *'Alam al-Dīn*, 1, pp. 7-8.
45. Ibid.
46. Nadīm's quotation is from 'Ali al-Ḥadīdi, *'Abdullah al-Nadīm: Khaṭīb al-Waṭaniyyah* (Cairo, Maktabat Miṣr, 1964), p. 12.
47. This appeared on 6 June 1881 and continued only until 23 October 1881, when 'Urābi asked him to change its name to *"Lisān al-Ummah"* and even obtained permission for the new magazine, as indicated in the last issue of *al-Tankīt*, XVIII, 23 October 1881. Any further reference to this magazine in the main text is appreviated to *Tankīt*.
48. After the closure of his first magazine, and on the recommendation of 'Urābi, he launched *al-Ṭā'if* on 20 November 1881, and it continued until the fall of the 'Urābi revolution on 6 September 1882.
49. After ten years of disguise and exile, Nadīm was pardoned, and he started *al-Ustādh* on 23 August 1892, which continued until his second exile on 13 June 1893.
50. Levin L. Schücking, *The Sociology of Literary Taste* (London, Routledge and Kegan Paul, 1966), p. 35.
51. *Al-Tankīt wa-l-Tabkīt*, I, 6 June 1881.
52. Q. D. Leavis, *Fiction and the Reading Public* (London, Chatto & Windus, 1965), p. 104.
53. Ian Watt, *The Rise of the Novel*, p. 49.
54. 'Abbās Khaḍr, *al-Qiṣṣah al-Qaṣīrah fī Miṣr: Mundh Nash'atihā Ḥattā Sanat 1930* (Cairo, al-Dār al-Qawmiyyah, 1966), p. 35.
55. *Al-Tankīt wa-l-Tabkīt*, I, 6 June 1881.
56. Ibid., II, 13 June; V, 10 July; and XIII, 11 September 1881.
57. The letter was published in *al-Ustādh*, 25 October 1892.
58. Ibid.
59. In the tenth issue of *al-Ustādh*, 25 October 1892, Nadīm published a narrative episode, by Ṣalīb Iṣṭafānūs, entitled *"Yūsuf al-Qammāsh wa-Salāmah al-Ṣayyād wa-Zawjatuh Khaḍrah"*, which deals with Nadīm's favourite theme of reform, and emulates his style in writing and even in titling the piece. In a number of other issues, Nadīm mentions that he received other similar works.
60. See *al-Tankīt wa-l-Tabkīt*, VI, 17 July 1881.
61. Watt, op. cit., p. 10.
62. In his essay "the Storyteller" in Walter Benjamin, *Illuminations*, trans. Harry Zohn (London, 1973).
63. Ali al-Ḥadīdi, op. cit., p. 115.
64. The magazine became very much involved in the 'Urābi revolution, in which Nadīm played an important role.
65. *Al-Tankīt wa-l-Tabkīt*, I, 6 June 1881, pp. 4-7.
66. Afaf Lutfi al-Sayyid, *Egypt and Cromer: A Study in Anglo-Egyptian Relations*, (London, John Murray, 1968), p. 1.
67. *Al-Tankīt wa-l-Tabkīt*, I, 6 June 1881, pp. 7-8.
68. C. Wright Mills, *Power, Politics, and People: The Collected Essays*, ed. Irving Louis Horowitz (Oxford, Oxford University Press, 1963), p. 300.
69. *Al-Tankīt wa-l-Tabkīt*, I, 6 June 1881, pp. 8-11.
70. Such as *"Majlis Uns"* (A Great Party), Ibid., III, 26 June1881; *"'Umdah Sakrān"* (A Drunken Mayor), V, 10 July 1881; *"al-Mazzah al-Muṭaharrah"* (Cleaned Snacks), VIII, 31 July 1881; *"Dhihāb al-'Aql"* (Losing Sense), IX , 7 August 1881; and *"Majlis Adabi"* (Learned Gathering), X, 15 August 1881.
71. *Al-Tankīt wa-l-Tabkīt*, I, 6 June 1881, pp. 11-13.

72. See in particular *"al-Nabīh wa-l-Fallāḥ"* (The Crafty Swindler and the Peasant), and *"al-Tājir al-Ḥimār wa-l-Fallāḥ al-Makkār"* (The Stupid Usurer and the Cunning Peasant), Ibid., VI, 17 July 1881, and *"Avocāto Jāhil wa-Fallāḥ Mughaffal"* (Ignorant Lawyer and Foolish Peasant), VIII, 31 July 1881. There are also a number of articles on this subject in the issues of X, 15 August, and XI, 22 August 1881.

73. Ibid., I, 6 June 1881, pp. 13-15.

74. In addition to those mentioned before, there are *"al-Mutayyam al-Mathūf"* (Highly Drugged), Ibid., X, 15 August 1881; *"Rawā 'an Ummat al-Takhrīf"* (Stories on a Mindless Nation), III, 26 June 1881.

75. Ibid., VIII, 31 July 1881, pp. 130-1.

76. Such as *"Salṭanat al-Takhrīf"* (The Sultanate of Mindlessness), and *"Taghfīlah wa-Jahālah"* (Negligence and Ignorance), Ibid., X, 15 August 1881; *"Amātak man Aslamak"* (Killing You by Giving You Up), XI, 21 August 1881 and *"Ṣiyām al-Shaikh"* (The Fasting of the Sheikh), XIV, 18 September 1881.

77. Such as *"Naqd al-Musha'widhīn"* (Criticizing the Quacks) by Muḥammad al-Ḥakīm, Ibid., VII, 24 July 1881; and *"al-Wilāyah al-Khurāfiyyah"* (Illusory Sainthood) by what Nadīm called *aḥad nubahā' Būr-Sa'īd* (one of the bright intellectuals of Port Said), XIII, 11 September 1881.

78. Ibid., IV, 3 July 1881, pp. 56-58.

79. Ibid., VII, 24 July 1881, pp. 111-112.

80. Ibid., III, 26 June, p. 35, and VI, 17 July 1881, p. 90.

81. See *"Iẓhār al-Mukhaba'"*, Ibid., IV, 3 July 1881, p. 63.

82. See *"al-'Āqil man Itta'aẓ bi-Ghayrih"* (The WiseOne Is He Who Learns from Others), Ibid., VIII, 31 July 1881, pp. 126-7.

83. 'Ali al-Ḥadīdi, op. cit., p. 115.

84. The nature of Nadīm's second magazine, *al-Ṭā'if,* which was the mouthpiece of the 'Urābi revolution, did not allow the publishing of fiction.

85. *Al-Ustādh,* 27 September and 8 November 1892.

86. Ibid., 4 and 25 October 1892.

87. Ibid., 18 October 1892.

88. Ibid., 6 and 20 September 1892, 8, 15, 29 November 1892, and 6, 13, 27 December 1892. This type of narrative has some precedent in *Tankīt* in the form of dialogues between Nadīm and his students, *al-Tankīt wa-l-Tabkīt,* IV, 3 July 1881, pp. 53-6 and XVII, 19 October 1881, pp. 267-72.

89. *Al-Ustādh,* 1, 15, and 29 November 1892, 6 and 13 December 1892.

90. Such as the dialogues between Ḥafṣah and her daughter Salmā; Zakiyyah and Nafīsah; Bahānah and Sitt al-Dār; and Sharīfah and Bahānah in this series.

91. *Al-Ustādh,* 13 September 1892.

92. Ibid., 20 September 1892, and 11 and 18 October 1892.

93. Ibid., 22 November 1892.

94. Q.D. Leavis, op. cit., p. 94.

95. As is the case in *"al-Murāfa'ah al-Waṭaniyyah"* (The Patriotic Defence), and *"Iyyāk A'ni yā Nafs fa-Isma'i wa-'i"* (I Am Only Talking to Myself, So Listen Carefully!), in *al-Tankīt wa-l-Tabkīt,* VII, 24 July 1881.

96. As is the case in *"'Arabi Tafarnaj"* and *"Majlis Ṭibbi li-Muṣāb bi-l-Afranji"*.

97. See, for example, *"Sahrat al-Anṭā'"* and *"al-Murāfa'ah al-Waṭaniyyah"*.

98. See, e.g., *"Majlis Ṭibbi li-Muṣāb bi-l-Afranji"* and *"al-Dhi'āb Ḥawl al-Asad"*.

99. Such as *"Majlis Ṭibbi li-Muṣāb bi-l-Afranji"*, *"al-Murāfa'ah al-Waṭaniyyah"*, and *"al-Dhi'āb Ḥawl al-Asad"*.

100. See, for example, *"Ḥanīfah wa-Laṭīfah"*, *"Laṭīfah wa-Dimyānah"* and the series of *"Madrasat al-Banāt"*.

101. Masīḥah Ilyās, one of the outstanding intellectuals of Asyut, as *al-Ustādh* described him, published an interesting comment on this phenomenon: "*al-Ustādh* was right in putting its advice into the mouths of women because they are the partners of men in pleasure and sadness. Their essential role in society and first-hand experience give them priority in advising men. If women's advice does not affect men and guide them to the right path, there is no hope of their recovery", *al-Ustādh,* 8 November 1892.

102. *Al-Ustādh* ceased publication on 13 June 1893 as a result of pressure from the occupying forces. Nadīm was exiled in the same month, and remained outside the country until he died in Constantinople on 11 October 1896.

103. Najm wrote his MA thesis on "*Aḥmad Fāris al-Shidyāq Rā'id al-Mujaddidīn fi al-Adab al-'Arabi al-Ḥadīth*" at the American University in Beirut, 1948. He also studied his narrative in *al-Qiṣṣah*, pp. 225-9.

104. Muḥammad Yūsuf Najm, *al-Qiṣṣah*, p. 226.

105. Aḥmad Fāris al-Shidyāq, *al-Sāq 'alā al-Sāq*, I, ch. 2.

106. Ibid., ch. 4.

107. Ibid., ch. 6.

108. Ibid., ch. 7.

109. Ibid., ch. 10.

110. Ibid., ch. 15.

111. *'Alam al-Dīn*, I, pp. 6-8.

112. 'Ā'ishah Taymūr, *Natā'ij al-Aḥwāl fi al-Aqwāl wa-l-Af'āl* (Cairo, al-Maṭba'ah al-Bahiyyah, 1305AH/1888), p. 4.

113. For a detailed comparison between Taymūr's work and *Télémaque* see Muḥammad Rushdi Ḥasan, *Athar al-Maqāmah fi Nash'at al-Qiṣṣah al-Miṣriyyah al-Ḥadīthah* (Cairo, al-Hay'ah al-Miṣriyyah al-'Āmmah li-l-Kitāb, 1974), pp.138-9.

114. *Al-Masāmīr* was written in three volumes, but only one survived.

115. Abū-l-Hudā al-Ṣayyādi, a religious leader from Aleppo, who was one of the most powerful advisers of Sultan Abdül-Hamid.

116. The work was serialized in *Miṣbāḥ al-Sharq* between 17 November 1898 and 15 June 1900 and appeared in book form in 1907; the edition used here is that of Maṭba'at al-Sa'ādah (1923).

117. Although *al-Masāmīr* was written in Turkey, the manuscript was smuggled into Egypt and printed in Alexandria in 1894. It contains significant innovations, including the appearance of Satan as a major character who is inferior in cunning and vice to the hero.

118. See 'Abd al-Muḥsin Ṭaha Badr, *Taṭawwur al-Riwāyah al-'Arabiyyah al-Ḥadīthah* (Cairo, Dār al-Ma'ārif, 1963), pp. 67-77; Yahya Ḥaqqi, *Fajr al-Qiṣṣah al-Miṣriyyah* (Cairo, Dār al-Qalam, 1960), pp. 14-27; and 'Ali al-Rā'i, *Dirāsāt fi al-Riwāyah al-Miṣriyyah* (Cairo, al-Dar al-Miṣriyyah li-l-Ta'līf, 1965), pp. 7-22.

119. *Ḥadīth 'Īsā Ibn Hishām*, pp. 72-3 and 475 ff.

120. Ibid., pp. 21-2, 96-8, 105-7.

121. Ibid., pp. 272 ff.

122. For a detailed study of this work, see Roger Allen, *Muḥammad Ibrāhīm al-Muwayliḥi: A Study of Ḥadīth 'Īsā Ibn Hishām*, on microfiche (Albany, State University of New York, 1974), pp. 114-64.

123. The work started to appear in *Miṣbāḥ al-Sharq* on 22 June 1899.

124. When he published his three works, *'Adhrā' al-Hind* (The Virgin of India, 1896) which is also entitled *Tammadun al-Farā'inah* (The Civilization of the Pharaohs, 1896); *Lādyās* or *Ākhir al-Farā'inah*, (The Last of the Pharaohs, 1898); and *Waraqat al-Ās* (The Ace, 1899).

125. *Fi Wādi al-Humūm*, p. 4.

126. Ibid., p. 6.

127. Ibid., pp. 8-14.

128. Ibid., p. 22.

129. In the magazine *al-Bayān*, I, 1897, p. 299. This was significantly republished in 1912 in *al-Mukhtārāt* by al-Manfalūṭi, who was clearly influenced by some of its ideas in his own work discussed below.

130. Published by Dār al-Hilāl in 1904.

131. Al-Khālidi was the Turkish counsellor in Bordeaux for a number of years, during which he familiarized himself with French literature and witnessed the elaborate celebration of Victor Hugo's (1802-1885) centenary in 1902.

132. For a detailed discussion of this book and its impact on the literary movement see, Isḥāq Mūsā al-Ḥusaini, op. cit., pp. 33-51.

133. See Shukri Muḥammad 'Ayyād, op cit., p. 91 Some of the works he mentioned are discussed later in this chapter.

134. 'Ayyād, op. cit., p. 92.
135. Muḥammad Rushdi Ḥasan, op. cit., p. 160.
136. Such as *"Narjis al-'Amya'"* (Narjis the Blind), *"Ṣadīqi 'Ali"* (My Friend Ali), *"al-Akhwāt al Thalāth"* (The Three Sisters), and *"al-Fākihah al-Muḥarramah"* (Forbidden Fruit).
137. 'Ayyād, op. cit., pp. 95, 97 and 98.
138. *Layāli al-Rūḥ al-Ḥā'ir,* pp. 42-50.
139. Ibid., pp. 51-61.
140. Philip Hitti, *The Middle East in History,* pp. 488-9.
141. These were collected later in his famous book, *al-Naẓarāt.*
142. *Al-Ḍiyā',* I (1898), p. 634.
143. She published *"al-Fawz ba'd al-Mawt"* (Victory After Death), *al-Ḍiyā',* II (1899), p. 508, and *"Jazā' al-Khiyānah"* (The Outcome of Treason), *al-Ḍiyā',* V (1902), p. 282.
144. Na'īm al-Yāfi, *al-Taṭawwur al-Fanni li-Shakl al-Qiṣṣah al-Qaṣīrah fi-l-Adab al-Shāmi al-Ḥadīth* (Damascus, Manshūrāt Ittiḥād al-Kuttāb al-'Arab, 1982), p. 58.
145. See the epilogue of *'Arā'is al-Murūj* by Amīn al-Gharīb (Beirut, Dār al-Andalus, n. d.), p. 69
146. See the introduction of Amīn al-Gharīb to *al-Arwāḥ al-Mutamarridah,* (Beirut, Dār al-Andalus, n.d.), pp. 13-14.
147. Amīn al-Gharīb, *al-Arwāḥ al-Mutamarridah,* p. 16.
148. Jibrān Khalīl Jibrān, *'Arā'is al-Murūj,* pp. 7-25.
149. Jibrān, *al-Arwāḥ al-Mutamarridah,* pp. 17-38.
150. Ibid., pp. 54-67.
151. Jibrān, *'Arā'is al-Murūj,* pp. 26-44. Bān is a beautiful little village in the north of Lebanon.
152. Ibid., pp. 45-76.
153. Jibrān, *al-Arwāḥ al-Mutamarridah,* pp. 68-130.
154. The writers of this group are numerous. Some did not publish their names, others used only their initials (M. Sh.) or a pseudonym ('Irāqi Amīn), and others used their full names such as Muḥammad Fā'iq al-Kīlāni and 'Aṭā' Amīn. The last named continued to experiment with other forms and is considered one of the pioneers of the Iraqi short story and the author of the works signed under the pseudonym of 'Irāqi Amīn.
155. For a detailed account of their work and a sample of their texts, see 'Abd al-Ilāh Aḥmad, *Nash'at al-Qissah wa-Taṭawwuha fi-l-'Irāq* (Baghdad, Maṭba'at Shafīq, 1969), pp. 32-55 and 327-59.
156. Such as *Lughat al-'Arab* (Baghdad, IV, October 1913; V, November 1913, and VIII, February 1914); *Dār al-Salām* (Baghdad, II, August and September 1919); *al-Lisān* (Baghdad, I, May 1919); and *al-'Iraq* (Baghdad, I, May 1921), pp. 283-90.
157. 'Abd al-Ilāh Aḥmad, op. cit., p. 39.
158. See Ibid., and Yūsuf 'Izz al-Dīn, *al-Qiṣṣah wa-Taṭawwuruhā fi al-'Irāq* (Cairo, Ma'had al-Buḥūth wa-l-Dirāsāt al-'Arabiyyah, 1974), p. 42.
159. *Tanwīr al-Afkār,* Baghdad, I, 1-6, 1328AH (1909), pp. 68-120. The full text was published as an appendix to 'Abd al-Ilāh Aḥmad, op. cit., pp. 327-33.
160. Muḥammad Fā'iq al-Kilāni, *"Ru'yah Adabiyyah"* (A Literary Dream), *Lughat al-'Arab,* IV, 1913, and in 'Abd al-Ilāh Aḥmad, op. cit., pp. 334-5.
161. *Dār al-Salām,* II, September 1919, p. 388, and 'Abd al-Ilāh Aḥmad, op. cit., p. 345.
162. Abd al-Ilāh Aḥmad, op. cit., has published an anthology of the pioneering narrative texts in Iraq which includes all the *ru'yā* texts and a couple of stories by Amīn, as well as a wide range of early narrative texts from Iraq which appeared only in periodicals and had not been collected in book form before.
163. *Al-'Irāq,* I, 1921, pp. 283-90, and Abd al-Ilāh Aḥmad, op. cit., pp. 351-9.
164. *Dār al-Salām,* III, 1, 1920 and Abd al-Ilāh Aḥmad, op. cit., pp. 360-4.
165. Ibid., III, 8-10, 1920, and Abd al-Ilāh Aḥmad, op. cit., pp. 365-72.
166. This is *'Ajā'ib al-Zamān fi Ṣarḥ 'Arūs al-Buldān* by Ākūb Kibir'īl; see Abd al-Ilāh Aḥmad, op. cit., p. 55.

167. The didacticism is even more crudely evident in Ḥammād's longer work, *Ibnati Saniyyah* (My Daughter Saniyyah, 1910).
168. In fact most of the works collected in *al-Naẓarāt* (Contemplations) and *al-'Abarāt* (Tears) had been published in periodicals and newspapers, *al-Mu'ayyad* in particular, several years before their appearance in book form.
169. 'Ayyād, op. cit., pp. 101-38.
170. *Al-Naẓarāt,* vol. I, p. 65.
171. Ibid., p. 64.
172. Sayyid Ḥāmid al-Nassāj, *Taṭawwur Fann al-Qiṣṣah al-Qaṣīrah fi Miṣr* (Cairo, Dār al-Kātib al-'Arabi, 1968), p. 68.
173. Ṣāliḥ Ḥamdi Ḥammād, *Aḥsan al-Qaṣaṣ,* p. 135.
174. Ḥammād was the holder of the title Bey which indicates a high social status.
175. Ḥammād, op. cit., p. 63.
176. Al-Nassāj, op. cit., p. 69.
177. Ḥammād, op. cit., pp. 63-86.
178. Ibid., p. 63.
179. Ibid., pp. 97-106.
180. Ibid., p. 116.
181. See al-Nassāj, op. cit., pp. 66-7.
182. Ṭaha Ḥusain was in fact the first to cast doubt on al-Manfalūṭi's style in a series of articles entitled *"Naẓarāt fi al-Naẓarāt"* (Ruminations on *Contemplations),* in *al-Sha'b,* 19-22 April 1910. Then came the severe attack of al-'Aqqād and al-Māzini in *al-Diwān* (II, 1921, p. 22 ff), and this was followed by that of Maḥmūd Taymūr who attacked his works in *al-Shaikh Sayyid al-'Abīṭ,* pp. 44-45, and praised his style in *Fir'awn al-Ṣaghīr,* p. 12. Aḥmad Luṭfi al-Sayyid also thought highly of his stylistic merits (see *al-Jarīdah,* 3 April 1910).
183. In his introduction to the first edition of *al-Naẓarāt* (1910), Aḥmad Ḥāfiẓ 'Awaḍ discusses al-Manfalūṭi's poetry and publishes ten of his poems, see recent editions of *al-Naẓarāt,* pp. 22-34.
184. Yaḥyā Ḥaqqi, *Khallīhā 'alā al-Lah* (Cairo, Dār al-Taḥrīr, 1956), p. 127.
185. Nāji Najīb, *Kitāb al-Aḥzān: Fuṣūl fi al-Tārīkh al-Nafsi wa-l-Ijtimā'i li-l-Fi'āt al-Mutawasiṭah al-'Arabiyyah* (Beirut, Dār al-Tanwīr, 1983).
186. 'Abbās Maḥmūd al-'Aqqād, *Murāja'āt fi al-Ādāb wa-l-Funūn* (Cairo, al-Maṭba'ah al-Salafiyyah, 1925), p. 155.
187. There is ample evidence to suggest that the literary movement was aware of the emergence and needs of this new public. See Aḥmad Ḥasan al-Zayyāt, "Ḥayāt Ḥāfiẓ" in *fi Dhikrā Ḥāfiẓ* (Cairo, 1957), pp. 104-6; Yaḥyā Ḥaqqi, *Khuṭuwāt fi al-Naqd* (Cairo, Dār al-'Urūbah, 1960), pp. 190-1; and *"Ashjān 'Ūdw Muntasib"*, his introduction to the new edition of *Qindīl Umm Hāshim* (Cairo, al-Hay'h al-Miṣriyyah al-'Āmmah lil-Kitāb, 1975), pp. 62-70.
188. *Al-Sufūr* was one of the most important avant-garde literary magazines of that period which encouraged the new forms of writing. It was edited by 'Abd al-Ḥamīd Ḥamdi, and its first issue came out on Friday, 21 May 1915.
189. *Al-Sufūr*, 21 May 1915.
190. A glance through the issues of *al-Sufūr* illustrates that this awareness was a common phenomenon among the younger generation of writers.
191. Especially in *al-'Abarāt,* tenth edition (Cairo, al-Maktabah al-Tujāriyyah, 1946) see, for example, *"al-Yatīm"* (The Orphan), pp. 3-21; *"al-Ḥijāb"* (The Veil), pp. 49-70; *"al-Hāwiyah"* (The Abyss), pp. 93-110; and *"al-'Iqāb"* (Retribution), pp. 133-58.
192. *Al-Masākīn,* ninth edition (Beirut, Dār al-Kitāb al-'Arabi, 1973), pp. 88-100.
193. He also wrote and published many poems; in *al-Masākīn* itself there is one entitled *"'alā al-Kawkab al-Ḥāwi"* (On the Planet), pp. 227-31.
194. *Al-Masākīn,* pp. 145-97.
195. For a detailed discussion of the intentional fallacy, see W.K. Wimsat, *The Verbal Icon: Studies in the Meaning of Poetry* (London, Methuen, 1970), pp. 3-18.
196. For a detailed account of this movement see 'Ali 'Abd al-Rāziq, *min Āthār Muṣṭafā 'Abd al-Rāziq* (Cairo, Dār al-Ma'ārif, 1957), pp. 41-8.

197. This is *"Mudhakkirāt al-Shaik al-Fazzāri"* whose first section appeared in *al-Jarīdah,* on 2 May 1914 and continued in the following issues of 7, 13, 20 and 27 May, 3, 13, 17 and 24 June, 2, 7, 15, and 22 July, 1, 9 and 27 August 1914. The text is an amalgam of narrative sketches, commentary and autobiographical material which is marked by its lucid style and reformative outlook.

198. He published in the first issue his essay *"al-Intiḥār"* (Suicide), *al-Sufūr,* 21 May 1915, and continued to contribute regularly to it afterwords. In the fourth issue (11 June 1915) he published an article entitled *"Naqd al-Sufūr"* (The Response to *al-Sufūr*) in which he discusses the various responses to the magazine and answers the criticism directed against it. This artlcle reveals in its tone, style and content that he was one of the inner group editing the magazine, and was speaking on behalf of its editorial board. Two years later he published an article, *"Nāshi'at al- Kuttāb"* (New Writers), *al-Sufūr,* 28 May 1917, in which he comments on the articles sent to *al-Sufūr* in manner that confirms that he is one of the editorial board, if not the real editor.

199. *Al-Sufūr,* 16 July 1917.

200. See Walter Benjamin, op. cit., p. 89.

201. *Al-Sufūr,* 4 June 1915, and *min Āthār Muṣṭafā 'Abd al-Rāziq,* pp. 153-5.

202. Ibid., 25 February 1916, and *min Āthār Muṣṭafā 'Abd al-Rāziq,* pp. 216-17.

203. Ibid., 7 July 1916, and *min Āthār Muṣṭafā 'Abd al-Rāziq,* pp. 254-6.

204. Ibid., 3 March 1916, and *min Āthār Muṣṭafā 'Abd al-Rāziq,* pp. 217-18.

205. Ibid., 2 July 1917, and *min Āthār Muṣṭafā 'Abd al-Rāziq,* pp. 360-2.

206. Ibid., 19 May 1916, and *min Āthār Muṣṭafā 'Abd al-Rāziq,* pp. 237-8.

207. Ibid., 16 June 1916, and *min Āthār Muṣṭafā 'Abd al-Rāziq,* pp. 242-8.

208. The section entitled "The Impact of Russian Literature".

209. It was probably under the influence of Pushkin that he added the word *al-'aṣriyyah* (the contemporary) to its title in the following year, making it *al-Nafā'is al-'Aṣriyyah.*

210. Ṣidqi was a student of Baydas who graduated from the Russian Seminary and went to study in Russia. Upon his return he wrote extensively on Russian literature, and introduced Chekhov and other Russian writers to the Arab reader, before embarking on writing his own narrative texts.

211. Najāti Ṣidqi, *Pushkin* (Cairo, Dār al-Ma'ārif, 1945), p. 91.

212. Mikhā'il Nu'aymah, *Sab'ūn* (Beirut, Dār Ṣādir, 1959), vol. I, p. 231.

213. *Al-Nafā'is,* II, 12, 1909, p. 10.

214. The magazine stopped at the outbreak of World War I, then resumed publication in 1919 and continued until it ceased publication altogether in 1923.

215. He translated Jūrji Zaydān's *al-Mamlūk al-Shārid* (The Wandering Mamluk) into Russian.

216. Imperial Russia was among the first European countries to establish modern schools in Palestine and other parts of the Levant and even a teacher training college in Nazareth in the mid-nineteenth century. The Tsar, members of his family and the Russian Orthodox Church were patron members of the Palestinian Orthodox Society, which played a major educational and cultural role in the area. By the turn of the century Russian schools were among the best and most reputable in the Levant. Bydas and many of the translators in his magazines, such as Anṭūn Ballān, Sulaymān Būlis, Ibrāhīm Jābir, 'Abd al-Karīm Sam'ān, Luṭf-allah al-Khūri Ṣarrāf, and Fāris Niqūlā Mudawwar were the product of such schools.

217. Na'īm al-Yāfi saw his stories as an extension of his translated work and praises his style and understanding of the language of fiction. See Na'īm al-Yāfi, op. cit., p. 37.

218. *Al-Nafā'is,* I, 1, 1908, p. 1.

219. K. Bydas, *Masāriḥ al-Adhhān* (Cairo, al-Maṭba'ah al-'Aṣriyyah, 1924), p. 4.

220. The Arabic word means "theatres" as well as "perambulate" and "wander freely", and associating both meanings with the mind suggests even freer roaming.

221. *"Al-Muqābalah al-Khafiyyah"* (Secret Meeting), *Masāriḥ al-Adhhān,* p. 329.

222. As in the stories *"Ayn al-Ḥaqīqah"* (Where is Truth?), *"al-Nūr al-Muqaddas"* (Divine Light), *"Alihat al-Jamāl"* (Goddess of Beauty), and *"Muḥāwarah bayn al-Ālihah"* (Conversation between Gods).

223. As in the stories *"al-Ab"* (The Father), *"al-Mūmyā'"* (The Mummy), *"Junūn al-Ḥubb"* (Love's Madness), and *"al-Sa'ādah"* (Happiness).
224. As in the story *"Ḥajar al-Falāsifah"* (The Philosophers' Stone).
225. As in the stories *"Ayyatuha al-Shams"* (O! Sun), *"Zawjah Nadirat al-Mithāl"* (A Unique Wife) and *"al-'Ilāj al-Shāfi"* (The Effective Cure).
226. As in the story *"Mu'tamar al-Ḥayawānāt"* (Animals' Conference).
227. As in the stories *"al-Zawj al-Makhdū'"* (The Cheated Husband), *"al-Dhikrā al-Akhīrah"* (The Last Memory), *"Hadiyyat al-'Īd"* (Christmas Present), and *"al-Liṣṣ"* (The Thief).
228. For a detailed discussion of his work, see 'Abd al-Raḥmān Yāghi, *Ḥayāt al-Adab al-Filasṭīni al-Ḥadīth: min Awwal al-Nahḍah ḥattā al-Nakbah* (Beirut, al-Maktab al-Tijāri, 1968), p. 439-56.
229. Yāghi, op. cit., p. 453.
230. For a detailed account of their work, see Najm, *al-Qiṣṣah*, and 'Abd al-Muḥsin Badr, op. cit.
231. A discussion of his novels is in 'Abd al-Ilāh Aḥmad, op. cit., pp. 56-66.
232. A detailed account of their plays can be found in Muḥammad Yūsuf Najm, *al-Masraḥiyya fī al-Adab al-'Arabi al-Ḥadīth* (Beirut, 1956), pp. 366-93, and in M.M. Badawi, *Early Arabic Drama*, pp. 43-64.
233. For a detailed account of their plays, see Najm, *al-Masraḥiyyah*, pp. 293-365.
234. For a detailed discussion of their work see Najm, *al-Masraḥiyyah*, pp. 396-442, and Badawi, *Early Arabic Drama*, pp. 68-100.
235. Hitti, op. cit., pp. 488-9.

Chapter 4

1. See Yaḥyā Ḥaqqi's introduction to Maḥmūd Ṭāhir Lāshīn, *Sukhriyat al-Nāy* (Cairo, Dār al-Kātib al-'Arabi, 1963?), p. v.
2. The theatre companies of this period were generally known by the name of their leading actor, who was, in most cases, the director too. The famous companies of this period were those of 'Abd al-Raḥmān Rushdi, Salāmah Ḥijāzi, Jūrj Abyaḍ, 'Abdullah 'Ukāshah, 'Azīz 'Īd, 'Ali al-Kassār, Aḥmad al-Shāmi, Rūz al-Yūsuf, Najīb al-Riḥāni and Sharikat al-Tamthīl al-'Arabi. There were, however, many smaller companies in small towns; for a detailed account see Muḥammad Yūsuf Najm, *al-Masraḥiyya fī al-Adab al-'Arabi al-Ḥadīth* (Beirut, 1956), pp. 168-86.
3. Such as Shibli Shumayyil (1853-1917), Jurji Zaydān (1861-1914), Niqūlā Ḥaddād (1870-1954), Faraḥ Anṭūn (1874-1922), and Anṭūn al-Jumayyil (1878-1948).
4. *Al-Siyāsah al-Usbū'iyyah*, 17 December 1927 and 7 January 1928.
5. For a detailed discussion of the relationship between the short story as a literary genre and the state of defeat and frustration, see F. O'Connor, *The Lonely Voice: A Study of the Short Story* (London, 1964).
6. There was another factor, mentioned by 'Īsā 'Ubaid in his introduction to his first collection *Iḥsān Hānim* (Cairo, Maktabat al-Wafd, 1921), which played a significant role in delaying the appearance of the early examples of the short story. This was the acute shortage of paper caused by World War I. He says: "The reason for our writers' interest in theatre and neglect of fiction is that theatre is more materially and literarily rewarding, and also because the war has created a paper crisis and destroyed the printing industry, thus preventing writers from writing fiction", *Iḥsān Hānim*, p. 3. This is certainly an important factor which exerted a devastating effect on the rising literary movement; the announcement of several forthcoming publications in the final pages of most of the creative works of that time may serve as an additional indication of the effect of this factor which caused the accumulation of manuscripts in writers' drawers.
7. Such as the novel, drama, the short story and narrative sketches.
8. He published, for example, *"al-Thu'bān"* (The Snake), in *al-Hilāl*, October 1917.
9. He published, for example, *"Ḥukm al-Hawā"* (The Rule of Passion) in *al-Hilāl*, February 1926, and *"al-Shaikh Ḥasan"*, *al-Hilāl*, April 1926.

10. He published *"Majma' al-Aḥyā'"* (The Academy of the Living) in *al-Hilāl*, March 1917, in addition to his novel *Zaynab*, which was published under the pseudonym *Miṣri Fallāḥ* (An Egyptian Peasant).
11. For a detailed study of this group, see chapter 6 below.
12. Muḥammad Taymūr, 'Īsā 'Ubaid, Shiḥātah 'Ubaid, Maḥmūd Taymūr and Maḥmūd Ṭāhir Lāshīn.
13. The elder brother of Maḥmūd Ṭāhir Lāshīn and an important but neglected pioneer who had a considerable influence upon Taymūr and many other young writers, but, unfortunately, his premature death in his late twenties prevented him from developing his own work.
14. Taymūr's major contribution is in the dramatic field. His works in this field not only paved the way for future development, but also were the beginning of indigenous Egyptian drama. His plays *al-'Uṣfūr fī al-Qafaṣ* (A Swallow in a Cage, 1918) and *'Abd al-Sattār Effendi* (Mr. Abd al-Sattar, 1918) are considered by many scholars to be the real debut of Egyptian drama. See, for example, 'Ali al-Rā'i, *Funūn al-Kumīdyā* (Cairo, Dār al-Hilāl, 1971), pp. 138-60, and M.M. Badawi, *Early Arabic Drama* (Cambridge, Cambridge University Press, 1988), pp. 101-20.
15. From 1914 until his premature death on 24 February 1921.
16. This was entitled *"Shakhṣiyyatunā"* (Our National Character) and first appeared in *al-Sufār*, 10 August 1918, and later on in *Wamīḍ al-Rūḥ* (Cairo, Maṭba'at al-I'timād, 1922), pp. 176-8.
17. Ibid., p. 177.
18. *"Al-'Āmm al-Jadīd"* (New Year) appeared in *al-Sufūr*, 8 January 1920 and *Wamīḍ al-Rūḥ*, pp. 180-3.
19. *"Al-Khawf min al-Ḥayāh"* (Fear of Life), *Wamīḍ al-Rūḥ*, pp. 167-71.
20. Ibid.
21. Most of these stories which were published in *al-Sufūr* throughout 1917 were collected and appeared posthumously in the first volume of his collected works in 1922, and then appeared as a separate collection of short stories in 1927 with the same title.
22. Apart from his father, his aunt was the eminent writer 'Ā'ishah Taymūr.
23. *Al-Sufūr*, 7 June 1917.
24. See Maḥmūd Taymūr's introduction to *Wamīḍ al-Rūḥ*, p. 38.
25. Most of the second volume of his collected works, *Ḥayātunā al-Tamthīliyyah* (Cairo, Maṭba'at al-I'timād, 1922), is devoted to his articles on drama, acting, and other theatrical matters.
26. Muḥammad Taymūr, *Wamīḍ al-Rūḥ*, p. 50.
27. "Moonlight" is indeed one of Maupassant's best-written and most poetic short stories. It tells the story of the Abbé Marignan, a zealous and conscientious believer who is absolutely convinced that everything in nature is subject to an infallible logic. He hates women for, to him, they are a source of sin. He has a niece, whom he is determined to make a Sister of Charity. But one day he is told that she has taken a lover and meets him every night by the river. He goes out at night to catch them, but, to his surprise, he is captivated and enchanted by the beauty of nature bathed in the softness of moonlight. When he sees them enveloped in such splendour, he realizes that God has created such nights to veil the loves of men with ideal beauty and flees, almost ashamed, as if he has entered a temple where he has no right to be.
28. Robert Scholes, *Elements of Fiction* (Oxford, Oxford University Press, 1968), pp. 53-4.
29. Yahya Ḥaqqi, *Fajr al-Qiṣṣah al-Miṣriyyah* (Cairo, Dār al-Qalam, 1960), p. 59.
30. See *Wamīḍ al-Rūḥ*, p. 170.
31. See Ibid., pp. 171-3.
32. Ibid., pp. 224-30 and *al-Sufūr*, 21 June 1917.
33. *Wamīḍ al-Rūḥ*, pp. 230-8 and *al-Sufūr*, 2 August 1917.
34. *Wamīḍ al-Rūḥ*, pp. 271-348.
35. Ibid., pp. 262-9.
36. Ibid., pp. 363-5.
37. Ibid., pp. 270-2.
38. Ibid., pp. 250-3.

39. It is considered by some critics to be the first indigenous Egyptian short story, see: 'Abbās Khaḍr, *Muḥammad Taymūr: Ḥayātuh wa-Adabuh* (Cairo, al-Dār al-Qawmiyyah, 1966), pp. 71-85, and Muḥammad Yūsuf Najm, *al-Qiṣṣah fī al-Adab al-'Arabī al-Ḥadīth* (Beirut, al-Maktabah al-Ahliyyah, 1966), pp. 271-84.

40. *Wamīḍ al-Rūḥ*, pp. 217-24 and *al-Sufūr*, 7 June 1919.

41. *Wamīḍ al-Rūḥ*, pp. 243-9.

42. Ibid., pp. 349-78.

43. Ibid., *"li-l-Fuqarā' Majjanā"* (Free for the Poor), pp. 354-7; *"'Urs wa-Ma'tam"* (A Wedding and a Funeral), pp. 361-2; *"Laban bi-Qahwah wa-Laban bi-l-Turāb"* (Coffee with Milk and Coffee with Dust), pp. 368-9; and *"Sāriq wa-Sāriq"* (A Thief and Another), pp. 373-5.

44. Ibid., pp. 358-60.

45. He was writing when al-Manfalūṭī was at the peak of his fame, and his style was increasingly popular.

46. Wayne Booth, *The Rhetoric of Fiction* (Chicago, University of Chicago Press, 1961), pp. 3-16.

47. In his narrative sketch *"al-'Āshiq al-Maftūn bi-l-Rutab wa-l-Nayāshīn"*.

48. In *"Ḥadīth Zahrah"* (The Talk of a Flower) in *Wamīḍ al-Rūḥ*, pp. 158-63.

49. The first edition of his collection *Kān mā Kān* included seven stories, but in subsequent editions he omitted one of them, *Jam'iyyat al-Mawtā* (The Association of the Dead), and continued to publish it with only six.

50. Na'īm al-Yāfī, *al-Taṭawwur al-Fannī li-Shakl al-Qiṣṣah al-Qaṣīrah fi-l-Adab al-Shāmī al-Ḥadīth* (Damascus, Manshūrāt Ittiḥād al-Kuttāb al-'Arab, 1982), pp. 210-1.

51. The author has some doubts about these dates and was unable to locate copies of the magazines in which they were published. It seems that the first to suggest these dates was Najm in *al-Qiṣṣah,* and others, such as Suhayl Idrīs, *al-Qiṣṣah fī Lubnān* (Cairo, Ma'had al-Dirāsāt al-'Arabiyyah, 1957), and al-Yāfī, op. cit., followed suit. The dates suggested by Najm, who states that he received a letter from Nu'aymah on 16 September 1950, confirming the publication of these stories first in *al-Funūn* and *al-Sā'iḥ* (*al-Qiṣṣah,* p. 281), have been widely accepted to the extent that they appear at the end of the stories in the subsequent editions of *Kān mā Kān.* Nu'aymah's letter was not published, and the fact concerning the publication of the stories in New York is not in question here. What is doubtful are the dates suggested for some of them, for they contradict the facts. One example suffices to demonstrate the point: Najm suggests that the second story, *"al-'Āqir"*, was published in 1915, and this is also the date mentioned at the end of the story in the fourth edition of *Kān mā Kān* (Beirut, Dār Ṣādir, 1956), while Nu'aymah himself gives the exact date of its writing as 8 July 1916 and adds that he mailed it to *al-Funūn* three days later on 11 July 1916: see Mikhā'īl Nu'aymah, *Sab'ūn* (Beirut, Dār Ṣādir, 1959), II, p. 59.

52. Nu'aymah, *Sab'ūn,* II, pp. 269-79.

53. Ismā'īl Adham, "Mīkhā'īl Nu'ymah", *al-Ḥadīth* (Aleppo), 3, 1944, p. 146.

54. Mikhā'īl Nu'aymah, *Kān mā Kān,* 4th ed. (Beirut, Dār Ṣādir, 1956), pp. 40-53.

55. This signified the refusal of any member of the family to leave the country as an emigrant or expatriate. The term "Columbus" is used to indicate the two Americas to which most of the Lebanese immigrated.

56. Mikhā'īl Nu'aymah, *Kān mā Kān,* pp. 54-87.

57. Ibid., pp. 88-98. The main meaning of the word is supply or munitions, it also mean a holy relic or even an amulet or a talisman.

58. Ibid., pp. 99-109.

59. Ibid., pp. 110-31.

60. Ibid., pp. 7-39.

61. 'Arīḍah was also from the same town, Hims, and married Ḥaddād's sister shortly after the foundation of the Association.

62. *al-Rābiṭah al-Qalamiyyah* was founded in New York on 20 April 1920 and included Jibrān, Nu'aymah, 'Arīḍah, Ḥaddād, Rashīd Ayyūb, Nudrah Ḥaddād, Īlyā Abū-Māḍī, Wadī' Bāḥūṭ, Ilyās 'Aṭallah and Willaim Kātsiflīs. It elected Jibrān as its president, Nu'aymah and Kātsiflīs as its two secretaries and made its aim the promotion of new writing.

63. For a detailed study of the work of the prose writers of the *mahjar* see: ʻAbd al-Karīm al-Ashtar, *al-Nathr al-Mahjarī* (Cairo, Maʻhad al-Dirāsaāt al-ʻArabiyyah, 1961), 2 vols, and Jūrj Ṣaydaḥ, *Adabunā wa-Udabāʼuna fī al-Mahājir al-Amrīkiyyah* (Beirut, al-Maktabah al-Ahliyyah, 1957).

64. Nuʻaymah, *Sabʻūn*, II, p. 182.

65. Nuʻaymah says that, presumably apart from himself, the two most cultured and widely read among the group were ʻArīḍah, who was fluent in Russian, and Jibrān, who was fluent in English. ʻArīḍah's readings were mainly in Russian and Arabic literature, while Jibrān was fluent in English and read various Western literatures, including Russian, in English translation. M. Nuʻaymah, *Sabʻūn*, II, pp. 182, and *Jibrān Khalīl Jibrān: Ḥayatuh, Mawtuh, Adabuh, Fannuh* (Beirut, Dār Ṣādir, 1934), pp. 201-2.

66. ʻAbd al-Masīḥ Ḥaddād, *Ḥihāyāt al-Mahjar* (New York, Maṭbaʻat al-Funūn, 1920), p. 3.

67. ʻAbd al-Karīm al-Ashtar, op. cit. II, p. 58.

68. ʻAbd al-Masīḥ Ḥaddād, op. cit., pp. 42-3.

69. Ibid., pp. 228-33.

70. In his introduction to *Iḥsān Hānim*, p. 12, ʻĪsā ʻUbaid refers to Taymūr as our "friend the late Muḥammad Taymūr who sparked off a significant revolution in art". But beyond this brief reference, written shortly after Taymūr's death, for the introduction is dated December 1921, there is no evidence as to whether they influenced each other's views and ideas. Indeed, apart from various speculations based on ʻĪsā's narrative world and a single article by his contemporary Niqūlā Yūsuf (*al-Masāʼ*, Cairo, 12 July 1962), there is very little information on his personal life and cultural background.

71. Only in the 1960s, and as a result of Yaḥyā Ḥaqqi's effort, were his two published books republished, but his other unpublished works are lost.

72. At the end of his two collections, ʻĪsā ʻUbaid advertised his forthcoming publications including two novels, *Bayn al-Ḥubb wa-l-Fann* (Between Love and Art) and *Yaqẓt Miṣr* (Egypt's Awakening); a collection of short stories, *al-ʼUsrah* (The Family); another collection in French, *Sur les bords du Nil;* a collection of critical essays, *Naẓarāt wa-Mulāḥaẓāt Fannyyah* (Artistic Reflections); and several plays. It was customary at this time for writers to fill the final page of their books with what seems more like a declaration of their literary intentions than an authentic list of completed works awaiting publication. But in ʻĪsā's case, one is inclined to take his list seriously, not only because his advertisements were very detailed and because he succeeded in publishing in 1922 the first book on the list which appeared in the final page of his first collection, but also because Muḥammad Bāqir ʻUlwān of Harvard University discovered in Cairo in 1973 the manuscripts of two of his lost plays.

73. Needless to say, he published these three volumes almost entirely at his own expense.

74. See his seminal work *Fajr al-Qiṣṣah al-Miṣriyyah*, pp. 101 ff.

75. However, it is very likely that ʻĪsā was the younger brother, for in his dedication to *Iḥsān Hānim*, p. 1, he refers to his older brother without giving his name.

76. A brief obituary on ʻĪsā ʻUbaid which appeared in *al-Sufūr*, 8 October 1922, refers to his originality and commends his pioneering achievements. This proves that he was known only to the narrow circle of literary innovators among the intellectuals.

77. *Al-Sufūr*, which appeared in 1915 and was edited by ʻAbd al-Ḥamīd Ḥamdi, was one of a few magazines which encouraged new writing; others were *al-Fajr al-Jadīd* and *al-Fajr*.

78. See the stories *"Mudhakkirāt Ḥikmat Hānim"* (The Memoirs of Her Ladyship Hikmat), in *Iḥsān Hānim* and *"al-Ṣalāh"* (Prayer) in *Dars Muʻlim*.

79. In this dedication which runs for two pages ʻĪsā says: "I wished to be able to dedicate to Your Excellency [i.e. Saʻd Zaghlūl] my novel *Yaqẓat Miṣr* in which I shall illustrate some facets of our glorious patriotic movement ... but my patriotism urged me to dedicate the first of my works to you as an acknowledgement of the great patriotic services which you have rendered to the Egyptian nation ... from a beginner and an unknown writer who lives in hope of witnessing the complete independence of his Egyptian homeland and the development and growing distinction of Egyptian art", *Iḥsān*

Hānim, pp. 1-2. However, this significant dedication, which appeared in the first edition of 1921, was deleted from the second edition when the collection was reprinted in 1964.

80. 'Īsā 'Ubaid, *Iḥsān Hānim*, p. 12.
81. This is the title of the introduction to *Iḥsān Hānim*, pp. 3-18.
82. *Iḥsān Hānim*, p. 6.
83. Ibid., p.7.
84. Ibid.
85. Ibid.
86. Ibid., pp. 4-5. The emphasis on psychology and psychoanalysis can be understood only in their literary sense and not as a specialized knowledge of the subject. They are meant as an interest in the character's psyche through artistic and intuitive insight into the personality and its motivation for the action taken.
87. Ibid.
88. Ibid.
89. 'Īsā 'Ubaid, *Thurayyā*, p. 7.
90. 'Īsā 'Ubaid, *Iḥsān Hānim*, pp. 15-16.
91. Ibid.
92. Ibid., p. 17.
93. Ibid., p. 18.
94. Shiḥātah 'Ubaid, *Dars Mu'lim*, p. 7.
95. Ibid., p. 11.
96. Ibid., pp. 7-8.
97. Ibid., p. 12.
98. Ibid., pp. 7-8.
99. Niqūlā Yūsuf praised, in his article on 'Īsā 'Ubaid (*al-Masā'*, Cairo, 12 July 1962), 'Īsā's excellent knowledge of French language and literature. It seems that he had, like many Levantines, a proper French education, to the extent that he felt competent enough to write his short stories in French, for he advertised a forthcoming collection entitled *Sur les bords du Nil: recueil de nouvelles sur l'Égypte contemporaine;* see *Iḥsān Hānim*, p. 92.
100. In addition, Shiḥātah referred to Shakespeare's *Hamlet* and *Romeo and Juliet.*
101. Yaḥyā Ḥaqqi, *Fajr al-Qiṣṣah al-Miṣriyyah*, p. 107.
102. 'Īsā 'Ubaid, *Iḥsān Hānim*, p. 76, and Shiḥātah 'Ubaid, *Dars Mu'lim*, p. 114.
103. Kenneth Burke, *Counter-Statement* (Berkeley, University of California Press, 1968), pp. 124-38.
104. The vernacular of the Egyptianized Levantines was a unique mixture of Egyptian and Levantine colloquial language and was marked by its subjugation of one dialect to the grammar and syntax of the other.
105. As in his *"Ma'sāt Qarawiyyah"* (A Tragedy of a Country Woman) in *Iḥsān Hānim*, pp. 42-60.
106. The special nature of Egyptian Christian family life with its specific ceremonies and rituals had to wait more than twenty-five years to find a writer, Yūsuf al-Shārūni, who could illustrate its unique and distinct problems.
107. See *"Anā Lak"* (I Am Yours), *"Mudhakkirāt Ḥikmat Hānim"*, and the title story of *Iḥsān Hānim*, and *"al-Ṣalāh"* and *"Maw'id Gharām"* in *Dars Mu'lim.*
108. 'Īsā 'Ubaid, *Iḥsān Hānim*, p. 78.
109. Ibid., p. 29.
110. Shiḥātah 'Ubaid, *Dars Mu'lim*, pp. 21-44.
111. Īsā 'Ubaid, *Iḥsān Hānim*, pp. 42-60.
112. Ibid., pp. 72-90.
113. Shiḥātah 'Ubaid, *Dars Mu'lim*, pp. 85-9.
114. Ibid., pp. 89-98.
115. 'Īsā 'Ubaid, *Thurayyā*, pp. 153-61.
116. 'Īsā 'Ubaid, *Iḥsān Hānim*, pp. 61-70.
117. Their contemporary, Ḥasan Maḥmūd, who adopted a similar approach to incompatibility in marriage, was keen to dissociate himself from this approach to adultery. In one of his stories, *"Khārij al-Insāniyyah"* (Outside Humanity), he warns the reader against sympathizing with such behaviour (*al-Sufūr*, 24 March 1922).

118. See, for example, the title story of *Iḥsān Hānim*, *"Maw'id Gharām"*, and the title story of *Dars Mu'lim*, pp. 1-20.

119. *Al-Sufūr*, 9 January 1922.

120. *Al-Sufūr*, 23 March 1922.

121. *Al-Sufūr*, 17 April 1922.

122. See *Iḥsān Hānim*, p. 55.

123. These criteria of female beauty were common among a number of writers in this period. Ḥasan Maḥmūd introduced similar criteria into his stories despite the fact that he was not of Levantine background. The justification for such attitudes may lie in the social structure of Egypt at that time, when the foreigners — the Turks and the Europeans — with their blonde and fair-skinned women occupied the highest status in the social scale in Egypt. The dreams and aspirations of the middle class, especially the *petite bourgeoisie*, were directed towards these foreign ideals and the hybrid local aristocracy, and this class was motivated by an amalgam of snobbery and desire for retaliation. It may be argued that the 'Ubaids were influenced by the standard *shāmiyyah* (Levantine woman), but this cannot explain other writers' adoption of the same attitude.

124. *Al-Sufūr*, 31 March 1922.

125. *Dars Mu'lim*, pp. 67-80.

126. Yaḥyā Ḥaqqi, *Fajr al-Qiṣṣah al-Miṣriyyah*, p. 113.

127. This story is also significant for it provides both the background and the backbone of another story which is the culmination of the Arabic short-story writer's search for maturity and authenticity, i.e. *"Ḥadīth al-Qaryah"* by Lāshīn to which the present book devotes chapter 7. However, despite the resemblance in the main plots of the two stories, there is not much evidence as to whether Lāshīn had read this story or not, before writing his.

128. This has been commented upon by Aḥmad Haykal, *al-Adab al-Qaṣaṣi wa-l-Masraḥi fī Miṣr: min A'qāb Thawrat 1919 ilā Qiyām al-Ḥarb al-Kubrā al-Thāniyah* (Cairo, Dār al-Ma'ārif, 1970), p. 43; al-Nassāj, op. cit., pp. 137, 140-1; and 'Abbās Khaḍr, *al-Qiṣṣah al-Qaṣīrah fī Miṣr: Mundh Nash'atihā Ḥattā Sanat 1930* (Cairo, al-Dār al-Qawmiyyah, 1966), p. 152.

129. They used several psychological terms in their narrative such as neurasthenia, monomania, neurosis, etc.

130. *Iḥsān Hānim*, pp. 19, 23, 25, 29, 63, 64, 77, etc.

131. Ibid., pp. 28-41.

132. This feature appeared, in different forms, in other works, e.g., *"Iḥsān Hānim"*, *"Dars Mu'lim"*, *"Mabrūk yā Umm Muḥammad"* (Congratulations, Umm Muhammad), in *Dars Mu'lim*, pp. 81-4, and *"Ḥadīqat al-Asmāk"* in *Thurryyā*, pp. 142-54.

133. See *"Iḥsān Hānim"*, *"al-Bā'inah"*, and *"al-Ṣalāh"* in *Dars Mu'lim*, pp. 55-66.

134. See al-Nassāj, op. cit. pp. 135-6.

135. *Dars Mu'lim*, pp. 55-66.

136. In *"al-Ṣalāh"*, for example, Shiḥātah was keen to give elaborate details of the patriotic occasion he described in the story. He gave the date of the party, the real names of the public personalities who took part, the full name of the lady who painted a portrait of Sa'd Pasha Zaghlūl which was auctioned at the party, the full name and profession of the man who bought it and the exact price paid. His keenness in giving all these somewhat irrelevant details betrays a lack of ability to master his art and eliminate unnecessary details, yet he manifests on several other occasions an ability to control his narrative and exclude unnecessary data. But these explicit patriotic references are due, in 'Īsā's case as well as in his brother's, to their longing both to integrate the new genre into the national movement and to use it as a means of participation in the national struggle.

137. See, for example, 'Abbās Khaḍr, *al-Qiṣṣah al-Qaṣīrah*, pp. 168-9, and Aḥmad Haykal, op. cit., p. 51

138. For detailed studies of his life and work, see: Maḥmūd al-'Abṭah, *Maḥmūd Aḥmad al-Sayyid* (Baghdad, Maṭba'at al-Ummah, 1961); 'Ali Jawād al-Ṭāhir, *Maḥmūd Aḥmad al-Sayyid: Rā'id al-Qiṣṣah al-'Irāqiyyah* (Beirut, Dār al-Ādāb, 1969?); Jamīl Sa'īd, *Naẓarāt fī al-Tayyārāt al-Adabiyyah al-Ḥadīthah fī al-'Irāq* (Cairo, Maṭbū'āt

Ma'had al-Dirāsāt al-'Arabiyyah, 1954), pp. 8 ff; and 'Abd al-Qādir Ḥasan Amīn, *al-Qiṣaṣ fī al-Adab al-'Irāqī al-Ḥadīth* (Baghdad, Dār al-Ma'ārif, 1956), pp. 29 ff.

139. 'Abd al-Ilāh Aḥmad, *Nash'at al-Qissah wa-Taṭawwuha fi-l-'Irāq* (Baghdad, Maṭba'at Shafīq, 1969), p. 115.

140. See *al-Ṣaḥīfah,* I, 3, February 1925, and 'Abd al-Ilāh Aḥmad, op. cit., p. 201.

141. See *al-Ma'raḍ,* II, 1, December 1926, and 'Abd al-Ilāh Aḥmad, ibid.

142. Al-Sayyid, *"Naz'ah min Naza'āt al-Adab al-Qaṣaṣī al-Turkī", al-Istiqlāl,* VII, p. 1095, July 1927. Quoted in 'Abd al-Ilāh Aḥmad, op. cit., p. 202.

143. Al-Sayyid, *al-Ḥadīth,* 7, quoted in 'Abd al-Ilāh Aḥmad, op. cit., p. 203.

144. See 'Abd al-Ilāh Aḥmad, op. cit., p. 28, and 'Umar al-Ṭālib, *al-Fann al-Qaṣaṣī fī al-Adab al-'Arabī al-Ḥadīth: al-Riwāyah al-'Arabiyyah fī al-'Irāq* (Baghdad, Maktabat al-Andalus, 1971), vol. I, p. 59. al-Ṭālib quotes a number of newspaper articles in *Lughat al-'Arab* (9, 1911); *al-Raqīb* (573, 1911); *al-'Irāq* (769, 1922) and *al-Ḥāṣid* (1, 1935), and discusses the nature and implication of this campaign.

145. Al-Sayyid, *al-Nakabāt,* p. 67.

146. As in his novel *fī Sabīl al-Zawāj* (For the Sake of Marriage) in 1921.

147. Ibid., p. 25.

148. See, for example, the stories of *"Nāṣiḥ al-Qawm"* (His People's Adviser), *"Qiṣṣat al-Ḍa'īf"* (The Story of the Weak), and *"Saṭrān min Ḥikāyah"* (A Couple of Lines from the Tale) in *al-Nakabāt,* pp. 58, 49, and 43 respecttively.

149. Ibid., p. 59.

150. Ibid., pp. 11-17.

151. Ibid., p. 58.

152. Ibid., p. 43.

153. A letter to Maḥmūd al-'Abṭah, *Mahmūd Aḥmad al-Sayyid,* p. 113.

154. Al-Sayyid, *al-Ṭalā'i',* pp. 46-56.

155. Quoted in 'Abd al-Ilāh Aḥmad, op. cit., p. 208.

156. Al-Sayyid, *al-Ṭalā'i',* pp. 67-74.

157. Ibid., p. 67.

158. Chapter 5 is devoted to the study of the early work of Taymūr.

159. 'Abd al-Ilāh Aḥmad, op. cit., pp. 208-9.

160. These are *"al-Ṭālib al-Ṭarīd"* (The Suspended Student), which was rewritten as *"Abū-Jāsim"*; *"al-Amal al-Muḥaṭṭam"* (The Broken Dream) rewritten as *"al-Daftar al-Azraq"* (The Blue Notebook); and *"Jimā' Hawā"* (Passion) rewritten as *"al-Dhikrā"* (Memory).

161. *"Nuktat al-'Imāmah"* (The Turban's Joke) in al-Sayyid, *al-Ṭalā'i',* pp. 95-7, and *fī Sā' min al-Zaman,* pp. 52-63.

162. These stories are published in the appendix of 'Abd al-Ilāh Aḥmad, op. cit., pp. 373-89, and are less mature than the rest of his work.

163. This is his *"Mujāhidūn"* in *al-Ṭalā'i',* pp. 30-45.

164. *"Fī al-Daftar al-Azraq"* (The Blue Notebook) and *"Dhikrā"* (Memory) in *fī Sā' min al-Zaman,* pp. 30-51 and 78-83 respectively.

165. *Al-Ṭalā'i',* pp. 3-8.

166. *Fī Sā' min al-Zaman,* pp. 17-29.

167. *Al-Ṭalā'i',* pp. 9-28.

168. Ibid., pp. 30-45.

169. Ibid., pp. 57-66.

170. *Fī Sā' min al-Zaman,* pp. 78-83.

171. Four of the seventeen stories in the two collections deal with this theme.

172. *Al-Ṭalā'i',* pp. 75-84.

173. *Fī Sā' min al-Zaman,* pp. 64-77.

174. *Al-Ṭalā'i',* pp. 86-94.

175. *Fī Sā' min al-Zaman,* pp. 94 ff.

176. Ibid., pp. 5-16.

177. Such as *Mudhakkirāt al-Arqash,* started in 1917, and *Liqā'* (1948).

178. Such as *al-Ābā' wa-l-Banūn* (1917).

179. The short novel is *Thurayyā* in 1922, and some of his lost plays were found in 1973, see note 72.

180. *Fi Sabīl al-Zawāj* (1921), *Maṣīr al-Ḍu'fā'* (1922) and *Jalāl Khālid* (1928).
181. Walter Benjamin, *Illuminations*, trans. Harry Zohn (London, 1973), p. 86.
182. Ibid., p. 87.
183. See chapters 1 and 2 of this study.
184. Benjamin, op. cit.
185. Aristotle, *The Poetics*, 60a, 22-6.
186. Benjamin, op. cit., p. 87.
187. For a detailed discussion of these differences, see Georg Lukács, *Writer and Critic*, trans. A. Khan (London, Merlin Press, 1970), pp. 110-48.
188. See Miriam Allot (ed.), *Novelists on the Novel* (London, Routledge & Kegan Paul, 1959), p. 71.

Chapter 5

1. The impact of Taymūr on the work of the Iraqi writer al-Sayyid has already been discussed in the previous chapter, but there were many others in Egypt (Ibrāhīm al-Miṣri, Tawfīq al-Ḥakīm, and al-Māzini), Lebanon (Sa'īd Taqiyy al-Dīn, Khalīl Taqiyy al-Dīn, Mārūn 'Abbūd and Tawfīq Yūsuf 'Awwād), Syria (Ṣubḥi Abū-Ghanīmah, 'Ali Khalqi and Fu'ād al-Shāyib), and Iraq (Dhū-l-Nūn Ayyūb, Ja'far al-Khalīli, 'Abd al-Ḥaqq Fāḍil, Anwar Shā'ūl and Shālūm Darwīsh) who were, in varying degrees, influenced by his work.
2. Manṣūr Fahmi and Aḥmad Zaki Abū Shādi introduced his first and second collections, respectively.
3. His friend, Ḥusain Fawzi, wrote the introduction for his third and last collection.
4. While Lāshīn published almost all his short stories in *al-Fajr*, Taymūr published only two stories from his first collection, i.e. *"al-Usṭā Shiḥātah"* (Shihatah the Foreman), *al-Fajr*, 10 February 1925, and *"al-Junūn Funūn"* (Madness Has Many Forms), *al-Fajr*, 13 March 1925, and three from his second collection, i.e. *"Ab wa-Ibn"* (Father and Son), *al-Fajr*, 12 July 1925, *"al-Waẓīfah Akhīrā"* (A Job at Last), *al-Fajr*, 2 August 1925, and *"Mughaffal"* (The Fool), *al-Fajr*, 20 September 1925.
5. See the introduction to his third collection, *al-Shaikh Sayyid al-'Abīṭ*, 1926.
6. *Al-Shaikh Jum'ah*, 2nd edn., p. 10.
7. *'Amm Mitwalli*, p. iii.
8. *Al-Shaikh Jum'ah*, pp. 7, 12.
9. *Al-Shaikh Sayyid al-'Abīṭ*, p. 12.
10. Ibid., p. 32.
11. Maḥmūd Taymūr, *Nushū' al-Qiṣṣah wa-Taṭawwuruhā* (Cairo, al-Maṭba'ah al-Salafiyyah, 1936), p. 39.
12. *Al-Shaikh Jum'ah*, 1st edn., pp. vii-viii.
13. *Al-Shaikh Jum'ah*, 2nd edn., pp. 6-7.
14. There is some evidence that he was introduced, albeit on a limited scale, to European literature in his father's salon and through his extensive library, which included some European books.
15. *Fir'awn al-Ṣaghīr*, pp. 22-3.
16. *Shifā' al-Rūḥ*, p. 16.
17. Ibid., p. 17.
18. *Al-Shaikh Jum'ah* (1925), *'Amm Mitwalli* (1925), *al-Shaikh Sayyid al-'Abīṭ* (1926), and *al-Ḥājj Shalabi* (1930).
19. This was *Rajab Afandi* (1928).
20. As in *"al-Usṭā Shiḥātah Yuṭālib bi-Ujratih"* (Shihatah the Foreman Demands his Wages) in *al-Shaikh Jum'ah*, pp. 3-18, where the wife is forced by the insensitive behaviour of her husband to make a prostitute of herself; in *"al-Junūn Funūn"*, ibid., pp. 62-4, she suffers expulsion from her rented flat; and in *"Mashrū' Kafāfi Afandi"* (Kafafi Effendi's Project), ibid., pp. 114-24, she escapes with her stepson, who matches her in age and inclinations, after they have stolen a sum of money.
21. As in *"Wasiṭat Ta'āruf"* (Introducing People to Each Other) in *al-Shaikh Jum'ah*, pp. 29-39; *"al-Junūn Funūn"*, *"al-Ḥājj Fayrūz"* in *'Amm Mitwalli*, pp. 118-38; *"al-Waẓīfah Akhīrā"*, ibid., pp. 142-77; *"Mughaffal"*, ibid., pp. 212-22; *"al-*

Malal" (Boredom) in *al-Shaikh Sayyid al-'Abīṭ*, pp. 110-24; "*Ṣadīqi Tilmīdhā wa-Muwaẓẓafā*" (My Friend at School and at Work), ibid., pp. 150-74; "*Khalf al-Sitār*" (Behind the Curtain) in *al-Ḥājj Shalabi*, pp. 97-109; "*Budūr*", ibid., pp. 179-93; and "*Ilā al-Ḥaḍīḍ*" (To the Abyss) in *Abū-'Ali 'Āmil Artist*, pp. 90-111, which is a new version with radical modifications of "*al-Waẓīfah Akhīrā*".

22. The most important of them were Mu'āwiyah Muḥmmad Nūr, e.g. his article on *al-Ḥājj Shalabi* in *Jarīdat Miṣr*, 29 September 1931, and Yaḥyā Ḥaqqi, e.g. his articles in *Kawkab al-Sharq* and *al-Majallah al-Jadīdah* in November 1930.

23. In Muḥammad Taymūr's fictional sketch, "*Dars fi Kuttāb*".

24. In Ḥasan Maḥmūd's two short stories, "*Jarīmah*" (Crime) and "*al-Zawjah al-Āthimah*" (The Adulterous Wife).

25. *Al-Shaikh Jum'ah*, pp. 2-7.

26. *'Amm Mitwalli*, pp. 2-16.

27. *Al-Shaikh Sayyid al-'Abīṭ*, pp. 50-108.

28. *'Amm Mitwalli*, pp. 42-53.

29. *Abū-'Ali 'Āmil Artist*, pp. 66-87 and *al-Majallah al-Jadīdah*, 1 February 1930.

30. See, for example, "*Sayyidunā*" (Our Master) in *al-Shaikh Jum'ah*, pp. 19-26.

31. As in "*al-Imām al-Mizwāj*" (The *Imām* Who Marries Often) in *al-Ḥājj Shalabi*, pp. 163-70.

32. See "*man Fāt Qadīmah Tāh*" (It is Unwise to Abandon Your First Wife) in *'Amm Mitwalli*, pp. 180-209.

33. See "*Abū Darsh*" in *al-Shaikh Sayyid al-'Abīṭ*, pp. 126-48.

34. For detailed information, see Shawqi Ḍayf, *al-Adab al-'Arabi al-Mu'āṣir fi-Miṣr* (Cairo, Dār al-Ma'ārif, 1961), p. 265; 'Abd al-Muḥsin Ṭaha Badr, *Taṭawwur al-Riwāyah al-'Arabiyyah al-Ḥadīthah* (Cairo, Dār al-Ma'ārif, 1963), pp. 231 ff; 'Abbās Khaḍr, *Muḥammad Taymūr: Ḥayātuh wa-Adabuh* (Cairo, al-Dār al-Qawmiyyah, 1966), pp. 15-32; Anwar al-Jundi, *Qiṣṣat Maḥmūd Taymūr* (Cairo, Dār Iḥyā' al-Kutub al-'Arabiyyah, 1951), pp. 47-52; and Maḥmūd Bin Sharīf, *Adab Maḥmūd Taymūr li-l-Ḥaqīqah wa-l-Tārīkh* (Cairo, Maṭba'at al-Kīlāni al-Ṣaghīr, n.d.), pp. 18 ff.

35. *'Amm Mitwalli*, pp. 56-68.

36. *Abū-'Ali 'Āmil Artist*, pp. 46-66 and *al-Siyāsah al-Usbū'iyyah*, 19 April 1930.

37. *'Amm Mitwalli*, pp. 70-80.

38. *Wamīḍ al-Rūḥ*, pp. 257-61.

39. *'Amm Mitwalli*, pp. 84-116.

40. *Shabāb wa-Ghāniyāt*, pp. 163-79.

41. *Wamīḍ al-Rūḥ*, pp. 271-348.

42. *Al-Shaikh Jum'ah*, pp. 76-89.

43. *Al-Ḥājj Shalabi*, pp. 113-60.

44. *Abū-'Ali 'Āmil Artist*, pp. 114-62.

45. For more details, see M.H. Abrams, *The Mirror and the Lamp: Romantic Theory and Critical Tradition* (Oxford, Oxford University Press, 1953), pp. 201-17.

46. *Al-Ḥājj Shalabi*, pp. 197-225.

47. *Al-Shaikh Jum'ah*, pp. 42-7.

48. Ibid., pp. 50-9.

49. For example, the protagonists of "*al-Sā'iḥ*" (The Tourist) in *al-Shaikh Jum'ah*, pp. 126-37; "*al-Munāfasah*" (The Contest), ibid., pp. 140-201; "*Mahzalat al-Mawt*" (Death Farce) in *'Amm Mitwalli*, pp. 18-30; "*Majīd Afandi*", ibid., pp. 32-40; "*Khalat Sallām Bāshā*" (Sallam Pasha's Aunt) in *al-Shaikh Sayyid al-'Abīṭ*, pp. 176-95; and "*'Ifrīt Umm Khalīl*" (Umm Khalīl's Ghost) in *al-Ḥājj Shalabi*, pp. 31 -54.

50. *Al-Ḥājj Shalabi*, pp. 73-89.

51. Ibid., pp. 57-69.

52. Ibid., pp. 179-93.

53. Ibid., pp. 229-37.

54. *Abū-'Ali 'Āmil Artist*, pp. 30-43 and *al-Hilāl*, March 1928.

55. *Abū-'Ali 'Āmil Artist*, pp. 3-13 and *al-Majallah al-Jadīdah*, December 1929, under the title "*Umm Zayyān*".

56. J.D.L. Ferguson, *Themes and Variations in the Short Story* (New York, Books for Libraries Press, 1972), p. 12.

57. For a discussion of Taymūr's plays, see M.M. Badawi, *Modern Arabic Drama in Egypt* (Cambridge, Cambridge University Press, 1987), pp. 88-111.

58. Nazīh al-Ḥakīm, *Maḥmūd Taymūr Rā'id al-Qiṣṣah* (Cairo, Maṭba'at al-Nīl, 1944), p. 89. He records some of the defects of Taymūr's stories about the peasants and life in the Egyptian village.

59. Such as *"Bayn 'Abd al-'Azīz wa 'Amm Murjān"* (Between 'Abd al-'Azīz and 'Amm Murjān), published in *al-Tamthīl*, 5 June 1924, and *"Ḥākim al-Markaz"* (The Ruler of the District), published in *al-Balāgh*, 26 November 1926.

60. Such as the story entitled *"Ustādh al-Qur'ān"* (The Qur'ānic Teacher), published in *al-Mishkāh*, 1 March 1923 which he rewrote under a new title, *"Qalam al-Abanūs"*, and published in his collection *'Amm Mitwalli*, pp. 42-53; *"al-Waẓīfah al-Akhīrah"*, published in *al-Fajr*, 2 August 1925, and in *'Amm Mitwalli*, pp. 142-77, was rewritten and appeared in *Abū-'Ali 'Āmil Artist*, pp. 90-111, under the new title *"al-Ḥadīd"*; and the title story of *Abū-'Ali 'Āmil Artist* which was rewritten twice after its first publication in *al-Balāgh* in 1927.

61. As he did with most of the stories originally published in his first collection, *al-Shaikh Jum'ah*, when he issued the second edition in 1927.

62. Such as *"al-Sā'iḥ"* and *"Khitāb min Munīr Bik"* (A Letter from Munir Bey) in his first collection, *al-Shaikh Jum'ah*, which were, as he confirmed in the introduction, based on two English short stories, and *"Abū Darsh"* in his third collection, *al-Shaikh Sayyid al-'Abīṭ*, which he admitted he took from Maupassant.

63. See the various reviews of his early works in *Ṣaḥīfat al-Jāmi'ah al-Miṣriyyah*, May 1925; *al-Fajr*, 8 May 1925; *The Egyptian Gazette*, 29 October 1925; *al-Muqtaṭaf*, December 1925; *Rūz al-Yūsuf*, 7 December 1925; and *al-Hilāl*, January 1926.

64. Nazīh al-Ḥakīm, op. cit., p. 44.

65. Spero Socrates, review of *al-Shaikh Jum'ah* in *The Egyptian Gazette*, 29 October 1925.

66. Yaḥyā Ḥaqqi, *Fajr al-Qiṣṣah al-Miṣriyyah*, p. 69.

67. David Daiches, *Critical Approaches to Literature* (London, 1956), p. 53.

68. *'Amm Mitwalli*, p. 58.

69. Ibid., p. 102.

70. Ibid., p. 118.

71. In the title story of *al-Shaikh Sayyid al-'Abīṭ*.

72. *Al-Shaikh Sayyid al-'Abīṭ*, p. 67.

73. Ibid., p. 73.

74. S. O'Faolain, *The Short Story* (London, Collins, 1948), p. 137.

75. Ibid., p. 138.

76. *Al-Shaikh Jum'ah*, 1st edn, p. xiv.

77. That is to say literary Arabic, *fuṣḥā*, and Egyptian vernacular, *'Āmmiyyah*. It is worth noting that he used the word *lughatayn*, two languages, and did not consider the vernacular a corrupt form of the written literary Arabic.

78. *Al-Shaikh Jum'ah*, 2nd ed., pp. 14-15.

79. Such as Muḥmmad 'Abdullah 'Anān and Sayyid Quṭb.

80. Ḥusain Fawzi, *"Kitāb Jadīd wa-Adab Jadīd"*, *al-Fajr*, May 1925.

81. Salāmah Mūsā, *"al-Adab al-Miṣri fi Usrah Miṣriyyah"*, *al-Hilāl*, January 1929.

82. O'Faolain, op. cit., p. 192.

83. For a detailed discussion of the difference between telling and showing in works of narrative, see Wayne C. Booth, *The Rhetoric of Fiction* (Chicago, University of Chicago Press, 1961), pp. 3-16.

84. This was the case in *"al-Junūn Funūn"*, *"al-Munāfasah"*, *"Shahr al-'Asal ba'd al-Arba'īn"*, *"Ab wa-Ibn"*, and *"Mughaffal"*.

85. See, for example, *"al-Ḥājj Fayrūz"*, *"al-Waẓīfah Akhīrā"*, *"man Fāt Qadīmah Tāh"*, *"al-Thālūth al-Muqaddas"*, and *"al-Ḥājj Shalabi"*.

86. A. Kratcshkovsky was the first to draw Taymūr's attention to the seriousness of such a phenomenon (sentimentality), immediately after the publication of his first collection. See *"Urustaqrāṭi Fallāḥ"* (An Aristocratic Peasant) in Anwar al-Jundi's *Qiṣṣat Maḥmūd Taymūr*, pp. 5-18.

Chapter 6

1. Maḥmūd Ṭāhir Lāshīn was born on 7 June 1894 in a middle-class family living in one of Cairo's poorest and most overcrowded quarters, al-Sayyidah Zaynab, where he spent his childhood. After completing the ordinary course of his education in 1912 he went to the High School of Engineering (Cairo), from which he graduated in 1917 as a civil engineer. He worked at Maṣlaḥat al-Tanẓīm (City Planning Department) from 1918 until his retirement in 1953, and died after a few months' illness in April 1954.

2. This is not the only major change in literary sensibility in modern Arabic literature, though it is the first. There is another vital change from this realistic sensibility to a modernistic one, which started to germinate after World War II and reached its zenith with the work of the writers of the 1960s. For a detailed study of this, see Sabri Ḥāfiẓ, *al-Qiṣṣah al-'Arabiyyah wa-l-Ḥadāthah: Dirāsah fī Āliyyāt Taghayyur al-Ḥasāsiyah al-Adabiyyah* (Baghdad, Wizārat al-Thaqāfah, 1990). The whole book is devoted to the study of the change in literary sensibility, particularly the shift to modernistic representation and its manifestations in Arabic narrative discourse.

3. These eight years, 1917-25, were of special significance in the patriotic struggle of the country and the growth of its aspirations. See chapters 1 and 2.

4. Aḥmad Khayri Sa'īd applied for permission to issue a weekly paper as early as 1918, but as a result of both the complications of granting such permission for a paper, and the state of political unrest at that time, he obtained permission only in August 1924. Then he started collecting contributions from friends, and received valuable financial and material aid from al-Ḥizb al-Waṭani (the Nationalist Party) and its daily, *al-Liwā'*. On 8 January 1925, the first issue of *al-Fajr,* the first Egyptian weekly paper devoted entirely to literature, appeared. The paper continued to appear until 13 January 1927, or, to be precise, this is the date of the last issue of the only known remaining copy in Dār al-Kutub, the National Library, Cairo.

5. By the time *al-Fajr* ceased publication in 1927, the group had grown enormously. It included many short-story writers, e.g. Lāshīn, Ḥasan Maḥmūd, Ḥusain Fawzi, Aḥmad Khayri Sa'īd, Andria Jibrīl, Maḥmūd 'Uzzi, Yaḥyā Ḥaqqi, Sa'īd 'Abduh, Ḥabīb Zaḥlāwi and more than ten others, as well as several outstanding critics and translators.

6. There were two influential literary groups involved in modernizing and changing literary sensibility at that time: the first aimed to establish an Egyptian renaissance in thought and literature on the basis of European civilization and rationalism (that is, Hellenic culture and the achievements of the French intellectual establishment), and integrate these new trends from occidental culture into the Arabic literary tradition in a way which would create a new culture. Among the leading figures of this group were Aḥmad Luṭfi al-Sayyid, Muḥammad Ḥusain Haykal, Ṭaha Ḥusain, and Aḥmad Ḍaif. The second was the group of *al-Dīwān* with its heavily Anglo-Saxon background and leanings. The eminent members of this group were al-Māzini, al-'Aqqād, 'Abd al-Raḥman Shukri, 'Abbās Ḥāfiẓ and Muḥammad al-Sibā'i.

7. Aḥmad Khayri Sa'īd, *"al-Istiqlāl al-Fikri"*, *al-Fajr,* 8 January 1925.

8. Among the members of the group were Ḥusain Fawzi, Muḥammad Shukri and Zakariyyā Muhrān, who were fond of Western classical music and were interested in developing Arabic music along similar lines. Sayyid Darwīsh also attended many of their meetings in one of 'Imād al-Dīn's cafés.

9. For a fuller list, see Yaḥyā Ḥaqqi, *Fajr al-Qiṣṣah al-Miṣriyyah* (Cairo, Dār al-Qalam, 1960), pp. 80-1.

10. Ibid., p. 81.

11. See Ḥusain Fawzi's article on the cultural formation of the group, *al-Ahrām,* 30 April 1965.

12. Aḥmad Khayri Sa'īd, *"al-Madhāhib al-Kitābiyyah"*, *al-Shabāb,* April 1921.

13. In several issues of *al-Fajr,* 'Ā'ishah Fahmi al-Khalafāwi, one of the most talented and learned critics of the group, wrote articles on Turgenev and Dostoevsky. Zakiyy al-Dīn al-Siwaifi and 'Abd al-Ḥamīd Sālim wrote on the schools of Russian literature and introduced other Russian writers.

14. Most of the leading members of this school read Russian literature in English or French translation. Ḥusain Fawzi emphasized the role of the translations of Muḥammad al-Sibā'i, Aḥmad Ḥasan al-Zayyāt, Ibrāhīm al-Māzini and Anṭūn al-Jumayyil in the cultural origins of the group. He attributes to their translations a dominant influence over the preceding Arabic narrative in that respect (*al-Ahrām*, 30 April 1965).

15. Mu'āwiyah Muḥammad Nūr, in his article, *"Ṭāhir Lāshīn al-Qaṣaṣi", al-Siyāsah al-Usbū'iyyah*, 5 July 1930, censured Lāshīn's adaptation of Chekhov's one-act play *The Bear* in his short story *"wa-Lakinnahā al-Ḥayāh"*. He also mentioned another of Lāshīn's adaptations, this time Maeterlinck's one-act play *L'Intruse*, in his story *"al-Zā'ir al-Ṣāmit"*. Likewise, Yaḥyā Ḥaqqi in his series of articles on Lāshīn's first collection, *Sukhriyat al-Nāy*, which appeared in *Kawkab al-Sharq*, February 1927 (see also his *Khuṭuwāt fi al-Naqd*, pp. 9-33) criticized Lāshīn's adaptation in his story *"al-Infijār"* of one of Chekhov's short stories which had been translated by Muḥammad al-Sibā'i under the title *"Zawba'ah Manziliyyah"* (Domestic Quarrels).

16. Max Weber in S.S. Prawer, *Comparative Literary Studies* (London, Duckworth, 1973), p. 13.

17. This was a cliché used by almost all the members of the group when they discussed the literature which they wanted to write.

18. See the dedication of his only novel, *al-Dasā'is wa-l-Dimā'* (Cairo, D'ar al-Hilāl, 1935), p. 3, and many of his articles.

19. Although there is no statistical evidence as to the size of its readership, the reference to its articles and the debate with its views pervaded the literary circles and imposed itself on many other journals with an established record of extensive readership.

20. See 'Abbās Khaḍr'Abbās Khaḍr, *al-Qiṣṣah al-Qaṣīrah fi Miṣr: Mundh Nash'atihā ḥattā Sanat 1930* (Cairo, al-Dār al-Qawmiyyah, 1966), pp. 87-97; and Sayyid Ḥāmid al-Nassāj, *Taṭawwur Fann al-Qiṣṣah al-Qaṣīrah fi Miṣr* (Cairo, Dār al-Kātib al-'Arabi, 1968), pp. 177-8. They state that the wide appreciation which *al-Fajr* achieved, especially among serious writers and readers, encouraged well-known writers — e.g. Muḥammad Ḥusain Haykal and Salāmah Mūsā-and old — established periodicals — e.g. *al-Hilāl* and *al-Muqtaṭaf* — to publish short stories.

21. Lāshīn emphasized this point in his answer to a literary questionnaire, *"al-Kitābah al-Qaṣaṣiyyah fi Miṣr wa-Asbāb Rukudihā"* (Narrative Writing in Egypt and the Reasons for Its Stagnation), *al-Majallah al-Jadīdah*, June 1931, p. 968.

22. For a detailed discussion of these avant-garde ideas and critical criteria, see the numerous articles of Aḥmad Khayri Sa'īd in *al-Fajr*, 8 January 1925, 20 March 1926, 26 June 1925, 6 January 1927; Ibrāhīm al-Miṣri, *al-Fajr*, 24 January 1926; Ḥusain Fawzi, *al-Fajr*, 1 May 1926; and Yaḥyā Ḥaqqi, *Kawkab al-Sharq*, February 1927.

23. His contemporary, Maḥmūd Taymūr, was for the greater part of his career far removed from this fundamental support of a coherent literary school and thus did not discover the importance of this primary principle until he had published a number of collections. In order to accentuate the need for short-story writers to labour extremely hard to improve their work and tighten its structure, Lāshīn called, in the questionnaire mentioned in note 21, for the devotion of most of the writer's efforts and time to the writing of narrative texts, and emphasized the importance of *al-tafarrugh* (making the writing of literature the writer's only full-time job), in order for creative literature to attain high artistic quality.

24. Ḥasan Maḥmūd's introduction to Lāshīn's only published novel, *Ḥawwā' bilā Ādam*, suggests that Lāshīn's first attempt to write fiction was in 1921, while Aḥmad Zaki Abū Shādi's introduction to *Yuḥkā Anna* suggests 1922.

25. His first published short story is *"Ṣaḥḥ", al-Funūn*, September 1924.

26. Such as *al-Jadīd, al-Hadīth, Shahrazād, al-Majallah al-Jadīdah, and al-Hilāl.*

27. Unlike Taymūr's, his collecting of his works in book form was not a sign of wealth but of artistic confidence. His books were published by a commercial publisher and were introduced by some of the leading literary figures of the time, particularly those associated with breaking new ground in thought, such as Manṣūr Fahmi, or in poetry, such as Aḥmad Zaki Abū Shādi.

28. See his stories in *al-Fajr* such as *"Jināyat Umm 'alā Waladihā"* (A Mother's Offence against Her Son), 31 January 1925; *"Umm Shiḥātah"* (Shihata's Mother), 17

April 1925; *"min al-Kūkh ila al-Qaṣr"* (From Rags to Riches), 8 May 1925; *"Qiṣṣat Mukhaddir"* (The Story of a Drug), 10 July 1925; *"al-Sariqah al-Mashrū'ah"* (The Lawful Theft), 2 August 1925; *"'Arīs al-Ghaflah"* (Unexpected Bridegroom), 14 September 1925; *"al-Lughz"* (The Riddle), 14 October 1925; *"al-Jarīmah al-Akhīrah"* (The Last Crime), 28 October 1925; *"al-Thā'ir"* (The Rebel), 28 December 1925; *"fī Ḍaw' al-Qamar"* (In the Moonlight), 11 April 1926; *"al-Musha'widh"* (The Quack), 25 April 1926; and several other stories after the closing of *al- Fajr* in *al-Akhbār, Majallat al-Fukāhah,* and *al-Rāwi.*

29. See his stories in *al-Fajr* such as *"Ḥikāyah Qadīmah"* (An Old Story), 4 February 1925; *"Qiṣṣat Mariḍah"* (A Story of a Female Patient), 24 February 1925; *"al-Shaikh 'Awdah"*, 20 March 1925; *"al-Jamādāt"* (Inanimate Objects), 24 April 1925; and *"Nustāljiyā"* (Nostalgia), 10 October 1925. After that date his literary work was interrupted by an educational mission to France.

30. See his stories in *al-Fajr* such as *"Fullah-Mishmish-Lūlū"*, 15 July 1926; *"al-Sukhriyah"* (Mockery), 16 September 1926; *"Muḥammad Bik Yazūr 'Izbatah"* (Muḥammad Bey Visits His Estate), 28 October 1926; and *"Shakir Afandi"*, 25 November 1926-13 January 1927.

31. The first editions of these two collections are undated, but Manṣūr Fahmi's introduction to the first collection is dated 6 November 1926, and the first review of it appeared in January 1927. From the reviews of the second collection in Egyptian periodicals, it would appear that the end of 1929 or the beginning of 1930 is the probable date of its publication.

32. Nevertheless, he published two more short stories: *"al-Ḥubb Yalhū"* (Love's Frivolities), *al-Majallah al-Jadīdah,* April 1930, and *al-Hilāl,* April 1934; and *"Taḥt 'Ajalat al-Ḥayāh"* (Under the Yoke of Life), *al-Hilāl,* January 1933. These two stories appeared with his third short story, *"Aḥraj Sā'ah fī Ḥayāti al-Madrasiyyah"* (The Most Critical Moment in My School Years), and his novelette, *"al-Niqāb al-Ṭā'ir"* (The Flying Veil), in his third book, *al-Niqāb al-Ṭā'ir,* 1940. He also serialized his novel *Ḥawwā' bilā Ādam* in *al-Hilāl,* June and July 1933, which then appeared in book form in the following year. After his third collection he published only one short story, *"mā lam Aqulhu li-Aḥad"* (What I Said to No One), *al-Hilāl,* November 1945.

33. The life of Muḥammad 'Abd al-Raḥim, Lāshin's elder brother, strikingly resembles that of Muḥammad Taymūr. He graduated from Madrasat al-Mu'ullimin al-'Ulyā (teacher training school), and then went to Europe to further his studies and literary knowledge. When he came back around 1920, he established a theatre group, for which he wrote or translated the necessary texts, and acted and directed most of the group's productions. His fondness for literature, and his artistic activities and ideas had a seminal influence on his young brother, Maḥmūd Ṭāhir Lāshin, and on many of his friends, who later formed *Jamā'at al-Madrasah al-Ḥadīthah.* For more details, see Yaḥyā Ḥaqqi's introduction to the second edition of *Sukhriyat al-Nāy*, 1964, p. xvi.

34. In his one-page preface to *Sukhriyat al-Nāy,* Lāshin mentioned with admiration and appreciation the work of both his predecessors and his contemporaries.

35. Ian Watt, *The Rise of the Novel* (Berkeley, University of California Press, 1957), p. 27.

36. T. O. Beachcroft, *The Modest Art: A Survey of the Short Story in English* (London, Oxford University Press, 1968), p. 260.

37. *Sukhriyat al-Nāy,* pp. 1-16. Ḥaqqi suggests that this story reflects upon the life of Lāshin's elder brother, Muḥammad 'Abd al-Raḥim, who also came back from Europe with tuberculosis.

38. *Sukhriyat al-Nāy,* pp. 89-107.

39. *Yuḥkā Anna,* pp. 25-31.

40. *Sukhriyat al-Nāy,* pp. 17-37.

41. Ibid., pp. 59-88.

42. Ibid., pp. 129-38.

43. *Yuḥkā Anna,* pp. 11-22.

44. Ibid., pp. 83-87.

45. Ibid., pp. 47-56.

46. Ibid., pp. 157-66.

47. Ibid., pp. 123-34.
48. Ibid., pp. 166-75.
49. Ibid., pp. 39-58.
50. *Bayt al-Ṭā'ah* is a legal term denoting the abode of a married couple which contains the bare minimum furnishings and implements to become legally accepted as the marital home, and the woman is thus forced to live in it under the contractual obligations of her marriage.
51. *Yuḥkā Anna*, pp. 137-47.
52. Ibid., pp. 97-107.
53. Ibid., pp. 150-4.
54. Ibid., pp. 59-70.
55. They are the protagonists of *"Mifistūfūlīs"* in *Sukhriyat al-Nāy*, pp. 139-66 and *"al-Shaikh Muḥammad al-Yamāni"* in *Yuḥkā Anna*, pp. 91-4.
56. The protagonist of *"Minṭaqat al-Ṣamt"* (The Domain of Impenetrable Silence) in *Sukhriyat al-Nāy*, pp. 168-84.
57. Although Maḥmūd Taymūr's stand *vis-à-vis* the religious sheikhs was almost identical with Lāshīn's, one cannot say that Lāshīn's excoriation of these religious figures was influenced by Taymūr's work. *"Mifistūfūlīs"* was published in *al-Fajr*, 30 August 1925. Lāshīn was the only writer to attack both sheikhs and clergymen. His story *"Minṭaqat al-Ṣamt"*, in which he gave Christian clergymen the same severe treatment, had no precedent and no successors for many years to come.
58. *Yuḥkā Anna*, pp. 39-44.
59. *Al-Niqāb al-Ṭā'ir*, pp. 107-80.
60. On the margins of his world one meets a considerable number of these wretched creatures: the public barber, the cobbler, the office boy, the news-vendor, the peasant, the watchman, the waiter of the poor *trottoir* café, the shoeshine boy, the tram conductor, the servant, the incense fumigator, the cemetery keeper, the matchmaker of the poor, the various types of vendor, the street trader, the procurer, the beggar, and those who do similar work.
61. See, for example, *Sukhriyat al-Nāy*, pp. 39, 59.
62. Malcolm Bradbury, *What is a Novel?* (Manchester, Manchester University Press, 1969), p. 40.
63. Ibid., p. 39.
64. The one exception is *"Ḥadīth al-Qaryah"*, in which the reader sees the village through the eyes of a visitor from the town. It seems that Lāshīn's post as a civil engineer in Maṣlaḥat al-Tanẓīm provided him with a wide knowledge of the streets and alleys of the poor quarters of Cairo, and this, combined with his lack of knowledge about the homes of the poor and lower class, guided him to situate the action in alleys and streets, if the story took him to the poor side of the city.
65. See *"Sukhriyat al-Nāy"*, *"fī Qarār al-Hāwiyah"*, and *"al-Zā'r al-Ṣāmi."*.
66. See *"Bayt al-Ṭā'ah"*, *"Manzil li-l-Ījār"*, *"Jawlah Khāsirah"*, and *"Alwu"*.
67. See *"Ḥadīth al-Qaryah"*, *"al-Ḥubb Yalhū"*, and *"al-Wiṭwāṭ"*.
68. The examples given in the three previous notes do not imply that the other two methods of presenting the scene are not used in the given stories, but only indicate that the features of one particular method are more in evidence and probably more prominent than those of others.
69. *Al-Fajr*, 27 January 1925.
70. *Al-Funūn*, September 1924.
71. *Al-Majallah al-Jadīdah*, April 1930, and *al-Hilāl*, April 1934.
72. *Sukhriyat al-Nāy*, pp. 139-66.
73. Ibid., pp. 168-84.
74. See the characters of Umm Bikhāṭirhā in *"Bayt al-Ṭā'ah"*, and Umm Sayyid in *"fī Qarār al-Hāwiyah"*.
75. See the heroines of *"Yuḥkā Anna,"* *"Bayt al-Ṭā'ah"*, and *"Lawn al-Khajal."*
76. See the heroines of *"wa-Lakinnahā al-Ḥayāh,"* *"Manzil li-l-Ījār"*, and *"Mādhā Yaqūl al-Wada'"*.
77. See *"Alwū"*, *"al-Wiṭwāṭ"*, *"wa-Lakinnahā al-Ḥayāh"*, and *"Ḥadīth al-Qaryah"*.

78. See *"al-Zā'ir al-Ṣāmit"*, *"al-Ḥubb Yalhū"*, and *"al-Niqāb al-Ṭā'ir"*. See also Aḥmad Khayri Sa'īd's story *"Jināyat Umm 'alā Waladihā"*, *al-Fajr*, 30 April 1925, in which he treats the same theme and manifests the dramatic consequences of the mother's excess of tenderness.

79. See *"al-Shabaḥ al-Māthil fi al-Mir'āh"*, *"Ḥadīth al-Qaryah"*, *"fi Qarār al-Hāwiyah"*, and *"Mifistūfūlīs"*.

80. As in *"fi Qarār al-Hāwiyah"*.

81. As in *"Bayt al-Ṭā'ah"*.

82. As in *"al-Infijār"* and *"Yuḥkā Anna"*.

83. As in *"Mifistūfūlīs"* and *"Minṭaqat al-Ṣamt"*.

84. As in *"al-Shāwīsh Baghdādi"*.

85. See *"Lawn al-Khajal"* and *"wa-Lakinnahā al-Ḥayāh"*.

86. See *"Alwū"*, *"Manzil li-l-Ījār"*, and *"al-Kahlah al-Mazhuwwah"*.

87. Ḥusain Fawzi, in his introduction to *al-Niqāb al-Ṭā'ir*, blames this satirical attitude for the critics' neglect of Lāshīn's work and for their deliberate attempt to hide his work from the European orientalists so it would not deface their spotless image of Egyptian social life. See *al-Niqāb al-Ṭā'ir*, p. 8.

88. Ibid., p. 9.

89. In his introduction to 2nd edition of *Yuḥkā Anna*, Maḥmūd Taymūr mentions that Lāshīn read Russian literature in English translation (*Yuḥkā Anna*, 1964), p. ii.

90. W. Somerset Maugham, *Points of View* (London, Heinemann, 1958), p. 171.

91. See e.g *"al-Kahlah al-Mazhuwwah"*, *"Lawn al-Khajal"*, *"al-Wiṭwāṭ"*, and *"fi Qarār al Hāwiyyah"*.

92. In his story *"Qiṣṣat 'Ifrīt"*, for example, he starts with the following dialogue:
Have you ever seen a ghost, dear reader?
No!
Have you ever had an encounter with a ghost that was invisible, dear reader?
No! No!
Do you believe in the existence of ghosts at all, dear reader?
No! No! No!
Pardon me, dear reader!
Note the sense of humour in this preamble, *Yuḥkā Anna*, p. 157.

93. In his introduction to Lāshīn's last collection, *al-Niqāb al- Ṭā'r*, Ḥusain Fawzi states that Lāshīn resumed writing at the close of the 1930s, after an interval of nearly seven years, because of a favourable remark about his work in a critical study. Though Fawzi declines to mention the book, it seems that he was referring to Ismā'īl Adham and Ibrāhīm Nāji's book, *Tawfiq al-Ḥakīm* (1938).

94. S. O'Faolain, *The Short Story* (London, Collins, 1948), p. 137.

95. E.R. Mirrielaes, *The Story Writer* (Boston, Little Brown & Co., 1939), p. 163.

96. Some of these features are at variance with Lāshīn's rare theoretical statements, in which he favours the realistic representation and claims that his narrative discourse is a whole world away from gratuitous local colour. See for example the interesting interview with him in *al-Majallah al-Jadīdah*, 1931, p. 966.

97. For example, Ḥusain Fawzi in his introduction to *al-Niqāb al- Ṭā'ir*.

98. For example, Mu'āwiyah Muḥammad Nūr in *"Ṭāhir Lāshīn al-Qaṣaṣi: Ārā' wa-Mulāḥaẓāt"*, *al-Siyāsah al-Usbū'iyyah*, 5 July 1930.

99. G. Lukács, *Writer and Critic* (London, Merlin Press, 1970), p. 132.

100. Ibid.

101. See Yaḥyā Ḥaqqi's introduction to the second edition of *Sukhriyat al-Nāy* (1964), pp. iv-v.

102. Northrop Frye, *Anatomy of Criticism* (Princeton, N.J., Princeton University Press, 1957), p. 304.

103. See, for example, his two works *"al-Shāwīsh Baghdīdi"* and *"al-Shaikh Muḥammad al-Yamāni"*. Although they are more narrative sketches than proper short stories, their vivid comic spirit enables them to stand up to criticism.

104. See, for example, *"fi Qarār al-Hāwiyah"* and *"Taḥt 'Ajalat al-Ḥayāh"*.

105. There is a detailed discussion in Yaḥyā Ḥaqqi's article on "*Sukhriyat al-Nāy*", published in *Kawkab al-Sharq*, February 1927, and in Ḥaqqi's book *Khuṭwāt fī al-Naqd*, (Cairo, Dar al-'Urūbah, 1962).

106. Lukács, op. cit., p. 116.

107. Mu'āwiyah Muḥammad Nūr, op. cit., discusses this in detail.

108. Yaḥyā Ḥaqqi, introduction to the 2nd edition of *Sukhriyat al-Nāy* (1964), p. i.

109. See, for example, *Yuḥkā Anna*, p. 169, when he says: "*al-anṣāb yanṣibūn wa-l-azlām yazlimūn wa-kull rijs min 'amal al-shyṭān yartakibūn*", and *al-Niqāb al-Ṭā'ir*, p. 20, when he says: "*wa-humm fī nahār ka-l-layl ya'mahūn*".

110. There are many examples throughout his three collections. In *Sukhriyat al-Nāy*, for example, one finds on page 4 a deliberate attempt to juxtapose decorative phrases full of puns, paronomasia and internal rhyme alongside colloquial words to show the absurdity of such a decorative style: "*al-qulal al-anīqah wa-l-abārīq al rashīqah, wa-l-azyār al ḍakhmah wa-l-balālīṣ al fakhmah. Bayn bayḍā' bilā ṭilā', wa-manqūshah bi-i'tinā', wa ḥamrā' dhāt bahā' wa-ṣafrā' fī zuhā' wa-raqṭā' fanṭaziyyat al-ruwā'.*"

111. Muḥammad Luṭfī Jum'ah, *al-Majallah al-Jadīdah*, April 1930, p. 776.

112. Yaḥyā Ḥaqqi, Introduction to *Sukhriyat al-Nāy*, pp. i-ii.

113. Even when there is an Arabic equivalent, he uses many of these foreign words in Arabic transcription, e.g. *automobile, orchestra, imperial, bonjour, propaganda, shake hands, mechanical, bravo, utopia, melancholy, bourse*, etc.

114. For a detailed discussion of the difference between the two, see I.A. Richards, *Principles of Literary Criticism* (London, Routledge & Kegan Paul, 1924), p. 267.

115. D. Daiches, *A Study of Literature* (London, André Deutsch, 1968), p. 34.

116. A. Yarmolinsky, *Letters of Anton Chekhov* (New York, Viking, 1973), p. 71.

117. Anonymous review of *Ḥawwā' bilā Ādam, al-Majallah al-Jadīdah*, March 1934, p. 133.

118. For details on the difference between various types of first-person narrative, see W. Hildick, *Thirteen Types of Narrative* (London, Macmillan, 1968), pp. 29-52.

119. F.L. Lucas, *Style* (London, Cassell, 1955), p. 272.

120. Yaḥyā Ḥaqqi, Introduction to *Sukhriyat al-Nāy*, p. x.

121. Such as Yaḥyā Ḥaqqi, Tawfīq al-Ḥakīm, Ṭaha Ḥusain and Maḥmūd Taymūr.

122. Such as Najīb Maḥfūẓ, Maḥmūd al-Badawi, Yūsuf Idrīs, 'Ādil Kāmil, Iḥsān 'Abd al-Quddūs, 'Abd al-Raḥman al-Sharqāwi, Tawfīq Yūsuf 'Awwād, Ḥannā Mīnā, Ghā'ib Ṭi'mah Firmān, Fu'ād al-Takarli, Jabrā Ibrāhīm Jabrā and 'Abd al-Raḥmān Munīf, to mention but a few.

Chapter 7

1. *Yuḥkā Anna*, pp. 71-82. The story has been republished in Sabry Hafez and Catherine Cobham (eds.), *A Reader of Modern Arabic Short Stories*, (London, Saqi Books, 1988), pp. 136-44. An English translation of the story is provided in the appendix of this study. But a different and more literal translation of certain phrases is used in the analysis, for the close reading of the text demands a greater awareness of certain linguistic connotations, some of which are lost in a more literary translation.

2. Some of Lāshīn's contemporaries perceived the importance of his short stories; see, for example, Aḥmad Zaki Abū Shādi's Introduction to *Yuḥkā Anna*, p. 9.

3. See the elaboration of Goldmann's concept in the Introduction of this book.

4. Helmut Bonheim, *The Narrative Modes: Techniques of the Short Story* (Cambridge, D.S. Brewer, 1982), p. 91.

5. Roland Barthes, "Introduction to the Structural Analysis of Narrative", in his *Image, Music, Text*, trans. Stephen Heath (New York, Hill & Wang, 1977), p. 116.

6. Bonheim, op. cit., p. 99.

7. Edward Said, *Beginnings: Intention and Method* (New York, Columbia University Press, 1985), p. 183.

8. For a discussion of the difference between the two, see Barthes, op. cit., p. 112.

9. These three terms are used in their Russian form because their translation into English is always a form of approximation, and the terms suggested by various critics suffer from their previous association with certain uses and critical approaches.

10. Particularly in Mikhail Bakhtin, *Problems of Dostoevsky's Poetics*, trans. Caryl Emerson (Manchester, Manchester University Press, 1984).

11. Particularly in Roland Barthes, *S/Z*, trans. Richard Miller (New York, Hill & Wang, 1974), and also in his, "Introduction to the Structural Analysis of Narrative".

12. Gerard Genette, *Figures*, vols. I, II and particularly III (Paris, Éditions du Seuil, 1966) and *Nouveau discours du récit* (Paris, Éditions du Seuil, 1983).

13. Tolstoy's quotation is taken from Victor Erlich, *Russian Formalism: History and Doctrine* (New Haven, Yale University Press, 1965), p. 241.

14. See Genette, *Nouveau discours du récit*, pp. 48-52.

15. V. Propp, *Morphology of the Folktale*, trans. L. Scott and L. Wagner (Austin, University of Texas Press, 1968).

16. For a detailed discussion of the nature of utopian thinking, see Karl Mannheim, *Ideology and Utopia* (London, Routledge & Kegan Paul, 1960), pp. 36-40, 173-74.

17. Ibid., p. 36.

18. Fredric Jameson, *The Political Unconscious: Narrative as a Socially Symbolic Act* (London, Methuen, 1981), pp. 289 and 291.

19. Edward Said, "Molestation and Authority in Narrative Fiction," in J. Hillis Miller (ed.), *Aspects of Narrative*, p. 55.

20. Ibid., pp. 57-8.

21. Seymour Chatman, *Story and Discourse* (Ithaca, New York, Cornell University Press, 1978), p. 148.

22. Edward Said, "Molestation and Authority in Narrative Fiction," in J. Hillis Miller, *Aspects of Narrative* (New York, Colombia University Press, 1971), p. 60.

23. See Barthes, "Introduction to the Structural Analysis of Narrative", p. 112, for a detailed discussion of the difference between the two.

24. The comparison with the structural principles of *The Arabian Nights* is based on Ferial Jaboury Ghazoul, *The Arabian Nights: A Structural Analysis* (Cairo, National Commission for UNESCO, 1980). This section of the analysis is inspired by her seminal work.

25. Ghazoul, op. cit., p. 36.

26. Ibid., p. 43.

27. René Wellek, *The Attack on Literature* (Brighton, Harvester, 1982), p. 128.

28. Hafez and Cobham, op. cit., p. 133.

29. *Yuḥkā Anna*, p. 77.

30. Ibid., p 79.

31. In his analysis of this story (*Fajr al-Qiṣṣah al-Miṣriyyah*, pp. 91-100), Yaḥyā Ḥaqqi interprets the narrator's comment, "I wish I had been with them", as meaning that the narrator was terrified by the peasants' primitive solutions to the extent of wishing himself dead along with the two victims (p. 99). Ḥaqqi bases his interpretation, it would seem, on Lāshīn's usage of the plural pronoun, *ma'ahum* (them), instead of the singular, *ma'ah* (him), which means "with 'Abd al-Samī'". The narrator's comment does not occur in the story immediately after the description of the killing — there are the peasants' several comments of sanction or disapprobation, and nature's response expressed through frogs croaking and a great stillness — but after the description of how 'Abd al-Samī' made himself a pot of tea and spent the night drinking tea and smoking. Here the narrator's friend comments *"ayy hawl hadhā"* (what a horror), and then comes the narrator's response followed this time by the villagers' reactions of revulsion. This series of comments confirms that the narrator's remark was about 'Abd al-Samī''s conduct after the killing; he was fascinated by the cobbler's ability to stay beside the two corpses throughout the night. The narrator's desire to be with him during that night demonstrates his craving to explore the inner psyche of this character and indicates that he has started to admit his lack of understanding of the villagers' logic. Ḥaqqi's interpretation does not draw its justification from the action. It seems to be based on Lāshīn's usage of the plural pronoun in *ma'ahum*, even though this usage does not justify Ḥaqqi's interpretation, because the pronoun in *ma'ahum* refers to both 'Abd al-Sami' and the two corpses. It

does not mean the two corpses alone; if he meant the latter, Lāshīn would have used the dual pronoun, *ma'ahumā,* and not the plural *ma'ahum,* especially if one knows that Ḥaqqi gives Lāshīn credit for being meticulous in choosing his words (p. 99).

32. G. Lukács, *Writer and Critic,* p. 132.

33. Ferial Jaboury Ghazoul, op. cit., p. 55.

34. N. Hale, *The Realities of Fiction* (London, Macmillan, 1963), p. 35.

35. Yaḥyā Ḥaqqi, op. cit., p. 99.

36. D. Lodge, *Language of Fiction* (London, Routledge & K. Paul, 1966), p. 29.

37. Wellek, op. cit., p. 39.

38. Helmut Bonheim, op. cit., p. 94.

39. Ibid., p. 119.

40. Ibid., p. 120.

41. This type of observation is a result of the analysis of more than 600 short stories from the nineteenth and twentieth centuries studied in Bonheim, op. cit.

42. Bonheim, op. cit., p. 94.

43. For a discussion of the use of the *and*-sentence see, Ibid., pp. 151-3.

44. Michel Foucault, *The Archaeology of Knowledge and the Discourse on Language,* trans. A.M. Sheridan Smith (New York, Pantheon Books, 1972), p. 233.

Bibliography

1. Books in Arabic

'Ā'ishah Taymūr, *Natā'ij al-Aḥwāl fī al-Aqwāl wa-l-Af'āl* (Cairo, al-Maṭba'ah al-Bahiyyah, 1888).
Mir'āt al-Ta'ammul fī al-Umūr (Cairo, al-Maṭba'ah al-Bahiyyah, 1893).
'Abbās Khaḍr, *al-Qiṣṣah al-Qaṣīrah fī Miṣr: Mundh Nash'atihā Ḥattā Sanat 1930* (Cairo, al-Dār al-Qawmiyyah, 1966).
Muḥammad Taymūr: Ḥayātuh wa-Adabuh (Cairo, al-Dār al-Qawmiyyah, 1966).
'Abbās Maḥmūd al-'Aqqād, *Murāja'āt fī al-Adāb wa-l-Funūn* (Cairo, al-Maṭba'ah al-Salafiyyah, 1925).
Muḥammad Abduh (Cairo, Maṭa'bat Miṣr, 1962).
'Abd al-'Azīz al-Disūqī, *Tārīkh al-Ḥarakah al-Naqdiyyah* (Cairo, al-Hay'ah al-Miṣriyyal al-'Āmmah li-l-Kitāb, 1977).
'Abd al-'Azīz Rifa'ī, *Thawrat Miṣr Sanat 1919* (Cairo, Dār al-Kātib al-'Arabī, 1966).
'Abd al-'Aẓīm Muḥammad Ramaḍān, *Taṭawwur al-Ḥarakah al-Waṭaniyyah fī Miṣr: 1918-1936* (Cairo, Dār al-Kātib al-'Arabi, 1968).
'Abd al-Ilāh Aḥmad, *Nash'at al-Qiṣṣah wa-Taṭawwuruhā fī-l-'Irāq* (Baghdad, Maṭba'at Shafīq, 1969).
'Abd al-Karīm al-Ashtar, *al-Nathr al-Mahjarī*, 2 vols. (Cairo, Ma'had al-Dirāsāt al-'Arabiyyah, 1961).
'Abd al-Masīḥ Ḥaddād, *Ḥihāyāt al-Mahjar* (New York, Maṭba'at al-Funūn, 1920).
'Abd al-Muḥsin Ṭaha Badr, *Taṭawwur al-Riwāyah al-'Arabiyyah al-Ḥadīthah fī Miṣr* (Cairo, Dār al-Ma'ārif, 1963).
'Abd al-Qādir Ḥasan Amīn, *al-Qaṣaṣ fī al-Adab al-'Irāqī al-Ḥadīth* (Baghdad, Dār al-Ma'ārif, 1956).
'Abd al-Razzāq al-Hilālī, *Tārīkh al-Ta'līm fī al-'Irāq fī al-'Ahd al-'Uthmānī: 1638-1917* (Baghdad, Sharikat al-Ṭab' wa-l-Nashr al-Ahliyyah, 1959).
'Abd al-Raḥman al-Jabartī, *'Ajā'ib al-Āthār fī al-Tarājim wa-l-Akhbār*, vols. IV and V (Cairo, Dār Iḥyā' al-Kutub al-'Arabiyyah, n.d.).
'Abd al-Raḥman al-Rāfi'ī, *Tārīkh al-Ḥarakah al-Qawmiyyah wa-Taṭawwur Niẓām al-Ḥukm fī Miṣr* (Cairo, Maṭba'at al-Nahḍah, 1929), vol. I.
'Aṣr Ismā'īl (Cairo, Maṭba'at al-Nahḍah, 1932), vols. I and II.
'Abd al-Raḥmān Yāghī, *Ḥayāt al-Adab al-Filasṭīnī al-Ḥadīth: min Awwal al-Nahḍah ḥattā al-Nakbah* (Beirut, al-Maktab al-Tijārī, 1968).
'Abd al-Raḥīm 'Abd al-Raḥmān 'Abd al-Raḥīm, "al-Qaḍā' fī Miṣr al-'Uthmāniyyah", in *Buḥūth fī Tārīkh Miṣr al-Ḥadīth* (Cairo, 'Ayn Shams University, 1976).
'Abd al-Ḥamīd Ibrāhīm, *al-Qiṣṣah al-Miṣriyyah wa-Ṣūrat al-Mujtama' al-Ḥadīth* (Cairo, Dār al-Ma'ārif, 1973).
'Abullah Nadīm, *al-Tankīt wa-l-Tabkīt* (Alexandria, 1881-2).
Al-Ustādh (Cairo 1892-3).

Al-Masāmīr (Cairo, 1894).
Aḥmad Fāris al-Shidyāq, *al-Sāq 'alā al-Sāq Fīmā Huwa al-Fāriyāq* (Beirut, 1855).
Aḥmad Ḥasan al-Zayyāt, "Ḥayāt Ḥāfiẓ"in *Fi Dhikrā Ḥāfiẓ* (Cairo, 1957).
Aḥmad Haykal, *al-Adab al-Qaṣaṣi wa-l-Masraḥi fi Miṣr: Min A'qāb Thawrat 1919 ilā Qiyām al-Ḥarb al-Kubrā al-Thāniyah* (Cairo, Dār al-Ma'ārif, 1970).
Aḥmad Khayri Sa'īd, *al-Dasā'is wa-l-Dimā'* (Cairo, Dar al-Hilāl, 1935).
Aḥmad Ṣādiq Sa'd, *Nash'at al-Takwīn al-Miṣri li-l-Ra'smāliyyah wa-Taṭawwuruh: Fi Ḍaw' al-Namṭ al-Āsyawi li-l-Intāj* (Beirut, Dār al-Ḥadāthah, n.d.).
Tārīkh Miṣr al-Ijtimā'i al-Iqtiṣādi (Beirut, Dār Ibn Khalhūn, 1979).
Taḥawwul al-Takwīn al-Miṣri min al-Namaṭ al-Āsyawi ilā al-Namaṭ al-Ra'smāli (Beirut, Dār al-Ḥadāthah, 1981).
Aḥmad Shawqi, *'Adhrā' al-Hind, aw Tamaddun al-Farā'inah* (Cairo, 1896).
Lādyās aw Ākhir al-Farā'inah (Cairo, 1898).
Waraqat al-Ās (Cairo, 1899).
Shayṭān Bintā'ūr (Cairo, 1901).
'Ali 'Abd al-Rāziq, *Min Āthār Muṣṭafā 'Abd al-Rāziq* (Cairo, Dār al-Ma'ārif, 1957).
'Ali al-Rā'i, *Dirāsāt fi al-Riwāyah al-Miṣriyyah* (Cairo, al-Dar al-Miṣriyyah li-l-Ta'līf, 1965).
Funūn al-Kumīdyā (Cairo, Dār al-Hilāl, 1971).
'Ali al-Ḥadīdi, *'Abdullah al-Nadīm: Khaṭīb al-Waṭaniyyah* (Cairo, Maktabat Miṣr, 1964).
'Ali Jawād al-Ṭāhir, *Maḥmūd Aḥmad al-Sayyid: Rā'id al-Qiṣṣah al-'Irāqiyyah* (Beirut, Dār al-Ādāb, 1969?).
'Ali Mubārak, *'Alam al-Dīn* (Cairo, 1879).
Anwar 'Abd al-Malik, *Nahḍat Miṣr* (Cairo, al-Hay'ah al-Miṣriyyah al-'Āmmah li-l-Kitāb, 1983).
Anwar al-Jundi, *Qiṣṣat Maḥmūd Taymūr* (Cairo, Dār Iḥyā' al-Kutub al-'Arabiyyah, 1951).
Anīs al-Maqdisi, *al-Ittijāhāt al-Adabiyyah fi al-'Ālam al-'Arabi al-Ḥadīth* (Beirut, Dār al-'Ilm lil-Malāyīn, 1952).
Fihris al-Khizānah al-Taymūriyyah (Cairo, Maṭba'at Dār al-Kutub al-Miṣriyyah, 1948).
Fihris Maktabat 'Umar Makram (Cairo, Maṭba'at Dār al-Kutub al-Miṣriyyah, 1933).
Filīb Ṭarrāzi, *Tārīkh al-Ṣiḥāfah al-'Arabiyyah* (Beirut, al-Maṭba'ah al-Adabiyyah, 1913).
Fārūq Khūrshīd, *Fi al-Riwāyah al-'Arabiyyah fi 'Aṣr al-Tajmī'* (Cairo, Dār al-Qalam, 1960).
George Hannā, *Qabl al-Maghīb: Tajārib wa-Dhikrāyāt min Ḥayāti* (Beirut, Dār al-Thaqāfah, [1960]).
Ḥasan al-Fiqi, *al-Tārīkh al-Thaqāfi lil-Ta'līm fi Miṣr* (Cairo, Dār al-Ma'ārif, 1971).
Ḥaydar Ḥāj Ismā'īl, *Francis Marrāsh* (London, Riad El-Rayyes Books, 1989).
Ḥilmi Marzūq, *Taṭawwur al-Naqd wa-l-Tafkīr al-Adabi al-Ḥadīth fi al-Rub' al-Awwal min al-Qarn al-'Ishrīn* (Cairo, Dār al-Ma'ārif, 1966).
Ḥusain Fawzi al-Najjār, *Rafā'ah al-Ṭahṭāwi* (Cairo, al-Dār al-Qawmiyyah, 1966).
Ḥāfiẓ Ibrāhīm, *Layāli Saṭīḥ* (Cairo, 1906)
Ibrāhīm 'Abduh, *Taṭawwur al-Ṣiḥāfah al-Miṣriyyah: 1797-1951* (Cairo, Maktabat al-Ādāb, 1951).
'Īsā 'Ubaid, *Iḥsān Hānim* (Cairo, 1921).
Thurayyā (Cairo, 1922).
Isḥāq Mūsā al-Ḥusaini, *al-Naqd al-Adabi al-Mu'āṣir fi al-Rub' al-Awwal min al-Qarn al-'Ishrīn* (Cairo, Dār al-Ma'rifah, 1967).
Jamāl Ḥamdān, *Shakhṣiyyat Miṣr*, 4 vols. (Cairo, 'Ālam al-Kutub, 1968-80).
Jamīl Sa'īd, *Naẓarāt fi al-Tayyārāt al-Adabiyyah al-Ḥadīthah fi al-'Irāq* (Cairo, Maṭbū'āt Ma'had al-Dirāsāt al-'Arabiyyah, 1954).
Jamīl Sulṭān, *Fann al-Qiṣṣah wa-l-Maqāmah* (Beirut, Dār al-Anwār, 1967).

Jibrān Khalīl Jibrān, *'Arā'is al-Murūj* (Beirut, Dār al-Andalus, 1906).
Al-Arwāḥ al-Mutamarridah (Beirut, Dār al-Andalus, 1908).
Al-Ajniḥah al-Mutakassirah (Beirut, 1912).
Jurji Zaydān, *Tārīkh Ādāb al-Lughah al-'Arabiyyah,* 4 vols. (Cairo, Maṭba'at al-Hilāl, 1914).
Jāk Tājir, *Ḥarakat al-Tarjamah fi Miṣr Khilāl al-Qarn al-Tāsi' 'Ashar* (Cairo, Dār al-Ma'ārif, 1945)
Jūrj Ṣaydaḥ, *Adabunā wa-Udabā'una fi al-Mahājir al-Amrīkiyyah* (Beirut, al-Maktabah al-Ahliyyah, 1957).
Kamāl al-Yāziji, *Ruwwād al-Nahḍah al-Ḥadīthah fi Lubnān* (Beirut, Maktabat Ra's Beirut, 1961).
Khalīl Bydas, *Masāriḥ al-Adhhān* (Cairo, al-Maṭba'ah al-'Aṣriyyah, 1924).
Labībah Hāshim, *Qalb al-Rajul* (Beirut, 1904).
Liwīs 'Awaḍ, *al-Mu'aththirāt al-Ajnabiyyah fi al-Adab al-'Arabi al-Ḥadīth* (Cairo, Dār al-Ma'rifah, 1963).
Dirāsāt fi Adabinā al-Ḥadīth (Cairo, Dār al-Ma'rifah, 1961).
Maḥmūd al-'Abṭah, *Maḥmūd Aḥmad al-Sayyid* (Baghdad, Maṭba'at al-Ummah, 1961).
Maḥmūd Aḥmad al-Sayyid, *Fi Sabīl al-Zawāj* (Baghdad, 1921).
Al-Nakabāt (Baghdad, 1922).
Jalāl Khālid (Baghdad, 1928).
Al-Ṭalā'i' (Baghdad, 1929).
Fi Sā' min al-Zaman (Baghdad, 1935).
Maḥmūd Bin Sharīf, *Adab Maḥmūd Taymūr li-l-Ḥaqīqah wa-l-Tārīkh* (Cairo, Maṭba'at al-Kilāni al-Ṣaghīr, n.d.).
Maḥmūd Muḥammad Shākir, *al-Mutanabbi* (Cairo, Maktabat al-Khānji, 1964).
Risāla fi al-Ṭarīq ila Thaqāfatina (Cairo, Dār al-Hilāl, 1987).
Maḥmūd Taymūr, *al-Shaikh Jum'ah* (Cairo, 1925).
'Amm Mitwalli (Cairo, 1926).
Al-Shaikh Sayyid al-'Abīṭ (Cairo, 1926).
Rajab Afandi (Cairo, 1928).
Al-Ḥājj Shalabi (Cairo, 1930).
Abū-'Ali 'Āmil Artist (Cairo, 1934).
Nushū' al-Qiṣṣah wa Taṭawwuruha (Cairo, al-Maṭba'ah al-Salafiyyah, 1936).
Maḥmūd Ṭāhir Lāshīn, *Sukhriyat al-Nāy* (Cairo, 1927).
Yuḥkā Anna (Cairo, 1929).
Ḥawwā' Bilā Ādam (serialized in *al-Hilāl,* June and July 1933).
Al-Niqāb al-Ṭā'ir (Cairo, 1940).
Mīkhā'īl Nu'aymah, *Mudhakkirāt al-Arqash* (Beirut, 1917).
al-Ābā' wa-l-Banūn (1917).
Jibrān Khalīl Jibrān: Ḥayatuh, Mawtuh, Adabuh, Fannuh (Beirut, Dār Ṣādir, 1934).
Kān mā Kān (Beirut, Dār Ṣādir, 1937).
Liqā' (1948).
Sab'ūn, 2 vols. (Beirut, Dār Ṣādir, 1957).
Muḥammad Anīs, *Thawrat 23 Yūlū 1952 wa-Uṣūluhā al-Tārīkhiyyah* (Cairo, Dār al-Nahḍah al-'Arabiyyah, 1964).
Muḥammad Ibrāhīm al-Muwailiḥi, *Ḥadīth 'Īsā Ibn Hishām: Aw Fatrah min al-Zaman* (Cairo, 1898)
Muḥammad Luṭfi Jum'ah, *Fi Buyūt al-Nās* (Cairo, 1904).
Fi Wādi al-Humūm (Cairo, 1905).
Layāli al-Rūḥ al-Ḥā'ir (Cairo, 1912).
Muḥammad Muḥammad Ḥusain, *al-Ittijāhāt al-Waṭaniyyah fi-l-Adab al-Mu'āṣir,* 2 vols. (Cairo, al-Maṭba'ah al-Namūdhajiyyah, 1956).
Muḥammad Rushdi Ḥasan, *Athar al-Maqāmah fi Nash'at al-Qiṣṣah al-Miṣriyyah al-Ḥadīthah* (Cairo, al-Hay'ah al-Miṣriyyah al-'Āmmah li-l-Kitāb, 1974).
Muḥammad Taymūr, *al-'Uṣfūr fi al-Qafaṣ* (Cairo, 1918).
Abd al-Sattār Effendi (Cairo, 1918).

Mā Tarāh al-'Uyūn (Cairo, Maṭba'at al-I'timād, 1922).
Wamīḍ al-Rūḥ (Cairo, Maṭba'at al-I'timād, 1922).
Muḥammad Yūsuf Najm, *al-Masraḥiyya fi al-Adab al-'Arabi al-Ḥadīth* (Beirut, 1956).
Al-Qiṣṣah fi al-Adab al-'Arabi al-Ḥadīth (Beirut, al-Maktabah al-Ahliyyah, 1958).
"Aḥmad Fāris al-Shidyāq rā'id al-Mujaddidīn fi al-Adab al-'Arabi al-Ḥadīth" MA thesis submitted to, the American University of Beirut, 1948.
Muḥammad Ṭal'at 'Īsā, *Atbā' Sān Simon: Falsafatuhum al-Ijtimā'iyyah wa-Taṭbīquha fi Miṣr* (Cairo, al-Dār al-Qawmiyyah, 1957).
Muṣṭafā Luṭfi al-Manfalūṭi, *al-Naẓarāt* (1910-12).
Al-'Abarāt (Cairo, 1915).
Muṣṭafā Ṣādiq al-Rāfi'i, *al-Masākīn* (Cairo, 1917).
Na'īm al-Yāfi, *al-Taṭawwur al-Fanni li-Shakl al-Qiṣṣah al-Qaṣīrah fi-l-Adab al-Shāmi al-Ḥadīth* (Damascus, Manshūrāt Ittiḥād al-Kuttāb al-'Arab, 1982).
Najāti Ṣidqi, *Pushkin* (Cairo, Dār al-Ma'ārif, 1945).
Najīb Maḥfūẓ, *Zuqāq al-Madaq* (Cairo, Maktabat Miṣr, 1946).
Nazīh al-Ḥakīm, *Maḥmūd Taymūr Rā'id al-Qiṣṣah* (Cairo, Maṭba'at al-Nīl, 1944).
Nāji Najīb, *Kitāb al-Aḥzān: Fuṣūl fi al-Tārīkh al-Nafsi wa-l-Ijtimā'i li-l-Fi'āt al-Mutawasiṭah al-'Arabiyyah* (Beirut, Dār al-Tanwīr, 1983).
P.L. Cheikho, *al-Ādāb al-'Arabiyyah fi al-Qarn al-Tāsi' 'Ashar* (Beirut, al-Maṭba'ah al-Yasū'iyyah, 1910), 2 vols.
Rif'at al-Sa'īd, *al-Asās al-Ijtimā'i li-l-Thawrah al-'Urābiyyah* (Cairo, Dār al-Thaqāfah al-Jadīdah, 1967).
Rūfā'īl Buṭṭi, *Tārīkh al-Ṣiḥāfah fi al-'Irāq* (Cairo, Dār al-Ma'rifah, 1955).
Ṣabri Ḥāfiẓ, *al-Qiṣṣah al-'Arabiyyah wa-l-Ḥadāthah: Dirāsah fi Āliyyāt Taghayyur al-Ḥasāsiyah al-Adabiyyah* (Baghdad, Wizārat al-Thaqāfah, 1990).
Ṣalāḥ 'Īsā, *al-Thawrah al-'Urābiyyah* (Beirut, al-Mu'assasah al-'Arabiyyah li-l-Dirāsāt wa-l-Nashr, 1972).
Ṣubḥi Waḥīdah, *Fi Uṣūl al-Mas'alah al-Miṣriyyah* (Cairo, Maktabat al-Anglū, 1958).
Ṣāliḥ Ḥamdi Ḥammād, *Aḥsan al-Qaṣaṣ* (Cairo, 1910).
Ibnati Saniyyah (Cairo, 1910).
Sayyid Ḥāmid al-Nassāj, *Taṭawwur Fann al-Qiṣṣah al-Qaṣīrah fi Miṣr* (Cairo, Dār al-Kātib al-'Arabi, 1968).
Shawqi Ḍayf, *al-Adab al-'Arabi al-Mu'āṣir fi-Miṣr* (Cairo, Dār al-Ma'ārif, 1961).
Shiḥātah 'Ubaid, *'Dars Mu'lim* (Cairo, 1922).
Shukri Muḥammad 'Ayyād, *al-Qiṣṣah al-Qaṣīrah fi Miṣr: Dirāsah fi Ta'ṣīl finn Adabi* (Cairo, Dār al-Ma'rifah, 1968).
Suhayl Idrīs, *Muḥāḍarāt 'an al-Qiṣṣah fi Lubnān* (Cairo, Dār al-Ma'rifah, 1957).
Ṭaha 'Abd al-Bāqi Surūr, *al-Taṣawwuf al-Islāmi wa-l-Imām al-Sha'rāni* (Cairo, Maktabat al-Nahḍah, 1955).
Ṭaha Ḥusain, *al-Ayyām*, vol.I (Cairo, Dar al-Ma'ārif, 1929).
Ṭal'at Ḥarb, *'Ilāj Miṣr al-Iqtiṣādi wa-Inshā' Bank lil-Miṣriyyīn* (Cairo, 1913).
Tawfīq al-Ṭawīl, *al-Sha'rāni: Imām al-Taṣawwuf fi 'Aṣrih* (Cairo, 'Īsā al-Bābi al-Ḥalabi, 1945).
'Umar al-Daqqāq, *Funūn al-Adab al-Mu'āṣir fi Sūriyyah* (Beirut, Dār al-Sharq, 1971).
'Umar al-Ṭālib, *al-Fann al-Qaṣaṣi fi al-Adab al-'Arabi al-Ḥadīth: al-Riwāyah al-'Arabiyyah fi al-'Irāq* (Baghdad, Maktabat al-Andalus, 1971).
Yaḥyā Ḥaqqi, *Fajr al-Qiṣṣah al-Miṣriyyah* (Cairo, Dār al-Qalam, 1960).
Khallīhā 'alā al-Lah (Cairo, Dār al-Taḥrīr, 1956).
Khuṭuwāt fi al-Naqd (Cairo, Dār al-'Urūbah, 1960).
Introduction to Maḥmūd Ṭāhir Lāshīn, *Sukhriyat al-Nāy* (Cairo, Dār al-Kātib al-'Arabi, 1963?).
Introduction to the new edition of, *Qindīl Umm Hāshim* (Cairo, al-Hay'h al-Miṣriyyah al-'Āmmah lil-Kitāb, 1975).

Yusūf Ilyās Sarkīs, *Mu'jam al-Maṭbū'āt al-'Arabiyyah wa-l-Mu'arrabah* (Cairo, Maṭba'at Sarkīs, 1928).
Yūsuf 'Izz al-Dīn, *al-Qiṣṣah wa-Taṭawwuruhā fi al-'Irāq* (Cairo, Ma'had al-Buḥūth wa-l-Dirāsāt al-'Arabiyyah, 1974).
Yūsuf As'ad Dāghir, *Qāmūs al-Ṣiḥāfah al-Lubnāniyyah: 1858-1974* (Beirut, Lebanese University Press, 1978).
Zaki Mubārak, *al-Taṣawwuf al-Islāmi fi al-Adab wa-l-Akhlāq*, 2 vols. (Cairo, Maṭba'at al-Risālah, 1946).

2. *Books in Other Languages*

Abdel Wahab, Farouq (ed.), *Modern Egyptian Drama: an Anthology* (Minneapolis, Bibliotheca Islamica, 1974).
Abrams, M.H., *The Mirror and the Lamp: Romantic Theory and Critical Tradition* (Oxford, Oxford University Press, 1953).
Adams, Charles, *Islam and Modernisation in Egypt, A Study of the Modern Reform Movement Inaugurated by Muhammad Abdu* (London, 1930)
Al-Biheiry, Kawthar A, *L'Influence de la littérature française sur le roman arabe* (Quebec, 1980).
Al-Khozai, Mohamed A., *The Development of Early Arabic Drama: 1847-1900* (London, Longman,1984).
Al-Sayyid, Afaf Lutfi, *Egypt and Cromer: A Study in the Anglo-Egyptian Relations* (London, John Murry, 1968).
Ali, Muhsin Jassim, "The Socio-Aesthetics of Contemporary Arabic Fiction", *Journal of Arabic Literature* (*JAL*), vol. XIV.
Allen, Roger, *Muḥammad Ibrāhīm al-Muwayliḥi: A Study of Ḥadīth 'Īsā Ibn Hishām*, on Microfiche, (New York, Albany State University, 1974).
The Arabic Novel: An Historical Introduction (Manchester, MUP, 1982)
Allot, Miriam, *Novelists on the Novel* (London, Routledge and Kegan Paul, 1959).
Antonius, George, *The Arab Awakening: The Story of the Arab National Movement* (London, Hamish Hamilton, 1938).
Aristotle, *The Poetics*, 60a, 22-26.
Atiyah, Aziz S., *A History of Eastern Christianity* (London, Methuen, 1968).
Aycock, Wendell M. (ed.), *The Teller and the Tale: Aspects of the Short Story* (Lubbock, Texas, Texas Tech Press, 1982).
Badawi, M.M., *Early Arabic Drama* (Cambridge, Cambridge University Press, 1988).
Modern Arabic Drama in Egypt (Cambridge, Cambridge University Press, 1987).
Modern Arabic Literature and the West (London, Ithaca Press, 1985).
Baer, Gabriel, "Social Change in Egypt: 1800-1914"in P.M. Holt.
Bakhtin, M.M., *Problems of Dostoevsky's Poetics*, trans. Caryl Emerson (Manchester, Manchester University Press, 1984).
The Dialogic Imagination: Four Essays, ed. Michael Holquist, trans. Caryl Emerson and Michael Holquist (Austin, University of Texas Press, 1981).
Marxism and the Philosophy of Language, with V.N. Volosinov, trans. L. Matejka and I.R. Titunik (New York, Simenar Press, 1973).
The Formal Method in Literary Scholarship: A Critical Introduction to Sociological Poetics, with P.M. Medvedev (Cambridge, Mass., Harvard University Press, 1985).
Barthes, Roland, *S/Z*, trans. Richard Miller (New York, Hill & Wang, 1974).
Image, Music, Text, trans., Stephen Heath (New York, Hill & Wang, 1977).
Beachcroft, T.O., *The Modest Art: A Survey of the Short Story in English* (London, Oxford University Press, 1968).
Benjamin, Walter, *Illuminations*, trans. Harry Zohn (London, Fontana/Collins, 1973).
Berque, Jacques, *Cultural Expression in Arab Society Today* (Austin, University of Texas Press, 1978).

Egypt: Imperialism and Revolution, trans. Jean Stewart (London, Faber and Faber, 1972).
"The Establishment of the Colonial Economy"in William R. Polk and Richard L. Chambers.
Beyerl, Jan, *The Style of the Modern Arabic Short Story* (Prague, Charles University Press, 1971).
Bonheim, Helmut, *The Narrative Modes: Techniques of the Short Story* (Cambridge, D.S. Brewer, 1982).
Booth, Wayne, *The Rhetoric of Fiction* (Chicago, University of Chicago Press, 1961).
Bottomore, T.B., *Elites and Society* (London, Penguin Books, 1973).
Bradbury, Malcolm, *What is a Novel?* (Manchester, Manchester University Press, 1969).
Brugman, J., *An Introduction to the History of Modern Arabic Literature* (Lieden, Brill, 1984).
Bullata, Isa (ed), *Critical Perspective on Modern Arabic Literature* (New York, Three Continents Press, 1980).
Burke, Kenneth, *Counter-Statement* (Berkeley, University of California Press, 1968).
Cachia, Pierre, *Ṭaha Ḥusayn: His Place in the Egyptian Literary Renaissance* (London, Luzac, 1956).
Charmes, Gabriel, *Voyage en Syrie.*
Chatman, Seymour, *Story and Discourse* (Ithaca, New York, Cornell University Press, 1978).
Chevallier, Dominique, "Western Development and Eastern Crisis in the Mid-Nineteenth Century: Syria Confronted with the European Economy"in William R. Polk and Richard L. Chambers.
Coleridge, *Biographia Literaria,* ed. Shawcross (London, 1907), i.
Corelli, Marie, *The Romance of Two Worlds* (1886).
Croce, Benedetto, *Estetica,* 2nd edition (Bari, 1906).
Culler, Jonathan, *The Pursuit of Signs: Semiotics, Literature, Deconstruction* (London, Routledge & Kegan Paul, 1981).
Daiches, David, *Critical Approaches to Literature* (London, Longman, 1956).
A Study of Literature (London, Andre Deutsch, 1968).
Erlich, Victor, *Russian Formalism: History and Doctrine* (New Haven, Yale University Press, 1965).
Ferguson, J.D.L., *Themes and Variations in the Short Story* (New York Books for Libraries Press, 1972).
Foucault, Michel, *Les mots et les choses,* translated into English as *The Order of Things; An Archaeology of the Human Sciences* (New York, Vintage Books, 1970).
The Archaeology of Knowledge and the Discourse on Language, trans. A.M. Sheridan Smith, (New York, Pantheon Books, 1972).
Friedman, Norman, *Form and Meaning in Fiction* (Athens, Georgia, The University of Georgia Press, 1975).
Frow, John, *Marxism and Literary History* (Oxford, Basil Blackwell, 1986).
Frye, Northrop, *Anatomy of Criticism* (Princeton, N.J., Princeton University Press, 1957).
Genette, Gerard, *Figures,* Vols. I, II and particularly III (Paris, Éditions du Seuil, 1966).
Nouveau discours du récit (Paris, Éditions du Seuil, 1983).
Ghazoul, Ferial Jaboury, *The Arabian Nights: A Structural Analysis* (Cairo, National Commission for UNESCO, 1980).
Gibb, H.A.R., "The Nineteen Century", *Bulletin of the School of Oriental and African Studies (BSOAS),* Vols IV (1926-8).
"Manfaluti and the New Style", *BSOAS,* Vol V (1928-30).
"The Egyptian Novel", *BSOAS,* Vol VII (1933-35).

Giddens, Anthony, *New Rules of Sociological Method (*London, Hutchinson, 1976).

Girard, René, *Mensonge romantique et vérité romanesque* (Éditions Bernard Grasset, 1961) translated into English as *Deceit, Desire, and the Novel,* by Yvonne Freccero (Baltimore, Johns Hopkins University Press, 1965).

Goldmann, Lucien, *Le Dieu Câché* (Paris, Gallimard, 1956), English translation as *The Hidden God,* trans. Philip Thody (London, Routledge& Kegan Paul, 1964).

Method in the Sociology of Literature, trans. William Q. Boelhower (Oxford, Basil Blackwell, 1980).

*Pour une sociologie du roman (*Paris, Éditions Gallimard, 1964), English translation as *Towards a Sociology of the Novel,* trans. Alan Sheridan (London, Tavistock Publications, 1975).

Gran, Peter, *Islamic Roots of Capitalism: Egypt 1760-1840 (*Austin, University of Texas, 1979).

Greimas, A.J. & Courtés, J., *Semiotics and Language: An Analytical Dictionary,* trans L. Crist & others (Bloomington, Indiana University Press, 1982).

Hafez, Sabry, and Cobham, Catherine (ed.), *A Reader of Modern Arabic Short Stories (*London, Saqi Books, 1988).

Hale, N., *The Realities of Fiction (*London, Macmillan, 1963).

Heyworth-Dunne, J., *An Introduction to the History of Education in Modern Egypt (*London, Luzac, 1938), pp. 96-285.

Hildick, W., *13 Types of Narrative (*London, Macmillan, I968).

Hirsch, E.D., *Validity in Interpretation (*New Haven, Yale University Press, 1967).

Hitti, Philip, *The Middle East in History (*Princeton, D. Van Nostrand, 1961).

Holt, P.M. (ed.), *Political and Social Change in Modern Egypt (*Oxford, Oxford University Press, 1968).

Hopwood, Derek, *The Russian Presence in Syria and Palestine: 1843-1914 (*Oxford, Clarendon Press, 1969).

Hourani, Albert, *Arabic Thought in the Liberal Age (*Oxford, Oxford University Press, 1962).

"Ottoman Reform and the Politics of Notables", in William R. Polk and Richard L. Chambers.

Huart, Clément, *A History of Arabic Literature (*Beirut, Khayats, 1966).

Issawi, Charles, "Economic Change and Urbanization in the Middle East,"in Ira M. Lapidus (ed.), *Middle Eastern Cities.*

Jameson, Fredric, *The Political Unconscious: Narrative as a Socially Symbolic Act (*London, Methuen, 1981).

Jauss, Hans Robert, *Towards an Aesthetic of Reception,* trans. Timothy Bahti (Minneapolis, University of Minnesota Press, 1982).

Kilpatrick, Hilary, *The Modern Egyptian Novel: A Study in Social Criticism,* (London, Ithaca Press, 1974).

Kohn, Hans, *Western Civilization in the Near East (*London, George Routledge & Sons, 1936).

Krachkovski, *Nad arabskimi rukopisyami (*Moscow, 1946).

Kristeva, Julia, *Semeiotikè: Recherches pour une sémanalyse (*Paris, Éditions du Seuil, 1969).

Landes, David S., *Bankers and Pashas: International Finance and Economic Imperialism in Egypt* (London, 1958).

Lane, Edward William, *Manners and Customs of Modern Egyptians (*London, 1836).

Lapidus, Ira M. (ed.), *Middle Eastern Cities: A Symposium on Ancient, Islamic and Contemporary Middle Eastern Urbanism (*Berkeley, University of California Press, 1969).

*A History of Islamic Societies (*Cambridge, Cambridge University Press, 1988).

Leavis, Q.D., *Fiction and the Reading Public (*London, Chatto & Windus, 1965).

Locke, *Essay Concerning Human Understanding* (1690).
Lodge, David, *Language of Fiction* (London, Routledge & Kegan Paul, 1966).
Lucas, F.L., *Style* (London, Cassell, 1955).
Lukács, Georg, *Writer and Critic*, trans. A. Khan (London, Merlin Press, 1970).
The Theory of the Novel, trans. Anna Bostock (London, Merlin Press, 1971).
Mabro, Robert, *The Egyptian Economy* (Oxford, Clarendon Press, 1974).
Mannheim, Karl, *Ideology and Utopia* (London, Routledge & Kegan Paul, 1960).
Mansfield, Peter, *The British in Egypt* (London, Weidenfeld and Nicolson, 1971).
Manzalaoui, Mahmoud (ed.), *Arab Writing Today: The Short Story* (Cairo, American Research Center in Egypt, 1970).
Arab Writing Today: Drama (Cairo, American Research Center in Egypt, 1977).
Martin, Wallace, *Recent Theories of Narrative* (Ithaca, Cornell University Press, 1986).
May, Charles E. (ed.), *Short Story Theories* (Ohio, Ohio University Press, 1976).
Medvedev, P.M., *The Formal Method in Literary Scholarship: A Critical Introduction to Sociological Poetics*, with M.M. Bakhtin (Cambridge, Massachusetts, Harvard University Press, 1985).
Miller, Owen, "Intertextual Identity,"in *Identity of the Literary Text* (ed.) Mario Valdés & Owen Miller (Toronto, University of Toronto Press, 1985).
Mirrielaes, E.R., *The Story Writer* (Boston, Little Brown, 1939).
Moosa, Matti, *The Origins of Modern Arabic Fiction* (Washington, Three Continents Press, 1983).
O'Brien, Patrick, "The Long-term Growth of Agricultural Production in Egypt: 1821-1962", in P.M. Holt.
O'Connor, Frank, *The Lonely Voice: A Study of the Short Story* (London, 1964).
O'Faolain, S., *The Short Story* (London, Collins, 1948).
Ostle, R.C. (ed.), *Studies in Modern Arabic Literature* (Warminster, Aris & Philips, 1976).
"The City in Modern Arabic Literature", *BSOAS* vol. XLIX, part 1, 1986, pp.193-202.
Peres, Henry, "Le Roman, le conte et la nouvelle dans la littérature arabe moderne", *Annales de l'Institut d'Études Orientales*, vol. 3, 1937.
Polk, William R., and Chambers, Richard L. (ed.), *Beginning of Modernization in the Middle East: The Nineteenth Century* (Chicago, The University of Chicago Press, 1968).
Prawer, S.S., *Comparative Literary Studies* (London, Duckworth, 1973).
Propp, V., *Morphology of the Folktale*, trans. L. Scott and L. Wagner (Austin, University of Texas Press, 1968).
Richards, I.A., *Principles of Literary Criticism* (London, Routledge & Kegan Paul, 1924).
Rivoyre, Denis de, *Les vrais Arabes et leur pays*.
Sabry, Muhammad, *Genèse de l'esprit national* (Paris, 1924).
Said, Edward, *Beginnings: Intention and Method* (New York, Columbia University Press, 1985).
"Introduction"to *Days of Dust*, by Halim Barakat, trans. Trevor Le Gassick (Wilmette, Illinois, The Medina University Press, 1974).
"Molestation and Authority in Narrative Fiction"in J. Hillis Miller (ed.), *Aspects of Narrative* (New York, Colombia University Press, 1971).
The World, the Text, and the Critic (Cambridge, Massachusetts, 1983).
Scholes, Robert, *Elements of Fiction* (New York, Oxford University Press, 1968).
Schulze, Reinhard, "Mass Culture and Islamic Cultural Production in 19th Century Middle East", in George Stauth, Sami Zubaida (ed.), *Mass Culture, Popular Culture and Social Life in the Middle East* (Frankfurt am Main, Campus Verlag, 1987).
Schücking, Levin L., *The Sociology of Literary Taste* (London, Routledge & Kegan Paul, 1966).
Somerset Maugham, W., *Points of View* (London, Heinemann, 1958).

Spearman, Diana, *The Novel and Society* (London, Routledge & Kegan Paul, 1966).
Stephen, Leslie, *English Literature and Society in the Eighteenth Century* (London, 1904).
Steppat, Fritz, "National Education Projects in Egypt before the British Occupation", in William R. Polk and Richard L. Chambers.
Swingewood, Alan, *Sociological Poetics and Aesthetic Theory* (London, Macmillan, 1986).
Tomiche, Nada, *Histoire de la Littérature Romanesque de l'Egypte Moderne* (Paris, 1981).
"The Situation of Egyptian Women in the First Half of the Nineteenth Century", in William R. Polk and Richard L. Chambers.
Vatikiotis, P.J., *The Modern History of Egypt* (London, Weidenfeld and Nicolson, 1969).
Volosinov, V.N., *Marxism and the Philosophy of Language*, with M.M. Bakhtin, trans. L. Matejka and I.R. Titunik (New York, Simenar Press, 1973).
Watt, Ian, *The Rise of the Novel* (Berkeley, University of California Press, 1957).
Weedon, Chris, *Feminist Practice and Poststructuralist Theory* (Oxford, Basil Blackwell, 1987).
Wellek, René, *The Attack on Literature* (Brighton, The Harvester Press, 1982).
Wimsat, W.K., *The Verbal Icon: Studies in the Meaning of Poetry* (London, Methuen, 1970), pp. 3-18.
Wolff, Janet, *Aesthetics and the Sociology of Art* (London, George Allen and Unwin, 1983).
The Social Production of Art (London, Macmillan, 1982).
Wright Mills, C., *Power, Politics, and People*, the Collected Essays, ed. Irving Louis Horowitz (Oxford, Oxford University Press, 1963).
The Sociological Imagination (London, Penguin Books, 1970).
Yarmolinsky, A., *Letters of Anton Chekhov* (New York, The Viking Press, 1973).
Zeine, Zeine N., *Arab Turkish Relations and the Emergence of Arab Nationalism* (Beirut, 1958).

3. Periodicals

Al-'Iraq (Baghdad, 1921-2).
Al-Adīb (Beirut, 1946-9).
Al-Ahrām (Cairo, 1881-1965).
Al-Akhbār (Cairo, 1920s).
Al-Bayān (Baghdad, 1897).
Al-Ḍiyā' (Beirut / Cairo, 1898-1902).
Al-Fajr (Cairo, 8 January 1925-13 January 1927)
Al-Funūn (Cairo, 1924).
Al-Ḥadīth (Cairo, 1920-8).
Al-Ḥadīth (Aleppo, 1944).
Al-Ḥāṣid (Baghdad, 1935).
Al-Hilāl (Cairo, 1897- 1934).
Al-Istiqlāl (Baghdad, 1927).
Al-Jadīd (Cairo, 1920-2)
Al-Jarīdah (Cairo, 1910).
Al-Jinān (Beirut, 1870-4).
Al-Lisān (Baghdad, 1919).
Al-Liwā' (Cairo, 1925).
Al-Ma'raḍ (Baghdad, 1926).
Al-Ma'rifah (Damascus, 80).
Al-Majallah al-Jadīdah (Cairo, 1920-34).
Al-Masā' (Cairo, 1962).
Al-Mu'ayyad (Cairo, 1910).
Al-Muqtaṭaf (Cairo, 1883-25).
Al-Nafā'is al-'Aṣriyyah (Jerusalem, 1908-23).

Al-Raqīb (Baghdad, 1911).
Al-Rāwi (Cairo, 1922-4).
Al-Ṣaḥīfah (Baghdad, 1925).
Al-Sha'b (Baghdad, 1910).
Al-Shabāb (Cairo, 1921).
Al-Siyāsah al-Usbū'iyyah (Cairo, 1928-30).
Al-Sufūr (Cairo, 1915-7).
Al-Tankīt wa-l-Tabkīt (Alexandria, 1881-2).
Al-Ustādh (Cairo, 1892-3).
Dār al-Salām (Baghdad, 1919-20).
Jarīdat Miṣr (Cairo, 1931).
Kawkab al-Sharq (Cairo, 1926-30).
Kenyon Review (1968-70).
Lughat al-'Arab (Baghdad, 1913-4).
Majallat al-Fukāhah (Cairo, 1902-5).
Nafīr Sūriyyā (Beirut, 1860-1).
Rūz al-Yūsuf (Cairo, 1925-31).
Ṣadā Bābil (Baghdad, 1910).
Ṣaḥīfat al-Jāmi'ah al-Miṣriyyah (Cairo, 1925).
Shahrazād (Cairo, 1920-4).
Tanwīr al-Afkār (Baghdad, 1909).
The Egyptian Gazette (Cairo, 1925).

Index

Abāẓah, Sulaymān 81
'Abbās Halîm, Khedive of Egypt 77
'Abbās I, Khedive of Egypt 48
'Abbūd, Mārūn 171
'Abd al-Malik, Anwar 60
'Abd al-Raḥman 53–4
'Abd al-Rāziq, 'Ali 102; *al-Islām wa-'Uṣūl al-Ḥukm* 102
'Abd al-Rāziq, Ḥasan 149
'Abd al-Rāziq, Muṣṭafa 15, 149–52; *'Abd al-'Alîm* 151–2; *Ḥādithah Faẓî'ah* 151; *Ḥasrah 'alā al-Shabāb* 151; *Ḥubb al-Nisā' wa Ḥubb al-Māl* 151; *'Ibrah ba'd Ibtisām* 151; *Min Tadhkār al-Māḍi* 151; *Ṣaḥîfah fi al-Ṭarîq* 151
'Abduh, Muhammad 61, 75, 100, 102, 110, 145, 149; *Risālat al-Tawḥîd* 100
'Abduh, Sa'id 161
'Abduh, Ṭanyūs 90, 108
Abdül-Ḥamîd, Sultan 76, 132
al-'Abṭah, Maḥmūd 191
Abū-Ghanîmah, Ṣubḥi 161, 171
Abū-l-Barakāt 110
Abū-l-Fawz al-Suwaydi 110
Abū-l-Rūs, Idāl 95, 96
Abū-l-Su'ūd, 'Abdullah 88, 97
Abyaḍ, Jūrj 158
al-Afghāni, Jamāl al-Dîn 75, 115, 116, 120
al-Aḥdab, Ibrāhîm 110
Aḥmad, 'Abd al-Ilāh 140, 192
Aḥmad Pasha al-Jazzār 42
Al-Ahrām 110
Alexander II, Tsar 91–2
Alf Laylah 171
Alf Laylah wa-Laylah (The Arabian Nights) 14, 19, 21–2, 107, 109, 127, 131, 136, 140, 141, 156, 250–1, 259
'Ali 146
'Ali, Muḥammad Kurd 90
Almaẓ 57
al-Alūsi, Abū-l-Thanā' Maḥmūd 110
al-Alūsi, Khayr al-Dîn, *al-Iṣābah fi Man' al-Nisā' min al-Kitābah* 70
Amîn, 'Aṭā' 141; *'Āqibat al-Ḥayāh* 141; *Lawḥah min Alwāḥ al-Dahr* 141; *Ru'yā Ṣādiqah* 141; *Waqfah 'alā Diyālā* 141
al-Amîn, 'Abd al-Wahhāb 161
Amîn, Qāsim 67, 70, 71, 158, 190; *al-Mar'ah al-Jadîdah* 70; *Taḥrîr al-Mar'ah* 70
al-Amîr Riḍwan al-Jalfi 41
Antāki, 'Abd al-Masîḥ 156
'Antar 106
Antonius, George 72
Anṭūn, Faraḥ 90, 156
Anwar, 'Ali 156
al-'Aqîli, Ḥasan ibn Ibrāhîm al-Jabarti 39
al-'Aqqād, 'Abbās Maḥmud 50, 145, 159, 161, 190; *al-Dîwān* 159
al-'Aqqād, Muḥammad 57

Arabian Nights, The see Alf Laylah wa Laylah
'Arîḍah, Nasîb 95, 171, 175
'Ārif, Muḥammad 80–1
Aristotle 254
Arslān, Shakîb 102
Artin, Ya'qūb 81
Artzybashev, Mikhail 190, 217
al-'Asali, Shukri 112
'Āṣim, Ismā'îl 156
'Aṭallah Pasha 54
Athanase IV, Patriarch 55
'Aṭiyyah, Farîdah 156; *Bayn 'Arshayn* 76
al-'Aṭṭār, Ḥasan 45, 56, 163; *Maqāmāt fi Dukhūl al-Faransāwiyyîn ilā al-Diyār al-Miṣriyyah* 109
Aṭwāq al-Dhahab 109
'Awaḍ, Liwîs 98
'Awdah, Kalthūm Naṣr 90, 96
'Ayyād, Rāghib 158
'Ayyād, Shukri 135, 136, 142
'Āzūri, Najîb, *Le Réveil de la nation arabe* 76

al-Badawi, Maḥmūd 210
al-Baghdādi, 'Abd al-Qādir ibn 'Umar, *Khizānat al-Adab* 39
al-Baḥari, Jamîl 161
al-Bājūri, Ibrāhîm Muḥammad 56
Bakhtin, Mikhail 14, 17, 23–5, 28, 33, 239
al-Bakri, Tawfîq 230
Ballān, Anṭūn 90, 96
Balzac, Honoré de 134, 181, 217
Bani Hilāl 106
al-Bāqi, Ḥasan 'Abd 110
al-Barbîr, Aḥmad 'Abd al-Laṭîf 109
Barthes, Roland 236, 239
Bashîr II, Emir of Lebanon 51
Baṭṭi, Salîm 90
Baudelaire, Charles 217
Baydas, Khalîl 15, 90, 95–6, 152–5, 172, 217; *Ahwāl al-Istibdād* (version of A. Tolstoy) 153–4; *Ibnat al-Qubṭān* (tr. of Pushkin) 95, 152–3; *Masāriḥ al-Adhhān* 154–5

Benjamin, Walter 120, 150, 195, 247
Berque, Jacques 22–3
Bible 47, 54
Biktāsh, Khalîl 110
al-Bîtūshi, 'Abdullah 39
Boccaccio, Giovanni 217
Bonheim, Helmut 236, 237
Bottomore, T.B. 66
Bradbury, Malcolm 221–2
Būlus, Sulaymān 96
Burke, Kenneth 182
al-Bustāni, Alîs 112
al-Bustāni, Buṭrus 47, 111–12
al-Bustāni, Sa'îd 112
al-Bustāni, Salîm 47, 70, 72, 97, 98, 111–13, 120, 156, 159, 231; *al-Huyām fi Jinān al-Shām* 111; *Asmā* 112; *Bint al-Aṣr* 112; *Fātinah* 112; *Ghānim wa-Amînah* 112; *Najîb wa-Laṭîfah* 112; *Ramyah min Ghayr Ram* 111; *Salmā* 112; *Sāmiyah* 112; *Zifāf Farîd* 112
al-Bustāni, Sulaymān 90; *Iliad* (tr. of Homer) 135
al-Bustāni, Yūsuf 110

Camus, Albert, *L'Etranger* 254
Carlyle, Thomas 217
Catherine II, Empress 152–3
Cervantes, Saavedra, Miguel de, *Don Quixote* 38
Chekhov, Anton 94, 172, 190, 192, 201, 207, 226–7, 230; *Death of a Civil Servant* 227; *The Three Sisters* 227, 258; *Uncle Vanya* 227, 258
Clot-Bey 68
Coleridge, Samuel Taylor 98
Comte, Auguste 102
Corneille, Pierre, *Le Cid* 88
Croce, Benedetto 33–4
Cromer, Earl of (Sir Evelyn Baring) 66–7, 72, 74

Dante Alighieri 217
Darwazah, Muḥammad 'Azzah 161
Darwîsh, Sayyid 58, 158, 183–4
Darwîsh, Shālūm 161
Daudet, Alphonse 182

Defoe, Daniel 117
Dhāt al-Himmah 106
Dickens, Charles 217
Dilthey 20
Dîrāni, Liyān 161, 171
al-Ḍiyā' 137
Dostoevsky, Fyodor 96, 172, 217
Dumas, Alexandre (*fils*) 217
Dumas, Alexandre (*père*) 217; *Les Trois Mousquetaires* 88
Dunlop, Douglas 66–7
Durkheim, Emile 149

L'Egyptienne 71
Enfantin, Barthélémy Prosper 102

Fahmi, Manṣūr, *La Condition des femmes en Islam* 71
al-Fajr: Ṣaḥîfat al-Hadm wa-l-Binā' 200, 216, 217, 218
Fakhr al-Dîn II 41
Fākihat al-Nudamā' 110
al-Falaki, Maḥmūd 97
al-Falaki, Shaikh Muḥammad al-Khashshāb 81
Faraḥāt, Jirmānūs 42
al-Faraj ba'd al-Shiddah 109
Fatāt al-Sharq 137
Fatḥallah, Ḥamzah 97
Faulkner, William 256
Fawwāz, Zaynab 70, 156
Fawzi, Ḥusain 213, 216, 219
Fayḍi, Sulaymān 161
Fayṣal, King of Iraq 78
Fénélon, François de Salignac de la Mothe, *Les Aventures de Télémaque* 58, 87, 110, 131
Fikri, 'Abdullah 97, 110, 113, 145, 213; *al-Maqāmah al-Fikriyyah al-Saniyyah fi al-Mamlakah al-Bāṭiniyyah* 110
Fitzgerald, F. Scott 256
Flaubert, Gustave 182, 217; *La Légende de Saint Julien l'Hospitalier* 254
Foucault, Michel 30–1, 234
al-Fukāhāt al-'Aṣriyyah 107
al-Funūn 95, 171, 175
Furāt 75

Genette, Gérard 239
Ghālib, 'Uthmān 102
Ghazoul, Ferial Jaboury 254
Giddens, Anthony 29
Girard, René 17
Goethe, Johann Wolfgang von 88
Gogol, Nikolai 96, 172, 190, 217; *The Overcoat* 227
Goldmann, Lucien 14, 18, 20, 24, 25–7, 234
Goncourt, Edmond and Jules de 182
Gorky, Maxim 96, 172, 190, 217
Gran, Peter 39, 109

al-Ḥaddād, 'Abd al-Masîḥ 95, 161, 162, 170, 171, 175–8, 194; *Ḥikāyāt al-Amal wa-l-Alam* 176–8; *Ḥikāyāt al-Mahjar* 175
al-Ḥaddād, Najîb 88, 89, 90, 110; *al-Bakhîl* (tr. of Molière) 88; *al-Fursān al-Thalāthah* (tr. of Dumas) 88; *Gharām wa Intiqām* or *al-Sayyid* (tr. of Corneille) 88; *Ḥimdān* (tr. of Hugo) 88; *Ḥiyal al-Rijal* (tr. of Shakespeare) 88; *Muqābalah bayn al-Shi'r al-'Arabi wa-l-Shi'r al-Afranji* 135; *Ṣalāh al-Dîn* (tr. of Scott) 88; *Shuhadā' al-Gharām* (tr. of Shakespeare) 88; *Thārāt al-'Arab* (tr. of Hugo) 88
Ḥaddād, Niqūlā 90, 156
al-Ḥaddād, Tāhir, *Imra-atunā fi al-Sharî'ah wa-l-Mujtama'* 71
Ḥadîqat al-Akhbār 107
Ḥadîqat al-Riwāyāt 107
al-Ḥadîth 192
Ḥāfiẓ 135
al-Ḥakîm, Nazîh 210
al-Ḥalabi, Sa'îd ibn Muḥammad 42
al-Ḥalabi, Sulaymān 43
al-Ḥalabi, Ta'ūfilis Antūn 110
al-Hamadhāni, Badî' al-Zamān 109, 132
Ḥammād, Ṣāliḥ Ḥamdi 90, 142, 143–4, 147, 148; *Aḥsan al-Qaṣaṣ* 142; *Fi*

al-Rîf 144; *min al-Faqr ilā al-Ghinā* 143; *S. Bey* 144
al-Ḥāmūli, 'Abduh 57
Ḥamzah, 'Abd al-Qādir 90
al-Hāni, Yūsuf 110
Ḥannā, George 93
Ḥaqqi, Yaḥyā 145, 178, 210, 217, 219
Ḥarb, Ṭal'at 60, 73
Hāshim, Labîbah 70, 137–8, 141; *Ḥasanat al-Ḥubb* 137; *Qalb al-Rajul* 137
Ḥassūn, Rizqallah 83, 107
Hawthorne, Nathaniel 256
Haykal, Muḥammad Ḥusain 156, 158, 161, 191; *al-Fann al-Miṣri* 159; *Zaynab* 183, 191
Heidegger, Martin 255
Ḥifni Nāṣif, Malak 70
Ḥijāzi, Salāmah 57
al-Hilāl 84–5
al-Himish al-Ghazri, Manṣūr 110
Hirsch, E.D. 33
Hitti, Philip 59, 104, 136
Homer 200; *Iliad* 135
Hopwood, Derek 94
Hugo, Victor 135, 217; *Les Burgraves* 88; *Hernani* 88
Humboldt, Wilhelm von 86
Ḥusain, Sharîf 77, 78
Ḥusain, Ṭaha 106, 159, 190; *Fi al-Shi'r al-Jāhili* 102, 159
Ḥusain, Kāmil, Sultan of Egypt 77–8
al-Ḥusaini, Isḥāq Mūsā 161
al-Ḥusayni, Muḥammad ibn 'Abd al-Razzāq (al-Murtaḍā al-Zubaydi), *Tāj al-'Arūs* 39
Ḥusni, Dāwūd 57
Ḥusni, Maḥmūd 110

Ibkāryūs, Yūḥannā 110
Ibn al-Muqaffa' 230
Ibrāhîm, 'Ali 65
Ibrāhîm, Ḥāfiẓ 90; *Layāli Saṭîḥ* 134
Ibrāhîm Pasha 46, 52
al-Ibyāri, 'Abd al-Hādi Najā 97
'Īd, 'Azîz 158
Iddah, Ilyās 47
al-'Idil, Ḥasan Tawfîq 110
'Iffat, Muḥammad, *Tasliyat al-Qulūb fi Riwāyat Mérope* 88
Ignatev, Count 93
al-Īrāni, Maḥmūd Sayf al-Dîn 161
Iskandar, Ḥusain Su'ūdi 161
Iskandar, Yūsuf 161
Ismā'îl, Khedive of Egypt 48–52, 56, 57, 58, 60–1, 65, 66, 69, 72, 81, 83, 93, 98, 100–1, 102, 111, 115, 149, 158

al-Jabarti, 'Abd al-Raḥmān 41, 42, 46, 102, 163
Jābir, Ibrāhîm 96
al-Jāḥiẓ 230
Jalāl, Aḥmad 88
Jalāl, Muḥammad 'Uthmān 58, 89, 108, 120; *al-Amāni wa-l-Minnah fi Ḥadîth Qabūl wa-Ward Jannah* (tr. of Saint-Pierre) 88; *al-Riwāyat al-Mufîdah fi 'Ilm al-Tirājîdah* (tr. of Racine) 88; *al-Shaikh Matlūf* (tr. of Molière) 88; *al-'Uyūn al-Yawāqiẓ fi al-Ḥikam wa-l-Mawā'iẓ* (tr. of La Fontaine) 88
al-Jalfi, al-Amîr Riḍwān 41
Jamā'at al-Madrasah al-Ḥadîthah 15
al-Jarîdah 150
Jauss, Hans Robert 14, 32, 33, 34, 35, 105
al-Jawā'ib 47, 130
Jawhari, Ṭanṭāwi 102
al-Jazā'iri, Muḥammad 110
Jazārîn, Zakariyya 161
Jibrān, Jibrān Khalîl 136, 138–40, 149, 156, 170, 171, 174, 243; *al-Ajniḥah al-Mutakassirah* 170; *'Arā'is al-Murūj* 136; *al-Arwāḥ al-Mutamarridah* 136; *Khalîl al-Kāfir* 139; *Maḍja' al-'Arūs* 138–9; *Martā al-Bāniyyah* 139; *Ramād al-Ajyāl wa-l-Nār al-Khālidah* 138; *Wardah al-Hāni* 138–9; *Yūḥannā al-Majnūn* 139
Jiddi, Salîm 110
al-Jinān 70, 111
Joyce, James 256; *Dubliners* 237

Jum'ah, Muḥammad Luṭfī 134–6; *Fi Buyūt al-Nās* 134; *Fi Wādi al-Humūm* 134; *Layāli al-Rūḥ al-Ḥā'ir* 134, 135, 142; *Narjis al-'Amyā'* 136; *Ṣadîqi 'Ali* 136
al-Jumayyil, Anṭūn 156

Kalîlah wa-Dimnah 109, 110, 127
Kamāl, Nāmiq 100; *Riwāyat al-Ru'yā* 140
Kāmil, Khalîl 156
Kāmil, Muṣṭafā 74
Kāmil, Yūsuf 158
Kapustin, Antonin 92
Karāmah, Buṭrus 47
al-Karmi, Aḥmad Shākir 161
al-Karmil 77
Karr, Jean-Baptiste Alphonse 181
al-Kassār, 'Ali 158
al-Kawākibi, 'Abd al-Raḥmān 75–6; *Ṭabā'i' al-Istibdād wa Maṣāri' al-Isti'bād* 76; *Umm al-Qurā* 76
Kenyon Review, The 13
al-Khālidi, Rawḥi, *Tārikh 'Ilm al-Adab 'Ind al-Ifrinj wa-l-'Arab* 135
Khalqi, 'Ali 171
Khayrat, Maḥmūd 156
al-Khayyāt, Yūsuf 57
Khilqi, 'Ali 161
al-Khula'i, Kāmil 57
al-Khūri, Khalîl 107
Kîlāni, Kāmil 161
al-Kilāni, Rashîd 'Ali 78
Krachkovski, A. 94
Kristeva, Julia 27
Kuzmā, Iskandar 92
Kyrillos I, Patriarch 48
Kyrillos IV, Patriarch 69

La Fontaine, Jean de, *Fables* 58, 88, 217
al-Lā'iḥah al-Waṭaniyyah 50
Lane, Edward William 106
Lāshîn, Maḥmūd Ṭāhir 9, 15–16, 199–200, 201, 202, 210, 215–32; *Alwū* 220, 222–3, 224, 225; *Bayt al-Ṭā'ah* 220, 221, 223, 224, 225; *al-Fakhkh* 220, 224; *Fi Qarār al-Hāwiyah* 220, 223, 225; *Ḥadîth al-Qaryah* 9, 15, 224, 226, 234–61, 262–8; *Ḥawwā' bilā Ādam* 231–2; *al-Ḥubb Yalhū* 223; *al-Infijār* 220, 224; *Jawlah Khāsirah* 220, 224; *al-Kahlah al-Mazhuwwah* 220, 223, 224; *Lawn al-Khajal* 220, 223; *Mādhā Yaqūl al-Wadā'* 220, 224, 225; *Manzil li-l-Ījār* 220, 223, 224; *Mifistūfūlis* 223–4; *Minṭaqat al-Ṣamt* 224; *al-Qadar* 220, 224, 225; *Qiṣṣat 'Ifrît* 220, 223, 224; *Ṣaḥḥ* 223; *al-Shabaḥ al-Māthil fi al-Mir'āh* 223; *al-Shaikh Muḥammad al-Yamāni* 224; *al-Shāwîsh Baghdadi* 224; *Sukhriyat al-Nāy* 219, 220, 225; *Taḥt 'Ajalat al-Ḥayāh* 221; *Wa-Lakinnahā al-Ḥayāh* 220; *al-Wiṭwāṭ* 220, 223, 224; *Yuḥkā Anna* 219, 220, 223, 234; *al-Zā'ir al-Ṣāmit* 221, 223, 224
Lāshîn, Muḥammad 'Abd al-Raḥîm 162, 219
Lawrence, D.H. 256
Leavis, Q.D. 17, 84, 124
Lenin, V.I. 94
Lermontov, Mikhail 95, 217
Locke, John 89, 101
Lukács, Georg 17, 19–20, 230; *To Narrate or To Describe* 254
Lumière, Auguste Marie and Louis Jean 60

McMahon, Sir Henry 77
al-Mahdi, Muḥammad al-Ḥifni, *Tuḥfat al-Mustayqiẓ al-Ānis fi Nuzhat al-Mustanîm al-Nā'is wa Maqāmāt al-Bîmāristān* 109
Maḥfūẓ, Najîb 106–7, 232;
al-Mahjar 138
Maḥmūd, Ḥasan 161, 183, 202, 216; *Bint al-Mā'* 185; *Ḥayāt al-Zahr* 184; *Khārij al-Insāniyyah* 184; *al-Zawjah al-Āthimah* 184
Maḥmūd, Muḥammad 150
al-Maḥrūsah 116
Majdi, Ṣāliḥ 97
Makram, 'Umar 55, 56

Mallāt, Shibli 90
Malraux, André 27
al-Manfalūti, Muṣṭafā Luṭfi 36, 144–9, 150, 151, 180, 213, 230; *al-'Abarāt* 142, 144, 146; *al-Naẓarāt* 142
Mannheim 20
Mansfield, Katherine 256
al-Manyalāwi, Yūsuf 57, 190
al-Maqāmah al-Sundusiyyah 109
Maqāmāt al-Hamadhāni 109
Maqāmāt al-Harîri 109
al-Maqāmāt al-Luzūmiyyah 109
Maqāmāt al-Rāzi 109
Maqāmāt al-Ṣuyūṭi 109
Maqāmāt al-Tilmisāni 109
Maqāmāt al-Wardi 109
Maqāmāt al-Zamakhshari 109
Maqāmāt Ibn al-Mu'aẓẓam 109
Marcel, J., *Contes du Cheykh el-Mohdy* (tr. of Mahdi) 109
Marie, Tsaritsa 92
Marrāsh, Francis 46, 47, 58, 76; *Durr al-Ṣadaf fi Gharā'ib al-Ṣudaf* 48; *Ghābat al-Ḥaqq* 48
al-Marṣafi, Ḥusain 97
Marx, Karl 20, 24, 39
Marya Aleksandrovna, Tsarina 69
Maṣāri' al-'Ushshāq 109
Mash'alāni, Nasîb 90, 112
Mattā, Yūsuf 161
Maupassant, Guy de 182, 196, 200, 201, 205, 217, 226; "Moonlight" 164–6
Maẓhar, Muḥammad 102
al-Māzini, Ibrāhîm 'Abd al-Qādir 159, 190; *al-Dîwān* 159
Melville, Herman 256
Midḥat Pasha 53, 68
Mill, John Stuart 102
Mills, C. Wright 121
Miṣbāḥ al-Sharq 133
al-Miṣri, 'Azîz 80
al-Miṣri, Ibrāhîm 217
Molière (Jean-Baptiste Poquelin), *L'Avare* 57, 88; *Tartuffe* 58, 88
al-Mu'ayyad 136
Mubārak, 'Ali 65, 97, 113, 131; *'Ālam al-Dîn* 58, 62, 113, 130–1
Mubārak, Buṭrus 42
Mudawwar, Fāris 96
Muḥammad 'Ali, Viceroy of Egypt 40, 41, 44–5, 46, 49, 52, 55, 63, 65, 66, 68, 71, 72–3, 102, 158
al-Mukhalla', Jibrā'îl 110
Mukhtār, Maḥmūd 158
Mukhtār, Murād, *Qiṣṣat Abi-'Ali Ibn Sinā wa-Shaqîqih Abi-l-Ḥārith wa-ma Ḥaṣal minhumā min Nawādir al-'Ajā'ib wa-Shawārid al-Gharā'ib* 88
al-Munîr, Ḥanāniyā 42, 109
Muntakhabāt al-Riwāyāt 107
al-Muqtaṭaf 80, 85
Murzūbān Nāmah 110
Mūsā, Salāmah 159, 161, 190, 213
Musāmarāt al-Mulūk 107
Musāmarāt al-Nadîm 107
Musāmarāt al-Sha'b 107
al-Musāmarāt al-Usbū'iyyah 107
al-Mūṣili, Sulaymān Fayḍi 156
al-Muṭṭalib, Muḥammad 'Abd 156
al-Muwailiḥi, Ibrāhîm 74, 81, 133; *Ḥadîth Mūsā Ibn 'Isām (Mir'āt al-'Ālam)* 133
al-Muwailiḥi, Muḥammad 132–3, 134, 140, 167; *Fatrah min al-Zaman (Ḥadîth 'Īsā Ibn Hishām)* 132–3, 140

Nadîm, 'Abdullah 15, 72, 74, 81, 84, 102, 113–29, 130, 131–3, 136, 138, 139, 140, 142, 148, 149, 155–6, 166, 167, 169, 183, 191, 196, 222, 231, 259; *al-Dhi'āb Ḥawl al-Asad* 123; *al-Mazzah al-Muṭaharrah* 122; *al-Murāfa'ah al-Waṭaniyyah* 125; *'Arabi Tafarnaj* 121; *Ghiflat al-Taqlîd* 122; *Ḥanîfah wa-Laṭîfah* 124; *'Imārah wa-Zanāti* 125; *Laṭîfah wa-Dimyānah* 124; *Madrasat al-Banāt* 124; *Madrasat al-Banîn* 124, 125; *Majlis Ṭibbi 'alā Muṣāb bil-Afranji* 121; *al-Masāmîr* 131–2; *Muḥtāj Jāhil fi Yad Muḥtāl Ṭami'* 122; *Nahāyat al-Balādah* 123; *Sahrat al-Anṭā'* 122; *Sa'îd wa-Bakhîtah* 125; *Ṭarîq al-*

Wuṣūl ilā al-Ra'y al-'Āmm 64; *Zubaidah wa-Nabawiyyah* 124
al-Nafā'is al-'Aṣriyyah 95, 107, 152, 154, 217
al-Nafathāt 107
Najm, Muḥammad Yūsuf 108, 129, 130
Nāmiq Pasha 54, 70
Napoleon I, Emperor 42, 43, 54, 97
al-Naqqāsh, Mārūn 47, 57, 156; *al-Bakhîl* 57
al-Naqqāsh, Salîm 57, 90, 110
Nāṣif, Ḥifni 145
Naṣṣār, Najîb 77
Naumov, Cyril 91
Nawādir Juḥā 109
Nawfal, Hind 70
Niva 94
Nu'aymah, Mîkha'îl 93, 95, 96, 153, 161, 162, 169–75, 176, 194; *al-Ghirbāl* 102; *al-'Āqir* 173–4; *Kān mā Kān* 171; *Sa'ādat al-Baik* 174; *Sā'at al-Kūkū* 174; *Sanatuhā al-Jadîdah* 171, 172–3; *Shūrti* 174; *al-Zakhîrah* 174

Peter the Great, Tsar 93
Pirandello, Luigi 217
Poe, Edgar Allan 217, 256
Propp, Vladimir 242
Pugachev, Emelian 152–3
Pushkin, Alexander 95, 96, 152–3, 217; *The Captain's Daughter* 95, 152

al-Qabbāni, Aḥmad Abū-Khalîl 57, 156
al-Qabbāni, Ibrāhîm 57
Qadri, Muḥammad 88
al-Qasāṭili, Nu'mān 112
Qilfāt, Nakhlah 156
Qur'ān 148, 230, 247, 248, 249, 257

Racine, Jean 88
al-Rāfi'i, Amîn 158
al-Rāfi'i, Muṣṭafa Ṣādiq 146–9, 150, 159; *al-Masākîn* 142, 143, 146; *Miskînah...Miskînah* 146–8; *Saḥq al-Lu'lu'* 147
Ramzi, Ibrāhîm 156
Rawḍat al-Madāris 97
al-Rāwi 107
Richardson, Samuel 117
Riḍā, Rashîd 61, 102
Rifā'ah, 'Ali Fahmi 97
al-Rîḥāni, Najîb 158
Rimbaud, Arthur 217
al-Riwāyāt al-Jadîdah 107
al-Riwāyāt al-Kubrā 107
al-Riwāyāt al-Shahriyyah 107
Rolland, Romain 182
al-Ruṣāfi, Ma'rūf, *Riwāyāt al-Ru'yā* (tr. of Kamal) 140
Ru'yā al-'Arabiyyah 140

al-Ṣabbān, Muḥammad 41
Ṣabri, Aḥmad 158
Sa'd, Aḥmad Ṣādiq 39
Sa'îd, Khedive of Egypt 48, 65
Sa'îd, Aḥmad Khayri 216, 218, 219; *al-Dasā'is wa-l-Dimā'* 231–2
Said, Edward 19, 21–2, 237, 248
Sa'îd, Maḥmūd 158
Saif Ibn Dhi-Yazan 106
al-Sā'iḥ 95, 171, 175, 176
Saint-Pierre, Jacques-Henri Bernardin, *Paul et Virginie* 58, 88
Saint-Simon, Claude Henri, Comte de 102
al-Salîm, 'Abd al-Ḥamîd 161
al-Samāni, Yūsuf Sam'ān 42
al-Samîr 107
Ṣannū, Ya'qūb 57, 117, 156
Ṣaqqāl, Anṭūn 110
Ṣarrāf, Luṭf-allah al-Khūri 96
Ṣarrūf, Ya'qūb 156
Saussure, Ferdinand de 30, 34
Ṣawāyā, Labîbah Mîkhā'îl, *Ḥasnā' Sālūnîk* 76
al-Ṣayyādi, Abū al-Hudā 130
al-Sayyid, Aḥmad Luṭfi 158
al-Sayyid, Maḥmūd Aḥmad 90, 161, 162, 189–94; *A wa-Tasharîn* 193; *Abṭāl al-Khamrah* 191; *Abū-Jāsim* 192; *al-Amal al-Muḥaṭṭam* 192;

Ātîkah 193; *Baddāy al-Fāyiz* 193–4; *al-Dhikrā* 193; *Fi Sā'min al-Zaman* 191, 192; *Inqilāb* 192, 193; *Jalāl Khālid* 191, 192; *Jimāḥ Hawā* 193; *Mujāhidūn* 192; *al-Nakabāt* 190; *Nāṣiḥ al-Qawm* 191; *Risālat Hajr* 193; *Ṣaḥîfah Sawdā' fi Tārîkh Aswad* 190; *Sakrān* 192, 193; *Saṭrān min Ḥikāyah* 191; *al-Ṣu'ūd al-Hā'il* 190; *al-Ṭalā'i'* 191, 192; *al-Ṭālib al-Ṭarîd* 192; *Ṭālib Effendi* 193
Schücking, Levin L. 115
Scott, Sir Walter 134, 217; *Tales of the Crusaders* 88
Sergei, Grand Duke 92
Shadîd, Bishārah 88
Shakespeare, William 217; *Othello* 88; *Romeo and Juliet* 88
Shākir, Maḥmūd 39
Sha'rāwi, Hudā 71, 137
Sharîf, Muḥammad 110
al-Sharqāwi, Shaikh 'Abdullah 50
Shā'ūl, Anwar 90, 161
Shawqi, Aḥmad 156; *Shayṭān Bintā'ūr* 134
al-Shāyib, Fu'ād 161
al-Shidyāq, Aḥmad Fāris 46, 47, 48, 129–30; *al-Jāsūs 'alā al-Qāmūs* 47; *al-Sāq 'alā al-Sāq fi ma Huwa al-Fāryāq* 47, 129; *Ḥimār Nahhāq wa Safar wa-Ikhfāq* 130; *Ighāb Shawāfin wa-Inshāb Barāthin* 130; *Intikāsah Khāfiyah wa-'Imāmah Wāqiyah* 130; *Kashf al-Mukhabbā 'an Aḥwāl Ūrūbbā* 47; *Mamshiyyah* 130; *Muq'adah* 130; *Muqîmah* 130; *Qiṣṣat Qissîs* 130; *Shurūr wa-Ṭanbūr* 130; *Sirr al-Layāli fi al-Qalb wa-l-'Ibdāl* 47; *Ṭa'ām wa-Iltihām* 130
Shukri, 'Abd al-Raḥmān 136
Shumayyil, Amîn 110
Shumayyil , Shibli 77, 190
Ṣidqi, Luṭfi Bakr 161
Ṣidqi, Najāti 90, 96, 153, 161
Silsilat al-Fukāhāt 107
Silsilat al-Riwāyāt 107
Silsilat al-Riwāyāt al-'Uthmāniyyah 107
Sirri Pasha 54
Smith, Eli 52
Sovremennik 152
Spiridon, Patriarch of Antioch 93
Stevenson, Robert Louis 217
al-Sufūr 146, 150, 162, 164, 179, 209
Sulṭān Pasha 81
al-Suwaydi, 'Abdullah 39
al-Suwaydi, Abū-l-Fawz 39

Tādurus, Wahbah, *'Iqd al-Anfās* 110
al-Ṭahṭāwi, Aḥmad 'Ubaid, *al-Rawḍ al-Azhar fi Tārîkh Buṭrus al-Akbar* (tr.) 93
al-Ṭahṭāwi, Rifā'ah Rāfi' 45–6, 47, 50, 55, 58, 72, 89, 97, 98, 102, 108, 120; *Manāhij al-Albāb al-Miṣriyyah fi Mabāhij al-Ādāb al-'Aṣriyyah* 45, 70, 97, 102; *Takhlîṣ al-Ibrîz fi Talkhîṣ Bārîz* 45, 97; *Waqā'i' al-Aflāk fi Ḥawādith Tilîmak* (tr. of Fénelon) 58, 87, 131
al-Ṭā'if 115
Taine, Hippolyte 182
al-Tankît wa-l-Tabkît 115, 116, 118, 120–3
al-Ṭanṭāwi, 'Ali 161
Tanwîr al-Afkār 140
Tarrād, Najîb 90
Tawfîq, Khedive of Egypt 61
Taymūr, Aḥmad 55, 56, 163, 190
Taymūr, 'Ā'ishah, 70; *Mir'at al-Ta'ammul fi al-Umūr* 131; *Natā'ij al-Aḥwāl fi al-Aqwāl wa-l-Af'āl* 131
Taymūr, Maḥmūd 15, 55, 56, 161, 190, 192–3, 194, 199, 200–14, 226; *Ab wa Ibn (Kabsh al-Fidā)* 204, 211; *Abū Darsh* 206; *Abū-Ali 'Āmil Artist* 201, 205; *'Amm Mitwalli* 202; *al-'Awdah* 207–8; *Budūr* 206; *Fatāt al-Jîrān* 204; *Hiya al-Ḥayāh* 205, 206; *Jaḥîm Imra'ah* 203; *Man Fāt Qadîmah Tāh* 203; *Mashrū' Kafāfi Afandi* 202, 203; *al-Qalam al-Abanūs* 202; *Qaswat al-Shabāb* 206; *al-Rajul al-Marîḍ* 206; *Ṣabîḥah*

206; *Salîm Afandi al-Ṭālib al-Adîb* 205–6; *Shahr al-'Asal Ba'd al-Arba'în* 203, 204, 211; *al-Shaikh Jum'ah* 202; *al-Shaikh Sayyid al-'Abîṭ* 202; *al-Shayṭān* 202; *al-Sitt Tawaddud* 206; *al-Thālūth al-Muqaddas* 205; *al-Usṭā Shiḥātah Yuṭālib bi-Ujratih* 203; *Wāsiṭat Ta'āruf* 204; *al-Waẓîfah* 205; *Yuḥfaẓ fi al-Būsṭah* 206
Taymūr, Muḥammad 55, 56, 161, 162–70, 171, 174, 178, 181, 189, 190, 200, 201, 202, 203, 219; *al-Āshiq al-Maftūn bi-l-Rutab wa-l-Nayāshîn* 167; *'Aṭfat al...Manzil Raqam 22* 167; *Bayt al-Karam* 167; *Dars fi Kuttāb* 168; *Fi al-Qiṭār* 167; *Kān Ṭiflā fa-Ṣār Shābbā* 204; *Khawāṭir* 167–8; *Mā Tarāh al-'Uyūn* 163, 164; *Rabbi li-man Khalaqt Hādha al-Na'îm* (after Maupassant) 164–6; *Ramaḍān fi Qahwat Matātyā* 167; *Rayyān yā Fijl* 167; *al-Shabāb al-Dā'i'* 167, 205; *Sirr min Asrār Ta'akhkhur al-Miṣriyyîn* 167; *Ṣuffārat al-'Īd* 167–9
Thackeray, William Makepeace 217
Times, The 51, 72
Tolstoy, Alexei, *Prince Serebriany* 153
Tolstoy, Leo 95, 134, 153, 164, 172, 192, 201, 217, 239
Turgenev, Ivan 94–5, 172, 190, 201, 217
al-Tūnsi, Khayr al-Dîn 100
al-Turk, Niqūlā 47, 110
al-Turk, Wardah 70
Twain, Mark 217

'Ubaid, 'Īsā 161–2, 178–89, 191, 194, 201, 203, 212, 219, 223, 225; *Anā Lak* 188; *al-Ghîrah* 184; *Iḥsān Hānim* 178, 184; *Kalimah 'an al-Fann wa-l-Adab al-Ḥadîth fi Miṣr*179–80; *Ma'sāt Qarawiyyah* 184, 185–8 *Mudhakkirāt Ḥikmat Hānim* 184, 188, 189; *al-Naz'ah al-Nisā'iyyah* 184; *Thurayyā* 178
'Ubaid, Shiḥātah 161–2, 178–9, 181–5, 188–9, 191, 194, 201, 203, 212, 219, 223, 225; *al-Bā'inah* 184, 188; *Dars Mu'lim* 178; *al-Ikhlāṣ* 184; *Maw'id Gharām* 184; *al-Ṣalāh* 189
al-Ujaymi, Yuḥannā 42
'Urābi, Aḥmad 72, 75, 101, 111, 124, 221
Uspenski, Porfiri 91
al-Ustādh 84, 115, 120, 124, 129
'Uthmān, Muḥammad 57

Voltaire, François-Marie Arouet, *Mérope* 88

Wahbi, Yūsuf 158
Wajdi, Farîd 102
al-Waqā'i' al-Miṣriyyah 47
Wāṣif, Maḥmūd 156
Watt, Ian 17, 98, 101, 219
Weber, Max 217
Wilde, Oscar 217
Wittfogel 39
Wolff, Janet 31

Yakan, Waliy al-Dîn 158
al-Yāziji, Ibrāhîm 80, 137
al-Yāziji, Khalîl 156
al-Yāziji, Nāṣîf 47, 72, 97, 98, 110; *Majma' al-Baḥrain* 110
al-Yāziji, Wardah 70

Zaghlūl, Sa'd 94, 179
al-Zahāwi, Jamîl Ṣidqi 70
al-Zahrāwi, 'Abd al-Ḥamîd 156
al-Zaibaq, 'Ali 106
Zaki, Aḥmad 88
al-Zawrā' 53
Zaydān, Jurji 112, 156; *al-Inqilāb al-'Uthmāni* 76
Znaniya 95
Zola, Emile 134, 182